A Time to Speak
and a Time to Listen

Teacher's Guide

Celia Warren

Schofield & Sims

Icons used in this book: an at-a-glance guide

 Speaking

 Listening

 Interacting

 Performing

A time to be sensitive

The poems in **A Time to Speak and a Time to Listen** touch upon some of the most profound human experiences – including birth and death, love and hate, war and peace. The majority of pupils will benefit greatly from exploring their feelings concerning major life events. However, if a family member or close friend of any of the pupils has recently died or is seriously ill, be sensitive to that pupil's needs and decide whether or not it will be helpful for the class to study a poem focusing specifically on death. The discussions that the poem engenders will usually offer comfort and relief – but if you are in doubt, keep the poem for another occasion.

First published in 2013

Copyright © Schofield & Sims Limited 2013

Author: Celia Warren

Celia Warren has asserted her moral right under the Copyright, Designs and Patents Act, 1988, to be identified as the author of this work.

Schofield & Sims would like to thank Andrea Shavick for her description of the events on which her poem 'The Wind's Prize' is based (see page 34). This description is reproduced with the kind permission of the poet and is copyright © Andrea Shavick, 2013.

All registered trademarks (for example, Plasticine® and Lego® on page 32 and page 51, and Microsoft PowerPoint® on page 130) remain the property of their respective holders. Their names are used only to directly describe the products.

British Library Catalogue in Publication Data:
A catalogue record for this book is available from the British Library.

All rights reserved. Except where otherwise indicated, no part of this publication may be reproduced, stored in a retrieval system, or transmitted in any form or by any means, electronic, mechanical, photocopying, recording or otherwise, without either the prior permission of the publisher or a licence permitting restricted copying in the United Kingdom issued by the Copyright Licensing Agency Limited, Saffron House, 6–10 Kirby Street, London WC1N 8TS.

The photocopy masters in Part Four are exempt from these restrictions and may be photocopied after purchase, for use within the purchaser's institution only.

Commissioning by **Carolyn Richardson Publishing Services** (www.publiserve.co.uk)
Design by **Oxford Designers & Illustrators**
Printed in the UK by **Charlesworth Press**, Wakefield

ISBN 978 07217 1206 2

Contents

Introduction	**3**
Part One: Poem by Poem	**6**
Prologue	**6**
A time to be born (Poems 1 to 3)	7
A time to die (Poems 4 to 6)	10
A time to plant (Poems 7 to 9)	13
A time to pull up (Poems 10 to 12)	16
A time to kill (Poems 13 to 16)	19
A time to heal (Poems 17 to 20)	23
A time to tear down (Poems 21 to 23)	27
A time to build up (Poems 24 to 26)	30
A time to weep (Poems 27 to 29)	33
A time to laugh (Poems 30 to 34)	36
A time to mourn (Poems 35 to 39)	41
A time to dance (Poems 40 to 43)	46
A time to cast away stones (Poems 44 to 46)	50
A time to gather stones together (Poems 47 to 50)	53
A time to embrace (Poems 51 to 53)	57
A time not to embrace (Poems 54 to 57)	60
A time to find (Poems 58 to 60)	64
A time to lose (Poems 61 to 64)	67
A time to keep (Poems 65 to 68)	71
A time to cast away (Poems 69 to 72)	75
A time to tear (Poems 73 to 75)	79
A time to sew (Poems 76 to 79)	82
A time to be silent (Poems 80 to 83)	86
A time to speak (Poems 84 to 86)	90
A time to love (Poems 87 to 90)	93
A time to hate (Poems 91 to 93)	97
A time for war (Poems 94 to 96)	100
A time for peace (Poems 97 to 99)	103
Epilogue (Poem 100)	**106**

11   # The Ghosts of Weeds

SECTION **A time to pull up** (page 13)   POET **Nick Toczek**

This poem, published for the first time in the anthology, makes use of a strong, sustained rhythm that is characteristic of the poet's lyrical style, which demands to be read aloud. It might equally fit under the banner of **A time to kill**, as weed-killer helps the gardener to pull up the weeds.

Preparing to read this poem aloud

- Make the most of the strong rhythm of this poem. Stress *ghosts* and *weeds* (line 1), *plants* and *needs* (line 2), 'NEG-li-gence' and 'NUR-ture' (line 3) to establish the beat. Sustain this rhythm throughout.
- When the pupils practise performing this poem, you may wish to encourage them to repeat the last line, fading gradually to a whisper and silence.

When is a plant a weed?

- Tell a story about a mother who was weeding the garden with her two-year-old child. As the mother pulled out a plant, the child put her hands on her hips, and in outraged tones, began to wail, 'Hey! Stop pulling up that pretty plant!' Discuss what makes a plant a weed. (Weeds are flowers and plants that flourish in sparse conditions; dandelions and daisies that grow in the cracks of a tarmac drive; plants that produce many strong leaves and small flowers; plants that spread so widely and rapidly that they choke all the other plants around them; plants that are self-seeded.)
- Discuss why people may like to have certain weeds in their garden. (They have colourful flowers / they attract butterflies.)
- Reach a consensus that individuals may have different opinions on which plants are weeds. Some people pull up dandelions while others plant them to eat their leaves.
- Discuss ways of controlling weeds – digging them up, poisoning them systemically or superficially with proprietary weed-killers.
- Explain that the poet, Nick Toczek, explores the notion that weeds might have minds of their own. How do the weeds feel about being destroyed? What if they return as ghosts?
- Read the poem aloud. Invite the pupils to join in a choral speaking of the poem. Establish a strong beat, and try to maintain it.
- Gradually introduce some gentle percussion to emphasise the rhythm. Build this up to a crescendo in the final line, as though the ghosts are gathering ranks and attacking the gardener's conscience. Explain that the more tightly they can speak in chorus, the more menacing their message.
- When their speaking is confident, experiment with the pupils marching and stamping their feet, as if on a demonstration march, as they recite the poem.

> **EXTRA**: Invite the pupils to research the life-cycle of a dandelion, using books and websites. Ask them to organise their findings into a presentation to the whole class. Invite the audience to ask questions at the end. Alternatively, invite pupils to design placards with the ghosts' slogans on them. Slogans might include, for example, 'Ban weed-killer', 'Rescue our roots', 'Save our sap'. Each slogan might feature a different weed illustration, drawn from direct observation or adapted from a reference book on wildflowers.

12 Good Taste

SECTION A time to pull up (page 14) **POET Christopher Logue (1926–2011)**

In a dire situation, even the smallest pleasure is a solace. Such is the experience of the man in this poem as, faced with his inevitable demise, he reaches out to pick the tastiest strawberry ever.

Preparing to read this poem aloud

- This dark, but lightly told, story poem needs to be presented in a narrative tone of voice. Pause significantly at each line-ending and full stop to allow the pupils to picture the scene and absorb the impact of each successive event.
- Change the tone of voice for the tiger's proud thought, *How fast I run* (line 3) and, again, for the road's thought, *How long I am* (line 4). Some hand actions and a change of facial expressions will help younger pupils to visualise the events.
- Keep your voice light on such details as the colours of the mice, thus emphasising the bathos alongside the man's dire situation.
- Draw out the final four words, *How sweet it tasted!,* focusing on the ephemeral delight of that moment.

Perfect moments

- List these traditional sayings, 'Between the devil and the deep blue sea', 'Between a rock and a hard place' and 'Out of the frying-pan, into the fire'. Discuss their meaning and implications.
- Introduce the poem, explaining that the character is in just such a 'no-win' situation. Ask the pupils to try and picture the sequence of events as you read the poem aloud.
- Discuss the poem and ask, 'Can the poem have a happy ending?' 'How does the poet keep the events so light when they are really so serious?' (Through attention to irrelevant detail, bathos and a matter-of-fact storytelling voice.)
- Ask, 'Why does the man hug the root, even though the mice are gnawing it?' Introduce the concept of the survival instinct and the feeling of optimism in the face of contrary evidence.
- Now ask the pupils to imagine that it is a very cold day. They have been playing in the snow till their fingers hurt with the cold. When they come indoors, would they prefer a cup of hot chocolate or an ice-cream? Conversely, on a hot day on the beach, would they prefer an ice-cream or a cup of hot soup?
- Discuss how many foods – birthday cake, mince pies, toffee apples and ice-lollies – taste better in a traditional context. Can the pupils explain why the man's strawberry would taste extra sweet in his circumstances?
- Sort them into pairs, providing them with pencils and paper. Ask each to interview his or her partner, asking what would be a perfect menu for a perfect day. Explain that by 'menu' they may also think beyond food and look at the 'menu' as a timetable for their perfect day. (By way of example, you might explain that maths and PE are 'on the menu' for today.)
- Bring the pupils together and ask each one to describe his or her partner's 'menu'. Ask, if they could time-freeze one moment of their perfect day, which would it be, and why?

EXTRA: Challenge the pupils to plot and tell a story about characters who find themselves in a dilemma.

(13) Lovely Mosquito

SUITABLE FOR YOUNGER PUPILS

SECTION **A time to kill** (page 15)   POET **Doug MacLeod**

This poem exemplifies irony from its title to its last line. It is a poem that younger children will find easy to learn, with its ABAB rhyme scheme, and enjoyable to perform with zest. It cries out to be performed with actions that mimic the words.

Preparing to read this poem aloud

- Adopt a falsely pleasant, friendly tone and a false smile, miming the mosquito on your arm, and approaching it with your hand, slowly and gently.
- Use an ironically persuasive tone, drawing out reassuring words, such as *simply* (line 4), *nobody* (line 6) and *lovely* (line 7). Otherwise maintain a slow, even pace (so as not to startle the insect!).
- Pause at each dash. Pause slightly longer in verse two, in readiness for the contrast of speed, volume and tone in the final line. Swipe at and finally swat the imaginary mosquito as you speak the final two words.

Pros and cons

- Together, quickly compile a short list of common flying insects – bluebottle, mosquito, butterfly, bee, wasp, gnat and dragonfly.
- Do any seem more attractive, or unattractive, to us than others. Why is this? (Butterflies are pretty, bees make honey, wasps sting, mosquitoes bite, bluebottles lay eggs on our food and make us ill.)
- Point out that seemingly less attractive insects still have their place in the food chain, for example, many birds and bats eat mosquitoes, gnats and moths. Explain that our viewpoint is subjective and is based on our personal feelings about insects.
- Announce the title of the poem and discuss the choice of adjective to describe the mosquito. Is it a surprising one? If so, why? (Mosquitoes bite and can cause anything from an itch to painful allergic reactions and the transmission of dangerous diseases such as malaria and blood poisoning.)
- Invite the pupils to compare the title with the way we say something like 'Oh great!' when being bitten by a mosquito. Explain that this is irony and that the poem is written ironically. Ask them to listen to the narrator speaking to the mosquito as you read the poem aloud.
- Read the poem aloud and then discuss the poet's choice of vocabulary. Ask, 'Why does *desire* (line 4) work better in this context than "want"?' (The longer vowel prolongs the tension. The word half-rhymes with *quiet* [line 2] and *right* [line 3] in the previous lines, adding assonance that helps the poem – and the scenario it describes – to flow. The fact that it is a less common word than we would normally use adds to the poem's sense of falseness and irony.)
- Challenge the pupils to learn the poem by heart to perform to the rest of the class. Discuss criteria for a successful performance. These include clarity of voice, varying pace, volume and tone, use of actions to enhance the words, eye-contact with the audience and/or with the imaginary mosquito and dramatic staging of the poem. Hold a contest to decide who performs it best. Invite the winner to perform the poem to another class, perhaps a class who are doing a project on minibeasts.

> **EXTRA**: Invite the pupils to research and then present a two-minute talk on the life-cycle and habitat of the mosquito.

PART ONE

25 **Target**

SECTION **A time to build up** (page 27)   POET **Rachel Rooney**

This inspirational poem is all about high aspirations and aiming beyond our reach. From clods of mud beneath our feet to stars above and the future ahead, the poem encourages readers to see their potential as limited only by their own low ambition and self-expectation.

Preparing to read this poem aloud

- Look down as you read the opening of the poem, raising your head as you continue to emulate the rising viewpoint. At the same time, gradually increase volume, tone and tempo with each succeeding couplet.
- Be prepared to carry *slanted attic windows, rows* (line 10) on to the following couplet to retain the sense.
- Strongly emphasise the two closing words.

Personal challenges

- Ask the pupils what the word 'target' means to them, from personal goals and desires to physical targets such as in a game of darts or archery. Discuss how targets can relate to ambition and achievement, success and disappointment.
- Invite individuals to talk about their own personal targets in different fields, in sports such as judo, dancing and swimming, and in competitions such as 'Readathons'. Compare competing with others with beating one's own record.
- List methods of measuring self-improvement and personal challenges, such as increases in speed, quantity or quality.
- Suggest that, in most things, we need to aim higher than we think in order to improve or reach our target. Explain that it is not usually easy to improve in all areas at once and that any targets we set ourselves – or that teachers may set – should be realistic and achievable.
- Read the poem aloud and encourage the pupils to observe how the targets become not only physically higher, but also more wonderful. Invite them to compare a *clod of mud* (line 1) with a *star* (line 14) and a *rusted can* (line 3) with *church spires* (line 11).
- Ask the pupils to choose a partner. Explain that you want them to choose a poem – or a number of poems – to learn by heart. Each child must set a challenge for his or her partner and accept the challenge he or she is given in return.
- Suggest that they set a target of learning one longer poem word-perfect, by this time next week, or two short poems by home-time. Alternatively, suggest that their target is to see how quickly they can learn a four-line poem, or an eight-line poem. Their next target may be to reduce the time it takes.
- Suggest that younger or less confident pupils decide on a shared challenge of learning together a poem by heart. That is, each partner may wish to learn half the poem or they may prefer to recite together their chosen poem.
- Bring the class together and ask each pupil to declare their learning target. Ensure that all pupils are aiming high and stretching themselves. Add conditions to those who have chosen a target that is too easy. For example, suggest that they polish their presentation by developing use of voice variation rather than simply performing a memory exercise.

> **EXTRA:** Challenge the pupils to choose their own target in some other field of learning, such as spelling, times tables, memorising notable dates and subject-specific facts, doing press-ups or timed races, and to be ready to report back orally to the class in one week's time.

26 **The Trouble with Snowmen**

Roger McGough's poem is a bitter-sweet exploration of the ephemeral versus the permanent. It is a good example of how some materials lend themselves better to some purposes than others and how certain pleasures are not designed to last.

Before the lesson

- Find an empty flowerpot, upturn it and paint it sand-coloured. Alternatively, use it as a papier-mâché mould to make a model sandcastle. Glue or paint on shells and place a paper flag or feather in the top.

Preparing to read this poem aloud

- Adopt a slow, deliberate and thoughtful tone for the father's direct speech, which differs from the narrator's voice.
- Pause after the first three verses to allow empathy with the prospect of a permanent non-snow figure. Add a note of resignation to: *And that snowman still stands* (line 13).
- Ensure that the final line of the poem, *And then fade away*, sounds uplifting to echo the sentiment.

Happy memories, sad reminders

- Ask the pupils if they have ever made models that they were very proud of, from, for example, Plasticine® or Lego®. How much did they enjoy making them? Which models did they keep? For how long? Is it possible to use the same materials again and again to make different models?
- Talk about making sandcastles. Are they fun to make? Why don't they last long? Invite the pupils to share memories of how much effort they put into building a sandcastle. How did they feel when the sea washed it away? Have they ever baked a cake? Did it last long? If not, why? Would they like to build more castles or bake more cakes?
- Show the pupils your model sandcastle. Would they like to take it with them to the seaside, so saving the effort of making a real sandcastle? Why not? Discuss the tactile quality of sand, the creativity involved in sculpturing sand and their feelings as they watch the sea flow up into the moat.
- Ask, 'Have you ever built a snowman?' 'Are you sad when your snowman melts?' 'How would you feel if there were snow all the year round and never any warm sunshine?'
- Repeat the title of the poem. Ask, 'Is "trouble" a word you would normally associate with an enjoyable activity?' Invite the pupils to guess what might be the 'trouble'. Why does the title give a sense of foreboding?
- Invite the pupils to follow the words as you read the poem aloud. Discuss how the poet makes the cement snowman sound unattractive. Ask them, in groups, to discuss and list words to sum up the tone and mood of each succeeding verse. (Verse one: criticism, value judgement; verse two: promise, planning; verse three: rationale, explanation; verse four: morbid, deathly; verse five: threatening, sinister; verse six: enduring, tedious; and verse seven: envy, longing.)

> **EXTRA**: Offer a choice of title – 'The Trouble with Cakes / Sandcastles' – and invite the pupils to write a poem to read aloud, adopting a similar point of view to that of the father in Roger McGough's poem.

27 **What has Happened to Lulu?**

SECTION **A time to weep** (page 29)   POET **Charles Causley (1917–2003)**

This poem achieves its emotional poignancy through the poet's technique of using questions in presenting his scenario. As the younger sibling of the missing daughter questions her mother, it is left for the reader to infer the events of the previous night.

Preparing to read this poem aloud

- The first three verses largely comprise questions, apart from the observation in the opening verse about what is left on Lulu's bed. Adopt a bewildered, increasingly urgent tone, pausing briefly between each of these verses.
- In verse four, reduce pace and volume for *I woke to voices late last night, / I heard an engine roar* (lines 13 and 14) to suggest the speaker turning over the events in his or her mind before you introduce a note of frustration and, possibly, anger in lines 15 and 16, *Why do you tell me the things I heard / Were a dream and nothing more?*
- In verse five, introduce a conciliatory tone, conveying concern.
- Adopt a pleading, despairing tone for the final verse, stressing that final single beat.

Detective work

- Read the poem aloud twice, the second time asking the pupils to follow the text.
- Elicit who the speaker is. (Already asleep when Lulu leaves; uses familiar name 'Lu'; addresses 'mother'.)
- Explain that you are going to try and answer the title question by asking further questions.
- Ask the pupils to look for clues in the form and nature of the questions, and in the brief, but vivid, descriptions of the aftermath of Lulu's departure. Prompt with questions, asking the pupils to justify their responses with direct reference to the text. Did Lulu leave in a hurry? (A single shoe left on the bed.) How did she leave her home? (The window was wide open, the curtain flapping in the breeze.) Was it a spur-of-the-moment decision or had she planned to run away? (She left a note.) At what time did she leave? (Late last night.) Is Lulu planning to return? (She took her savings with her.)
- Open a class discussion as to why Lulu left in such a manner and why her mother crumpled and burned the note. Since she burned the note the following morning, does this suggest she had reread the letter – perhaps several times – before destroying it? Why did she destroy it? (She was hurt by its words, which were perhaps unkind, angry or reproachful.)
- Prompt with questions. Ask, 'Was someone waiting for Lulu?' 'What was the *engine roar* [line 14]?' (Boyfriend's motorbike? A car?) 'Why does the child not accept the mother's dismissive explanations?' 'In the child's position, would you believe it was just the sound of the rain or a dream?'
- Encourage the pupils to build a picture of the characters involved and the possible content of the letter. What was Lulu's relationship with her mother? Do relationships have ups and downs? What aspects of family relationships are constant? (Love, displayed in the mother's tears.)
- Finally, discuss how the poet's use of questions, rather than statements, enhances the feelings of bewilderment, hurt, anger, shock and, ultimately, love.

EXTRA: Challenge the pupils to write in the first person Lulu's note to her mother – in a way that makes Lulu's feelings clear. Will the note explain why she is leaving at night? Does it mention whether she will be back? Encourage them to take turns in reading their letters to the rest of the class.

Schofield & Sims   **A Time to Speak** and a Time to Listen   **Teacher's Guide**   33

37 Stop All the Clocks

SECTION **A time to mourn** (page 39)   POET **W H Auden (1907–1973)**

This poignant poem, made famous overnight when it was used in the 1994 film, *Four Weddings and a Funeral*, epitomises feelings of deep grief and mourning. Its sentiment of unremitting hopelessness in the face of losing a loved one is tempered by awareness that the very despair expressed makes it, equally, a love poem.

Preparing to read this poem aloud

- Read the first two verses as the list of instructions that it is, adopting a matter-of-fact tone of voice, and reading at a measured pace, pausing at commas and line-endings.
- Raise pitch at the onset of verse three, adding emotion to the words. Pause significantly before, and after, *I was wrong* (line 12).
- Adopt a tone of resignation for the final verse.

Love and loss

- Invite the pupils to think what it is like when they press the 'pause' button in the middle of watching a DVD. What happens? (All action, movement and sound stops instantaneously in mid-action.)
- Now ask them to imagine that happening in real life, in the middle of a lesson, or on their journey to school. It would be a very unreal feeling. Explain that the narrator in this poem is feeling the shock of losing a loved one, and wants the whole world to stop while he mourns.
- Read the poem aloud and share responses to the words. Do pupils who have lost someone close (or even a much-loved pet) empathise with the speaker's feelings?
- Elicit how the narrator's stance changes subtly throughout the poem. Initially, it is matter-of-fact, gradually admitting feelings and emotion into the description of his relationship with the person he mourns.
- Briefly discuss the generally accepted belief that mourning is how we deal with grief, and that the process has recognised stages, such as initial disbelief and lack of acceptance, followed by anger or feelings of guilt, depression and extreme sadness and, finally, a level of acceptance and hope. Elicit which stages of grief this poem represents.
- Reread the last line of the third verse, *I thought that love would last for ever: I was wrong* (line 12). Sort the pupils into groups and ask them to discuss this line in the light of the rest of the poem. Is he in fact wrong? Is it because love lasts forever that he is feeling the pain of his loss? Is this a love poem?
- Ask each group to discuss ways in which love can be channelled after a person has died, for example, through sharing happy memories, visiting a grave or a special place, collecting photographs and memorabilia, writing memoirs or a eulogy, painting or playing music that relates to the loved one.
- Bring the class together and invite a speaker from each group to sum up their thoughts. Elicit positive aspects to mourning, such as honouring a loved one's memory and celebrating his or her life.

> **EXTRA:** Challenge the pupils to write a verse modelled on the original poem, but this time thinking of positive things, to celebrate 'picking up the pieces' of life again. Begin, for example, 'Set your alarm clock, and leap out of bed / Take the dog for a walk, sing songs in your head'.

38 # When I am Dead, my Dearest

SECTION **A time to mourn** (page 40)   POET **Christina Rossetti (1830–1894)**

At the time this poem was written, it was a common Christian belief that, on death of the body, a person's soul lived on, in sleep, until the day of resurrection. The speaker is concerned that her absence should not interfere with her loved ones' lives, and they should carry on with their everyday occupations, remembering or forgetting her as and when their thoughts dictate.

Preparing to read this poem aloud

- Selfless and unsentimental, this poem invites a pragmatic tone of voice, accepting death as an inevitable separation, which is not 'the end of the world'.
- Ensure an upbeat optimism in your voice to reflect the speaker's feelings and a tone of acceptance, especially in the final two lines.

Our words reveal us

- Discuss why we mourn loved ones when they die. (Largely because we love them and miss their company.) Discuss how happy memories of someone help to comfort us. (They keep the person alive in our head; remind us of the person's value and influence on our life and that of others.) Encourage pupils to draw on their own experience, both of bereavement and missing people who live a long way away.
- After reading the poem aloud, reread *Be the green grass above me / With showers and dewdrops wet* (lines 5 and 6). What is special about grass after rain? (Strong-growing, full of life, extra green and bright after showers.) Introduce the word 'resilient' (full of spirit and life, bouncy and strong, unbeaten). Discuss how 'being' the grass becomes a metaphor for making the most of being alive, seizing the day, not wasting time worrying about the dead who are happy.
- Explain the archaic word *haply* (lines 15 and 16), which means 'perhaps' or 'maybe', not to be confused with 'happily'.
- Split the class into pairs and ask the pupils to share what they would miss about their partner if he or she moved to the other side of the world. What would they want their partners to remember about them?
- Encourage them to make notes and develop a eulogy about their partner, based on their own feelings, and their partner's wishes. Read aloud this example:

  Jack was always laughing, which made me laugh, too. He would want to be remembered for his rope-climbing and gymnastic skills. I miss walking to and from school with him. I always think about Jack in the autumn when I pass the horse-chestnut tree, where we used to find huge conkers. I don't think Jack will forget our friendship that began the day we both started school.

- Keep the tone as light as the poem to prevent the pupils from becoming over-sentimental. Remind them that this is a hypothetical event and that they should imagine their partners returning after some time, just as the poet did not see death as a permanent divider but as a temporary parting.
- Listen to a selection of eulogies from pupils willing to share their thoughts.

EXTRA: Ask the pupils to prepare a talk about someone whose temporary absence makes them sad. Encourage them to include plans for activities to enjoy when they are together again.

PART ONE

39   Do not Stand at my Grave and Weep

SECTION A time to mourn (page 41)	**POET Mary E Frye (1905–2004)**

This poem offers comfort and reassurance to mourners, allowing them to picture their loved one's life continuing in the beauty of the natural world.

Preparing to read this poem aloud

- Vary tone and pace to lift each fresh image in the lines beginning *I am*.
- Recognise *I am the swift uplifting rush* (line 8) by the briefest of pauses, so retaining the flow of meaning on to the following line.
- Close with a life-affirming, uplifting tone for the final line, *I am not there. I did not die.*

Life and death

- Discuss what purpose is served by graves and cemeteries, concentrating especially on their function to mourners in the process of grieving.
- If possible, visit a local churchyard and read some of the headstones. Suggest that friends and family of the deceased feel close to the person they love when visiting his or her grave and that is why they often leave flowers.
- Explain that sometimes bodies are cremated and ashes scattered. Discuss why this may be appropriate for some people. (They may like the idea of their remains becoming part of the natural world, integral to a loved place.)
- Introduce the poem by its title, establishing that the narrator is the one whose body has been placed in the grave, imploring mourners not to grieve, but rather to find the person still alive in all the things that he or she loved in life.
- Read the poem aloud. Then elicit and list the references to the natural world: *winds, snow, sunlight, rain, birds* and *star-shine*. Discuss what these images have in common. (They are peaceful / gentle / beautiful.)
- Invite suggestions as to the effect of the poem. (It is comforting / reassuring / positive.) Does the narrator want people to be unhappy as they mourn? Discuss why not.
- Ask the pupils to think about which part of nature they would like to be a part of, if they did not have their human body. Collect and list suggestions, inviting them to precede each suggestion with 'I am', for example, 'I am … the stream where you paddle in the park'.
- Return to the poem and, sharing ideas, together plan a eulogy based on what the pupils have learned of the person in the poem. Offer an opening such as 'Please do not cry, that's not what Mary would have wanted. She loved feeling the wind on her face.' Act as scribe, inviting suggestions and encouraging the pupils to embellish ideas based on the text. For example, they might decide on where she liked to walk. (On the downs / on a favourite beach / in her garden / by a lake.)
- Take turns to read the finished eulogy, changing reader at each new sentence. Do the pupils like the character they have built? Why? Is their eulogy 'true to the poem'? Does it reflect the implied personality in the poem?

> **EXTRA:** Challenge the pupils to imagine themselves old and at the end of a long and active life. Encourage them to imagine their ambitions fulfilled, for example, their flight into space or a life-changing invention accomplished. Ask them to present their own wishes for mourners when, at a great age, they die. Encourage them to concentrate on a celebration of their life, the qualities and achievements for which they would like to be remembered.

49 Philip Fox

SUITABLE FOR YOUNGER PUPILS

SECTION **A time to gather stones together** (page 50)   POET **Colin West**

A short, witty *epitaph* (words written in memory of someone), with an implied moral, this poem is an easy quatrain to learn by heart, and will doubtless raise a wry smile.

Preparing to read this poem aloud

- Pause briefly at the end of each line, and slightly longer at the end of the second line after *rocks*. A mock-serious tone would suit the subject well.

The bigger picture

- Explain that this humorous poem is an epitaph. Ask the pupils where such a verse might be found (on a gravestone or memorial tablet, or on a card tucked into a bunch of flowers and placed at the top of a cliff).
- Read the poem aloud. Can the pupils infer how Philip Fox died? Elicit their answers through a discussion of the nature, and weight, of rocks. How might he have been carrying them? (Perhaps in a backpack, which made him lose his balance?) What does a cliff imply? (A sheer drop.)
- Do the pupils believe this is a true story? Why not? (The flippant treatment of the subject and the catchy rhyme.)
- Point out that alliteration, as in the title, also makes for humour.
- Invite them to imagine that the story is to be reported on the television news. Explain that they will have to add a background story to the main event. They must determine more about the late Philip Fox. Did he have a family? If so, do they also have odd hobbies? Perhaps Philip Fox's weepy relative recounts how he wishes his brother had stuck to his earlier hobby of collecting feathers.
- Sort the pupils into groups to plan their report. Encourage them to role-play an interviewer and talk to neighbours, friends and relatives, building up a bigger picture of Philip Fox's life and personality. Stress that they are to use humour so that the report is in the same vein as the original poem.
- Listen to each group's planning and prompt with questions to elicit in-depth thinking. Suggest that they use comical props – perhaps Philip Fox's favourite rock, which he took to bed with him – or objects that rely on rhyme for humour. (For example, Philip Fox's Sunday 'sockses' / building blocks / his earlier collection of frocks. His twin brother's collection of clocks / locks / weathercocks.)
- Ensure that their report includes a brief introduction and a closing statement.
- Encourage them to include Colin West's original poem in the report.
- After planning and practice, allow the groups to perform their news report. Praise pupils' ability to retain a mock-solemn tone while keeping a straight face.

EXTRA: Challenge the pupils to write and then read aloud a short, humorous epitaph, inventing alliterative names that offer a choice of rhymes to inspire the 'story' behind the verse. Offer springboards of alliterative names to less imaginative pupils, for example, Billy Ball, Daisy Day, Griselda Green, Sajiv Singh. Provide rhyming dictionaries.

PART ONE

50 **Stone Circles**

SECTION **A time to gather stones together** (page 51)   POET **Tony Mitton**

This poem explores the mystery of prehistoric stone circles such as Stonehenge. Their meaning and purpose is now lost, and they, like the builders' own remnants, have become anonymous bones.

Before the lesson
- Prepare a collection of photographs of standing stones and circles, such as Stonehenge and Avebury. If possible, arrange to visit such a site.

Preparing to read this poem aloud
- Retain a measured pace throughout, pausing at each line-ending, and a little longer between verses.
- Identify west and east, so that you can point in these directions when you read, *would sink and rise* (line 7).
- In verse six, stress the word *why* (line 12).

Transience and eternity
- Read the poem aloud. Share the photographs of standing stones and circles. Discuss the age of the stones, their weight, and our lack of knowledge as to how and why they were positioned in that way. Elicit the clues that we have. (Alignment with stars and planets, and the movement of the sun and the moon.) Might these have influenced, or reflected, the builders' beliefs?
- Invite the pupils to compare the images of *blown away* (line 18), *vanished winds* (line 19) and *light as a leaf* (line 20). Such things are transient, ephemeral; cannot be kept. Elicit the contrast of the heavy permanence of the stones. Draw attention to how comparing the stones with *remnant bones* (line 25) links their existence to *The ones* (line 1) who put them there.
- Invite the pupils to reread the poem, noticing particularly the opening and closing lines. How are these linked? Is the poem as much about the people who positioned the stones as it is about the stone circles?
- Arrange the class in a well-spaced circle. Explain that they are to stand as still as stone, as if they were the stones in the ancient circle. Mark the four main compass points in the centre of the ring.
- Invite the pupils facing most directly east to say what they can see in their mind's eye, imagining they are outdoors in open countryside. Challenge them to describe the sunrise. What do they see first? The sky brightening in the general direction of the east? An intense bright spot on the horizon? Repeat with those looking west.
- Now, ask them to sit cross-legged and to keep as still as stone. Join them, and together, reread the poem.
- Explain that you are going to move around the circle, pointing to a pupil as you do so. He or she, in the persona of a stone, will make a wish and say something that the 'stone' wants to happen. For example, the pupil facing east may say, 'I invite the sun to rise' (rather than 'I can *see* the sun rise'). The next pupil may offer 'I persuade the birds to sing', and so on.
- If pupils find the activity difficult, ask them what they can see, hear, feel, taste or smell. If they say, for example, that they can smell smoke, hint at how this could become their wish fulfilled, 'I wish dry wood to burn'.

EXTRA: Challenge them in groups to plan and present an imaginary explanation for the stone circle's purpose. Is it spiritual or practical? Is the circle the world's soul or a big compass?

51 # Taking a Chance

SECTION **A time to embrace** (page 52)   POET **Roger Stevens**

Published for the first time in the anthology, this short motivational poem will encourage pupils to examine their understanding of the words 'chance' and 'embrace'. They may also want to research details of the Amazon, Kathmandu and the sport of white-water canoeing to understand the enormity of these feats of courage and endeavour.

Preparing to read this poem aloud

- Make sure that the title leads smoothly into the poem, from 'a' chance to 'the' chance, so setting it in context.
- Keep your tone of voice upbeat and inspirational, lifting your voice at the line-endings. Without the aid of punctuation, it is important to recognise where line-endings require pauses: after *The chance to swim the Amazon* and *To climb up Kathmandu* (lines 1 and 2), with a longer pause after *In a two-man crewed canoe* (line 4).
- Pause briefly after *So* (line 7) and emphasise the imperative verbs in the final line.

Risk and opportunity

- Together, and with the help of dictionaries, list definitions of the verb, 'to embrace', for example: 'to clasp', 'hug', 'receive gladly', 'accept willingly' (an idea), 'adopt' (a belief-set, lifestyle or profession), 'encircle' or 'contain', 'avail oneself of' (an opportunity).
- After reading the poem aloud, ask the pupils to identify the meaning of 'embrace' to which the poem's message applies.
- Look at the title. Discuss the double meaning of 'chance', which means both 'opportunity' and 'risk'. Offer, or invite, brief extreme examples of how life always carries risk. If you jump from a high building without a parachute you 'risk' death, while you 'risk' becoming ill through lack of exercise and sunshine if you never leave home.
- Break the class into groups and ask them to discuss when it is worth taking a risk in order to embrace an opportunity. They could begin by considering the opportunities cited in the poem or in other similar activities.
- Explain that each group is to come up with one or two examples of amazing opportunities that involve risk. Assess what risks are involved and whether the activity is worth the risk. Discuss, too, how they may reduce risks when having an adventure. Each group should nominate a reporter to act as spokesperson.
- Then ask each group to consider 'an event' that is high-risk, and discuss why it would *not* be worth taking the risk.
- Bring the class together to share opinions. Ask each group spokesperson to explain how the group justified the risk assessment.
- Encourage the class to form a consensus on how we should approach chances and balance risk with pleasure, the value of exploration and/or experience, at a personal and global level. (Learning to dive, say, compared with sending a manned flight to Mars.) Determine if there are grey areas or personal differences.

> **EXTRA**: Invite the pupils to set themselves a personal challenge and to keep a video journal of how far they are willing, and able, to complete the task. **Ensure that their challenges are not dangerous**.

63   The Sorrow of Socks

SECTION **A time to lose** (page 62)   POET **Wendy Cope**

The light and whimsical subject of this poem perfectly matches its form: a *triolet* (a poem of eight lines, patterned ABAAABAB). It begins and ends with a two-line refrain, the second line of which is – almost – repeated in the last line. The whole poem contains only two rhymes, A and B, making it an easy poem for children and young people to memorise and recite. The mysterious odd-sock experience will strike a universal chord, while the personification of these 'loners' offers a fresh and humorous perspective.

Before the lesson

- Prepare a mock washing-line of odd socks pegged up together. Make these as diverse as possible – a football sock, a thick boot sock, a decorative Christmas stocking, a walking sock, a baby's sock, stripy, spotty and plain socks, a bedsock, and so on. In addition, you could ask each pupil to bring an odd sock to school.

Preparing to read this poem aloud

- Before introducing the poem, ask the pupils if they have ever thought of clothes having feelings. Announce the title with exaggerated seriousness and reverence.
- Read the poem at a steady pace, pausing briefly at the end of each line. Allow your voice to echo the mystery of the odd-sock scenario – stressing *want to* (line 4), *puzzle* (line 5), and exaggerating the long vowels in *dark lairs* (line 6).
- Adopt an observant tone for the first appearance of the refrain and then a resigned tone of voice when (almost) repeating it at the end.

Extemporising stories

- Read the poem aloud. Then ask the pupils if they notice anything odd about the socks that you have pegged up on the washing-line. (They are singles, not pairs.)
- Discuss occasions when the pupils have experienced finding an odd sock and been unable to find its partner. Do the missing socks ever turn up? If so, where? (Under the bed / in the rubber door-seal of the washing machine / in their dad's sock drawer / in the car.)
- Explain that each individual sock has its own history. Ask each pupil to think of a sock. Explain that, in a few minutes, they are going to tell the story of that sock.
- Encourage them to use their imagination. For those lacking in inspiration, offer questions to set their minds working: Do they know the sock's owner? Did they find the sock? If so, where? Were they given the sock? If so, by whom? Does it fit or is it someone else's? Is it meant to be worn? Does it have any properties that can't be seen? Is there anything inside it? Does it have another purpose (as a glove-puppet / for polishing silver / hanging by the chimney / covering the nozzle of a vacuum cleaner to stop small things being sucked up)?
- Allow only five minutes for planning before inviting the pupils, in turn, to tell their stories. If they brought a sock in, ask them to hold it for the class to see. If necessary, give them starters such as 'One morning …' and ask them to finish with '… and that is the story of my sock'. Limit their storytelling time to no longer than two or three minutes.

> **EXTRA:** Challenge the pupils to retell their sock story in writing, using conventions such as paragraphs, a beginning, middle and an end, adding more detail to their original telling and then reading it to the class. Ask the rest of the class to give a score for each story read.

64 **The Loser**

SECTION **A time to lose** (page 63)   POET **Cynthia Castellan**

Anyone who competes in a sport will relate to the disappointment of under-achievement after weeks of practice and preparation. The unexpected applause given to 'the loser' exemplifies respect shown to those who 'get back in the saddle' – in this case literally.

Preparing to read this poem aloud

- Verse one requires a brisk, expectant and proud tone of voice, retained throughout the second verse's optimism.
- Slightly extend the usual pause between verses before stressing the word of foreboding that opens verse three, *Yet* (line 9); draw out the long 'oo' sounds in *loomed* and *doomed* (line 11).
- Increase pace in verses four and five, pausing at the ellipsis after *bright* (line 20), to allow listeners to anticipate the inevitable result.
- Reduce pace and lower pitch for the final verse, again allowing pride to creep into the final two lines.

Back in the saddle

- Read the poem aloud. Discuss the term 'getting back in the saddle' and how this is a literal example of an attitude to setbacks that can be applied metaphorically to a broader experience. Invite metaphorical examples that the pupils have experienced, or observed, of immediately reattempting an activity or recovering after a setback. Maybe their 'saddle' was also literal, relating to a bike or a pony?
- Invite the pupils to discuss how the speaker's feelings gradually change from verse one to the final verse, *They set me on my horse* (line 22). Make two contrasting lists of adjectives to reflect the changes, such as: proud, hopeful, optimistic, excited, eager / worried, distressed, disappointed, embarrassed, unhappy.
- Elicit adjectives that reflect the speaker's feelings at the end of the poem. (Surprised / pleased / comforted / restored.)
- List the following proverbs and ask the pupils to decide which may apply, directly or ironically, to events within the poem: 'Pride comes before a fall', 'Practice makes perfect', 'You can take a horse to water, but you can't make it drink', 'Failure teaches success', 'Never say die', 'Never hit a man when he's down', 'Fortune favours the brave', 'Hope springs eternal', 'Nothing ventured, nothing gained', 'The unexpected always happens' and 'Undertake no more than you can perform'.
- Ask them to discuss, in groups, questions to put to the show-jumper, based on these proverbs. For example, for the proverb 'Undertake no more than you can perform', they may ask, 'Do you think this course was too difficult for you?' Alternatively, they could use the proverb within their question: 'Is it true that practice makes perfect?'
- Choose one pupil within each group to role-play the show-jumper, while the rest of the group act as reporters, asking their planned questions. The pupil must reply, in role, justifying his or her participation and skills, explaining why he or she got back in the saddle, and so on, for example, 'I couldn't believe it when people applauded'. The rider may also draw on proverbs, including those listed above, within his or her response.

EXTRA: Invite the pupils to draw and annotate a graphic-story interpretation of the poem's events and to put together a presentation that describes, among other things, their method of illustration.

65 Lion

SECTION **A time to keep** (page 64)   POET **Celia Warren**

This fantasy poem describes the contents of an imaginary box, a source of emotional comfort in the narrator's mind. Although the poem describes the lion in the box as physical and tactile, it is nevertheless an imaginary creature, whose fanciful presence soothes the speaker in times of need.

Preparing to read this poem aloud

- Read verse one as simply as it is written.
- Introduce a tone of awe and wonder in verse two, modified by a logical explanatory tone that continues into verse three.
- Change to a confidential and quieter tone of voice for verse four, pausing before the final verse and holding on to each word in the alliterative last line.

Creating a comfort-zone

- Provide writing materials for the pupils and ask them to listen as you read a list of categories. The categories could include toy, possession, food, colour, place, living thing, memory, time of day, musical instrument, activity, garment.
- Explain that, for each category, you want them to write down something they love, value or treasure. These might be specific – from a teddy bear to a picture on their bedroom wall – or generic, like chocolate.
- Advise them not to think too long about their choices as you read the list since you are looking for spontaneous answers.
- Listen to some of the pupils' responses and discuss which items are physical and tactile, and which are abstract. Discuss how we can capture some abstract things, such as views, memories and sounds, through photographs, drawings or recordings.
- Ask them to imagine the world before the invention of cameras or electronic devices, and elicit how our minds, memories and imaginations were our only means of keeping abstract things. Discuss, too, how emotions cannot be stored except in our memories and experience of feelings. Give examples, such as 'We cannot store "love", but we can keep thoughts of people we love in our minds and hearts.'
- Read the poem aloud and elicit all that the poet's 'lion' represents – comfort, strength, reliability. Discuss how the imaginary box and its contents can accompany someone wherever they go, keeping them company in whatever circumstances they find themselves. Give examples: at the dentist, at the swimming baths, in the classroom, on a bus, in the playground, and so on.
- Ask the pupils, working in pairs, to tell each other which things from their list they would like to put in an imaginary box, and why. Encourage them to develop their list by combining elements, such as a living thing and a favourite colour – a purple tree with singing birds.
- As the pupils share ideas, encourage them to note the images they like. Invite them to share some of these images with the whole class, and elicit how and why these are comforting images.

> **EXTRA**: Challenge individual pupils to develop their notes into a poem, for reading aloud to the class.

75 **Shirt**

SECTION **A time to tear** (page 74)   POET **Carl Sandburg (1878–1967)**

In this deceptively simple poem, the poet explores what clothes say about us, the attention outfits invite, and how we feel about ourselves.

Preparing to read this poem aloud

- Read verse one as the simple statement that it is.
- Add a slight swaggering note of confidence to the subsequent verses. Make the most of the onomatopoeic *ripping razzly noise* (line 6), extending the 'r' sounds.
- Look your listeners especially hard in the eye for the final two lines.

Are we what we wear?

- Read the poem aloud and then open a discussion about how and why we choose to wear what we do, and how our choice influences others' opinions of us, reactions to us, and our own feelings about ourselves.
- Encourage the pupils to read 'The Emperor's New Clothes' by Hans Christian Andersen and to compare the story with this poem.
- Explore what the poet means by *a signal, / and a teller of souls* (lines 3 and 4). (We are what we wear.) Talk about why 'designer labels' appeal so widely and why labels appear on the outside of clothes for all to see, something which was unthinkable before the late twentieth century. Discuss the concept of being manipulated by both commercial designers and peer pressure.
- Ask how the speaker's shirt makes him feel (confident / in control / powerful). Discuss how the narrator recognises that he can make his own choices. Does this extend beyond what he wears, to the whole of his life? What can we infer about the character by 'reading between the lines'?
- Compare the second and third verses. The action of tearing suggests anger and the hint at the phrase 'keep your shirt on' indicates calm and patience. Discuss the effect of repeating *I can keep my shirt on* (line 9) in the final line. (It suggests the speaker has nothing to prove / that he doesn't need to fight to have confidence in himself.)
- Elicit a list of different kinds of outfit that we wear over the course of a year. This could include: play or casual; sports; club uniform; dressing-up costumes; sleepwear; swimwear; party; formal; school uniform; new / old clothes; hand-me-downs; matching outfits. Invite the pupils to copy the list, and to add one or two words about how they feel in each outfit.
- Sort the pupils into groups to compare and discuss why they chose the words they did. Is there common ground? Why do their responses differ, for example, when wearing sports gear as opposed to party clothes? In which clothes do they feel most at ease? Which clothes best reflect their personality? In which outfit do they feel most uncomfortable, not just physically but also emotionally and socially?
- Invite a spokesperson from each group to sum up their findings. Encourage whole-class debate based on their findings. Has it made them think more about their choice of clothes? Will it change how they look at others? Do they think clothes are important? Is it right to judge people by what they wear? Is it sensible to desire expensive designer labels? Elicit suggestions of how young people can be trendy while avoiding being pressured into extreme fashion.

> **EXTRA:** Hold a formal class debate on the pros and cons of wearing school uniform. Encourage the pupils to discuss as a team or individually issues such as cost, the levelling effect, sense of belonging, and so on.

76 Needle and Thread

SECTION **A time to sew** (page 75)	POET **Celia Warren**

The strong rhythm, rhyme and repetition in this light lyrical poem will make it easy for the pupils to learn by heart. The abstract nature of the requests that are voiced to the sewing implements suggests a retrospective mood of longing and regret. This poem has been especially written for the anthology, **A Time to Speak and a Time to Listen**.

Preparing to read this poem aloud

- The repeated rhythm of the refrain establishes a strong rhythm. Make the most of this, allowing it to echo in the second line of verses one, two and three.
- Do not pause too long between verses one, two and three. Pause slightly longer before the final verse.
- Pause at each comma in the final couplet, slowing pace and adding a remorseful, almost pleading tone to the words.

Learning by heart

- Read the poem together and elicit the common factor in all the speaker's requests. (All relate to the spoken word.) Discuss each request in turn, considering the mood of the speaker. (Does the speaker want a happy or sad song? Why? Is the speaker thinking about whether he or she will be remembered after death? Does the speaker have any regrets about what he or she has done?)
- Explain the meaning of 'sampler' and the sort of things that a traditional embroidered sampler would display (the alphabet, the name and date of birth of the needleworker, a quotation from a poem). In their opinion, would a sampler be attractive?
- Does the speaker hope to have only the good things remembered, not the bad? Kind words, not cruel ones, so that the sampler shows only the best side of his or her character?
- Point out that words are often spoken in haste, but cannot be unspoken. Ask, 'Should we think twice before saying something hurtful or unkind?'
- Ask the pupils, working in pairs, to share occasions when they have said something that they regret. Which words would they like to 'unpick'?
- As a whole class, ask the pupils whether they can quote a few lines, or an entire verse, from a favourite poem, words that 'sing in their head'. Invite them to share these lines or verses with the class, first introducing them with a brief explanation of why they chose them.
- Challenge the pupils to find examples of alliteration (*sew / song / sing / sampler / said; lyric / live*) and to discuss the value and purpose of this device, and how it helps the musicality of the words.

> **EXTRA:** Ask the pupils to add their own verse to the poem, using repetition to rhythmic effect. Then invite them to read it aloud. Encourage them to use the format of the first three couplets or to add a 'But …' couplet, as in the original poem. Offer end-rhymes (or cloze-procedure lines) for less confident pupils to complete, for example: 'Sew me … to keep by my bed'; 'Sew me … where I tread'; 'Sew me … to eat with my bread'.

77 # My Sock and an Old English Proverb

SECTION **A time to sew** (page 75)   POET **Celia Warren**

Published for the first time in the anthology, this short, lyrical poem describes a literal interpretation of the well-known proverb, which is usually used metaphorically.

Preparing to read this poem aloud

- The poem can be divided into three parts: a statement, in lines 1 to 4; a regret, in lines 5 to 8; and, in the final two lines, a conclusion in the wording of the old proverb. Keep the metre consistent throughout the first two parts, pausing briefly to acknowledge the line-breaks and rhymes.
- Pause a little longer before the concluding adage, stressing *time* and *nine*.

Literal and metaphorical

- Do the pupils know any fairytales or stories that are about needles and thread? ('Sleeping Beauty', 'The Elves and the Shoemaker' by the Grimm Brothers.)
- Read the poem aloud and ask the pupils to identify which words recreate the old English proverb, 'a stitch in time saves nine'. Write the proverb on the board.
- Reread the poem, making sure that the pupils recognise what the numbers 'eight' and 'nine' refer to (time of day; number of stitches, respectively).
- Clarify that mending a small hole requires fewer stitches and less time than mending a large hole. It also saves a considerable amount of effort and materials. Explain that, in this poem, the words are interpreted literally.
- Challenge the pupils to rephrase the poem's meaning as a metaphor, for example: it is quicker and easier to solve a problem if you take action straightaway.
- Together, think up examples of how the saying might be applied to other situations. Cite a couple of diverse examples:
  - A man has a small hole in his tooth. He doesn't go to the dentist for a filling, which is a small and painless procedure. The hole becomes bigger. He ends up with toothache and the tooth must be removed.
  - The paint on a wooden gate begins to peel. If it is fixed straightaway, it will be simply a matter of rubbing down and repainting the wood. If it is left to decay further, the wood will rot and the owner will have to buy, and fit, a brand new gate.
- Sort the pupils into groups. Ask each group to think up a scenario and storyline to act out a short script to illustrate the metaphorical meaning of the saying. For example, one character might nag another, who fails to act in time. The scene could conclude with one pupil quoting the saying.
- For older pupils, offer a choice of other common sayings to interpret metaphorically, such as 'Pride comes before a fall', 'Many hands make light work', 'Too many cooks spoil the broth', 'A bird in the hand is worth two in the bush' and 'Necessity is the mother of invention'. Can they add further sayings to this list?

> **EXTRA:** Challenge the pupils to write their scenario as a script, complete with details of props, costume, stage directions and list of characters.

87 Eighteenth Sonnet

SECTION **A time to love** (page 84)   POET **William Shakespeare (1564–1616)**

This is one of 154 sonnets written by Shakespeare, and one of a series addressing a youth whom he admired. Its continued popularity suggests that it still fulfils the promise of the final couplet: that as long as people live, so, through the poem, will its subject.

Preparing to read this poem aloud

- Read at a measured pace, pausing briefly at each line-ending, allowing your phrasing to reflect the regular *iambic pentameter*, which is the *di-dum*, *di-dum*, *di-dum*, *di-dum*, *di-dum* rhythm of every line. Pause slightly longer before reading the final couplet, adding emphasis to its summarising statement.

Compliments and comparisons

- Arrange the class in a circle. Explain that each pupil in turn must pay a compliment to the person on their left, moving clockwise, avoiding repetition and ending with the first speaker. Give examples: 'You have a lovely smile'; 'You are a great goalie'.
- Explain that the second time around the circle they are to create a simile, for example, 'Your smile is like sunshine'; 'You stop goals like a bulldozer'. Invite suggestions, encouraging them to be adventurous. Challenge them to invent metaphors, for example, 'You ARE sunshine'; 'You ARE a bulldozer'.
- Ask them which compliments they liked best and why. Discuss how it feels to be compared with a favourable thing.
- People who are cheerful have a 'sunny disposition'. Ask whether such a person would be better compared to a summer's day or a winter's day.
- Challenge the class to list every aspect of a perfect summer's day. (Warm, dry, flowers blooming, trees in leaf, birds singing, relaxing.) Quote George Gershwin's lyrics: 'Summertime, and the livin' is easy'. Consider why summer is said to be easier than winter (no fuel to fetch, no snow to clear, food harvested, and so on).
- Read aloud the sonnet. Then reread it, asking the pupils to listen for references to extreme weather conditions that can spoil a summer's day (such as the wind, which may damage buds [line 3], and the sun, which can be too hot [line 5]). Explain that the subject of the poem is lovelier than summer because he or she has none of these flaws.
- Ask them to explain the final couplet. Discuss how the poem is still relevant, that we are still able to see in it the person's perceived perfection even though hundreds of years have passed since Shakespeare wrote it.
- Return to the circle of compliments. Invite each pupil to adapt their comparison so that the compliment exceeds the comparison (for example, 'You run faster than lightning').

> **EXTRA**: Challenge the pupils to paraphrase the final couplet, incorporating the gist of their compliment, such as 'As long as feet can kick and goals are saved, / As long lives this, that shows how you behaved.'

88   # Flowers

SECTION **A time to love** (page 85)   POET **Wendy Cope**

Flowers are the classic gift to express love or affection. However, once cut, they are ephemeral. Memory, on the other hand, can last a lifetime. It is this juxtaposition that the poet explores, comparing the physical and tangible with the abstract and intangible.

Preparing to read this poem aloud

- Read the poem at a measured pace. Pause at each full stop to allow the words to make thought-provoking impact.
- Pause at each line-ending, allowing words such as *You thought* (line 7) space to breathe.
- At the word *look*, in the penultimate line, lift your tone of voice to stress the speaker's sudden realisation that memory outlasts cut flowers.

Nearly, but not quite

- Read the poem aloud. Briefly discuss the passage of time in the poem. Point out the use of *you'd* (line 3), showing how this 'nearly' bringing of flowers occurred a number of times. Discuss why the speaker can no longer hug the would-be giver. (Drifted apart / moved away / died.)
- In lines 9 and 10, ask how the meaning of the two smiles might differ – the first, in love and happiness; the second, wistful, wry or fond.
- Invite the pupils to suggest things that they, or someone they know, have 'nearly done'. It might be something about which they changed their mind, or something they started and didn't finish. Create a quick list, headed 'I nearly …':
  - baked a cake
  - knitted a scarf
  - visited my uncle
  - went skiing
  - bought an ice-cream
  - learned to swim.
- Return to the list and invite them to add a 'but …' clause to each event, such as '(I nearly) baked a cake (but) I dropped the bag of flour.' Explain that their images should be as inventive as possible. Ask them to read out their examples in turn, encouraging the rest of the class to offer suggestions and possible improvements.
- Select one example to develop into a shared, extemporised 'go on' story. Seat the pupils in a circle and ask them, in turn, to add an element to the 'nearly' story. For example, (Pupil 1): 'I nearly baked a cake, but I dropped the bag of flour, then …' / (Pupil 2): 'Then the dog rolled in the flour, so …' / (Pupil 3): 'So it looked like a ghost dog. When …', and so on. Prompt with a variety of link- and time-passing words. ('After that', 'then', 'as', 'because', 'soon', 'so', 'when', 'until', 'suddenly', 'but', 'only'.)
- Encourage the pupils either to repeat the story from the beginning or keep it flowing while you act as scribe, so that you can read it back to them after they have all made a contribution. Discuss a suitable ending and steer them towards an extemporised conclusion.

EXTRA: Ask the pupils to write the story in their own words, using paragraphs and adding description to enhance the basic events.

89 # Haiku

SECTION **A time to love** (page 85)   POET **Matsuo Bashō (1644–1694)**

Just as Shakespeare represents the sonnet, so Bashō represents the haiku. So well-known is he as the exponent of the form that he tends to be referred to by surname alone. He contemporised what was considered, in his time, an ancient form of poetry dating back to the end of the seventh century. This poem, which he cites as a love poem, is the exclamation of a woman who is upset when an expected male visitor is late.

Preparing to read this poem aloud

- Sometimes, when the Japanese original is translated into English, the classic 5–7–5 syllable count becomes imprecise. If you wish to read the poem aloud while maintaining the original count, try eliding the first two syllables in the middle line: 'tsa thor-ny way I'll send him'.
- Make the most of the passion and emotion of this short text, to show the exasperation, anger and frustration in the speaker's voice.

What's happening?

- Read the poem aloud. Ask, 'Who might be speaking the words?' 'Does the speaker sound happy or annoyed?' Share ideas of why the speaker may be angry, who the *wretched man* (line 1) may be, and his relationship to the speaker. Ensure the pupils explain the reasons for their suggestions. Invite comments from others as to the plausibility of the suggestions.
- Explain that this poem appears in **A time to love**. Does this surprise the pupils? Why isn't it in, for example, **A time to hate**? Talk about the two emotions. Discuss whether they overlap. If we think about someone all the time, allowing him or her to affect the way we feel and behave, is that born of love or hate?
- Discuss why Bashō classed it as a love poem, explaining the background. Is the woman upset because she loves the man? Ask them to share experiences of their parents being cross with them for being late home / not saying where they were going / saying something hurtful. Are they angry because they love, or hate, their children?
- Briefly practise reading the haiku aloud together. Encourage the pupils to show differing emotions until they know the words by heart.
- Divide the class into groups of five or six. Ask each group to plan a brief scene with a simple storyline that they will act out, improvising the dialogue. They may draw from experience or invent a scenario. Explain that the scene must conclude with the haiku spoken in their chosen context by a character. Allow them to change the word *man* (line 1) to suit their purpose – woman, girl, dog, boy, cat, and so on.
- For those who are more practised in improvisation, hand out small pieces of blank paper to each group member except one. Give this one pupil a piece of paper on which the haiku has been written. (Warn the pupils not to reveal who has the words.) The pupil with the haiku will be the one to deliver 'the punch line', with his or her peers not knowing who it will be. Their scenario, therefore, will be more spontaneous and less tightly planned.

> **EXTRA**: Challenge the pupils to find out more about Bashō, using reference books and websites. Then invite them to present a one-minute talk on the poet and his work.

99 # Adlestrop

SECTION **A time for peace** (page 95) POET **Edward Thomas (1878–1917)**

This is arguably one of the best-known and most popular poems of the twentieth century. It was written at a time when railway lines ran to many countryside places, stopping at platforms that now no longer exist as the lines have fallen into disuse. Nevertheless, pupils who have travelled by train will relate to seeing, through a window, place-names of locations they have not visited. They will, doubtless, have also experienced trains stopping 'unwontedly' in the middle of nowhere.

Preparing to read this poem aloud

- Introduce the poem as belonging to the early twentieth century, when trains ran on steam and travellers were accommodated in individual compartments, increasing feelings of isolation as they observed the passing countryside.
- Pause significantly after the first full stop in the opening line, implying that a question set off a response in the narrator's mind. Stress *name* (line 2).
- Similarly, pause at each full stop, allowing the memories to seem to return gradually. Increase tempo as commas replace full stops, and memories seemingly flood back.
- Slow down to a dreamy pace for the second half of verse three (lines 11 and 12). Pause a little longer before the final verse, stressing *And for that minute* (line 13) and adopting a tone of contentment and peace for the remainder.

Names and places

- Read the poem aloud and encourage the pupils to enjoy the atmosphere the words recreate. Together, locate Adlestrop on a map and note the county boundaries across which the speaker heard the birds' singing.
- Ask them to research Adlestrop on the internet and list a few facts about its size, location, population, nearest city, type of farming nearby. Is there woodland, arable or livestock farming nearby? Where might residents commute to for work?
- Demonstrate how facts can be found using the Contents page and Index of a reference book and search engines for websites. Sort the pupils into twos or threes. Provide atlases of Great Britain and give each group a different letter of the alphabet. Invite them to choose the name of a village or town that is a long way from where they live.
- Ask them to research their chosen village / town and to find it on the map, note which county it is in and, indeed, which country – England, Wales, Scotland, Ireland or an island that belongs to the British Isles.
- Challenge them to put together a short presentation to introduce the place to the rest of the class.
- With the class, prepare a list of questions to support the pupils as they write the presentation. Does the place have a special industry? Is it famous or did a person who was famous live there? Is it a holiday destination or generally regarded as a place of outstanding natural beauty? What leisure activities does it offer? How many schools does it have? How far is it from the sea?
- Bring the class together and ask them, in pairs or small groups, to present their place to the class.

> **EXTRA:** Ask the pupils, in groups, to prepare a poster advertising the place's attractions, as in a tourist bureau poster. Remind them of the importance of both words and layout, encouraging them to use snappy phrases, slogans and jingles, and pictures and fonts in varying sizes and colours.

100 # The Tree and the Pool

SECTION **Epilogue** (page 96)   POET **Brian Patten**

Time, in this poem, is the dictator, ignoring the wishes of human and inanimate objects alike. The poem provides a springboard for discussion of the nature of time and our lack of control over its passing and duration.

Preparing to read this poem aloud

- In the first two verses, aim to vary the tone, pace and volume of the different speakers. Alter where your stresses lie. In line 1, stress *leaves* and *drop*; in line 2, *I* and *freeze*; in line 3, *want*; and in line 4, *ever*.
- In the last verse, present lines 9 to 11 in a conspiratorial tone of voice, making the final line louder, more imperious, in the tone of a dictator.

Wishing

- Read the poem aloud and discuss the various wishes expressed. Ask, 'Which season do the tree and the pool like best?' 'Why is it foolish to wish never to cry?' (Crying brings relief / it heals / can only be avoided if we never love in the first place.)
- Elicit that we all have times that we want to last forever and times we want to end. Share a few of these experiences.
- Elicit that change is necessary. Cite the example of a bud, which is full of promise of what is to come, a hint of colour already visible, and of fruit following flower.
- Ask the pupils to think about Time. 'What sort of character does Time appear to be, judging by the last line of the poem?' (A dictator.) 'Is Time always harsh?' 'Can Time also be gentle and helpful, healing and patient?'
- Invite the pupils spontaneously to list three things that they do not want to happen – from the weather turning wet to the end of a birthday treat.
- Ask them to find a partner and to swap lists. To each of their partner's wishes, challenge them to add a tagline that turns the speaker into an inanimate object. For example, Pupil 1 writes, 'I don't want summer to end / to go to school / to have toothache'. Pupil 2 replies, 'said the daisy / the bus / the comb'.
- Next, invite them to choose one of the above examples and to discuss reasons for the wish. Encourage them to expand and develop their ideas into a short soliloquy. For example, the comb explains that he or she is made of gold, is priceless and belongs to long-haired Rapunzel, whose hair must not be allowed to tangle if she is to escape from the tower.
- Allow the pairs time to plan, before inviting them to tell their stories, taking turns to speak. Explain that you will be listening for imaginative scenarios and settings, convincing characterisation and vivid descriptive phrases.
- Invite members of the audience to ask two or three questions of each pair, to encourage them to improvise in role.

> **EXTRA:** Challenge the pupils to develop their inanimate character's feelings into a poem to read aloud to the class.

Poetry for Pleasure

A time to inspire

Background notes

If you were to ask poets what inspires their poems, they might well give a different answer for each poem. Generally, however, poems may be slotted into large categories: for example, sharing experience or feelings, a memory or a mood, evoking place or people, playing with words, entertaining through humour, telling a story, sharing a brief moment or painting a picture through vivid description.

Planning a programme of poetry to reflect its wide range of styles to suit different tastes is a challenge that the pupils will enjoy tackling.

This activity is suitable for any time of year, but would be especially well-timed if planned to coincide with National Poetry Day, which is usually held throughout the UK on the first Thursday in October.

Activity

- Sort the pupils into groups, appointing a scribe to each group, and distribute copies of the anthology.
- Explain that each group is to plan a poetry event as an evening's entertainment, to inspire an audience to enjoy poetry. Remind the pupils that they will need to find poems with a wide range of styles and subjects to appeal to different tastes. When planning their programme, they will also need to vary mood, pace, length and 'voice' to retain the audience's attention. Perhaps they can find some poems with a refrain with which the audience can join in?
- Hand out copies of the photocopy master 'Preparing a poetry event' to help each group to explore the diversity of poetry within the anthology and to select a range of poetic styles.
- Encourage participation of the whole group as one pupil acts as scribe to fill in the photocopy master.
- Bring the class together and compare the choice of poems, discussing the reasons for choices and inviting the pupils to explain why there may be overlap or differences in selection.
- Elicit a consensus of choices within each inspirational area, and discuss and plan a working running order for a whole-class performance programme.
- Ask the pupils to bear in mind that the event should begin and end on an optimistic note.
- Follow the planning through to a performance for another class, the rest of the school, parents or other invited guests. This will, of course, require rehearsal and continuous evaluation of the success of their choices, which can be modified if required.
- Encourage all the pupils to take part. Include solo performances, choral speaking and shared recitations. If possible, persuade the pupils to learn the poems by heart, ensuring that they make eye-contact with the audience. Decide which poems might involve audience participation and who will be responsible for inviting them to join in.
- Designate one group of pupils to orchestrate the smooth running of the presentation, perhaps designing and printing a programme, choosing Masters of Ceremonies to introduce each item, and so on.

Theme: Seasons

SUGGESTED POEMS: Spring: Poems 9 'Bulb' (Alison Chisholm), 18 'Thaw' (Edward Thomas), 43 'Daffodils' (William Wordsworth), 66 'Easter Monday' (Catherine Benson); **Summer:** Poems 47 'Shells and Stones' (Eric Finney), 99 'Adlestrop' (Edward Thomas); **Autumn:** Poems 8 'Plum' (Tony Mitton), 9 'Bulb' (Alison Chisholm), 14 'The Wind' (James Stephens); **Winter:** Poem 26 'The Trouble with Snowmen' (Roger McGough); **All seasons:** Poem 59 'The Kiss' (Sue Hardy-Dawson).

PREPARATION: Allow the pupils time to: practise reading one or two poems; draft or rewrite statements; practise speaking them; write own poems (optional); plan the running order and rehearse the whole assembly.

PROPS: Decorate the stage or a table with items according to the season: a hyacinth in a pot; vase of daffodils; bucket and spade; bowl of fruit; woolly hats and scarves. In addition, performers might hold a daffodil or wear a woolly hat, as appropriate.

A time to enjoy

- Explain that the aim of the assembly is to heighten enjoyment of the season.
- Read aloud the poems listed above and elicit which would be best to highlight the joys of that season, for example: a focus on new growth in spring; holiday and travel in summer; the fall of leaves and dying of flowers in autumn; the immediacy and pleasure of snow in winter. The pupils need not be limited to one poem.
- Depending on time, invite them to write their own poems on the theme of enjoyment of the season to complement their chosen poem. Remind them that the aim of their poem is to persuade others as to the season's attractions.
- Challenge younger pupils to find something to like in the current season, for example, 'I like seeing birds build nests.' Then encourage them to develop this simple sentence by dropping 'I like' at the onset, and replacing with 'In spring …', while substituting more exciting verbs and adjectives: 'In spring, birds gather soft moss to line their hidden nests.'
- Vote on the class's favourite six or so statements. Use these as an introduction, before asking pupils, working in pairs or small groups, to present the poem.
- Invite the pupils to lead a prayer of thanks and to choose a seasonal song / hymn.
- Close the assembly with another half-dozen statements that invite the listeners to share the season's joy. This time vary the opening words, replacing 'In spring …' with, for example, 'Let's look after our world / where baby birds chirp'; 'Remember to look for tiny green shoots as they burst through the soil', and so on.

Theme: Managing change

SUGGESTED POEMS (listed here in the order in which they are to be read): 1 'Haiku' (Celia Warren); 100 'The Tree and the Pool' (Brian Patten); 69 'These Old Shoes' (Tony Mitton); 78 'The Loom of Time' (Anonymous); 65 'Lion' (Celia Warren); 32 'Laugh and be Merry' (John Masefield).

PREPARATION: This assembly is useful if individual members of the class are coping with difficult changes at home – divorce, a new baby or the death of a grandparent – or at the end of the school year, before they start a new school or join a new class.

PROPS: Photographs of the pupils as babies, numbered and displayed around the classroom; photocopied lists of the names of pupils who brought photographs, one for each pair of pupils.

A time to change

- Read aloud Poem 1 'Haiku' and ask the pupils to imagine how their parents must have felt when they were born: excited, scared, tired, worried, pleased.
- Play a game. Distribute the photocopied list of pupils' names to each pair. Ask them to examine the baby photos and to match the photo with the classmate, writing the baby-photo number alongside the name of the pupil.
- Bring the class together and compare results, asking each pupil to claim their number in turn, while others tick off which they got right. Did anyone get all correct?
- Discuss how much the pupils have changed: they are bigger, taller, have more hair, more teeth. Elicit how their lives have changed – the activities they enjoy, their diet, maybe they have younger siblings. Ask if anyone has moved house. How did it feel? Has anyone changed school? Did it take time to get used to a new teacher?
- Remind the pupils that when they were born they faced the enormous change of suddenly coming into this world. Encourage them to see that all changes are manageable. Again, read together Poem 1 'Haiku'.
- Read the poems in the order in which they are listed above, introducing a fresh aspect to each one. Sometimes we don't like change but nothing 'stands still', Poem 100 'The Tree and the Pool'. Sometimes it's hard to let go of the old and welcome the new, Poem 69 'These Old Shoes'. We can't always see 'the big picture' but in the long run positive things result from difficult changes, Poem 78 'The Loom of Time'. Sometimes it helps to imagine putting our problems in a box and 'opening the lid' on them when we feel strong enough, Poem 65 'Lion'. Whatever we have to deal with, there's usually a way to be happy and smile, and enjoy our lives, Poem 32 'Laugh and be Merry'.
- Explain that the pupils are to use Poems 100, 69, 78, 65 and 32 in a class assembly on 'Change'. Sort them into five groups, with a scribe in each group. Invite them to plan a short introduction to each poem, similar to the examples above.
- Choose five poem readers and five narrators to lead the assembly. Invite them to add prayers or songs as appropriate. They may choose to close with Poem 98 'Prayer for Peace', which shows that we can also *choose* to change ourselves.

Theme: Self-belief

SUGGESTED POEMS: 21 'Demolition Worker' (Stanley Cook); 25 'Target' (Rachel Rooney); 51 'Taking a Chance' (Roger Stevens); 52 'Doubly my Ma' (Debjani Chatterjee); 64 'The Loser' (Cynthia Castellan); 75 'Shirt' (Carl Sandburg); 96 'When a Knight Won his Spurs' (Jan Struther); 98 'Prayer for Peace' (St Francis of Assisi).

PREPARATION: If the assembly is more than a week ahead, challenge each pupil to tackle a new task or to improve a skill. Note praiseworthy behaviour, such as one pupil helping another, the picking up of litter or returning a lost item to its owner.

PROPS: Examples of objects that symbolise the pupils' achievements, such as a skipping rope, an origami model, a page of neat writing.

A time to believe

- Explain that the pupils are to prepare an assembly that celebrates their own achievements, skills, prowess, abilities, staying power, and so on. Bring to their attention improvements in their interpersonal and social skills, and suggest that these reflect the pupils' growth as good citizens.
- Invite each pupil in turn to tell the class about some personal progress that he or she is aware of. This may relate to a specific challenge or to a more general improvement, for example, 'I really struggle with long multiplication but, even if I still find it hard, I keep on trying' or 'I didn't give up trying until I could climb a rope'.
- Ask them to write these statements onto small cards, which they will use as prompts in an assembly in which each will state their achievement.
- Add your own statements and observations of the pupils' social skills and behaviour. Be sure to include pupils who lack self-confidence or are slow to promote their own achievements.
- Invite a few pupils to demonstrate a new skill, or 'show and tell' something they have made or done.
- Ask the pupils which of the poems listed above they would like to include in their assembly, considering the merits of each. For example, Poem 21 'Demolition Worker' shows how something that we know requires great bravery and skill is made to look easy. Discuss how difficult things do not come easily until they have been thoroughly learned and practised.
- If the pupils wish to offer comfort to someone who is feeling discouraged, suggest Poem 52 'Doubly my Ma' followed by an aspirational poem such as Poems 25 'Target' or 51 'Taking a Chance'.
- Link the individual components of the assembly with a refrain, devised by the pupils, along the lines of, 'There's no such word as can't; / We thought we couldn't, but we can!' Keep to the same wording, using a memorable rhythm, so that the assembly can close with the audience joining in.
- Add a musical component to the poem so that the assembled pupils can join in, in the way that Poem 96 'When a Knight Won his Spurs' is performed to the folk melody, 'Stowey'.

Reading poetry aloud

Here is an example of how to annotate a poem before reading it aloud.

Daffodils – ⌒by **William Wordsworth**

I wandered <u>lonely</u> as a cloud ⌒→
That floats on high o'er vales and hills,
When < all at once I saw a <u>crowd</u>,
A <u>host</u>, of golden daff-o-dils;
5 > Beside the lake, beneath the trees,
<u>Fluttering</u> and <u>dancing</u> in the breeze.

Contin<u>u</u>ous as the stars that shine ⌒→
And <u>twinkle</u> on the milky way,
They stretched in never-ending line ⌒→
10 Along the margin of a bay:
< <u>Ten thousand</u> saw I at a glance,
Tossing their heads in sprightly dance.

> The waves beside them danced, but they ⌒→
<u>Out-did</u> the sparkling leaves in <u>glee</u>:
15 < A poet could not <u>but</u> be gay,
In such a <u>jocund</u> com-pan-y!
I gazed – and gazed – but little thought ⌒→
What <u>wealth</u> the show to <u>me</u> had brought:

For oft, when on my couch I lie ⌒→
20 > In vacant or in pensive mood,
They flash upon that inward eye ⌒→
Which is the <u>bliss</u> of <u>sol-i</u>-tude;
And then > my heart with <u>pleasure</u> fills,
And <u>dances</u> with the daffo<u>dils</u>.

⌒→ = continue without pause; <u>underlined</u> = stress whole word or syllable;
< = increase volume; > = reduce volume; - = syllable breaks within words.

Note: You may wish to use your own colour code and personal symbols as reminders.

From: **A Time to Speak and a Time to Listen: Teacher's Guide** by Celia Warren (ISBN 978 07217 1206 2), specially written to accompany the poetry anthology of the same title (ISBN 978 07217 1205 5/1225 3). Copyright © Schofield & Sims Ltd, 2013. Published by Schofield & Sims Ltd, Dogley Mill, Fenay Bridge, Huddersfield HD8 0NQ, UK (www.schofieldandsims.co.uk). This page may be photocopied after purchase for use within your school or institution only.

Prologue: A Time for Everything

There is a time for everything
And a season for every activity under heaven.
    A time to be born
        And a time to die
5   A time to plant
        And a time to pull up
    A time to kill
        And a time to heal
    A time to tear down
10   And a time to build up
    A time to weep
        And a time to laugh
    A time to mourn
        And a time to dance
15   A time to cast away stones
        And a time to gather stones together
    A time to embrace
        And a time not to embrace
    A time to find
20   And a time to lose
    A time to keep
        And a time to cast away
    A time to tear
        And a time to sew
25   A time to be silent
        And a time to speak
    A time to love
        And a time to hate
    A time for war
30 And a time for peace

Ecclesiastes 3: 2–8

From: **A Time to Speak and a Time to Listen: Teacher's Guide** by Celia Warren (ISBN 978 07217 1206 2), specially written to accompany the poetry anthology of the same title (ISBN 978 07217 1205 5/1225 3). Copyright © Schofield & Sims Ltd, 2013. Published by Schofield & Sims Ltd, Dogley Mill, Fenay Bridge, Huddersfield HD8 0NQ, UK (www.schofieldandsims.co.uk). This page may be photocopied after purchase for use within your school or institution only.

Preparing a poetry event

Name:	Class:	Date:

Choose a diverse selection of poems for a poetry event. Write the numbers and titles of the poems in the boxes provided. Sequence the poems so that you start and end with an uplifting poem.

Poems based on the poet's personal experience

Poems based on a shared memory

Poems that share and evoke strong feelings and emotions

Poems that entertain and amuse

Poems that play with language or involve wordplay

Poems that present a message or moral

Poems that are descriptive

Poems that are about celebration

Choosing a new theme

Name:	Class:	Date:

Find poems that fit into the themes or 'seasons' listed below. Write down their number and title and brief notes on how they fit into the theme.

A time to grow

Poem: number and title	Notes

A time to celebrate

Poem: number and title	Notes

A time to admire

Poem: number and title	Notes

A time to help

Poem: number and title	Notes

Index of poets

Agard, John 28, 91
Anonymous 62, 84
Armstrong, Martin 37
Assisi, St Francis of 104
Auden, W H 43

Bashō, Matsuo 95
Belloc, Hilaire 46, 68
Benson, Catherine 72
Benson, Gerard 85, 99
Binyon, Laurence 73
Blake, William 97
Brackenbury, Alison 16, 30
Brownlee, Liz 8

Castellan, Cynthia 70
Causley, Charles 33, 63
Chatterjee, Debjani 58
Chesterton, G K 9
Chisholm, Alison 15
Clarke, Jane 59
Cook, Stanley 27
Cope, Wendy 69, 94
Cornford, Frances 54
Cowling, Sue 39, 67
cummings, e e 64

Davies, W H 23
de la Mare, Walter 87, 103
Dean, Jan 51
Donne, John 11

Finney, Eric 10, 50, 53
Foster, John 101
Frye, Mary E 45

Gittins, Chrissie 26, 47

Hardy, Thomas 13, 22, 52
Hardy-Dawson, Sue 65
Hughes, Ted 60

Joseph, Jenny 96

Lear, Edward 79
Logue, Christopher 18

MacLeod, Doug 19
Magee, Wes 48
Masefield, John 38, 78
McGough, Roger 32
McNaughton, Colin 76
Mitchell, Cynthia 74
Mitton, Tony 14, 56, 75
Morgan, Michaela 42, 90

Nash, Ogden 61
Nicholls, Judith 100
Niven, Frederick 25
Noyes, Alfred 36

Owen, Gareth 35

Patel, Gieve 21
Patten, Brian 106
Phinn, Gervase 89

Rooney, Rachel 31
Rossetti, Christina 44
Rumble, Coral 40
Russell, Jane A 41

Sandburg, Carl 81
Scannell, Vernon 92
Shakespeare, William 93
Shavick, Andrea 34
Shelley, Percy Bysshe 29
Squire, J C 66, 88
Stephens, James 20, 98
Stevens, Roger 57
Stevenson, Robert Louis 77
Struther, Jan 102

Thomas, Edward 12, 24, 105
Toczek, Nick 17
Townsend, Jill 80

Umansky, Kaye 86

Warren, Celia 7, 71, 82, 83
West, Colin 55
Wordsworth, William 49

Index of titles

Adlestrop 105, 119, 123, 129
Algy Met a Bear 5, 62
Auguries of Innocence (extract) 97, 123

Ballet Teacher, The 47, 122, 126
Bulb 15, 108, 119, 129, 130
Bungalowner, The 92

Cargoes 78, 108, 126
Carol from Flanders, A 25, 115, 116,
    126, 130
Childhood 54, 122
Children and Sir Nameless, The 52, 108,
    109
Conference of Cows, A 5, 91, 122, 129
Creator 41, 123

Daddy Fell into the Pond 36, 109, 116,
    117, 124, 127
Daffodils 4, 5, 49, 108, 119, 129
Dandelion Time 5, 67, 108, 129
Death be not Proud 10, 11, 108
Demolition Worker 27, 121, 126
Discovery, The 66
Do not Stand at my Grave and Weep 45,
    128
Dog End Days 42, 108
Dog, The 5, 61, 108, 129
Donkey, The 5, 9
Doubly my Ma 58, 117, 121

Easter Monday 6, 72, 119
Eighteenth Sonnet 93, 108
Elephant is Born, An 8, 116, 124, 129
Evolution 100

Final Appointment, A 10, 11, 109, 116,
    128
Fishing for Compliments 59, 76, 108
Flowers 94, 129

Ghosts of Weeds, The 17, 109
Good Morning, Mr Croco-doco-dile 63,
    124, 127
Good Taste 18, 116
Got you, Pirate! 5, 74, 109, 116

Haiku 7, 95, 108, 117, 120, 130
Hate 98, 118

In the Misty, Murky Graveyard 48
It isn't Right to Fight 101, 109

Jacks 5, 51, 114, 117, 122

Kiss, The 65, 117, 119, 129

Laugh and be Merry 38, 108, 120, 128
Laughter Forecast, The 39, 108, 128
Leisure 5, 23, 123, 128
Lights Out 12, 108
Lion 71, 120
Loom of Time, The 84, 120
Loser, The 68, 70, 108, 116, 121
Lovely Mosquito 5, 19, 124

maggie and milly and molly and may 5,
    64, 122
Man he Killed, The 22
Mrs Reece Laughs 37
My Father is a Werewolf 5, 86, 117
My Sock and an Old English Proverb 83

Necklace 26, 116, 117, 125
Needle and Thread 5, 82, 122, 125
Nod 103, 108, 126, 129
Note, The 80, 116, 118
Nymph Considers the Garden, The 16,
    108, 123

On Killing a Tree 21, 123
Ozymandias 29, 52, 108

Pantomime Poem 40, 109, 126, 130
Philip Fox 5, 55, 108, 124
Plum 5, 14, 108, 119, 125, 129
Poet-trees 59, 108, 129
Prayer for Peace 104, 121, 125

Reminiscence 73, 127

Samantha is Sobbing 5, 35, 117, 118
Sea-anemone 60
Secret Love 89, 109, 118
Shells and Stones 53, 119, 129
Ship, The 88
Shirt 81, 121
Shirts for us Kids 85, 108, 117, 126, 130
Silver 87, 108, 129
Sorrow of Socks, The 5, 69
Spell of the Rose, The 13, 108, 116
Spiders Cast their Spell, The 28, 109, 123
Spinner 30, 108, 123, 129
Stone Circles 56, 108
Stony 50, 118

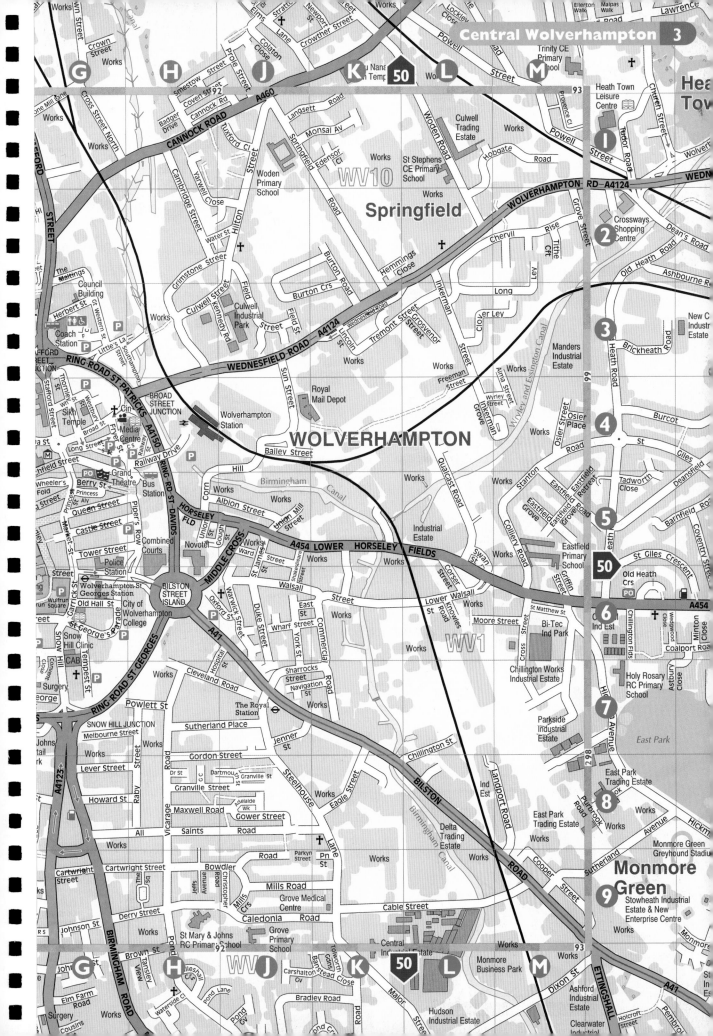

Springfield

WV10

St Stephens
CE Primary
School

WOLVERHAMPTON

WV1

Monmore
Green

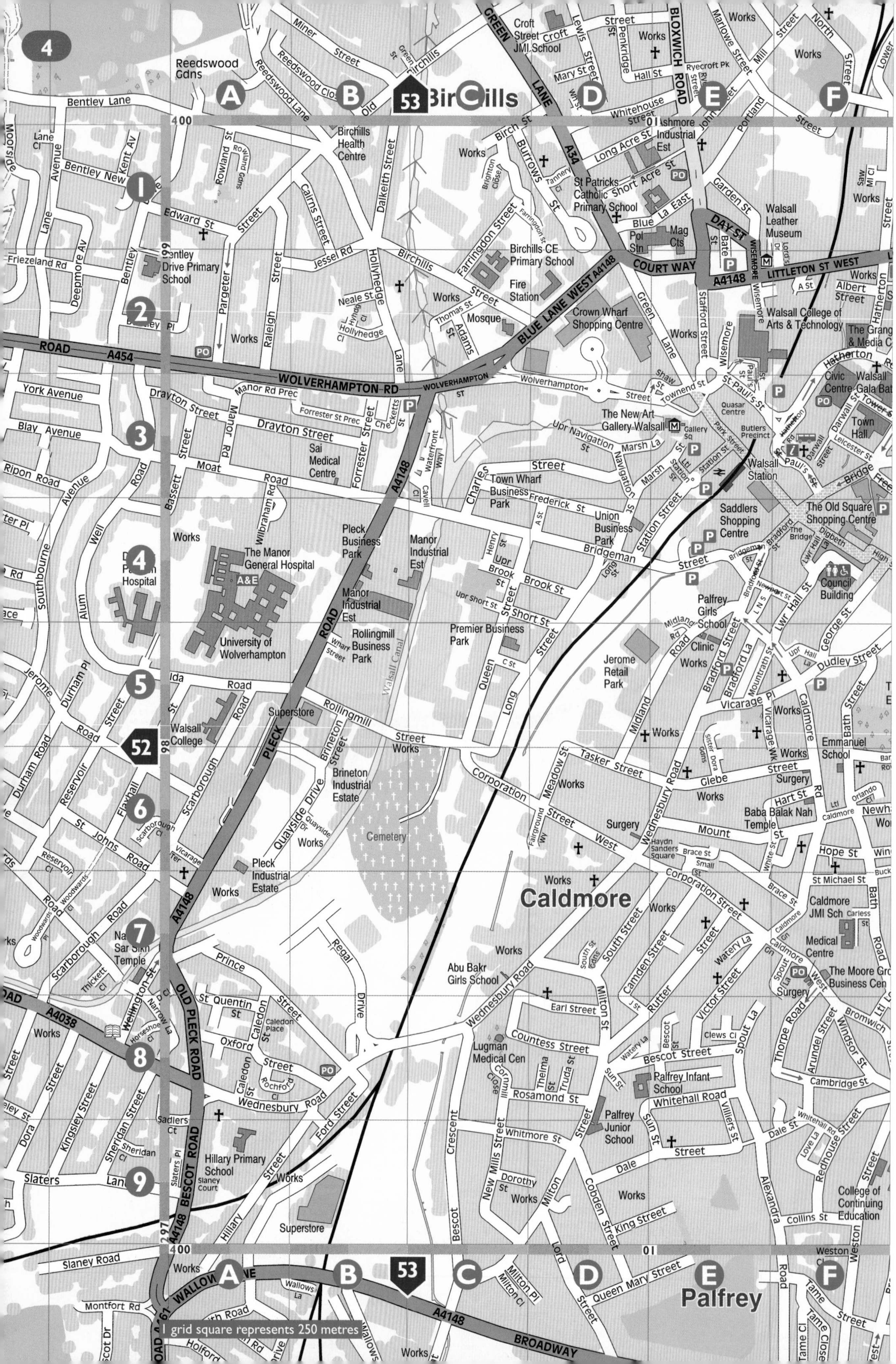
53
Birchills
Reedswood Gdns
Bentley Lane
Miner Street
Reedswood Close
Reedswood Lane
Green Lane
Croft Street JMI School
Lewis Street
Mary St
Penkridge Street
Works
Bloxwich Road
Ryecroft Pk
Hall St
Marlowe Street
Mill Street
North Street
Whitehouse Street
Ashmore Industrial Est
Long Acre St
Short Acre St
St Patricks Catholic Primary School
Blue La East
Pol Stn
Mag Cts
Day St
Walsall Leather Museum
Court Way
A4148
Littleton St West
Albert Street
Walsall College of Arts & Technology
The Grange & Media C
Hatherton Rd
Civic Centre
Walsall Gala Baths
Town Hall
Birchills Health Centre
Rowland St
Dalkeith Street
Cairns Street
Edward St
Bentley Drive Primary School
Friezeland Rd
Deepmore Av
Bentley New
Kent Av
Moorside
Jessel Rd
Hollyhedge Lane
Birchills Street
Farringdon Street
Birchills CE Primary School
Fire Station
Mosque
Blue Lane West A4148
Crown Wharf Shopping Centre
Green Lane
Stafford Street
Wisemore
Pargeter Street
Raleigh Street
Wolverhampton Road A454
Wolverhampton St
York Avenue
Drayton Street
Manor Rd Prec
Forrester St Prec
Checketts St
Blay Avenue
Ripon Road
Moat Road
Sai Medical Centre
Forrester Street
Waterfront Way
Town Wharf Business Park
Frederick St
Union Business Park
Upr Navigation St
The New Art Gallery Walsall
Gallery Sq
Marsh La
Station Street
Walsall Station
Saddlers Shopping Centre
The Old Square Shopping Centre
Digbeth
Bridgeman Street
Council Building
Bassett Street
Wilbraham Rd
The Manor General Hospital
A&E
University of Wolverhampton
Pleck Business Park
Manor Industrial Est
Pleck Road
Rollingmill Business Park
Premier Business Park
Brook St
Short St
Queen Street
Long Street
Palfrey Girls School
Clinic
Jerome Retail Park
Bradford Street
Lwr Hall St
George St
Dudley Street
Vicarage Pl
Caldmore Rd
Bath Street
Southbourne Avenue
Alum Well Road
Hospital
Jerome Road
Durham Pl
Ida Road
Walsall College
Superstore
Rollingmill Street
Brineton Street
Brineton Industrial Estate
Walsall Canal
Midland Road
Tasker Street
Glebe Street
Emmanuel School
Surgery
52
Durham Road
Reservoir Road
Flaxhall Street
Scarborough Road
Quayside Drive
Cemetery
Corporation Street West
Meadow St
Wednesbury Road
Hart St
Baba Balak Nah Temple
Mount Street
Haydn Sanders Square
St Johns Road
Vicarage Ter
Pleck Industrial Estate
Caldmore
Hope St
St Michael St
Caldmore JMI Sch
Medical Centre
Nanak Sar Sikh Temple
Thickett Cl
Prince Street
Regal Drive
South Street
Camden Street
Rutter Street
Victor Street
Watery La
Spout La
The Moore Gro Business Cen
Thorpe Road
Arundel Street
Windsor St
Wellington St
St Quentin St
Caledon St
Abu Bakr Girls School
Earl Street
Milton St
Countess Street
Bescot Street
Clews Cl
Lugman Medical Cen
Cambridge St
A4038
Old Pleck Road
Oxford Street
Rochford Cl
Wednesbury Road
Ford Street
Rosamond St
Palfrey Infant School
Whitehall Road
Kingsley Street
Sheridan Street
Sadlers Ct
Bescot Road
Hillary Primary School
Slaney Court
Whitmore St
Palfrey Junior School
Dale Street
Redhouse Street
Slaters Lane
Dorothy St
New Mills Street
Cobden Street
Alexandra Road
College of Continuing Education
Superstore
King Street
Collins St
Weston Street
Slaney Road
Wallows Lane
Milton Pl
Milton Cl
Queen Mary Street
Palfrey
Montfort Rd
A4148
Broadway
Tame Street
1 grid square represents 250 metres

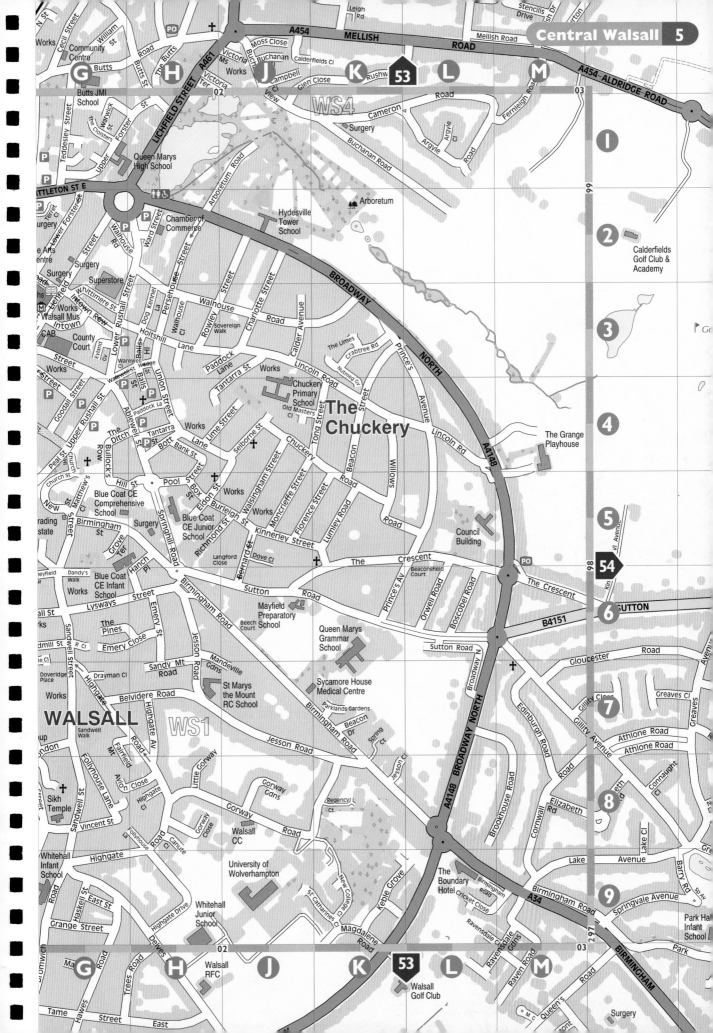

A454 MELLISH ROAD
Mellish Road

Central Walsall

A454—ALDRIDGE ROAD

Community Centre
Cecil Street
William St
Butts
The Butts
Butts Road
Moss Close
Calderfields Cl
PO
Campbell
Buchanan
Victoria Ms
Victoria Ter
02
Glen Close
View
Rushw
53
Cameron Road
Argyle Road
Argyle Cl
Fernleigh Road
03

WS4

Surgery

Teddesley Street
Warwick St
The Cloisters
Upper Forster
Lichfield Street
A461
Victoria Ter

Queen Marys High School

Buchanan Road

I

Calderfields Golf Club & Academy

2

LITTLETON ST E

P
P
Lower Forster St
Walhouse Rd
Ward Street
Chamber of Commerce
Arboretum Road
Hydesville Tower School
Arboretum

3

e Arts entre
Surgery
Surgery
Superstore
Whittimere St
Intown Row
Lower Rushall Street
Dog Kennel La
Persehouse Street
Walhouse Cl
Rowley
Charlotte Street
Walhouse Road
Calder Avenue
BROADWAY NORTH
Princes Avenue

4

M
Walsall Mus
Intown
CAB
County Court
Holtshill
Lane
Sovereign Walk
The Limes
Crabtree Rd
Nurmed Cv

The Chuckery

The Grange Playhouse

Street
Works
Warewell Cl
Warewell St
Wedge
Balls St
Paddock Lane
Tantarra St
Lincoln Road
Chuckery Primary School
Old Masters Cl
Lincoln Rd
A4148

5

Goodall Street
Upper Rushall St
Paddock La
The Ditch
Tantarra
Bott
P St
Works
Lime Street
Lane
Selborne St
Chuckery
Tong Street
Beacon Road
Willows Road
Council Building

PO

54

Peal St
Church St
church Street
New St
Matthews
St
Birmingham St
Bullock's Row
Hill St
Pool Street
Box St
Eldon St
Bank St
Walsingham Street
Moncrieffe Street
Florence Street
Works
Lumley Road
The Crescent
Beaconsfield Court
Vl Avenue

The Crescent

SUTTON

6

Blue Coat CE Comprehensive School
Surgery
Springhill Road
Blue Coat CE Junior School
Burleigh St
Richmond St
Kinnerley Street
Dove Cl
Bernard St
Langford Close
Prince's Av
Orwell Road
Boscobel Road
B4151

eyfield
Walk
Dandy's
Works
Grove Ter
Hanch Pl
Blue Coat CE Infant School
Street
Lysways
Emery St
Birmingham Road
Sutton Road
Beech Court
Mayfield Preparatory School
Sutton Road
Broadway N
Gloucester Road
Gillity Close
Gillity Avenue
Athlone Road
Greaves Cl

7

all St
rks
Sandwell Street
The Pines
Emery Close
R Cl
Sandy Mt Road
Mandeville Gdns
Queen Marys Grammar School
Sycamore House Medical Centre
Parklands Gardens
Athlone Road
Edinburgh Road
Cornwall Rd
Elizabeth Rd

WALSALL

WS1

Doveridge Place
dmill St
ie Cl
Drayman Cl
Highgate
Belvidere Road
Fairfield Mt
Avion Close
St Marys the Mount RC School
Highgate Av
Jesson Road
Birmingham Road
Beacon Dr
Spring Ct
Broadway North
A4148
Brookhouse Road

8

Sandwell Walk
London
up
Sikh Temple
Sandwell St
Vincent St
Follyhouse Lane
Highgate Cl
Little Gorway
Gorway Gdns
Regency Ct
Jesson Road
Beacon Dr
The Boundary Hotel
Cricket Close
Birmingham Road
A34
Birmingham Road
Lake Avenue
Lake Cl
Connaught

9

Whitehall Infant School
Haskell St
East St
Grange Street
Fairfield Mt
Follyhouse Drive
Highgate Road
Canute Cl
Gorway Close
Gorway Road
Walsall CC
University of Wolverhampton
Whitehall Junior School
Highgate Drive
St Catharines Cl
Keble Grove
New College Dr
Magdalene Road
Ravensdale
Ravensdale Gdns
Raven Road
Springvale Avenue
Park Hall Infant School
Queen's Road
Surgery

omwich
Ma
Road
Trees Road
Walsall RFC
Delves
02
Walsall Golf Club
53
M
297
03
BIRMINGHAM

G H J K 53 L M

Tame
Hawes Street
East

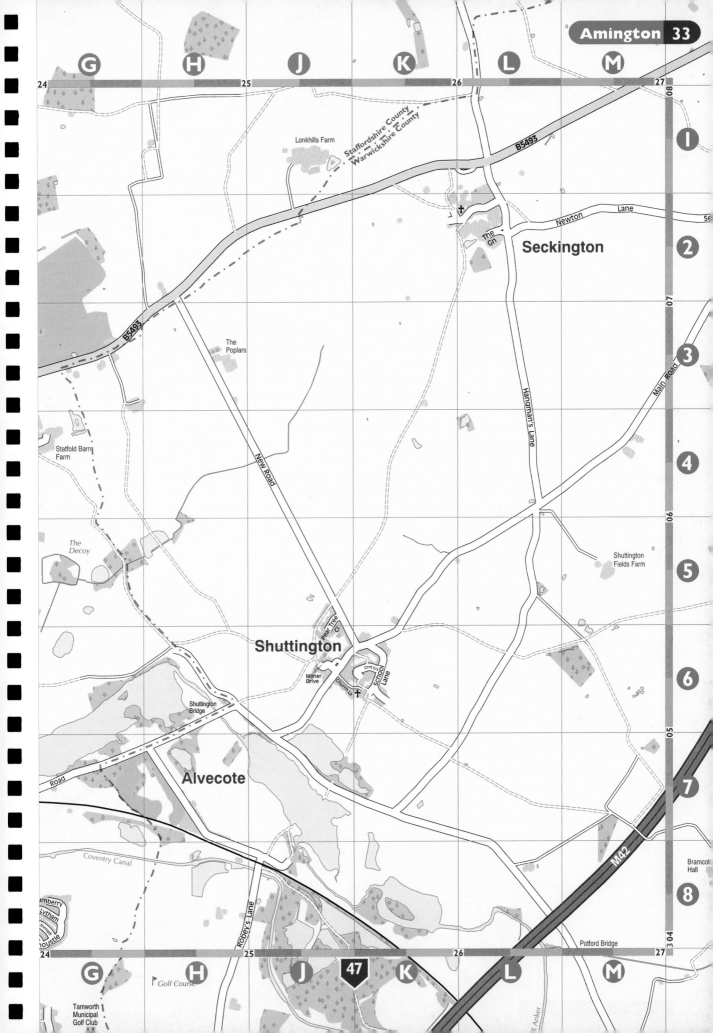

G H J K L M

24 25 26 27 08

I

Lonkhills Farm

Staffordshire County
Warwickshire County

B5493

Newton Lane Se

The Gn

2

Seckington

07

B5493

3

The Poplars

Hangman's Lane

Main Road

4

New Road

06

Statfold Barn
Farm

The
Decoy

Shuttington
Fields Farm

5

Pear Tree Cl

Shuttington

Milner
Drive

crnt crnt School Lane

Church La

6

05

Shuttington
Bridge

Road

Alvecote

7

M42

Coventry Canal

Bramcot
Hall

8

Rodey's Lane

Turnberry

Lytham

Carnoustie

Potford Bridge

3 04

24 25 26 27

G H J 47 K L M

Golf Course

Tamworth
Municipal
Golf Club

R Anker

A **B** **C** **D** **E** **F**

3 85   86   87

The Stockings

Moatbrook

Strawmoor Lane

Wood Road

Moat Brook Av

Fairfield Drive

Canford Crs

Cemetery

Mill Lane

Church Lane   Gunstone La

Staffordshire Way

River Penk

St Nicholas
CE VC First
School

CODSALL

Comm High
School

Lane Green
First Sch

Bilbrook CE
Middle School

I

Strawmoor
Farm

Oaken Lane

Monarch's Way

Oaken

Springfield
House

Oaken Drive

Chapel
Broadway

Wilkes Road

Arps Road

Wolverhampton Road

Station Road

Codsall
Station

Council
Offices

Codsall
Clinic

St Christophers RC
Primary School

Codsall
Middle School

Bilbrook
Medical
Centre

2

Manor
Fold

Hollybush Lane

Middle Shop Lane

Oaken Lanes

Lansdowne Av

Histons Hill

Princes Drive

Princes
Gdns

The Paddock

Suckling Green Lane

Oaken Park

Bilbrook
Station

Birches First
School

3

A41

Stafford

Greenhills

Stafford Lane

Meadow Wy
Hawthorne La

Wergs Hall Road

Keepers Lane

4

Wrottesley Hall

HOLYHEAD ROAD

Heath Road

Heath
House

River Penk

5

Monarch's Way

Park Road

Wergs Hall Road

Keepers Lane

Wergs
Golf Club

Golf Course

6

A41

Wergs
Drive

Chatsworth
Gdns

Popes Lane

7

Cranmoor

Wrottesley Park Road

The Parkway

Westcroft Road

Yew Tree Road

Wergs

Wrottesley Road

Cranmere Avenue

Woodthorne Road

Wergs Rd

West Lane

WERGS

8

Cranmoor Lodge
Farm

Turnberry Gv

St Andrews Drive

The Parkway

Shackleton Dr

Mercia Drive

Idsall Road

Wrekin Drive

Elviron
Drive

Redhouse

The Kings
CE School

3 00

3 85   86   87

A **B** **C** **48** **D** **E** **F**

Perton
Clnc

Sandown
First School

Gainsborough Drive

Woodthorne
Primary School

Perton

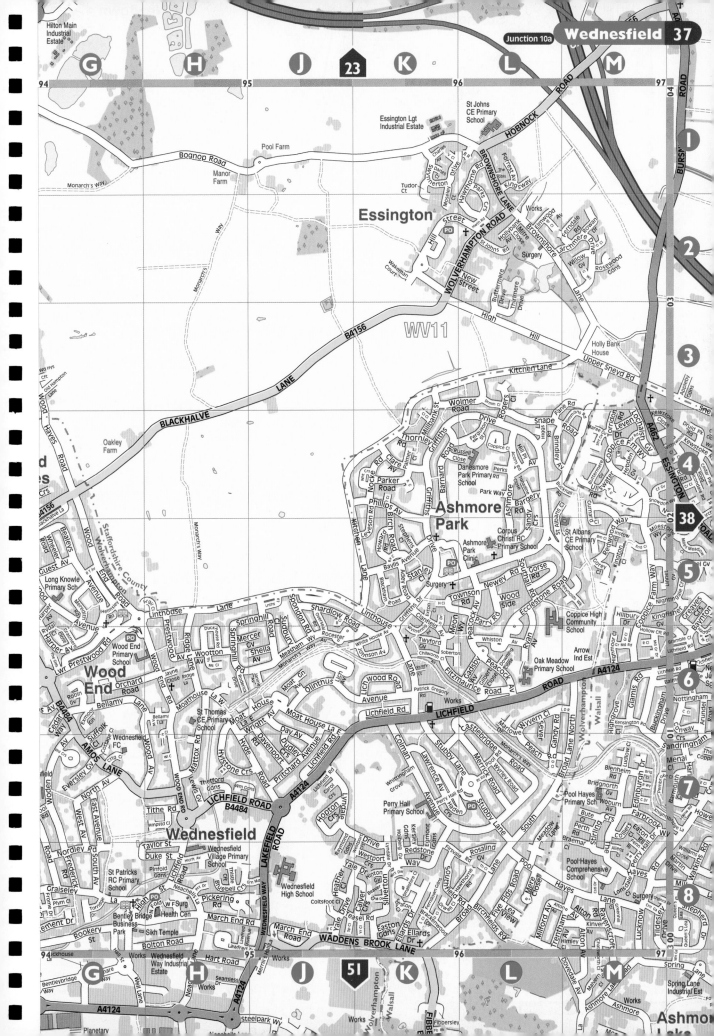

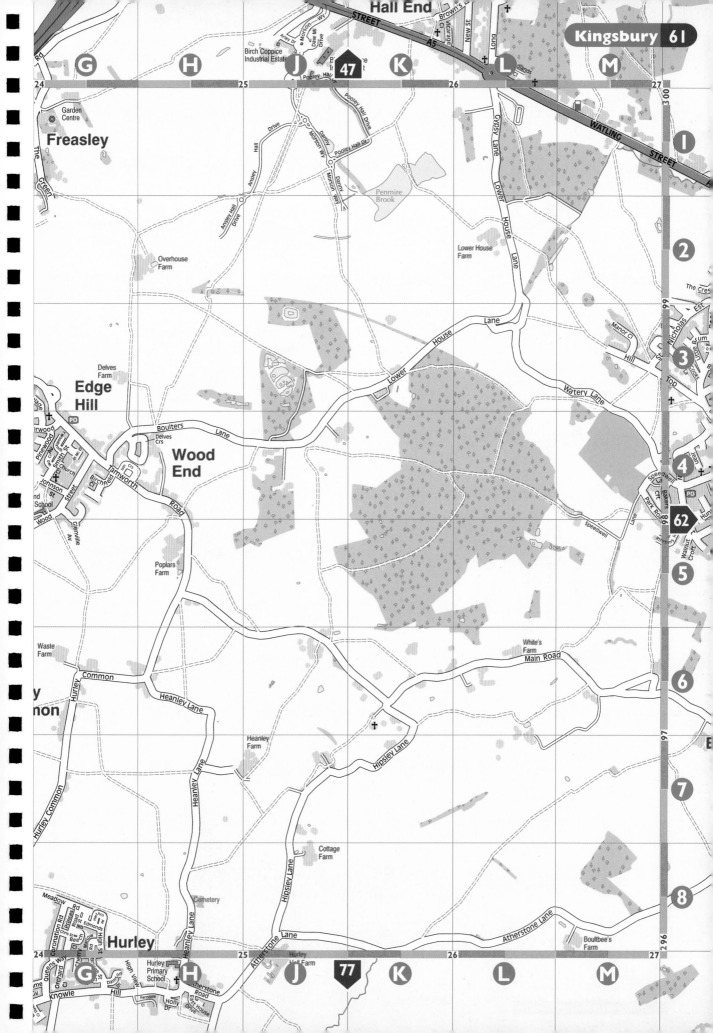

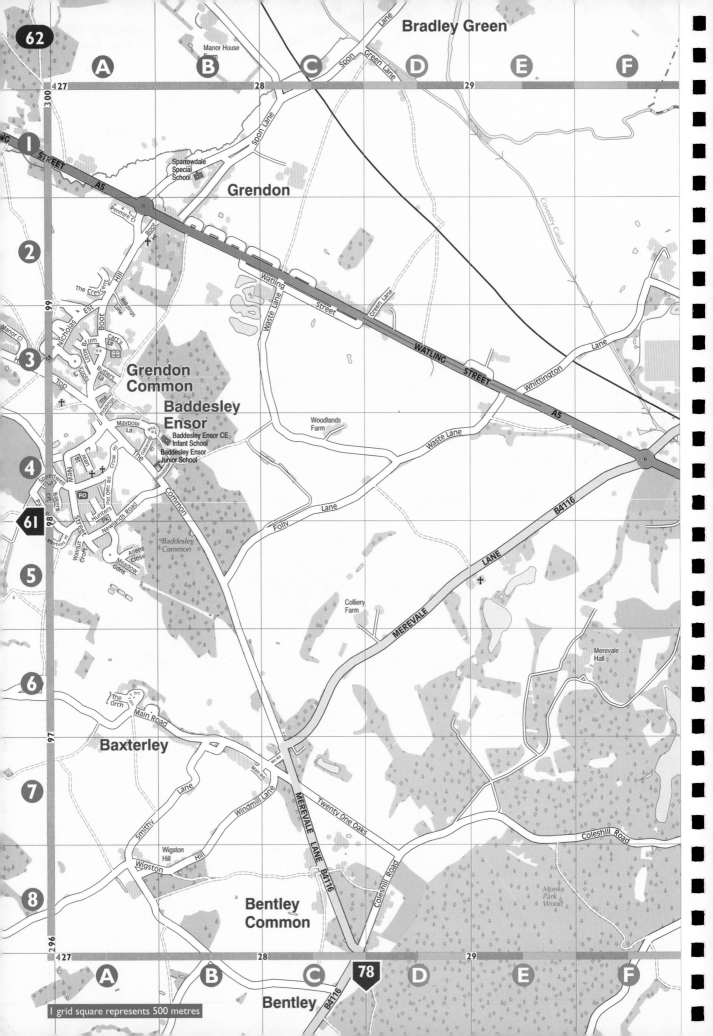

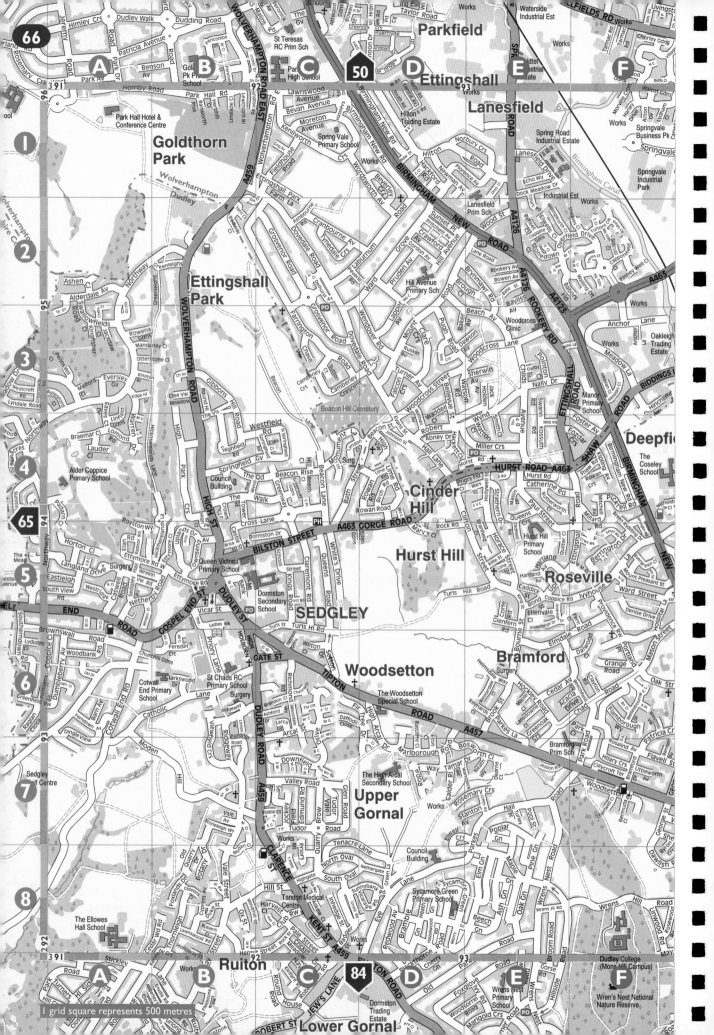

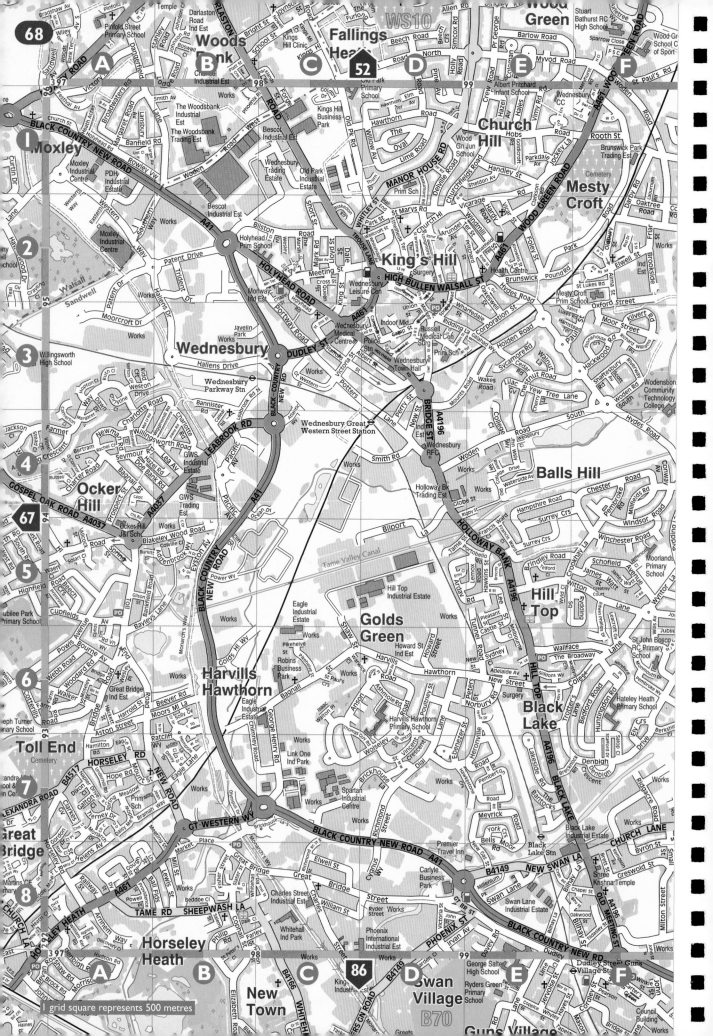

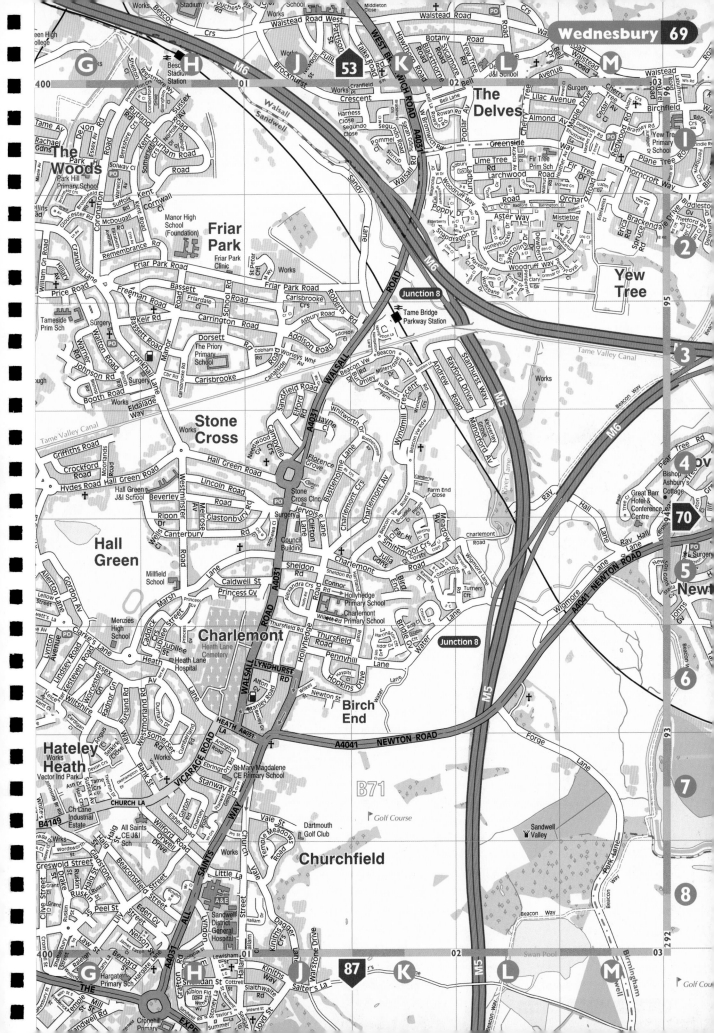

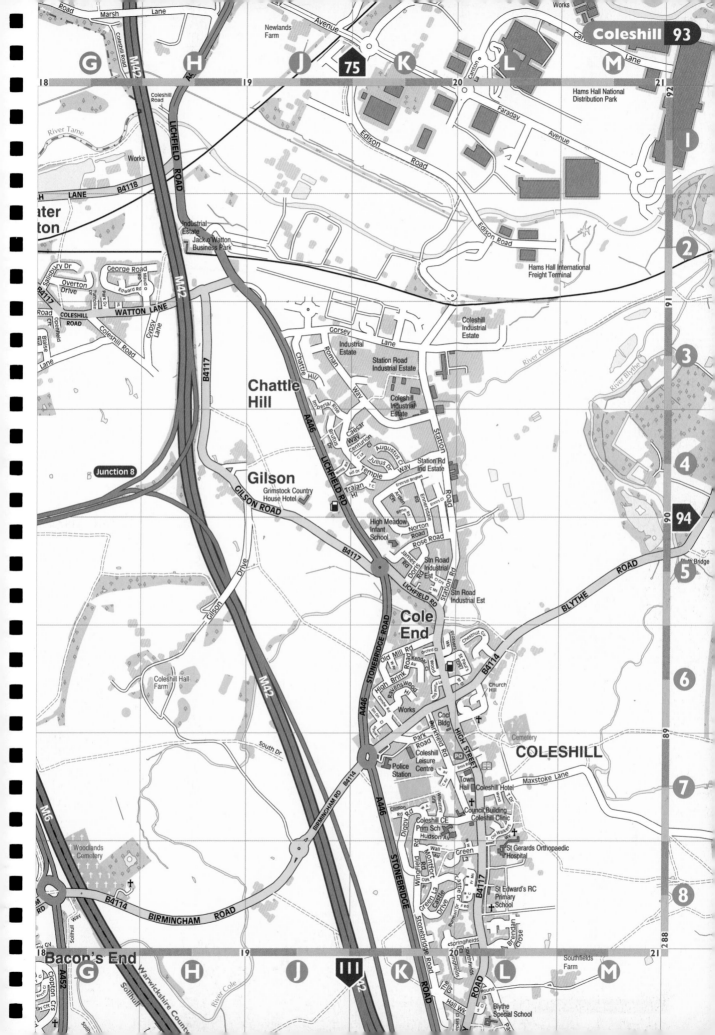

94

A   B   C   D **76** H**D**rill's End   E   F

421
92 91

1

Lane

Centenary Way
Dingle Lane
The Dingle
Reddings
Garden Centre
Ridley Lane
Old Farm Lane
Hill Farm
End Lane
Hogrills End Lane
Hogrills End

Station Road
Heart of England Way
Heart of England Way

2

Works
Watery La
Centenary Way
Shustoke Reservoir

Watery
Lane
COLESHILL   ROAD   B4114   CHURCH   ROAD
Bixhill Lane

Blyth End

3

River Blyth

Back La
The Green
Croxall Drive
Wilkinson Wy
Forge Rd
Shustoke CE Primary School

Shustoke

4

Moat House Farm
Moat House Lane

93
90

Hollyland

5

ROAD
Blyth Bridge

Hall Farm

Castle Lane

Heart of England Way

The Metlins

6

89

B46

Maxstoke Castle

7

Castle Farm

Maxstoke Park Golf Club
Golf Course
Dumble Farm

Castle Lane

8

Maxstoke Lane
Duke Bridge
Coleshill Road
Fillongley Road

288
421
A   B **112** C **Duke End** D   E   F
22   23
Road

1 grid square represents 500 metres

Duke End Farm

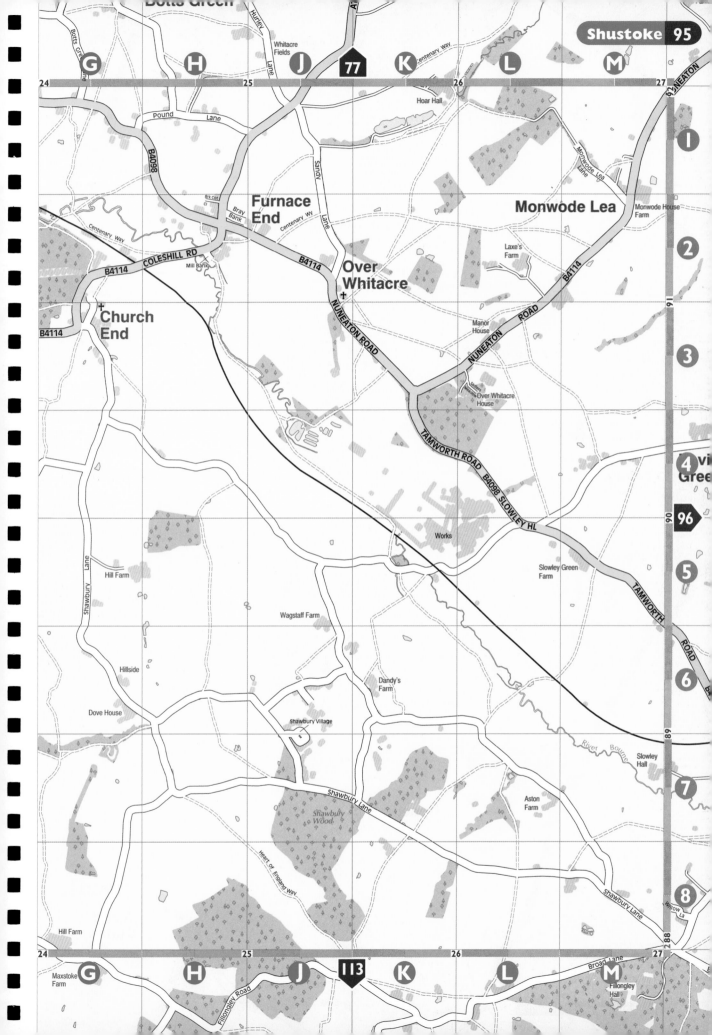

Botts Green

G   H   J   77   K   L   M

24   25   26   27

Hurley Lane

Whitacre Fields

Centenary Way

NUNEATON

I

Hoar Hall

Pound   Lane

Monwode Lea Lane

B4098

Monwode Lea

Monwode House Farm

2

Furnace End

Sandy Lane

Brk Cot

Bray Bank

Centenary Wy

B4114

Laxe's Farm

Centenary Way

COLESHILL RD

Mill Bank

B4114

Over Whitacre

NUNEATON ROAD

Manor House

ROAD

B4114

B4114

Church End

B4114

Over Whitacre House

TAMWORTH ROAD   B4098 SLOWLEY HL

vi Green

4

96

Works

Slowley Green Farm

5

TAMWORTH

Hill Farm

Shawbury Lane

Wagstaff Farm

Dove House

Hillside

Dandy's Farm

Shawbury Village

6

River   Bourne

Slowley Hall

ROAD

7

Shawbury Lane

Shawbury Wood

Aston Farm

Shawbury Lane

Wirow La

8

Heart of England Way

Fillongley Road

Hill Farm

Broad Lane

24   25   26   27

G   H   J   113   K   L   M

Maxstoke Farm

Fillongley Road

Fillongley Hall

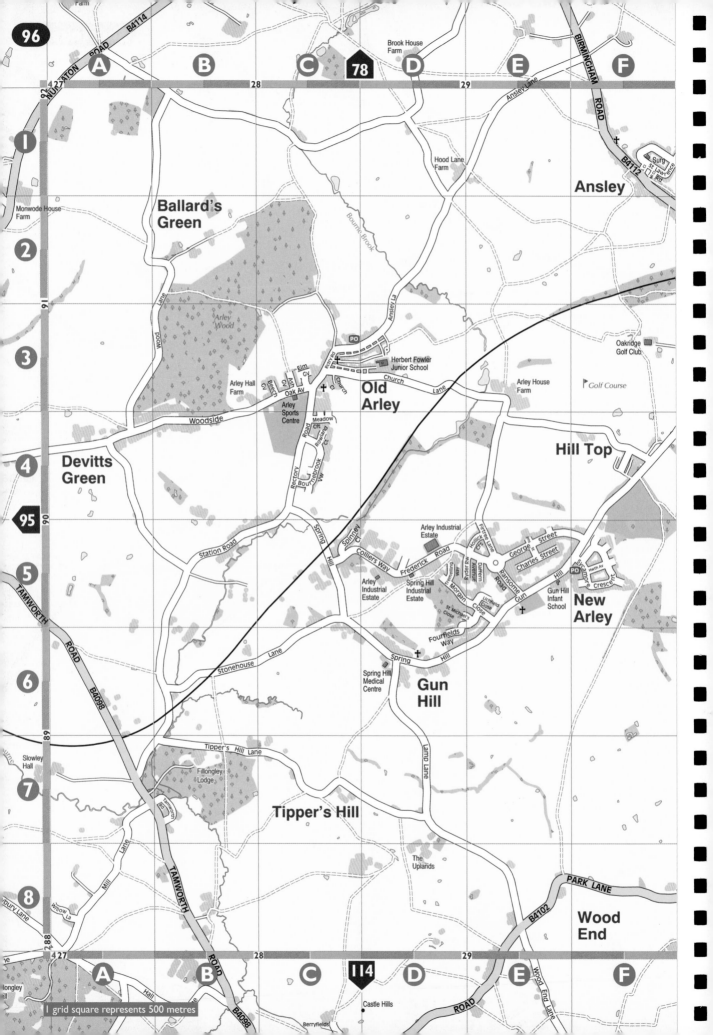

G
H
J
95
K
L
M

24
25
26
27

Hill Farm

Maxstoke Hall Farm

Filongley Road

Bentley's Farm

Bentley Lane

High House Farm

Hardingwood Lane

Heart of England Way

Broad Lane

Filongley Hall

1

Pump

2

87

Filong Mount

3

Wood Corner Farm

Manor House Farm

Blabers Hall Farm

Green End

Newhall Green

4

114

86

White House Farm

5

A4102

Daniels Wood

M6

MERIDEN ROAD

Chapel Green

6

85

Kinwalsey

Kinwalsey Lane

B4102

Birchley Hays Wood

7

Coventry Way

oods

Outwoods Farm

Butler's End

Close Wood

Meigh's Wood

Heart of England Way

Becks Lane

8

Ivy House Farm

284

24
25
26
27

G
H
J
131
K
L
M

High Ash Farm

Lodge Green Lane North

ROAD

Shaft L

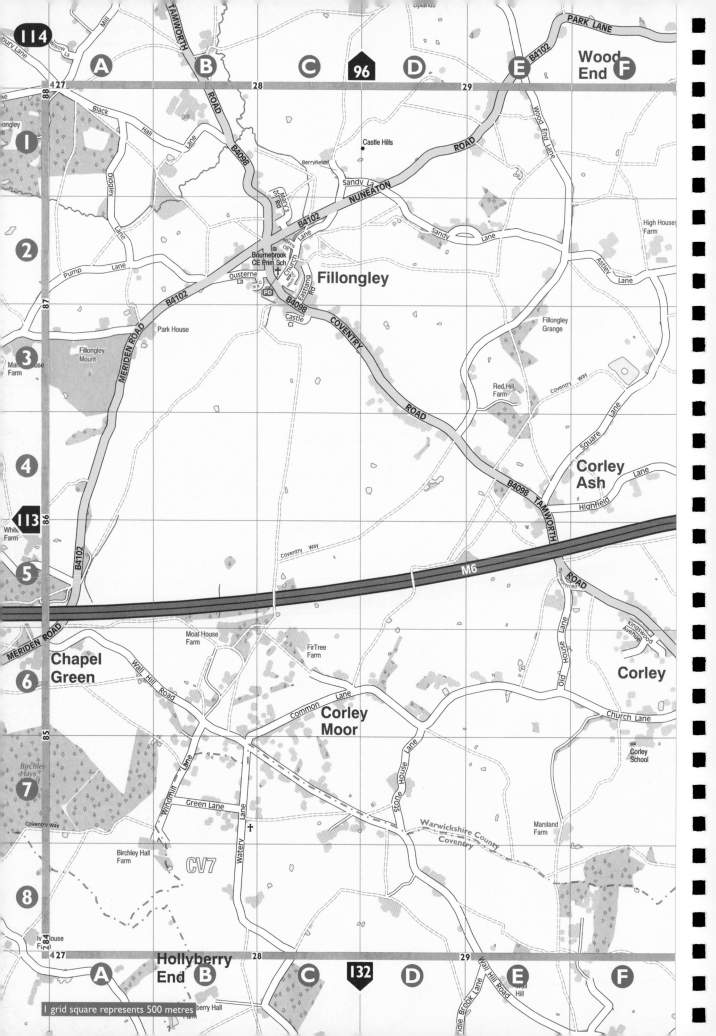

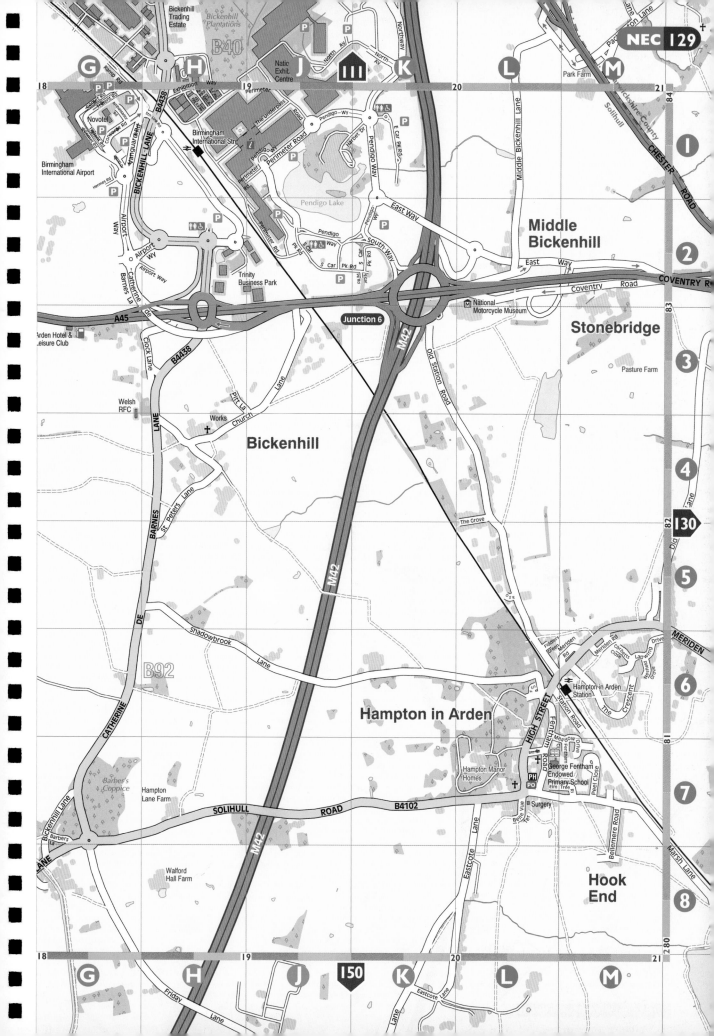

A B C 112 D E F

84 421 22 23

I

HESTER ROAD

River Blythe

Packington Park

Packington Hall

Hall Pool

Great Pool

The Decoy

The Dairy Farm

2

Road

COVENTRY ROAD

BIRMINGHAM ROAD

83

The Mill Farm

Shepherds Lane

Maxstoke Lane

Whitestitch

A45

3

Pasture Farm

Geary's Heath

Golf Course

BIRMINGHAM ROAD

Forest Hall

Maxstoke Lane

KENILWORTH ROAD

Warwickshire County

Solihull

Somers Wood Caravan Park

Stonebridge Golf Club

The Somers

Somers Road

B4104

MAIN

Kitwood Cl

Archer Road

Hampton Gra

Maxstoke Cl

4

Molands Bridge

HAMPTON LANE

North Warwickshire Golf Club

Heath Farm

Strawberry Fields

82

129

A452

B4102

5

River Blythe

Golf Course

6

MERIDEN ROAD

Drive

Lapwing Close

Crescent

Patrick Bridge

Cornets End Lane

Hornbrook Farm

Cornets End

81

7

Marsh Lane

Mercote Mill Farm

Corne

8

KENILWORTH ROAD

Park Farm

80

Arden House

421 Marsh Lane 22 23

I grid square represents 500 metres

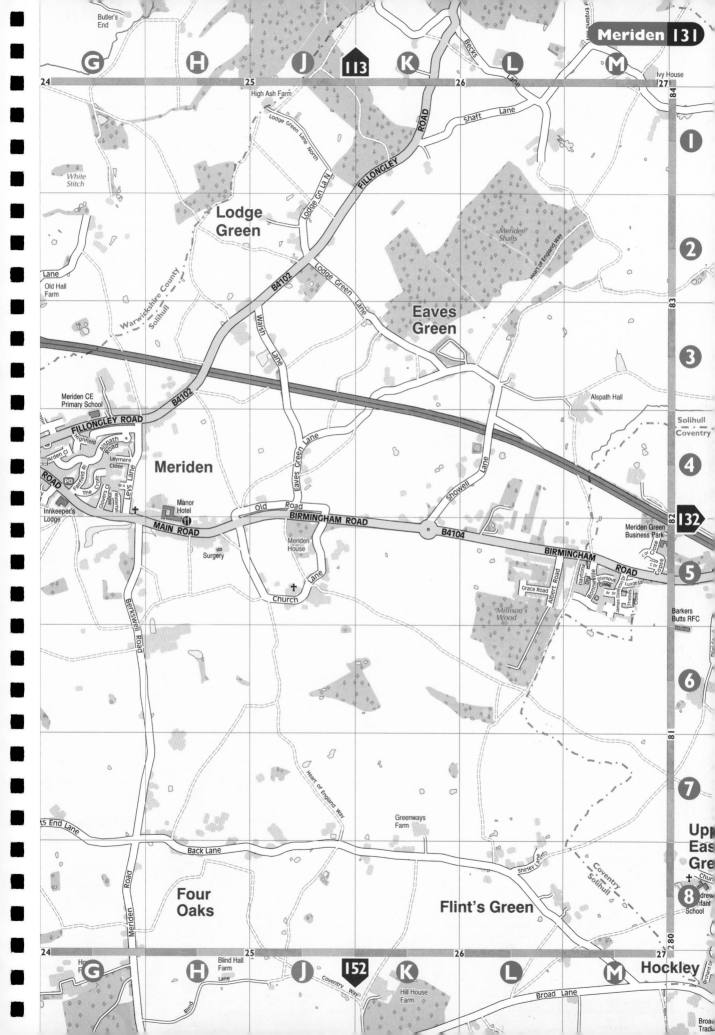

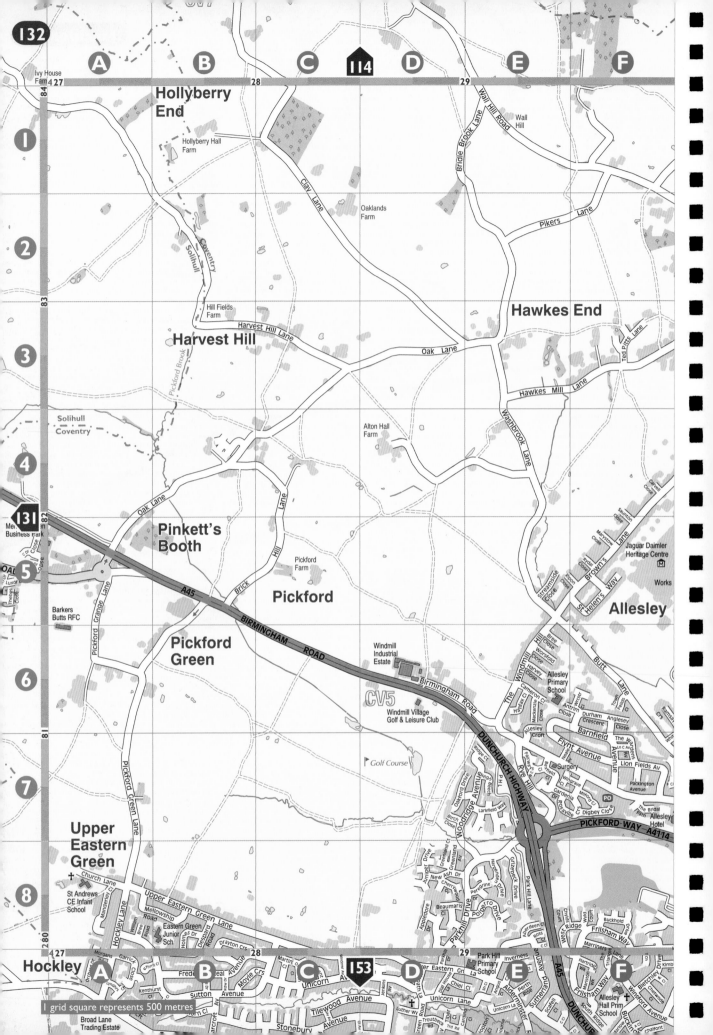

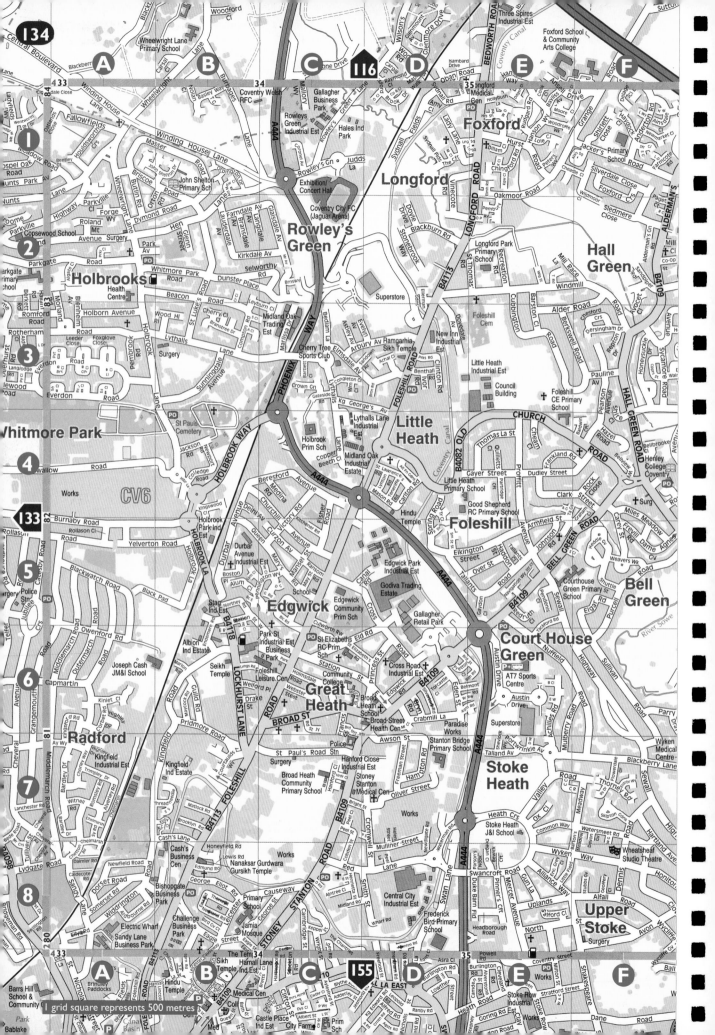

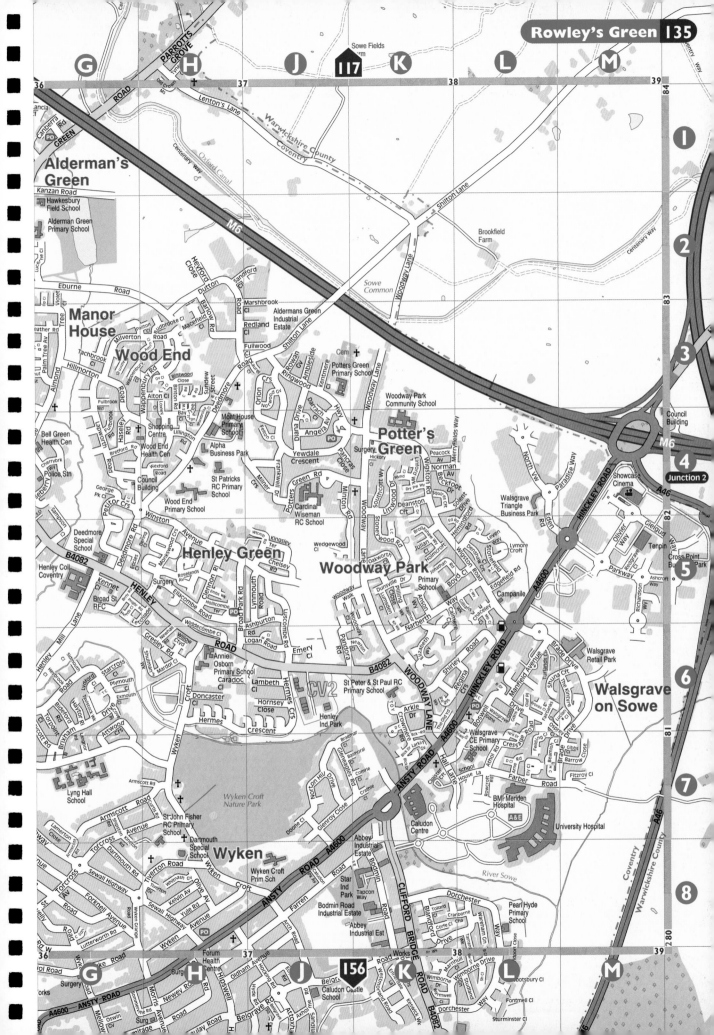

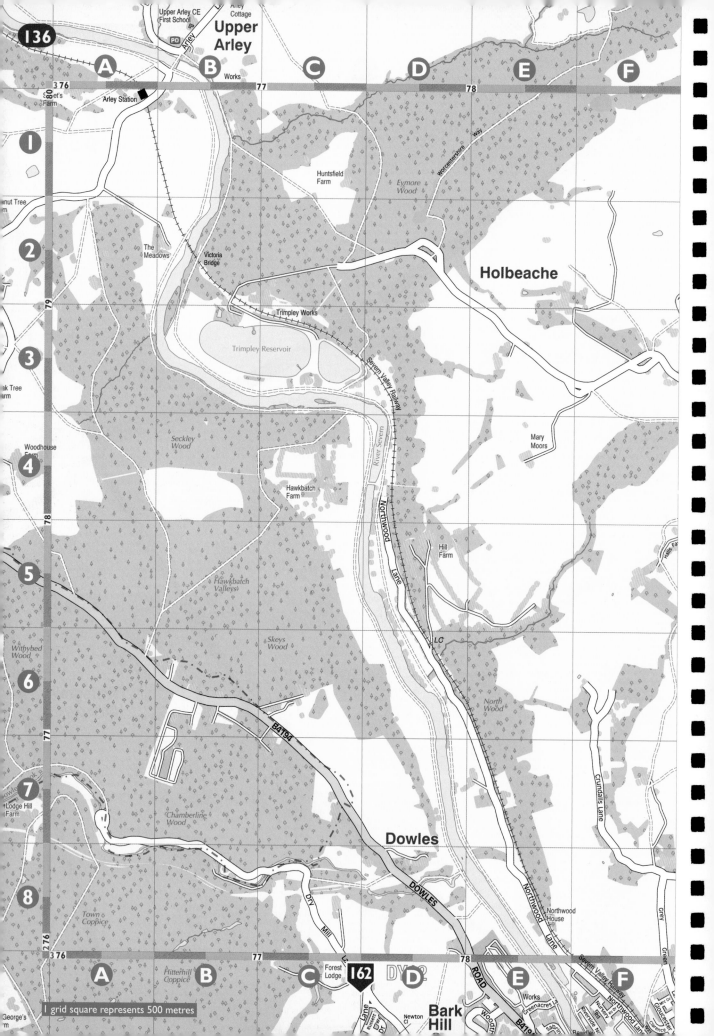

Upper Arley

Upper Arley CE First School
Arley Cottage
PO
Works

A 3 76 B 77 C 78 D E F

Arley Station

I

Chestnut Tree Farm

The Meadows

Victoria Bridge

Huntsfield Farm

Eymore Wood

Worcestershire Way

Holbeache

2

Trimley Works

Trimley Reservoir

Oak Tree Farm

3

Severn Valley Railway

Seckley Wood

River Severn

Mary Moors

Woodhouse Farm

4

Hawkbatch Farm

Northwood Lane

Hill Farm

5

Hawkbatch Valleys

LC

Skeys Wood

Withybed Wood

6

North Wood

B4194

Crundalls Lane

7

Lodge Hill Farm

Chamberline Wood

Dowles

8

Town Coppice

DOWLES

Dry Mill Lane

Northwood Lane

Northwood House

Severn Valley Railway

A 3 76 B 77 C 78 D E F

George's Farm

Hitterhill Coppice

Forest Lodge

162

DY12

Bark Hill

ROAD

Newton Cl

Works

Greenacres La

Grey Green

B4190

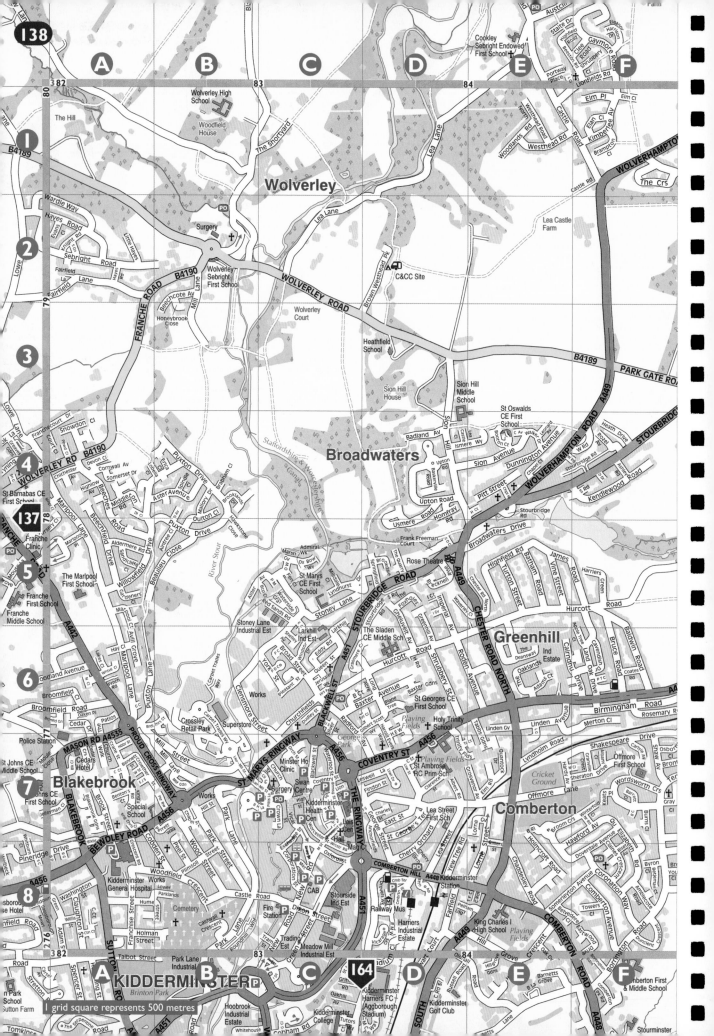

Five ways

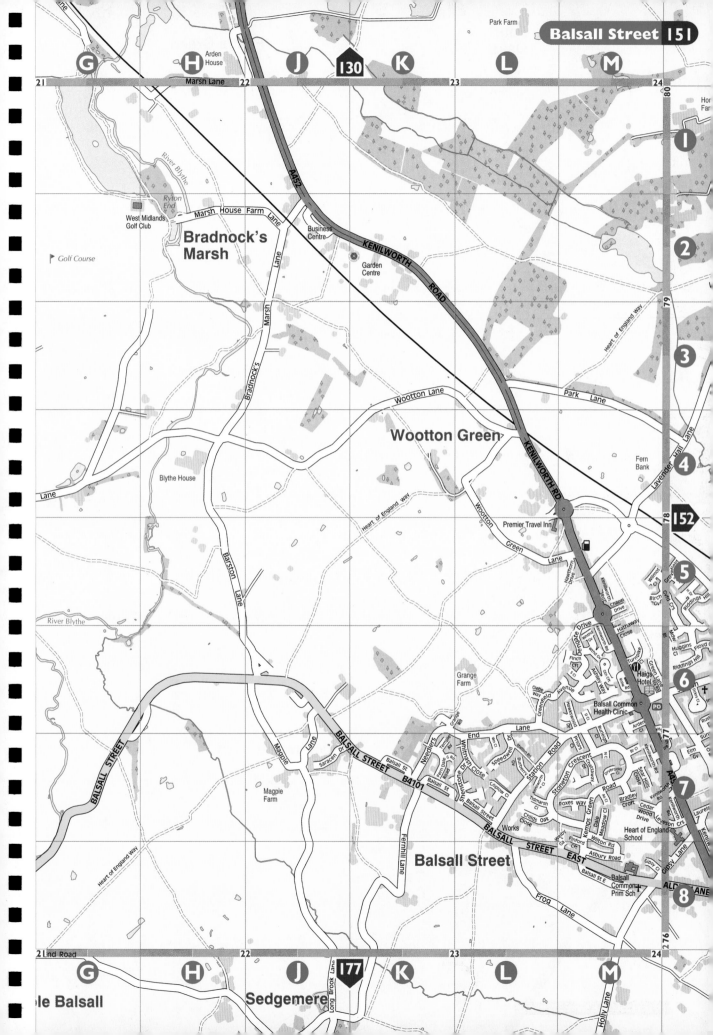

Bradnock's Marsh

Wootton Green

Balsall Street

Sedgemere

le Balsall

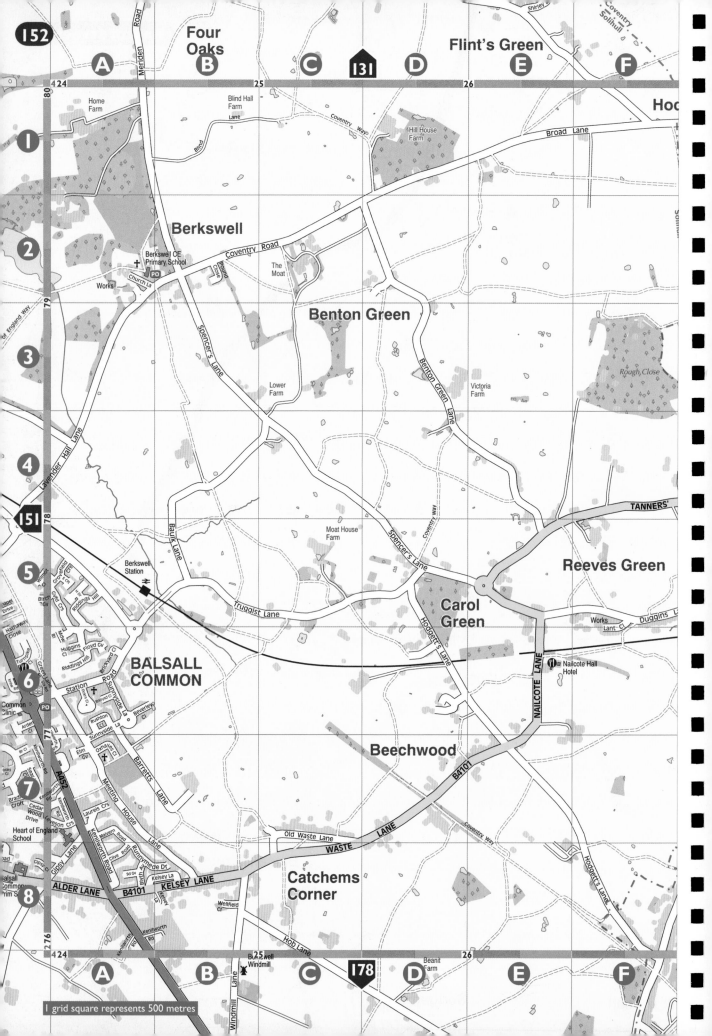

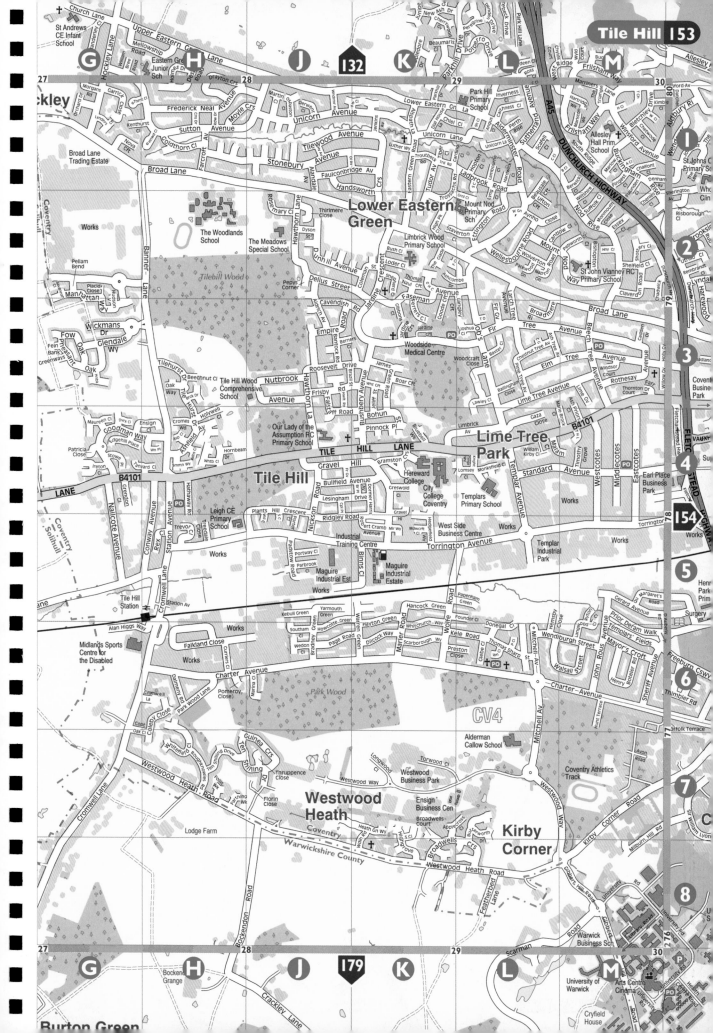

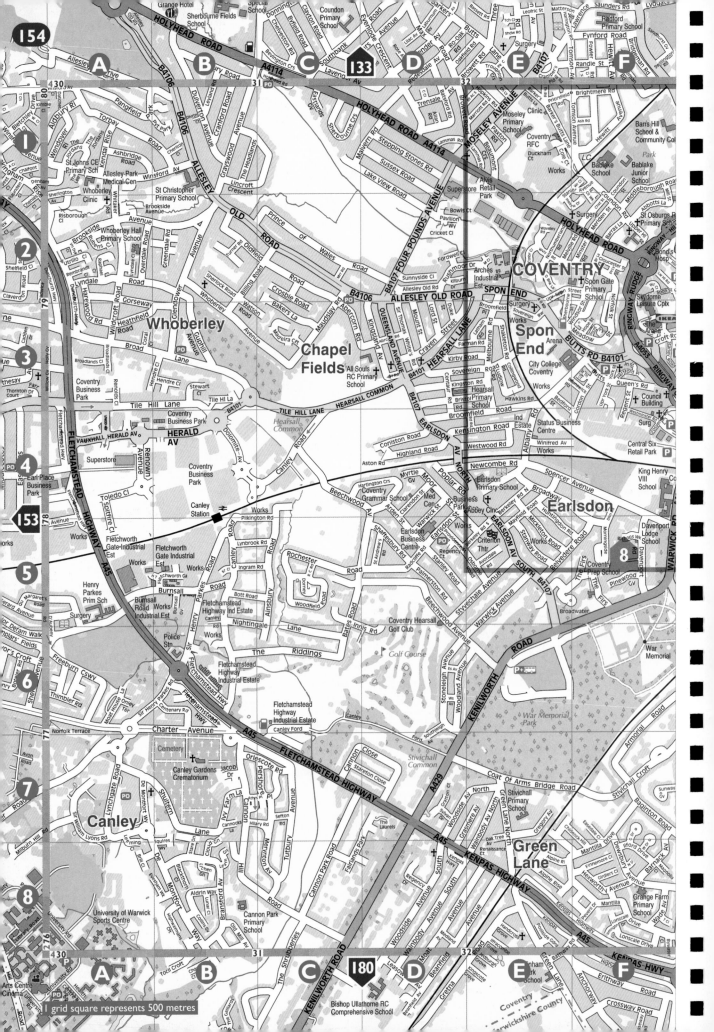

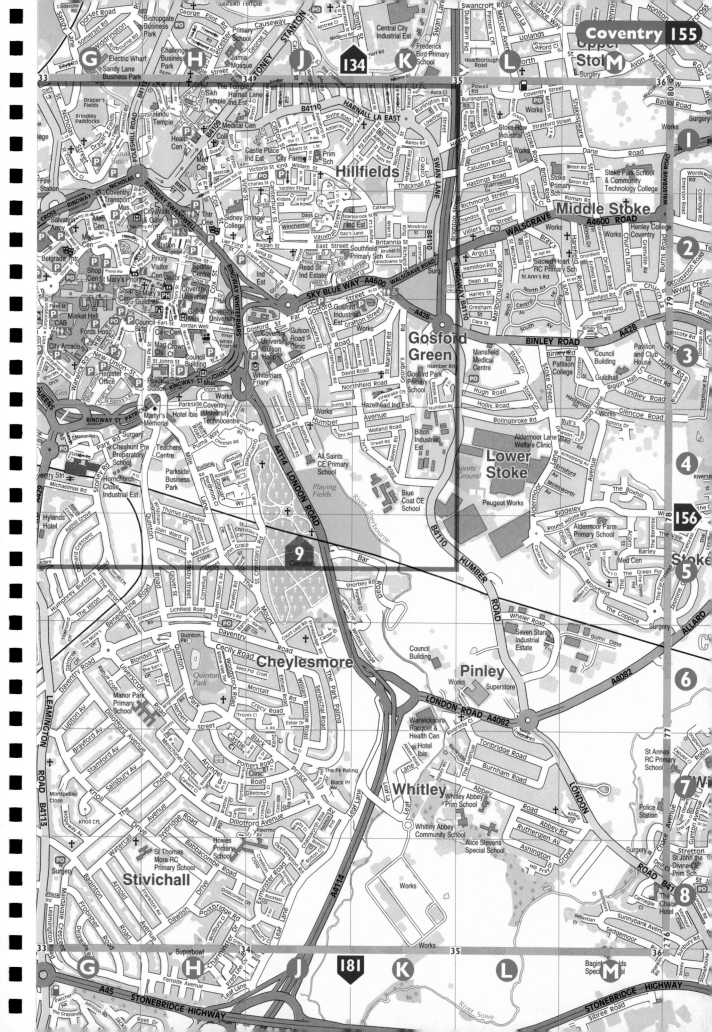

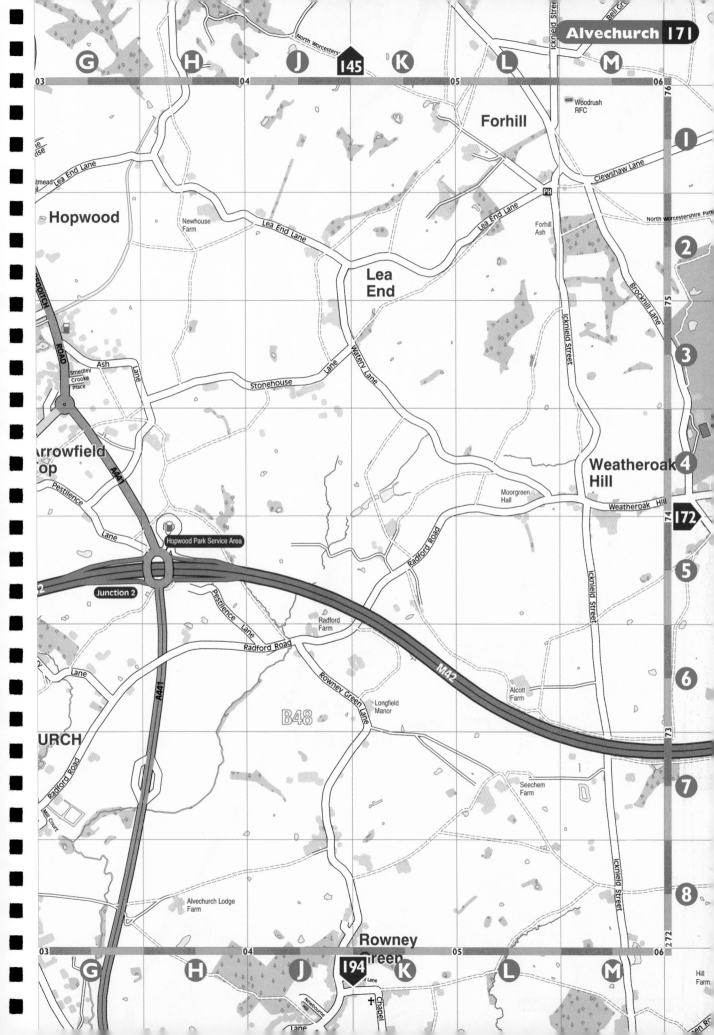

G H J 145 K L M

03 04 05 06 76

Woodrush
RFC

Forhill

I

Lea End Lane

Clewshaw Lane

PH

North Worcestershire Path

2

Lea End Lane

75

Forhill
Ash

North Worcesters'...

Newhouse
Farm

Hopwood

Lea End Lane

**Lea
End**

Watery Lane

3

Icknield Street

Stonehouse Lane

REDDITCH ROAD

Ash Lane

Smedley
Crooke
Place

Brockhill Lane

**Weatheroak
Hill**

4

Moorgreen
Hall

Weatheroak Hill

arrowfield
op

A441

172

74

Pestilence

Hopwood Park Service Area

Junction 2

Lane

Radford Road

5

Icknield Street

M2

Pestilence Lane

Radford
Farm

Radford Road

Alcott
Farm

6

A441

Lane

Rowney Green Lane

Longfield
Manor

M42

73

URCH

Radford Road

B48

Seechem
Farm

7

Mill Court

Icknield Street

8

Alvechurch Lodge
Farm

**Rowney
Green**

272

Hill
Farm

Newbourne
Hill

194

Chapel

G H J K L M

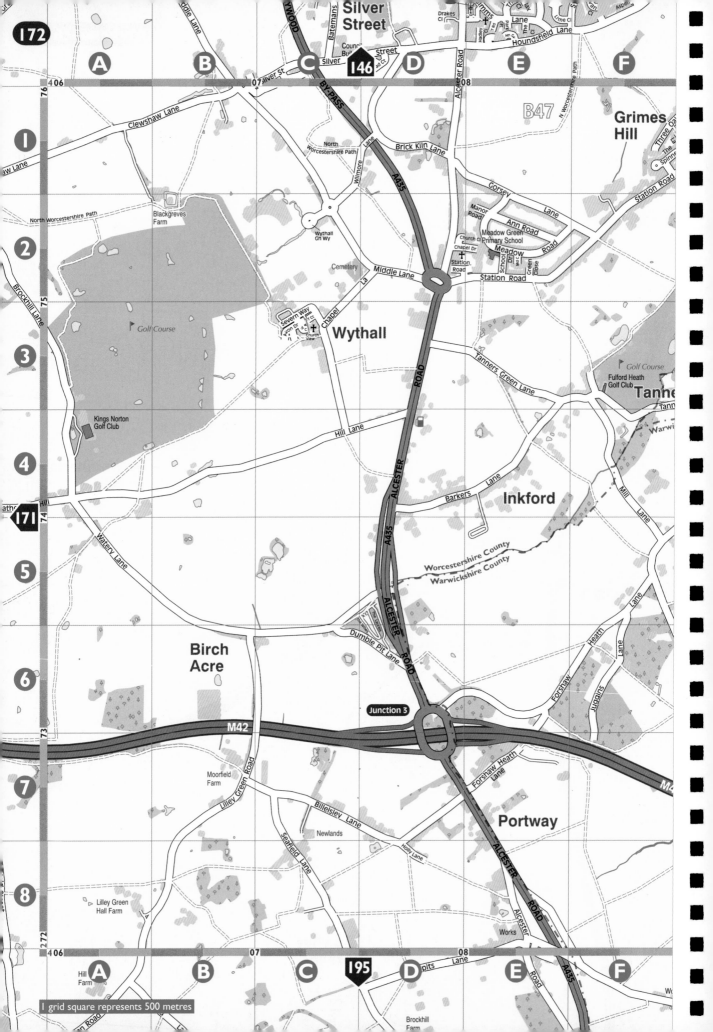

1 grid square represents 500 metres

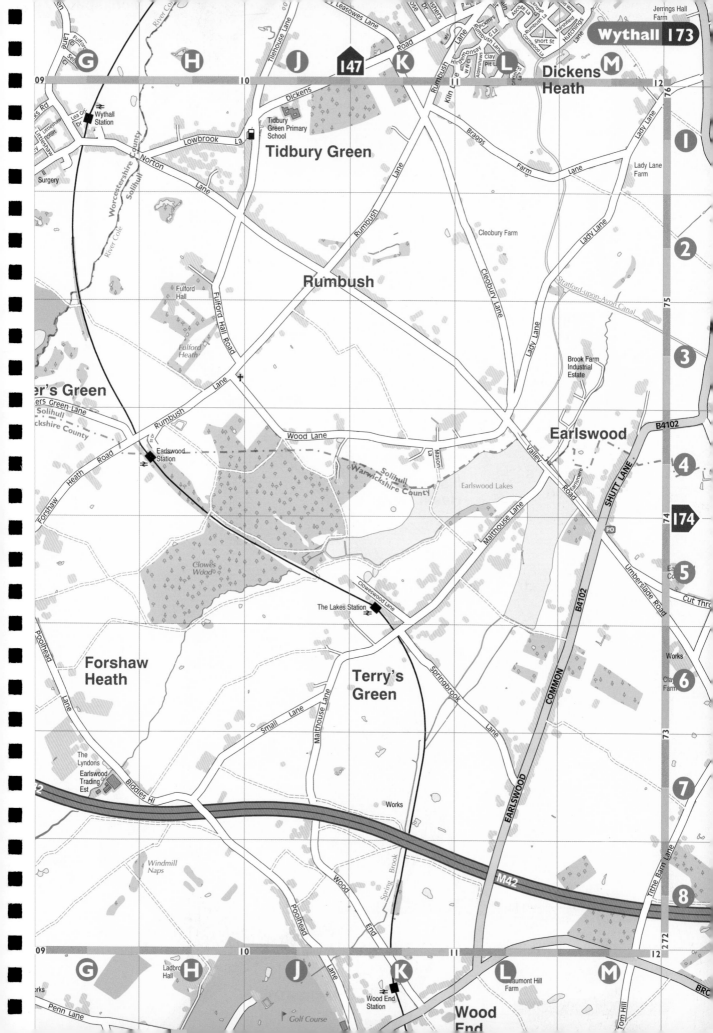

G H J 147 K L M

Dickens
Heath

Jerrings Hall
Farm

Leasowes Lane

Tilehouse Lane

River Cole

Fulford
Lane

Wythall
Station

Surgery

Lowbrook La.

Dickens

Tidbury
Green Primary
School

Tidbury Green

Norton

Lane

Solihull

Worcestershire County

River Cole

Fulford
Hall

Fulford Hall Road

Fulford
Heath

Rumbush

Rumbush

Lane

Cleobury Farm

Cleobury Lane

Lady Lane

Lady Lane
Farm

Stratford-upon-Avon Canal

Brook Farm
Industrial
Estate

Braggs
Farm
Lane

Rumbush
Lane

Kiln La.

er's Green

ers Green Lane

Solihull

ckshire County

Rumbush

Lane

Wood Lane

Earlswood
Station

Solihull
Warwickshire County

Mason

La.

Earlswood Lakes

Earlswood

B4102

Valley

Road

SHUTT LANE

Umberslade Road

PO

174

Ea

Co

Cut Thro

Clowes Wood

Forshaw

Heath

Road

The Lakes Station

Cloweswood Lane

Malthouse Lane

COMMON

B4102

Works

Cla
Farm

**Forshaw
Heath**

Poolhead

Lane

Small

Lane

Malthouse Lane

**Terry's
Green**

Springbrook

Lane

EARLSWOOD

The
Lyndons

Earlswood
Trading
Est

Biddles Hl

Works

Windmill
Naps

Wood

End

Spring Brook

Poolhead

M42

Trithe Barn Lane

BRC

G H J K L M

Ladbro
Hall

Golf Course

Penn Lane

Wood End
Station

aumont Hill
Farm

Tom Hill

**Wood
End**

Works

09 10 11 12

76 75 74 73 272

1 2 3 4 5 6 7 8

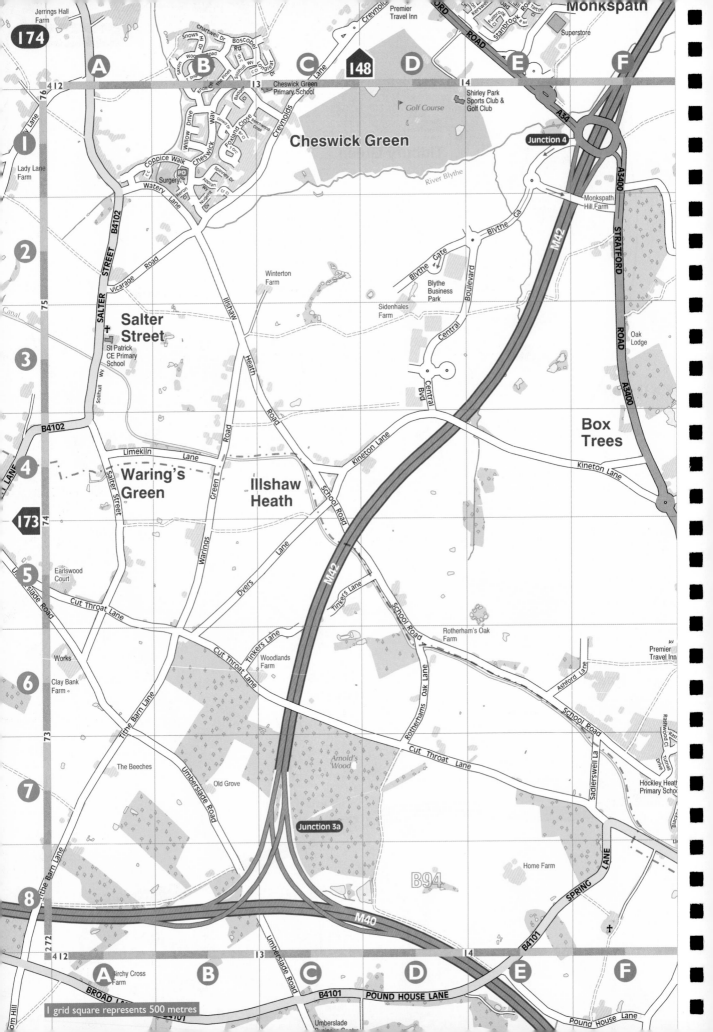

G H J **159** Lo **K** Lawford L M

Church Road

RUGBY ROAD
45 46 47 48
A428
COVENTRY ROAD
A428 RUGBY ROAD

Clayhill Lane
St John's La
Thomas Way
Cross Street
The Spinney
Round Aven
Long Lawford Primary School
Steeling Road
Thurnmill Rd
Judge Close
Holbrook
Elizabeth Way
Weaver Dr
Townsend
Cherwell Way
Lane

Badger Close
Chapel St
West St
Main
Railway Street
Baileys
School Street
PO
Back Lane
Tee Tong Rd
Redhill Rd
Briars Close

Livingstone Avenue
South View Road
Green Cl
The Green

Mount Pleasant

Bilton Lane

Estimated

Lawford Heath Lane

Lawford Hill Farm

Lodge Farm Campsite

Henry Hinde Junior School

Wilson Dr
Kenn Drive
Drayton Close
Lestock Close
Barrington Road
Keppel Cl
Cowan
Road
Froudster
Henry Infant

Berrybanks
Mulberry Road
Birch Dr
Rowan Dr
Acorn
Larch
Lilac Cl
Elder
Pear Tree Way
Wych elm Cl
Cornwallis

Whitefriars Drive
Cresw Cl
Pl
Cavendish

Cawston Grange Dr
Dorset
Devonshire
Lawford

Bilton High School

186
74

Ling Lane

Works

Lawford Heath Industrial Estate

The Ryelands

Lawford Heath

A4071

The Crescent

Potford's Dam Farm

Estimated completion end 2009

Cawston Grange Dr
Francis
Shenfield Rd
L Pl
Frewen Rd
Joyce
Alicia
Gerard
S Cl
Judith Wy
Caillier Cl
Scholars
Cawston Grange Primary School
Road
Wortley Cl
Brudenell Cl
Planter Cl
Blyth
Field VW

Cave Way
Trussell Wy
Clement
Noble Dr
Turchil Rd
Monks
Gold Av
Salawak Pl
Main Str

Durrell Dr
Calvestone
Edwin
COVENTRY ROAD
A4071
Cawston

Lime Tree Avenue
Alwyn Road
MAIN STR

COVENTRY ROAD

Cawston Lane

Marton
Wolston Ct
Napton Ct
Salemorton Ct
Cawston House
Thurlaston
Compton Ct

Dunkleys Farm

Heath Lane
Lawford Heath Lane

Travelodge
G
A45
Dunchurch Trading Esta
H
45 46 47 48

J K L M
Windmill Farm
272
COVENTRY ROAD

2
I
3
4
5
6
7
8
73
75
76

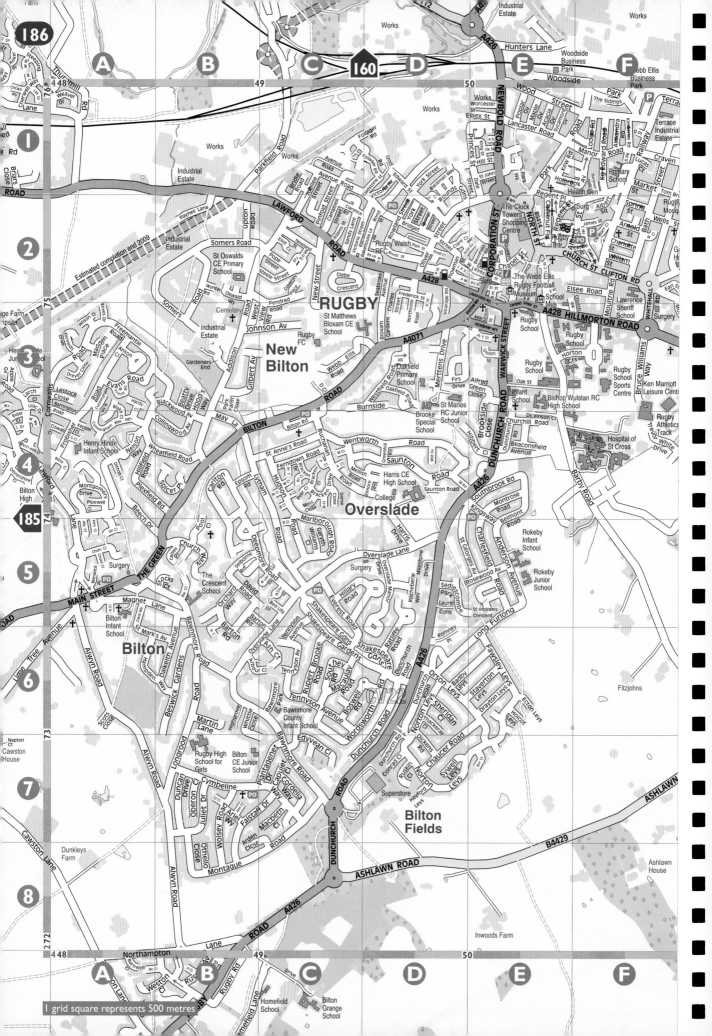

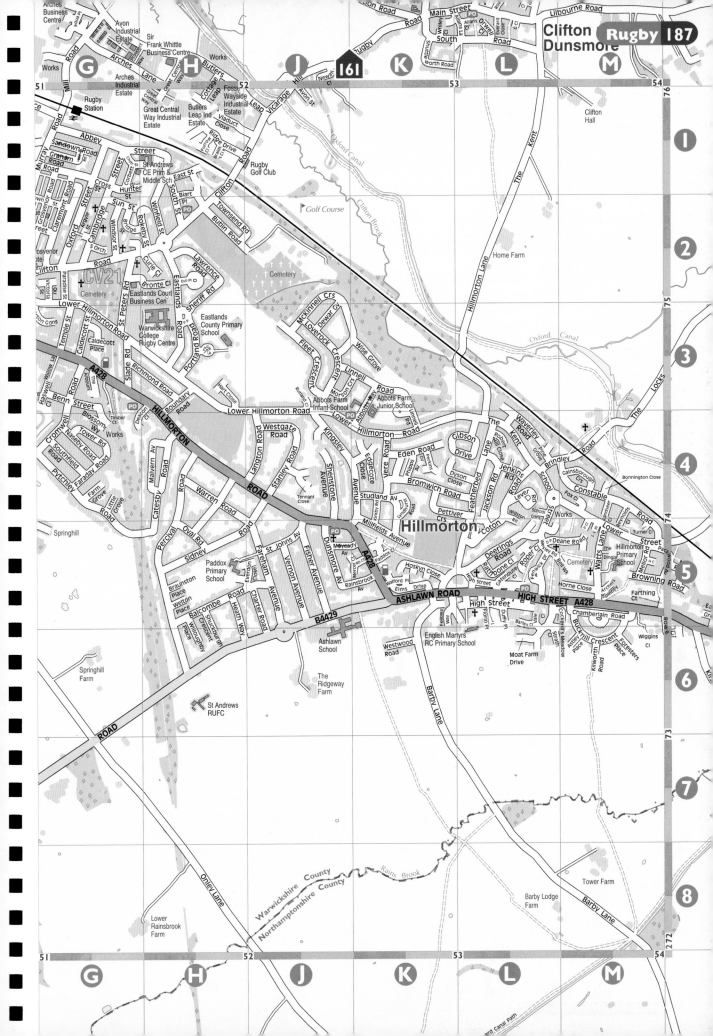

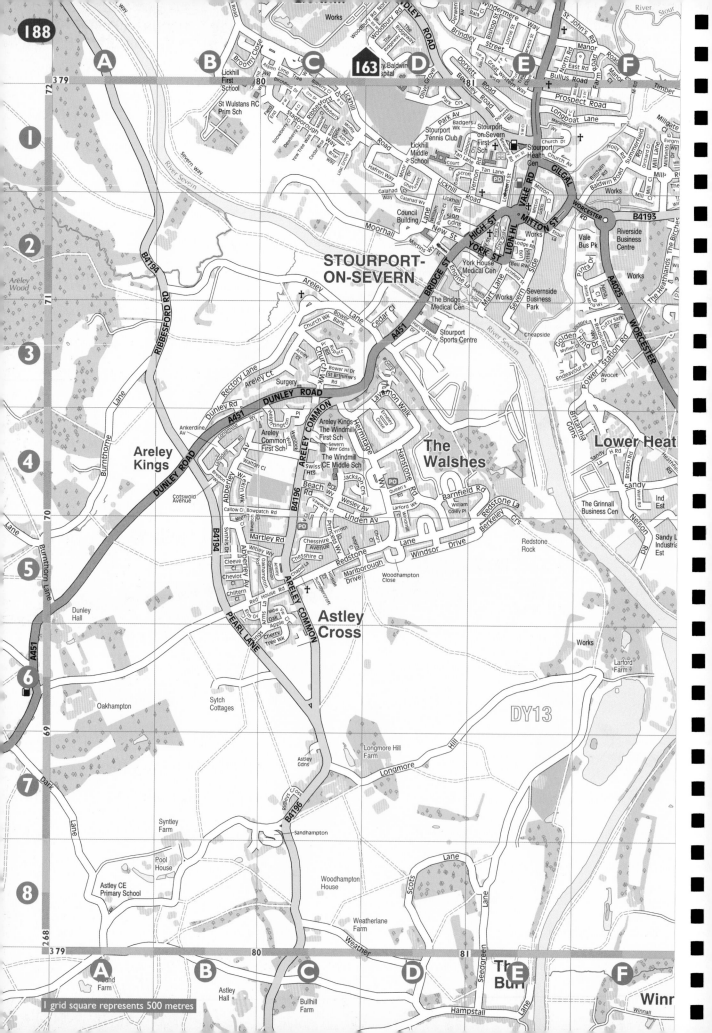

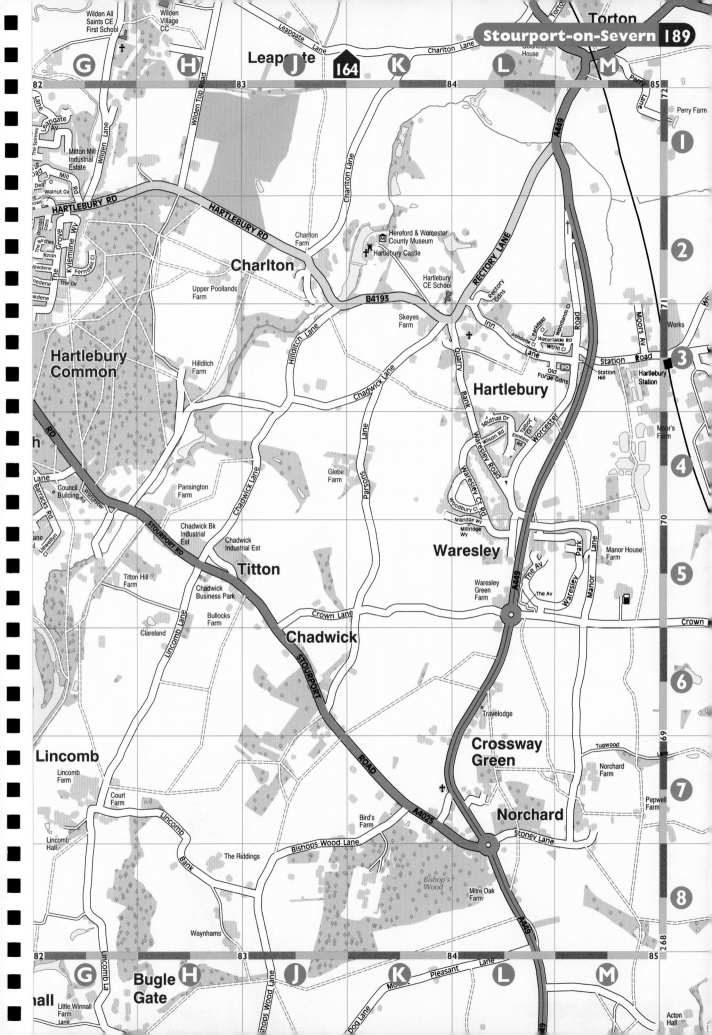

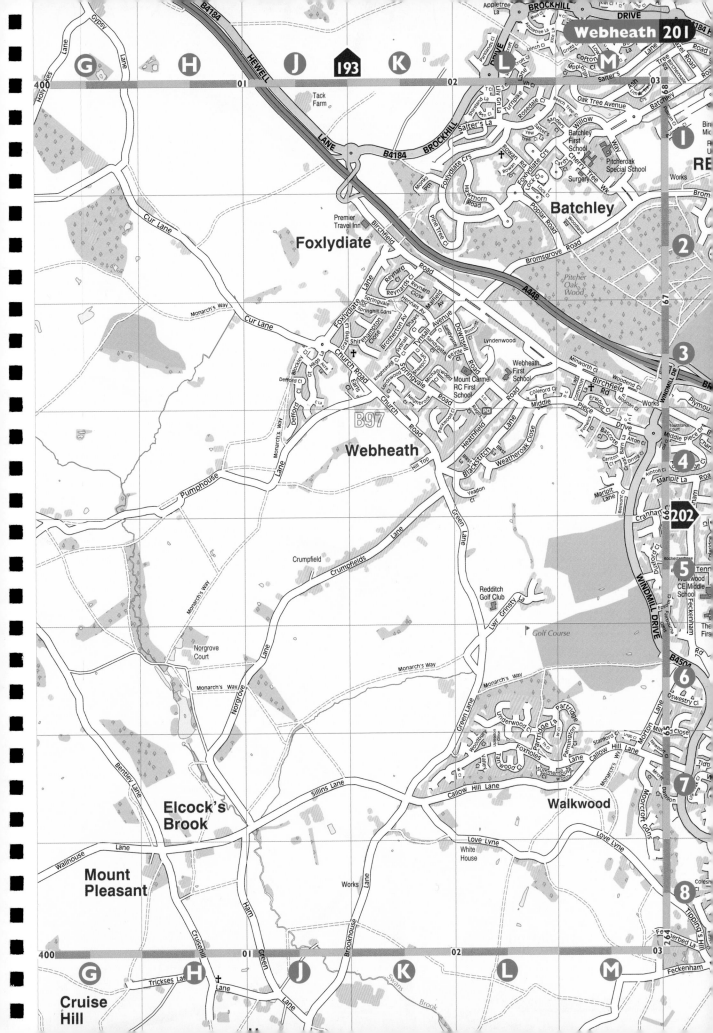

B4184

BROCKHILL

DRIVE

Appletree La

193

Batchley

Foxlydiate

Webheath

B97

Crumpfield

Crumpfields

Norgrove Court

Elcock's Brook

Mount Pleasant

Walkwood

White House

202

Cruise Hill

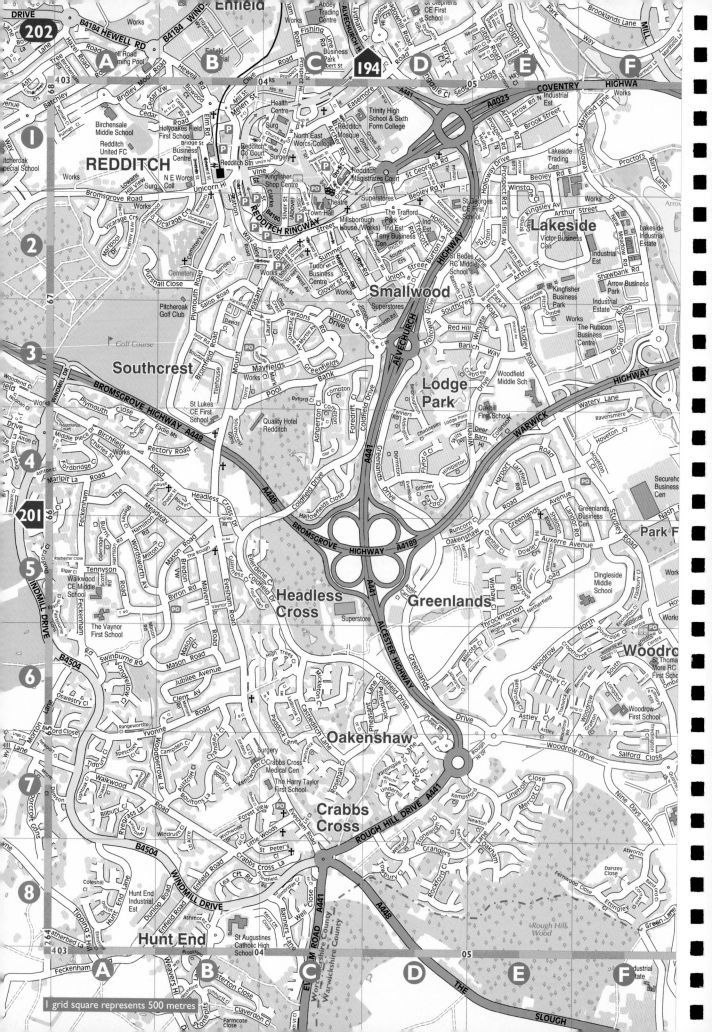

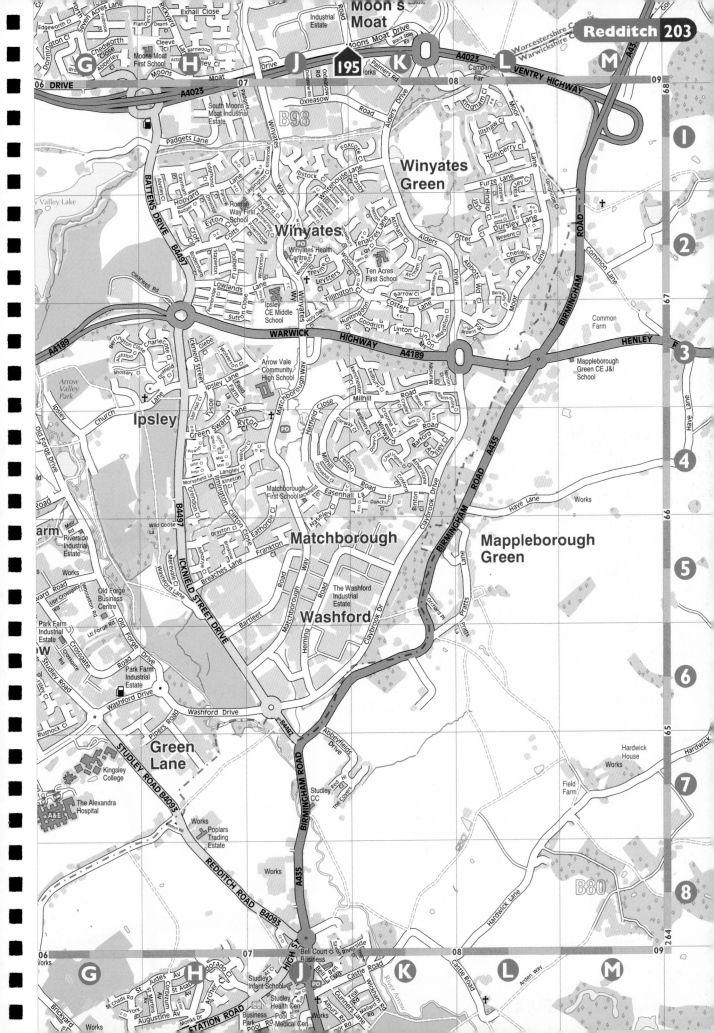

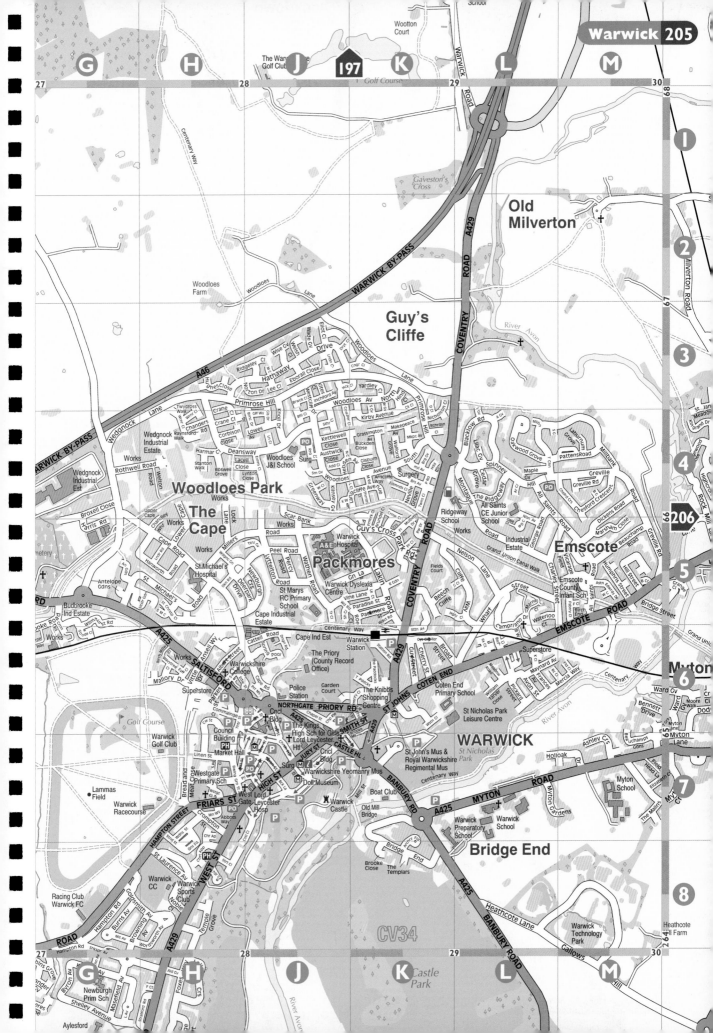

Church Pl BLOX/PEL WS3 39 H5
Church Rd ALDR WS9 41 J2
AST/WIT B6 89 L5
ATHST CV9 63 M6
BDMR/CCFT WV3 49 J6
BILS/COS WV14 67 H4
BLKHTH/ROWR B65 104 A2
BLOX/PEL WS3 39 L2
BNTWD WS7 19 H6
BRGRVW B61 191 K2
BRWNH WS8 26 D6
CDSL WV8 34 D1
CNCK/NC WS11 15 L4
CNCK/NC WS11 25 J1
CSHL/WTROR B46 94 E3
DUDS DY2 84 F8
DUNHL/THL/PER WV6 48 C1
EDG B15 106 E6
ERDE/BCHGN B24 90 E1
HAG/WOL DY9 102 C8
HAG/WOL DY9 141 H6
HALE B63 103 G6
KNWTH CV8 181 K3
LGN/SDN/BHAMAIR B26 110 A8
LICHS WS14 28 D8
MOS/BIL B13 125 L2
NFLD/LBR B31 144 E1
NUNW/HART CV10 79 M5
NUNW/HART CV10 98 A2
PBAR/PBCH B42 71 H8
PENK ST19 10 C4
POL/KGSB/FAZ B78 47 L8
REDW B97 201 J3
RRUGBY CV23 159 G8
SCFLD/BOLD B73 72 D5
SEDG DY3 82 C3
SHHTH WV12 38 B7
SHLY B90 147 M3
SMTHWKW B67 105 K1
STETCH B33 109 K3
STRBR DY8 101 H3
STRBR DY8 119 M2
TAM/AM/WIL B77 60 A1
WMBN WV5 64 F6
WOLVN WV10 23 G3
WOLVN WV10 36 A4
YDLY B25 109 H7
Church Rw ATHST CV9 * 62 A4
Churchside Vw ALDR WS9 40 F3
Church Sq OLDBY B69 86 E6
Churchstone Cl BRGRVW B61 168 D5
Church St ATHST CV9 63 H5
BILS/COS WV14 51 H8
BKHL/PFLD WV2 2 E7
BLOX/PEL WS3 38 F5
BNTWD WS7 18 C8
BRGRVW B61 191 K3
BRLYHL DY5 102 A3
BRWNH WS8 26 C8
CBHAMNW B3 6 F4
CDYHTH B64 103 J4
CNCK/NC WS11 16 B7
COV CV1 9 H1
CRTAM B79 31 M8
DARL/WED WS10 67 M1
DUDS DY2 85 G5
HAG/WOL DY9 119 L8
KIDD DY10 138 C7
LICH WS13 21 G5
LOZ/NWT B19 89 G6
NUN CV11 99 G1
OLDBY B69 86 E5
RLSS CV31 206 E6
RMSLY B62 104 B4
RRUGBY CV23 161 L8
RUGBYN/HIL CV21 186 E2
SEDG DY3 84 B2
STRBR DY8 101 L8
TPTN/OCK DY4 85 L3
WBROM B70 87 G1
WLNHL WV13 51 M3
WOLVN WV10 50 E1
WSL WS1 5 G5
WWCK CV34 205 J7
Church Ter MGN/WHC B75 * 57 G2
RLSS CV31 206 E6
STETCH B33 * 109 J4
Church V BFLD/HDSWWD B20 88 F4
CNCK/NC WS11 25 J1
HHTH/SAND B71 69 H7
Church Vw ALDR WS9 40 D2
BEWD DY12 162 E2
HLYWD B47 172 C3
KNWTH CV8 * 182 F4
Church View Cl BLOX/PEL WS3 39 G5
Church View Dr CDYHTH B64 103 K4
Church Vls
BFLD/HDSWWD B20 * 88 C3
Church Wk ATHST CV9 63 K6
BDMR/CCFT WV3 49 K6
COVW CV5 133 G7
DUNHL/THL/PER WV6 35 J8
KIDDW DY11 138 A7
RLSS CV31 206 D6
RUGBYN/HIL CV21 186 F2
RUGBYS/DCH CV22 186 B5
STRPT DY13 188 C3
WASH/WDE B8 90 E7
Churchward Cl STRBR DY8 101 M7
Churchward Gv WMBN WV5 64 E5
Church Wy BDWTH CV12 116 F2
RUSH/SHEL WS4 39 M3
Churchyard Rd TPTN/OCK DY4 67 M8
Churnet Gv
DUNHL/THL/PER WV6 48 D1
Churn Hill Rd ALDR WS9 54 E1
Churns Hill La SEDG DY3 82 F2
Churston Cl BLOX/PEL WS3 38 E2
Chylds Ct COVW CV5 132 E8
Cider Av BRLYHL DY5 102 C4
Cinder Bank DUDS DY2 85 G7
Cinder Rd BNTWD WS7 18 C6
SEDG DY3 83 M3
Cinder Wy DARL/WED WS10 68 C2
Cinquefoil Leasow
TPTN/OCK DY4 68 A7
The Circle NUNW/HART CV10 98 C1
Circuit Cl WLNHL WV13 51 M2
Circular Rd ACGN B27 127 G3
Circus Av
CHWD/FDBR/MGN B37 111 G3
Cirencester Cl BRGRVE B60 191 M3
City Ar LICH WS13 * 20 F6
City Plaza CBHAM B2 * 7 G5
City Rd LDYWD/EDGR B16 106 A3
OLDBY B69 85 M6
City Vw ERDW/GRVHL B23 90 C2
WASH/WDE B8 108 B1
Civic Cl CBHAMW B1 6 C5
Claerwen Av STRPT DY13 163 J6
Claerwen Gv NFLD/LBR B31 123 J8
Claines Crs KIDD DY10 138 F7
Claines Rd HALE B63 103 H8
NFLD/LBR B31 145 G1
Clairvaux Gdns HIA/OLT B92 127 H8
Clandon Cl
ALE/KHTH/YWD B14 145 M3
Clanfield Av WNSFLD WV11 37 K5
Clapgate Gdns BILS/COS WV14 66 E2
Clap Gate Gv WMBN WV5 64 C7
Clapgate La RIDG/WDGT B32 122 F3
Clap Gate Rd WMBN WV5 64 C6
Clapham Sq RLSS CV31 206 F6
Clapham St RLSS CV31 206 F7
Clapham Ter RLSS CV31 206 F6
Clapton Gv KGSTG B44 71 M4
Clara St COVE CV2 155 L3
Clare Av WNSFLD WV11 37 K4
Clare Cl RLSN CV32 207 G3
Clare Ct RUGBYN/HIL CV21 186 D2
Clare Crs BILS/COS WV14 66 D3
Clare Dr EDG B15 106 D5
Clarel Av WASH/WDE B8 108 A2
Claremont Cl BDWTH CV12 117 M1
Claremont Ms BDMR/CCFT WV3 49 L6
Claremont Pl WSNGN B18 * 88 E8
Claremont Rd BDMR/CCFT WV3 49 L6
CRTAM B79 31 K5
RLSS CV31 206 D7
RUGBYN/HIL CV21 187 G2
SEDG DY3 66 C5
SMTHWK B66 105 M1
SPARK B11 107 M6
WSNGN B18 88 E7
Claremont St BILS/COS WV14 51 G7
CDYHTH B64 103 J4
Claremont Wk COVW CV5 133 G7
Claremont Wy HALE B63 121 L2
Clarence Av HDSW B21 * 88 A5
Clarence Ct LGLYGN/QTN B68 105 G3
Clarence Gdns
FOAKS/STRLY B74 56 D3
Clarence Gv SHLY B90 147 M1
Clarence Rd BILS/COS WV14 51 J6
DUDS DY2 85 H7
ERDW/GRVHL B23 90 B2
FOAKS/STRLY B74 56 D2
HDSW B21 88 A5
HRBN B17 106 B7
MOS/BIL B13 125 L5
RUGBYN/HIL CV21 186 C2
WOLV WV1 2 E4
Clarence St COV CV1 9 K2
KIDD DY10 138 D7
NUN CV11 98 F1
RLSS CV31 206 E7
SEDG DY3 66 B7
WOLV WV1 2 E5
Clarence Ter RLSN CV32 * 206 D4
Clarence Wy BEWD DY12 162 F1
Clarenden Pl HRBN B17 106 A8
Clarendon Av RLSN CV32 206 D4
Clarendon Cl REDW B97 193 M8
Clarendon Ct RLSN CV32 * 206 D4
Clarendon Crs RLSN CV32 206 C4
Clarendon Dr TPTN/OCK DY4 68 B5
Clarendon Pl BLOX/PEL WS3 39 K1
RLSN CV32 206 C4
RMSLY B62 104 D7
Clarendon Rd KNWTH CV8 197 L2
LDYWD/EDGR B16 106 C4
MGN/WHC B75 57 G2
RUSH/SHEL WS4 40 A3
SMTHWKW B67 105 K1
Clarendon Sq RLSN CV32 206 C4
Clarendon St BDMR/CCFT WV3 2 B5
BLOX/PEL WS3 38 F4
COVW CV5 154 D4
RLSN CV32 206 E4
Clare Rd BLOX/PEL WS3 39 K7
WOLVN WV10 36 C6
Clare's Ct KIDDW DY11 138 A7
Clarewell Av SOLH B91 148 E4
Clarion Wy CNCK/NC WS11 12 C8
Clarke's Av HEDN WS12 12 C8
KNWTH CV8 197 L2
Clarkes Gv TPTN/OCK DY4 68 A7
Clarke's La HHTH/SAND B71 69 G6
WLNHL WV13 52 A3
Clarke St REDW B97 202 C1
Clark Rd BDMR/CCFT WV3 49 K3
Clarksland Gv
CHWD/FDBR/MGN B37 110 E5
Clarks La SHLY B90 147 L7
Clarkson Cl NUN CV11 99 H1
Clarkson Rd DARL/WED WS10 68 E2
Clark St COVN CV6 134 E4
LDYWD/EDGR B16 106 D3
STRBR DY8 101 J8
Clarry Dr FOAKS/STRLY B74 56 D5
Clary Gv DSYBK/YTR WS5 69 L2
Clatterbach La HAG/WOL DY9 141 L1
Clattercut La KIDD DY10 166 D8
Claughton Ct KIDDW DY11 138 A8
Claughton Rd DUDS DY2 85 H4
Claughton Rd North DUDS DY2 85 H4
Claughton St KIDDW DY11 138 A8
Clausen Cl GTB/HAM B43 71 J1
Clavedon Cl NFLD/LBR B31 123 J6
Claverdon Cl BRWNH WS8 26 E5
SOLH B91 148 C1
Claverdon Dr
FOAKS/STRLY B74 55 M1
GTB/HAM B43 70 B5
Claverdon Gdns ACGN B27 108 F8
Claverdon Rd COVW CV5 153 M2
Claverley Dr
ETTPK/GDPK/PENN WV4 49 H8
Clay Av NUN CV11 81 K6
Claybrook Dr REDE B98 203 K6
Claybrook St DIG/EDG B5 7 G8
Claycroft Ter DUDN DY1 66 F7
Claydon Gv
ALE/KHTH/YWD B14 146 E2
RWWCK/WEL CV35 204 C2
Claydon Rd KGSWFD DY6 83 G4
Clay Dr RIDG/WDGT B32 104 E8
Claygate Rd HEDN WS12 17 J2
Clayhanger La BRWNH WS8 26 B7
Clayhanger Rd BRWNH WS8 26 D7
Clayhill La RRUGBY CV23 159 K8
Clay La COVE CV2 155 L1
COVW CV5 132 C1
LGN/SDN/BHAMAIR B26 109 J8
OLDBY B69 104 E1
Claymore TAM/AM/WIL B77 46 B6
Claypit Cl WBROM B70 86 E2
Claypit La BRGRVW B61 168 E4
LICHS WS14 28 D1
Clay Pit La SHLY B90 147 L8
Claypit La WBROM B70 86 E2
Clay St PENK ST19 10 C4
Clayton Cl BKHL/PFLD WV2 50 A6
Clayton Dr BRGRVE B60 191 M6
CBROM B36 92 A5
Clayton Gdns RBRY B45 169 L3
Clayton Rd BILS/COS WV14 66 F6
COVN CV6 133 J8
WASH/WDE B8 90 B8
Clear Vw KGSWFD DY6 82 F7
Clearwell Gdns DUDN DY1 84 D2
Clearwell Rd REDE B98 203 G2
Cleasby TAM/AM/WIL B77 47 G4
Clee Av KIDDW DY11 164 A3
Clee Hill Dr BDMR/CCFT WV3 48 D4
Clee Hill Rd SEDG DY3 84 A1
Clee Rd DUDN DY1 84 E6
LGLYGN/QTN B68 105 G1
NFLD/LBR B31 144 E5
STRBR DY8 101 L7
Cleeton St HEDN WS12 17 H4
Cleeve TAM/AM/WIL B77 46 B2
Cleeve Cl REDE B98 195 H8
STRPT DY13 188 B5
Cleeve Dr FOAKS/STRLY B74 42 D7
Cleeve Rd ALE/KHTH/YWD B14 147 G1
BLOX/PEL WS3 38 D2
Cleeves Av WWCK CV34 206 B7
Cleeve Wy BLOX/PEL WS3 38 D3
Clee View Meadow SEDG DY3 66 B3
Clee View Rd WMBN WV5 64 C8
Clegg Rd BNTWD WS7 19 J6
Clematis TAM/AM/WIL B77 46 D2
Clematis Dr COVEN WV9 35 K2
Clemens St RLSS CV31 206 E6
Clement Pl BILS/COS WV14 * 51 H6
Clement Rd BILS/COS WV14 51 H6
RMSLY B62 104 B4
Clements Cl KNWTH CV8 179 L8
OLDBY B69 104 D1
Clements Rd YDLY B25 109 H5
Clements St COVE CV2 155 L2
Clement St CBHAMW B1 6 B4
NUN CV11 98 F2
WSLW WS2 4 C5
Clement Wy
RUGBYS/DCH CV22 185 L5
Clemson St WLNHL WV13 51 L3
Clennon Ri COVE CV2 135 H5
Clensmore St KIDD DY10 138 B6
Clent Av KIDDW DY11 163 M4
REDW B97 202 B6
Clent Dr HAG/WOL DY9 120 A7
NUNW/HART CV10 97 M2
Clent Hill Dr
BLKHTH/ROWR B65 85 L8
Clent Rd HDSW B21 88 B4
LGLYGN/QTN B68 105 G5
RBRY B45 143 J5
STRBR DY8 101 L7
Clent View Rd HALE B63 121 G1
STRBR DY8 119 G3
Clent Vls BHTH/HG B12 * 125 M1
Clent Wy RIDG/WDGT B32 122 D5
Cleobury Cl REDW B97 193 M8
Cleobury La HOCK/TIA B94 173 L2
Cleobury Rd BEWD DY12 162 C3
Cleton St TPTN/OCK DY4 85 M2
Clevedon Av CBROM B36 92 C4
Clevedon Rd BHTH/HG B12 107 J7
Cleveland Cl WLNHL WV13 51 H4
WNSFLD WV11 37 K4
Cleveland Dr CNCK/NC WS11 16 F1
RBRY B45 169 L3
Cleveland Pas WOLV WV1 2 F6
Cleveland Rd BDWTH CV12 117 M2
BKHL/PFLD WV2 3 H7
COVE CV2 155 L1
Cleveland St DUDN DY1 84 F4
STRBR DY8 119 J1
WOLV WV1 2 F6
Cleveley Dr NUNW/HART CV10 80 B6
Cleves Crs GTWY WS6 24 B4
Cleves Dr RBRY B45 143 J6
Cleves Rd RBRY B45 143 J5
Clewley Dr COVEN WV9 35 L2
Clewley Gv RIDG/WDGT B32 104 F8
Clews Cl WSL WS1 4 E8
Clewshaw La
HWK/WKHTH B38 171 M1
Clews Rd REDE B98 202 D6
Cley Cl DIG/EDG B5 107 H7
Cley Rd CNCK/NC WS11 16 F8
Clifden Gv KNWTH CV8 180 A7
Cliff Dr DARL/WED WS10 68 B5
Cliffe Dr STETCH B33 109 M2
Cliffe Rd RLSN CV32 206 B4
Cliffe Wy WWCK CV34 205 L5
Cliff Hall La
POL/KGSB/FAZ B78 59 M5
Clifford Bridge Rd COVE CV2 135 K7
COVS CV3 156 D3
Clifford Rd DOR/KN B93 175 K1
SMTHWKW B67 105 K4
WBROM B70 86 E3
Clifford St DUDN DY1 84 F5
DUNHL/THL/PER WV6 2 A2
LOZ/NWT B19 89 H6
TAM/AM/WIL B77 46 C2
Clifford Wk LOZ/NWT B19 89 H6
Cliff Rock Rd RBRY B45 143 M6
Clift Av SHHTH WV12 38 B6
Clift Cl SHHTH WV12 38 A7
Clifton Av ALDR WS9 41 G5
BRWNH WS8 26 B7
CNCK/NC WS11 16 A6
CRTAM B79 31 K6
Clifton Cl AST/WIT B6 89 K6
OLDBY B69 104 D1
REDE B98 203 H4
Clifton Crs SOLH B91 148 D4
Clifton Gdns CDSL WV8 35 G2
Clifton Gn HLGN/YWD B28 126 E8
Clifton La CRTAM B79 32 F2
HHTH/SAND B71 69 J5
Clifton Rd AST/WIT B6 89 K6
BHTH/HG B12 107 L8
CBROM B36 92 C5
DUNHL/THL/PER WV6 35 H8
KIDD DY10 139 G2
KIDDW DY11 163 L4
NUNW/HART CV10 98 D1
RMSLY B62 104 B5
RUGBYN/HIL CV21 186 F2
SCFLD/BOLD B73 72 E1
SMTHWKW B67 105 K1
Clifton St BDMR/CCFT WV3 2 C5
BILS/COS WV14 66 D4
CDYHTH B64 103 K4
COV CV1 9 J1
STRBR DY8 119 K1
Clifton Ter ERDW/GRVHL B23 * 90 D1
Clinic Dr HAG/WOL DY9 102 C8
NUN CV11 99 G2
Clinton Av KNWTH CV8 179 H7
RWWCK/WEL CV35 204 E6
Clinton Crs BNTWD WS7 18 F5
Clinton Gv SHLY B90 148 B4
Clinton La KNWTH CV8 179 H6
Clinton Rd BILS/COS WV14 51 L6
COVN CV6 134 D3
CSHL/WTROR B46 93 K7
SHLY B90 148 C5
Clinton St RLSS CV31 206 E6
WSNGN B18 88 C8
Clipper Vw LDYWD/EDGR B16 106 C4
Clipstone Rd COVN CV6 133 J7
Clipston Rd WASH/WDE B8 90 D8
Clissold Cl BHTH/HG B12 107 J8
Clissold Pas WSNGN B18 106 E1
Clissold St WSNGN B18 106 E1
Clive Cl MGN/WHC B75 57 H3
Cliveden Av ALDR WS9 40 F4
PBAR/PBCH B42 89 G1
Cliveden Coppice
FOAKS/STRLY B74 56 D4
Cliveden Wk NUN CV11 99 J5
Clivedon Wy RMSLY B62 103 L6
Cliveland St LOZ/NWT B19 7 G1
Clive Rd BNTWD WS7 18 E6
BRGRVE B60 191 M5
RCOVN/BALC/EX CV7 152 A8
REDW B97 194 B8
RIDG/WDGT B32 105 H6
Clive St HHTH/SAND B71 69 G8
Clockfields Dr BRLYHL DY5 101 L4
Clock La HIA/OLT B92 129 H3
Clockmill Av BLOX/PEL WS3 39 J2
Clockmill Pl BLOX/PEL WS3 39 K2
Clockmill Rd BLOX/PEL WS3 39 J2
Clodeshall Rd WASH/WDE B8 108 C1
Cloister Cft COVE CV2 135 K7
Cloister Crofts RLSN CV32 206 D2
Cloister Dr RMSLY B62 122 B2
The Cloisters RUSH/SHEL WS4 5 G1
Cloister Wy RLSN CV32 206 D2
Clonmel Rd BVILLE B30 124 E7
Clopton Crs
CHWD/FDBR/MGN B37 111 G1
Clopton Rd STETCH B33 110 A5
The Close DARL/WED WS10 68 C2
HALE B63 103 H7
HIA/OLT B92 127 K5
HLYWD B47 146 E8
HRBN B17 105 K6
KNWTH CV8 157 K8
LICH WS13 20 F5
RLSS CV31 206 E7
RMSLY B62 121 L6
SEDG DY3 82 C3
SEDG DY3 84 A1
SLYOAK B29 * 124 B5
Clothier Gdns WLNHL WV13 51 L2
Clothier St WLNHL WV13 51 L2
Cloud Br KNWTH CV8 181 J8
Cloudbridge Dr HIA/OLT B92 128 D6
Cloud Gn TLHL/CAN CV4 154 B8
Cloudsley Gv HIA/OLT B92 127 K2
Clovelly Gdns COVE CV2 135 G8
Clovelly Rd COVE CV2 134 F8
Clovelly Wy NUN CV11 81 J8
Clover Av
CHWD/FDBR/MGN B37 111 H3
Clover Cl RRUGBY CV23 161 H5
Cloverdale
DUNHL/THL/PER WV6 48 B1
Cloverdale Cl COVN CV6 133 M1
Clover Dr RIDG/WDGT B32 123 G3
Clover Hl DSYBK/YTR WS5 54 C5
Clover La KGSWFD DY6 82 E6
Clover Lea Sq WASH/WDE B8 90 E7
Clover Ley WOLVN WV10 3 L3
Clover Mdw HEDN WS12 17 G4
Clover Piece TPTN/OCK DY4 68 A7
Clover Rdg GTWY WS6 24 A2
Clover Rd SLYOAK B29 123 L6
Cloweswood La HOCK/TIA B94 173 K5
Club La WOLVN WV10 22 A7
Club Rw SEDG DY3 66 C8
Club Vw HWK/WKHTH B38 145 H3
Clud Dr ATHST CV9 76 F1
Clunbury Cft BKDE/SHDE B34 91 M8
Clunbury Rd NFLD/LBR B31 144 F5
Clun Cl OLDBY B69 85 K4
Clunes Av NUN CV11 81 J7
Clun Rd NFLD/LBR B31 123 K7
Clyde Av RMSLY B62 104 C5
Clyde Ms BRLYHL DY5 83 M7
Clyde Rd BDWTH CV12 117 L2
DOR/KN B93 175 L3
Clydesdale
LGN/SDN/BHAMAIR B26 109 L8
Clydesdale Rd
RIDG/WDGT B32 104 F7
Clyde St BHTH/HG B12 7 L8
CDYHTH B64 103 J4
Coalash La BRGRVE B60 200 A2
Coalbourn La STRBR DY8 101 K8
Coal Haulage Rd HEDN WS12 17 K5
Coalheath La RUSH/SHEL WS4 40 A5
Coalpit Fields Rd
BDWTH CV12 117 G3
Coalpit La KNWTH CV8 184 A1
Coal Pool La BLOX/PEL WS3 39 K8
Coalport Rd WOLV WV1 50 F4
Coalway Av BDMR/CCFT WV3 49 L7
LGN/SDN/BHAMAIR B26 128 A1
Coalway Gdns
BDMR/CCFT WV3 49 H6
Coalway Rd BDMR/CCFT WV3 49 H7
BLOX/PEL WS3 38 E4
ETTPK/GDPK/PENN WV4 49 H7
Coates Rd KIDD DY10 138 F6
Coat of Arms Bridge Rd
COVS CV3 154 E7
Cobb Cl COVE CV2 9 M2
Cobbett Rd BNTWD WS7 18 C7
The Cobbles CSCFLD/WYGN B72 73 G6
Cobble Wk WSNGN B18 * 88 E8
Cobbs Rd KNWTH CV8 179 H7
Cobden Av RLSS CV31 207 G8
Cobden Cl DARL/WED WS10 52 D7
HEDN WS12 13 G6
TPTN/OCK DY4 67 K5
Cobden Gdns BHTH/HG B12 107 J8
Cobden St COVN CV6 134 C8
DARL/WED WS10 52 A7
KIDDW DY11 138 A7
STRBR DY8 101 H7
WSL WS1 4 D9
Cobham Cl BRGRVE B60 191 K6
CVALE B35 91 K2
Cobham Court Ms
HAG/WOL DY9 120 B7
Cobham Crs BEWD DY12 162 E2
Cobham Rd BORD B9 108 B3
DARL/WED WS10 69 J3
HALE B63 121 M1
KIDD DY10 164 C1
STRBR DY8 119 L3
Cobia TAM/AM/WIL B77 46 B6
Cob La BVILLE B30 124 A6
Cobley Hl ALVE B48 193 J1
Cobnall Rd BRGRVW B61 168 E3
Cobs Fld BVILLE B30 124 A7
Coburg Cft TPTN/OCK DY4 68 A7
Coburn Dr MGN/WHC B75 57 H3
Cochrane Cl HAG/WOL DY9 120 A3
TPTN/OCK DY4 * 68 A7
Cochrane Rd DUDS DY2 84 C8
Cockerill's Meadow
RUGBYN/HIL CV21 187 L5
Cockermouth Cl RLSN CV32 206 B3
Cock Hill La RBRY B45 143 K5
Cocksheds La RMSLY B62 104 A5
Cockshut Hl
LGN/SDN/BHAMAIR B26 109 L5
Cockshutt La BKHL/PFLD WV2 * 50 B6
BRGRVW B61 168 B7
Cockshutts La BKHL/PFLD WV2 50 B6
Cocksmead Cft
ALE/KHTH/YWD B14 125 H8
Cocksparrow La HEDN WS12 12 A6
PENK ST19 15 L1
Cocksparrow St WWCK CV34 205 H6
Cockspur St
POL/KGSB/FAZ B78 47 J6
Cockthorpe Cl HRBN B17 105 K6
Cocton Cl DUNHL/THL/PER WV6 34 C8
Codsall Gdns CDSL WV8 34 C1
Codsall Rd CDSL WV8 35 G4
CDYHTH B64 103 J5
DUNHL/THL/PER WV6 35 H6
Cofield Rd SCFLD/BOLD B73 72 D4
Cofton Church La RBRY B45 170 B3
Cofton Cl REDW B97 193 M8
Cofton Ct RBRY B45 144 B6
Cofton Gv NFLD/LBR B31 144 C7
Cofton Lake Rd RBRY B45 170 A2
Cofton Rd NFLD/LBR B31 144 E6
Cokeland Pl CDYHTH B64 103 H5
Colaton Cl WOLVN WV10 50 C1
Colbek Ct NUNW/HART CV10 97 J1
Colbourne Gv RLSN CV32 206 B3
Colbourne Grove Dr
RLSN CV32 * 206 B3
Colbourne Rd
POL/KGSB/FAZ B78 45 L3
TPTN/OCK DY4 85 L1
Colbrook TAM/AM/WIL B77 46 B4
Colchester St COV CV1 9 J3
Coldbath Rd MOS/BIL B13 125 M5
Coldfield Dr REDE B98 202 B5
Coldridge Cl CDSL WV8 35 K4
Coldstream Dr STRBR DY8 101 J2
Coldstream Rd
WALM/CURD B76 73 J5
Cole Bank Rd HLGN/YWD B28 126 C5
Colebourne Rd MOS/BIL B13 126 B7
Colebridge Crs
CSHL/WTROR B46 93 K5
Colebrook Cl COVS CV3 156 D3
Colebrook Cft SHLY B90 147 K3
Colebrook Rd SHLY B90 147 J3
SPARK B11 108 B8
Coleby Cl TLHL/CAN CV4 153 H7
Cole Ct CHWD/FDBR/MGN B37 110 F3
COVN CV6 8 B2
Coleford Cl REDW B97 201 L3
STRBR DY8 101 G3
Coleford Dr
CHWD/FDBR/MGN B37 110 E3
Cole Gn SHLY B90 147 J3
Cole Hall La STETCH B33 109 L1
Colehill CRTAM B79 31 M8
Colehurst Cft SHLY B90 148 D7
Coleman Rd DARL/WED WS10 52 E8
Coleman St
DUNHL/THL/PER WV6 49 K1
TLHL/CAN CV4 153 K2
Colemeadow Rd
CSHL/WTROR B46 93 K6
MOS/BIL B13 125 M8
REDE B98 195 J7
Colenso Rd LDYWD/EDGR B16 106 A1
Coleraine Rd PBAR/PBCH B42 70 E7
Coleridge Cl BLOX/PEL WS3 * 25 L8
CRTAM B79 31 L7
REDW B97 202 A5
SHHTH WV12 38 C6
Coleridge Dr
DUNHL/THL/PER WV6 48 C1
Coleridge Pas CBHAMNE B4 7 H3
Coleridge Ri SEDG DY3 83 L1
Coleridge Rd COVE CV2 156 A1
GTB/HAM B43 70 C6
Colesbourne Av
ALE/KHTH/YWD B14 146 A3
Colesbourne Rd HIA/OLT B92 127 M2
Coleshill Cl REDW B97 202 A8
Coleshill Heath Rd
CHWD/FDBR/MGN B37 111 G7
Coleshill Rd ATHST CV9 62 D8
CHWD/FDBR/MGN B37 110 E6
CSHL/WTROR B46 92 F3
CSHL/WTROR B46 94 B3
MGN/WHC B75 57 H8
NUNW/HART CV10 79 G7
POL/KGSB/FAZ B78 45 L6
Coleshill St
CSCFLD/WYGN B72 57 G8
Coleside Av MOS/BIL B13 126 B6
Coles La CSCFLD/WYGN B72 73 G2
HHTH/SAND B71 68 E6
The Colesleys
CSHL/WTROR B46 93 L7
Cole St DUDS DY2 103 J1
Cole Valley Rd HLGN/YWD B28 126 B6
Coleview Crs STETCH B33 110 C2
Coleville Rd WALM/CURD B76 73 M7
Coleys La NFLD/LBR B31 144 E3
Colgreave Av MOS/BIL B13 126 B3
Colina Cl COVS CV3 156 A8
Colindale Rd KGSTG B44 71 L2
Colinwood Cl GTWY WS6 24 D4
Colledge Cl RRUGBY CV23 158 B2
Colledge Rd COVN CV6 134 B4
Colleen Av BVILLE B30 145 M2
College Cl DARL/WED WS10 68 E3
College Dr BFLD/HDSWWD B20 88 D3
RLSN CV32 206 D3
College Farm Dr
ERDW/GRVHL B23 72 B5
College Ga WASH/WDE B8 108 C1
College Gv
BFLD/HDSWWD B20 * 88 F6
College Hl SCFLD/BOLD B73 72 F1
College La CRTAM B79 31 M8
KNWTH CV8 177 J4
College Rd
BFLD/HDSWWD B20 88 C3
BRGRVE B60 191 L3
DUNHL/THL/PER WV6 49 H1
KGSTG B44 71 J8
KIDD DY10 164 C1
MOS/BIL B13 126 A3
RMSLY B62 104 E7
SCFLD/BOLD B73 72 B4
STRBR DY8 119 L1
WASH/WDE B8 108 C2
College St NUNW/HART CV10 98 F3
WSNGN B18 106 E1
College Vw
DUNHL/THL/PER WV6 49 H2
College Wk BRGRVE B60 191 L3

Collet Rd
 DUNHL/THL/PER WV6.....34 G4
Collets Brook MGN/WHC B75...57 L3
Collett TAM/AM/WIL B77 ...46 E3
Collett Cl STRBR DY8.....101 L7
Colletts Gv
 CHWD/FDBR/MGN B37.....110 D1
Collett Wk COV CV1.....8 C7
 KNWTH CV8 *.....197 K1
Colley Av WOLVN WV10....36 D5
Colley Ga HALE B63.....103 G7
Colley La HALE B63.....103 G7
Colley Orch HALE B63.....103 G7
Colley St WBROM B70.....87 H1
Collier Cl BRWNH WS8.....26 A6
 GTWY WS6.....24 B3
Colliers Cl SHHTH WV12....37 M7
Colliers Fold BRLYHL DY5.....83 M8
Colliers Wy HEDN WS12....12 A7
 RCOVN/BALC/EX CV7.....96 C5
Colliery Dr BLOX/PEL WS3....38 D2
Colliery La (North)
 RCOVN/BALC/EX CV7.....116 F4
Colliery Rd HHTH/SAND B71....87 L4
 WOLV WV1.....3 M1
Collindale Ct KGSWFD DY6....83 H7
Collingbourne Av CBROM B36....91 H6
Collingdon Av
 LGN/SDN/BHAMAIR B26....110 A3
Colling Dr LICH WS13.....20 D7
Collingtree Ct ACGN B27.....127 K3
Colling Wk
 CHWD/FDBR/MGN B37.....92 E8
Collingwood Av
 RUGBYS/DCH CV22.....186 A4
Collingwood Dr GTB/HAM B43...71 G1
Collingwood Rd BVILLE B30...146 B2
 COVW CV5.....8 A8
 WOLVN WV10.....36 C3
Collins Cl RIDG/WDGT B32...104 E8
Collins Gv TLHL/CAN CV4....154 E8
Collins Hl WS13.....20 E3
Collinson Cl REDE B98.....202 C3
Collins Rd BRWNH WS8.....26 A6
 DARL/WED WS10.....68 F2
 WWCK CV34.....206 B8
Collins St WBROM B70.....86 C2
 WSL WS1.....4 F6
Collis Cl BRGRVE B60.....191 J6
Collis St STRBR DY8.....101 K5
Collister Cl SHLY B90.....126 F8
Colly Cft CHWD/FDBR/MGN B37...92 C8
Collycroft Pl ACGN B27.....108 F8
Colman Av WNSFLD WV11....37 K7
Colman Crs LGLYGN/QTN B68...105 G3
Colman Hl HALE B63.....103 H8
Colman Hill Av HALE B63....103 H8
Colmore Av
 ALE/KHTH/YWD B14.....125 H6
Colmore Circ Queensway
 CBHAMNW B3.....3 J4
Colmore Crs MOS/BIL B13....125 M4
Colmore Dr MGN/WHC B75....57 L8
Colmore Flats LOZ/NWT B19 *...6 F1
Colmore Rd
 ALE/KHTH/YWD B14.....125 H6
 CBHAMNW B3.....6 F4
Coln Cl NFLD/LBR B31.....123 K7
Colonial Rd BORD B9.....108 D2
Colshaw Rd STRBR DY8....119 J1
Colston Rd ERDE/BCHGN B24...90 F2
Colt Cl FOAKS/STRLY B74....55 J6
Coltham Rd SHHTH WV12....38 A7
Coltishall Cft CVALE B35....91 K3
Coltman Cl LICHS WS14.....21 H6
Coltsfoot Cl WNSFLD WV11...37 J5
Coltsfoot Vw GTWY WS6.....24 C3
Colts La REDE B98.....203 H4
Columbia Cl DIG/EDG B5.....107 H6
Columbian Crs BDWTH CV12...117 H3
Columbian Gdns BDWTH WS7...118 D5
Columbian Dr CNCK/NC WS11...16 D2
Columbian Wy CNCK/NC WS11...16 D2
Columbine Cl DSYBK/YTR WS5...69 K2
Columbine Wy BDWTH CV12...116 C4
Columbus Av BRLYHL DY5....102 D2
Colville Cl TPTN/OCK DY4....68 F8
Colville Rd BKHTH/HG B12...107 M6
Colwall Rd SEDG DY3.....84 B1
Colwall Wk ACGN B27.....127 K1
Colworth Rd NFLD/LBR B31...144 C1
Colyere Cl
 RCOVN/BALC/EX CV7.....115 L7
Colyns Gv STETCH B33.....91 L4
Comber Cft MOS/BIL B13....126 B5
Comber Dr BRLYHL DY5.....83 M7
Comberford Ct
 DARL/WED WS10 *.....68 C2
Comberford Dr
 DARL/WED WS10.....69 H1
Comberford La CRTAM B79...31 L4
Comberford Rd CRTAM B79...31 L5
Comberton Av KIDD DY10....138 D8
Comberton Hl KIDD DY10....138 D8
Comberton Park Rd
 KIDD DY10.....164 F1
Comberton Pl KIDD DY10....138 D8
Comberton Rd KIDD DY10....164 F1
 LGN/SDN/BHAMAIR B26....109 M6
Comberton Ter KIDD DY10...138 D8
Combine Cl MGN/WHC B75....57 H1
Combroke Gv
 RWWCK/WEL CV35.....204 C3
Comet Rd
 LGN/SDN/BHAMAIR B26....129 G4
Comfrey Cl HEDN WS12.....12 M4
Commainge Cl WWCK CV34...205 H6
Commerce Dr PENK ST19....10 C4
Commercial Rd WOLV WV1...3 K6
 WSLW WS2.....38 C6
Commercial St CBHAMW B1....6 D7
Commissary Rd
 LGN/SDN/BHAMAIR B26....128 C2
Common Barn La KIDD DY10...118 B8
Commonfield Cft
 WASH/WDE B8.....90 B4
Common La CNCK/NC WS11...16 C2
 KNWTH CV8.....179 M6
 LGN/SDN/BHAMAIR B26....109 M6
 LICHS WS14.....30 B2
 POL/KGSB/FAZ B78.....47 L5
 RCOVN/BALC/EX CV7.....114 C6
 STUD B80.....203 M2
 WASH/WDE B8.....90 D2
Common Rd WMBN WV5....82 D1
Commonside BLOX/PEL WS3...39 L3
 BRLYHL DY5.....84 A1
Common Side BRWNH WS8...26 B6
 RUGE WS15.....18 C2
The Common COV CV1.....62 A4
Common Vw BNTWD WS7....18 E4
 HEDN WS12.....12 A3
Common Wy COV CV2.....134 D2
Communication Rw EDG B15....6 C1
Compass Wy BRGRVE B60...191 L6

Compton Cl REDE B98.....202 C3
 NUN CV32.....207 G2
 SOLH B91.....148 B1
Compton Ct
 RUGBYS/DCH CV22.....185 M7
Compton Cft
 BDMR/CCFT B37.....111 H4
Compton Dr DUDS DY2.....85 J6
 FOAKS/STRLY B74.....55 J4
 KGSWFD DY6.....83 H8
Compton Gv HALE B63.....121 G1
 KGSWFD DY6.....83 H8
Compton Hill Dr
 BDMR/CCFT WV3.....49 H3
Compton Pk BDMR/CCFT WV3...49 J3
Compton Rd BDMR/CCFT WV3...49 K3
 CDYHTH B64.....103 K4
 COVN CV6.....134 B3
 CRTAM B79.....31 K6
 ERDW/GRVHL B23.....90 C4
 HAG/WOL DY9.....120 B8
 RMSLY B62.....104 D8
Compton Rd West
 BDMR/CCFT WV3.....49 H3
Comrie Cl COVE CV2.....135 K7
Comsey Rd GTB/HAM B43....70 F3
Comwall Cl BLOX/PEL WS3....39 G6
Comyn St RLSN CV32 *.....206 F1
Conchar Cl CSCFLD/WYGN B72...73 G3
Conchar Rd CSCFLD/WYGN B72...73 G3
Concorde Rd
 LGN/SDN/BHAMAIR B26...129 L1
 WBROM B70.....87 H1
Condor Gv HEDN WS12.....17 G4
Condover Cl WSLW WS2.....52 B2
Condover Rd NFLD/LBR B31...144 F5
Conduit Rd CNCK/NC WS11...25 L1
Coneyford Rd BKDE/SHDE B34...92 A7
Coney Gn STRBR DY8.....101 M8
Coney Green Dr
 NFLD/LBR B31.....144 D5
Coneygree Rd TPTN/OCK DY4...85 L2
Coney La COVN CV6.....117 G7
Congleton Cl COVN CV6....134 C3
 REDW B97.....193 M8
Congreve Cl WWCK CV34....205 K3
Conifer Cl BDWTH CV12.....117 J5
 BRLYHL DY5.....102 A3
 HEDN WS12.....12 A7
Conifer Ct MOS/BIL B13....125 J3
Conifer Dr HDSW B21.....88 C6
 NFLD/LBR B31.....144 F2
Conifer Gv BRGRVW B61....191 K2
 RLSS CV31.....206 E8
Conifer Paddock COVS CV3...156 C5
 RMSLY B62.....104 C5
Conifer Rd FOAKS/STRLY B74...55 J5
The Conifers KNWTH CV8...197 M2
Coningsby Cl RLSS CV31....207 G7
Coningsby Dr KIDDW DY11...137 L1
Conington Gv HRBN B17....105 L8
Coniston TAM/AM/WIL B77...46 F6
Coniston Av HIA/OLT B92....127 K1
Coniston Cl BRGRVE B60....191 M4
 HLGN/YWD B28.....126 D6
 RUGBYN/HIL CV21.....161 H7
Coniston Crs GTB/HAM B43...70 F2
 STRPT DY13.....163 K7
Coniston Dr COVW CV5.....153 H1
 KGSWFD DY6.....82 F6
Coniston Rd COVW CV5....154 D2
 DUNHL/THL/PER WV6.....35 J3
 ERDW/GRVHL B23.....72 B8
 FOAKS/STRLY B74.....55 J4
 RLSN CV32.....206 B4
Coniston Wy BEWD DY12...162 D2
 CNCK/NC WS11.....16 C4
 NUN CV11.....81 K6
Connaught Av
 DARL/WED WS10.....69 G2
 KIDDW DY11.....164 A2
Connaught Cl DSYBK/YTR WS5...54 A6
Connaught Dr WMBN WV5....64 A4
Connaught Rd BILS/COS WV14...51 K1
 BRGRVE B60.....192 A4
 WOLV WV1.....3 H1
Connops Wy HAG/WOL DY9...102 C8
Connor Rd HHTH/SAND B71...69 J3
Conolly Dr RBRY B45.....143 M4
Conrad Cl BHTH/HG B12....107 L6
 RUGBYS/DCH CV22.....186 D7
Conrad Rd COVN CV6.....133 L6
Consort Crs BRLYHL DY5....84 A7
Consort Dr DARL/WED WS10...52 A2
Consort Pl CRTAM B79.....32 A8
Consort Rd BVILLE B30....145 L2
Constable Cl BDWTH CV12...98 E3
 GTB/HAM B43.....71 G2
Constable Rd
 RUGBYN/HIL CV21.....187 M4
The Constables
 LGLYGN/QTN B68.....104 F3
Constance Av WBROM B70....87 H4
Constance Cl BDWTH CV12...116 D5
Constance Rd DIG/EDG B5...107 H8
Constantine La
 CSHL/WTROR B46.....93 K4
Constantine Wy
 BILS/COS WV14.....67 L3
Constitution Hl DUDS DY2....85 H5
 LOZ/NWT B19.....6 E1
Constitution Hl East
 DUDS DY2.....85 H5
Consul Rd RUGBYN/HIL CV21...160 D6
Convent Cl ATHST CV9.....63 K6
 BKHL/PFLD WV2.....3 J8
 CNCK/NC WS11.....16 B5
 KNWTH CV8.....179 L6
Convent La ATHST CV9.....63 J6
Conway Av HHTH/SAND B71...68 F4
 RIDG/WDGT B32.....104 F7
 TLHL/CAN CV4.....153 G7
Conway Cl DUDN DY1.....85 G1
 KGSWFD DY6.....101 K1
 SHLY B90.....148 B4
Conway Dr
 BLKHTH/ROWR B65.....104 A3
Conway Gv GTB/HAM B43....70 B6
Conway Rd BRGRVE B60....191 K4
 CHWD/FDBR/MGN B37.....110 A2
 DUNHL/THL/PER WV6.....48 D2
 FOAKS/STRLY B74.....55 J4
 RLSN CV32.....206 B4
 SHLY B90.....148 B4
 SPARK B11.....108 A2
 STRBR DY8.....119 K8
 TPTN/OCK DY4.....68 B4
Coppice View Rd
 SCFLD/BOLD B73.....71 L1
 SHLY B90.....174 A1
Copplestone Cl
 BKDE/SHDE B34.....91 M7
Copps Rd RLSN CV32.....206 B5
Coppy Hall Gv WALM/CURD B76...40 F4
Coppy Nook La BNTWD WS7...18 E4
Copse Cl BLOX/PEL WS3....39 L1
Copse Dr COVW CV5.....131 M5
Copse Rd DUDS DY2.....102 F2
The Copse FOAKS/STRLY B74...56 D4
 MOS/BIL B13.....125 M3
 RCOVN/BALC/EX CV7.....116 B3

Cooke Cl PENK ST19.....10 C3
 WWCK CV34.....205 K3
Cookes Cft NFLD/LBR B31...145 K3
Cookesley Cl GTB/HAM B43...71 H1
Cooke St BKHL/PFLD WV2....50 A6
Cooks Cl ATHST CV9.....63 H5
Cooksey La KGSTG B44.....71 K1
Cooksey Rd SMHTH B10....107 M5
Cooks La ATHST CV9.....62 A3
 CHWD/FDBR/MGN B37.....110 C2
Cook St COV CV1.....8 F3
 DARL/WED WS10.....52 D7
 VAUX/NECH B7.....90 A6
Coombe Cft COVEN WV9 *....35 L2
Coombe Dr COVS CV3.....156 E3
 NUNW/HART CV10.....97 M1
Coombe Hl CDYHTH B64....103 M4
Coombe Pk FOAKS/STRLY B74...56 D6
Coombe Park Rd BFLD/HDSWWD B20...89 J4
 SHLY B90.....148 A3
Coombes La NFLD/LBR B31...144 D7
Coombe St COVS CV3.....155 M3
Coombs Rd RMSLY B62....103 M7
Coombswood Wy RMSLY B62...103 K5
Co-operative St COVE CV2...134 F2
Cooper Av BRLYHL DY5.....101 L3
Cooper Cl BRGRVE B60....191 J6
Coopers Bank Rd BRLYHL DY5...84 A4
Coopers Cl HEDN WS12 *....17 M1
Coopers Hl ALVE B48.....170 C7
Coopers La SMTHWK B66....87 L8
 SMTHWKW B67.....87 K8
Coopers Rd
 BFLD/HDSWWD B20.....88 D3
Cooper St BKHL/PFLD WV2....3 M9
 NUN CV11.....99 H1
 WBROM B70.....87 H2
Cope Arnolds Cl COVN CV6...134 D1
Copeland RUGBYN/HIL CV21...161 G6
Copeley Hl ERDW/GRVHL B23...90 A4
Copes Crs WOLVN WV10....36 E7
Cope's Dr CRTAM B79.....31 L6
Cope St BLOX/PEL WS3.....39 G7
 COV CV1.....9 H4
 DARL/WED WS10.....52 C7
 WSNGN B18.....106 E2
Cophall St DUDN DY4.....68 B2
Cophams Cl HIA/OLT B92....128 A3
Copland Pl TLHL/CAN CV4...153 J4
Coplow Cl
 RCOVN/BALC/EX CV7.....151 L7
Coplow Cottages
 LDYWD/EDGR B16 *.....106 D2
Coplow St LDYWD/EDGR B16...106 D2
Copnor Gv
 LGN/SDN/BHAMAIR B26...109 J7
Coppenhall Gv STETCH B33...109 L3
Copperas St COVE CV2....134 C2
Copperbeach Dr
 BHTH/HG B12.....107 L8
Copper Beech Cl COVN CV6...134 C4
Copperbeech Cl
 RIDG/WDGT B32.....105 K8
Copperbeech Dr
 BHTH/HG B12 *.....107 L8
Copper Beech Dr KGSWFD DY6...83 K8
 WMBN WV5.....64 F7
Copper Beech Gdns
 BFLD/HDSWWD B20.....88 D3
Copperfield Rd COVE CV2...155 M2
Copperfields LICHS WS14....21 H1
Coppermill Rd HEDN WS12...12 D6
Coppice Av HAG/WOL DY9...120 D2
Coppice Cl BNTWD WS7....18 D5
 ERDE/BCHGN B24.....90 D2
 GTWY WS6.....24 B1
 KNWTH CV8.....182 F5
 RBRY B45.....143 K6
 REDW B97.....202 A5
 SEDG DY3.....66 A6
 SHLY B90.....174 A1
 SOLH B91.....127 L6
 WNSFLD WV11.....37 L4
Coppice La
 BLKHTH/ROWR B65.....103 K1
 NFLD/LBR B31.....144 F1
 WALM/CURD B76.....73 M4
Coppice Rd
 BLKHTH/ROWR B65.....103 K1
 NFLD/LBR B31.....144 F1
 WALM/CURD B76.....73 M4
The Cornfield COVS CV3....156 A4
Cornfield Cl WOLVN WV10...22 B6
Cornflower Crs DUDS DY2....85 K5
Cornflower Rd RRUGBY CV23...161 G6
Cornflower Rd BRWNH WS8...26 B7
Cornforth Cl
 POL/KGSB/FAZ B78 *.....60 D7
Corngreaves Rd CDYHTH B64...103 H4
The Corngreaves
 BKDE/SHDE B34.....92 A7
Corngreaves Wk
 CDYHTH B64.....103 J6
Cornhampton Cl REDW B97...193 M8
Cornhill CNCK/NC WS11....12 C8
Corn Hl DSYBK/YTR WS5....54 C5
 WOLV WV1.....3 H5
Cornhill Gv BVILLE B30....180 A8
 KNWTH CV8.....180 A8
Cornish Cl NUNW/HART CV10...79 K5
Cornish Crs
 NUNW/HART CV10.....98 E3
Corn Mdw BDWTH CV12....117 G3
Corn Mill Cl RIDG/WDGT B32...123 J4
 WALM/CURD B76.....73 K4
Cornmill Cl WSL WS1.....4 C8
Cornmill Gdns BRGRVE B60...169 L8
Cornmill Gv
 DUNHL/THL/PER WV6.....48 B2
Cornovian Cl
 DUNHL/THL/PER WV6.....34 C8
Corns Gv WMBN WV5.....64 D5
Cornwall Av KIDDW DY11....138 A4
 LGLYGN/QTN B68.....104 F5
 POL/KGSB/FAZ B78.....45 L2
Cornwall Cl ALDR WS9.....40 F4
 DARL/WED WS10.....69 H1
 KGSWFD DY6.....83 H5
 WWCK CV34.....205 M4
Cornwall Ga SHHTH WV12...37 M8
Cornwallis Rd
 RUGBYS/DCH CV22.....185 M4
 WBROM B70.....86 E4
Cornwall Pl WSLW WS2....52 C2
Cornwall Rd
 BFLD/HDSWWD B20.....88 D3
 COV CV1.....9 K9
 DSYBK/YTR WS5.....69 K1
 DUNHL/THL/PER WV6.....49 G1
 HEDN WS12.....12 A3
 RBRY B45.....143 J3
 SMTHWK B66.....105 M1
 STRBR DY8.....101 H1
Cornwall St CBHAMNW B3....6 E4
Cornwell Cl REDE B98.....202 F3
Cornyx La SOLH B91.....148 C3
Coronation Av
 POL/KGSB/FAZ B78.....45 H4
 POL/KGSB/FAZ B78.....47 M3
 WLNHL WV13.....53 J1
Coronation Crs CRTAM B79...33 K6

Copsewood Av NUN CV11....99 M6
Copsewood Ter COVS CV3...156 A3
Copson Cl WBROM B70....86 E2
Copstone Dr DOR/KN B93...175 K2
Copston Gv SLYOAK B29....123 M5
Copthall Rd HDSW B21....88 A3
Copt Heath Cft DOR/KN B93...149 M6
Copt Heath Dr DOR/KN B93...149 L6
Copthorne Av BNTWD WS7....26 C4
Copthorne Rd BDMR/CCFT WV3...49 G6
 COVN CV6.....133 K5
 KGSTG B44.....71 K1
Copt Oak Cl TLHL/CAN CV4...153 G6
Copyholt La BRGRVE B60....200 A1
Coral Cl COVW CV5.....154 A3
Coralin Cl
 CHWD/FDBR/MGN B37.....110 F3
Corbet Dr COVN CV6.....134 A6
Corbett Cl BRGRVE B60....191 H6
Corbett Crs STRBR DY8....101 L6
Corbett Rd BRLYHL DY5....102 C4
 HLYWD B47.....146 E6
 KIDDW DY11.....137 L5
Corbetts Cl HIA/OLT B92....129 M6
Corbett St RUGBYN/HIL CV21...187 G1
 SMTHWK B66.....105 M1
Corbin Rd POL/KGSB/FAZ B78...47 K7
Corbison Ct WWCK CV34....205 G2
Corbridge Av KGSTG B44....71 K4
Corbridge Rd SCFLD/BOLD B73...72 D1
Corbyn Rd BORD B9.....108 F2
 DUDN DY1.....84 D5
Corbyns Cl BRLYHL DY5....83 M6
Corbyns Hall La BRLYHL DY5...83 M6
Corbyns Hall Rd BRLYHL DY5...83 M6
Cordelia Wy
 RUGBYS/DCH CV22.....186 C7
Cordle Marsh Rd BEWD DY12...137 J3
Cordley St WBROM B70....86 F1
Corfe Cl DOR/KN B93.....149 L8
 DUNHL/THL/PER WV6.....48 D2
 RIDG/WDGT B32.....105 K8
Corfe Rd BILS/COS WV14....66 L5
Corfton Dr
 DUNHL/THL/PER WV6.....35 J3
Coriander Cl RBRY B45....143 M3
Corinne Cl RBRY B45.....143 L7
Corinne Cft
 CHWD/FDBR/MGN B37.....110 E1
Corinthian Pl COVE CV2 *...135 K4
Corisande Rd SLYOAK B29...124 A3
Corley Av NFLD/LBR B31....144 A2
Corley Cl SHLY B90.....147 J4
Corley Vw
 RCOVN/BALC/EX CV7.....116 A6
Cormorant Gv KIDD DY10...164 E6
Cornbrook Rd SLYOAK B29...123 K7
Cornbury Gv SOLH B91....148 B1
Corncrake Cl
 CSCFLD/WYGN B72.....73 H3
Corncrake Dr CBROM B36....92 E5
Corncrake Rd DUDN DY1....84 C2
Corndon Cl KIDDW DY11....163 M3
Cornel Cl
 CHWD/FDBR/MGN B37.....111 G5
Cornelius St COVS CV3....155 H5
Corner La ALDR WS9.....201 J3
Cornerway SHLY B90.....148 B1
Cornets End La
 RCOVN/BALC/EX CV7.....130 C6
Cornfield CDSL WV8.....35 J4
Cornfield Av BRGRVE B60....191 H4
Cornfield Cl KGSWFD DY6...82 E5
Cornfield Cft
 CHWD/FDBR/MGN B37.....111 H2
 WALM/CURD B76.....73 J2
Cornfield Dr LICHS WS14....21 J6
Cotleigh Gv GTB/HAM B43...71 H2
Cot La KGSWFD DY6.....83 G8
Cotman Cl BDWTH CV12....116 E1
 GTB/HAM B43.....71 H1
Coton Gv SHLY B90.....147 J3
Coton La CRTAM B79.....31 H6
 ERDW/GRVHL B23.....90 A4
Coton Park Dr RRUGBY CV23...161 G4
Coton Rd CSHL/WTROR B46...76 B5
 ETTPK/GDPK/PENN WV4...49 M8
 NUN CV11.....99 C3
 RUGBYN/HIL CV21.....187 L5
 WALM/CURD B76.....75 M3
Cotstake Rd
 ETTPK/GDPK/PENN WV4...65 J2
Cotsford SOLH B91.....148 B2
Cotswold Av GTWY WS6....24 D2
Cotswold Cl ALDR WS9....41 G4
 KIDDW DY11.....164 A3
 OLDBY B69.....86 C8
 RBRY B45.....143 L7
Cotswold Cl BKHL/PFLD WV2...49 L7
Cotswold Crs
 NUNW/HART CV10.....97 M2
Cotswold Cft HALE B63....121 H1
Cotswold Dr COVS CV3....181 G2
Cotswold Gv SHHTH WV12...37 M4
Cotswold Rd BKHL/PFLD WV2...50 D6
 HEDN WS12.....12 B5
 STRBR DY8.....101 M7
Cotswold Wy BRGRVW B61...168 A8
Cottage Cl BNTWD WS7....18 D8
 HEDN WS12.....17 H1
 RLSS CV31.....207 J1
 WNSFLD WV11.....37 G7
Cottage Dr BRGRVE B60....169 G7
Cottage Farm La BRGRVE B60...169 G4
Cottage Farm Rd COVN CV6...133 L4
 TAM/AM/WIL B77.....46 B7
Cottage Gdns
 NUNW/HART CV10.....79 M3
 RBRY B45.....143 K7
Cottage La BNTWD WS7....18 D8
 BRGRVE B60.....169 G3
 CSHL/WTROR B46.....76 B7
 WALM/CURD B76.....74 B7
 WOLVN WV10.....36 B2
Cottage Leap
 RUGBYN/HIL CV21.....187 H1
Cottage Ms ALDR WS9....55 J1
Cottage Sq RLSS CV31.....207 G7
Cottage St BRLYHL DY5....102 B2
 KGSWFD DY6.....83 H6
Cottage Vw CDSL WV8.....34 F1
Cotterell Rd
 RUGBYN/HIL CV21.....160 D7
Cotteridge Rd BVILLE B30...145 L4
Cotterills Av WASH/WDE B8...108 A1
Cotterills La WASH/WDE B8...109 G1
Cotterills Rd TPTN/OCK DY4...67 M6
Cottesbrook Rd COVS CV3...156 C4
Cottesbrook Rd ACGN B27...127 G3
Cottesfield Cl WASH/WDE B8...108 F1
Cottesmore Cl HHTH/SAND B71...69 K5
Cottle Cl WSLW WS2.....52 D2
Cotton Arches Rbt NUN CV11...99 G3
Cotton Dr KNWTH CV8....180 A7
Cotton La MOS/BIL B13....125 L3
Cotton Mill Spinney
 RLSN CV32.....199 J7
Cotton Pool Rd BRGRVW B61...191 J3
Cottrell St HHTH/SAND B71...87 H1
Cottsmeadow Dr
 WASH/WDE B8.....109 G1

Cotwall End Rd SEDG DY3 83 M1
Cotysmore Rd MGN/WHC B75 57 H6
Couchman Rd WASH/WDE B8 108 C1
Coughton Dr RLSS CV31 207 H8
Coulson Cl BNTWD WS7 18 B4
Coulter Gv
DUNHL/THL/PER WV6 48 B1
Coulter La BNTWD WS7 19 J4
Coundon Gn COVN CV6 133 J5
Coundon Rd COV CV1 8 C2
Coundon St COV CV1 8 C3
Coundon Wedge Dr
COVW CV5 133 G7
Counterfield Dr
BLKHTH/ROWR B65 85 K8
Countess Dr RUSH/SHEL WS4 40 B6
Countess Rd NUN CV11 98 E1
The Countess's Cft COVS CV3 155 H6
Countess St WSL WS1 4 C8
Countinghouse Wy
BRGRVE B60 191 J7
Country Inn Ms RRUGBY CV23 159 L8
Country Park Vw
WALM/CURD B76 73 J4
County Cl BVILLE B30 125 G7
RIDG/WDGT B32 123 G2
County Dr POL/KGSB/FAZ B78 45 K4
County La STRBR DY8 119 H5
County Park Av RMSLY B62 122 A2
Courtaulds Wy COVN CV6 134 B7
Court Cl KIDDW DY11 137 M4
Court Crs KGSWFD DY6 83 G8
Court Dr LICHS WS14 42 D1
STRPT DY13 188 D1
Courtenay Gdns GTB/HAM B43 70 C3
Courtenay Rd KGSTG B44 71 J6
Court Farm Rd
ERDW/GRVHL B23 72 C7
Courthouse Cft KNWTH CV8 198 A1
Courtland Av COVN CV6 133 K8
Courtland Rd KGSWFD DY6 83 J5
Courtlands Cl DIG/EDG B5 107 G7
The Courtlands
DUNHL/THL/PER WV6 49 J1
Court La ERDW/GRVHL B23 72 C7
Court Leet COVS CV3 157 H6
Court Leet Rd COVS CV3 155 J6
Courtney Cl NUN CV11 81 K6
Court Oak Gv RIDG/WDGT B32 105 K7
Court Oak Rd RIDG/WDGT B32 105 J7
Court Pas DUDN DY1 * 85 G4
Court Rd BHTH/HG B12 107 J7
DUNHL/THL/PER WV6 49 K1
ETTPK/GDPK/PENN WV4 66 E1
SPARK B11 126 A1
Court St CDYHTH B64 103 J4
RLSS CV31 206 E6
Court Wy WSLW WS2 4 D2
Courtway Av
ALE/KHTH/YWD B14 146 F4
The Courtyard
CSHL/WTROR B46 * 93 K3
Cousins St BKHL/PFLD WV2 50 B6
Coveley Gv WSNGN B18 88 E8
Coven Cl BLOX/PEL WS3 25 L8
Coven Gv SLYOAK B29 123 M3
Coven Mill Cl COVEN WV9 22 A4
Coven St WOLVN WV10 3 H1
Coventry Hwy REDE B98 202 E1
Coventry Point COV CV1 * 8 F5
Coventry Rd BDWTH CV12 116 F4
CSHL/WTROR B46 76 D6
CSHL/WTROR B46 111 L2
HIA/OLT B92 129 M2
KNWTH CV8 179 L7
KNWTH CV8 181 G6
LGN/SDN/BHAMAIR B26 109 J7
NUNW/HART CV10 98 F7
POL/KGSB/FAZ B78 76 B1
RCOVN/BALC/EX CV7 114 C3
RCOVN/BALC/EX CV7 117 L5
RCOVN/BALC/EX CV7 152 B2
RLSN CV32 199 J5
RRUGBY CV23 158 B1
RRUGBY CV23 185 J1
SMHTH B10 7 M8
WKWCK CV34 205 K5
Coventry Road Exhall
RCOVN/BALC/EX CV7 116 E6
Coventry St COVE CV2 155 L1
DIG/EDG B5 7 J6
KIDD DY10 138 C7
NUN CV11 99 G1
STRBR DY8 101 L8
WOLV WV1 50 E3
Coventry Wy BDWTH CV12 115 L2
COVE CV2 117 K6
KNWTH CV8 179 G2
KNWTH CV8 183 K2
RCOVN/BALC/EX CV7 113 M7
RCOVN/BALC/EX CV7 152 C1
RRUGBY CV23 158 B4
Cove Pl COVE CV2 135 G6
Cover Cft WALM/CURD B76 73 L4
Coverdale Rd HIA/OLT B92 127 L1
Coverley Pl
RUGBYS/DCH CV22 186 C2
Covers La KINVER DY7 100 C4
The Covers STUD B80 203 J7
Covert La STRBR DY8 119 H4
The Covert CDSL WV8 35 J4
Covey Cl LICH WS13 21 H4
Cowan Cl RUGBYS/DCH CV22 185 M4
Cowdray Cl RLSS CV31 207 G6
Cow La POL/KGSB/FAZ B78 60 D2
Cowles Cft YDLY B25 109 J4
Cowley TAM/AM/WIL B77 46 C3
Cowley Cl CBROM B36 92 D4
PENK ST19 10 D6
Cowley Dr ACGN B27 127 H1
DUDN DY1 84 D3
Cowley Gn HEDN WS12 12 D5
Cowley Rd COVE CV2 156 B1
SPARK B11 108 C8
Cowper Cl SHHTH WV12 38 C6
WKWCK CV34 205 J3
Cowslip Cl HWK/WKHTH B38 145 K5
SLYOAK B29 123 L6
Coxcroft Av BRLYHL DY5 102 D5
Coxmoor Cl BLOX/PEL WS3 * 38 D2
Cox Rd BILS/COS WV14 67 J4
Cox's Cl NUNW/HART CV10 98 F2
Cox's La CDYHTH B64 103 K3
Cox St CBHAMNW B3 6 E2
COV CV1 9 H5
Coxwell Av WOLVN WV10 36 A8
Coxwell Gdns
LDYWD/EDGR B16 106 D3
Coyne Cl TPTN/OCK DY4 67 H8
Coyne Rd WBROM B70 86 F3
Cozens Cl BDWTH CV12 116 E1
Crabbe St HAG/WOL DY9 102 D8
Crabbs Cross La REDW B97 202 B8
Crab La CNCK/NC WS11 16 E2
SHHTH WV12 38 B4
Crabmill Cl DOR/KN B93 150 A6
Crab Mill Cl HWK/WKHTH B38 145 J6
Crabmill La COVN CV6 134 D6
HWK/WKHTH B38 146 A5
Crabourne Rd DUDS DY2 102 F3
Crabtree Cl HAG/WOL DY9 119 M7
HHTH/SAND B71 69 K5
NFLD/LBR B31 145 G3
REDE B98 202 D3
Crabtree Dr BRGRVE B61 191 K2
CHWD/FDBR/MGN B37 110 D2
Crabtree Gv RLSS CV31 207 G7
Crabtree La BRGRVW B61 191 J2
Crabtree Rd WSL WS1 5 K3
WSNGN B18 88 E8
Crackley Cottages
KNWTH CV8 * 179 M5
Crackley Hl KNWTH CV8 * 179 M5
Crackley La KNWTH CV8 179 J1
Crackley Wy DUDS DY2 84 E7
Crackthorne Dr RRUGBY CV23 161 H4
Craddock Dr NUNW/HART CV10 80 A6
Craddock Rd SMTHWKW B67 87 J7
Craddock St
DUNHL/THL/PER WV6 49 L1
Cradley Cl REDE B98 203 K3
Cradley Cft HDSW B21 88 B2
Cradley Flds HALE B63 103 H8
Cradley Forge HALE B63 102 E5
Cradley Park Rd DUDS DY2 103 G3
Cradley Rd CDYHTH B64 103 G5
Cradock Rd WASH/WDE B8 90 C8
Craig Cl RLSS CV31 206 F8
Craig Cft
CHWD/FDBR/MGN B37 111 H3
Craigends Av COVS CV3 156 C7
Crail Gv GTB/HAM B43 70 F2
Crakston Cl COVE CV2 156 C3
Cramlington Rd
PBAR/PBCH B42 70 E5
Cramnore Cl TPTN/OCK DY4 67 L5
Cramper's Fld COVN CV6 133 L8
Cramp Hl DARL/WED WS10 52 B7
Cranberry Dr STRPT DY13 188 C1
Cranborne Cha COVE CV2 135 K8
Cranbourne Av
ETTPK/GDPK/PENN WV4 66 C2
Cranbourne Cl RBRY B45 143 M3
Cranbourne Gv KGSTG B44 71 L5
Cranbourne Pl
HHTH/SAND B71 * 87 H1
Cranbourne Rd KGSTG B44 71 K4
STRBR DY8 119 L1
Cranbrook Gv
DUNHL/THL/PER WV6 48 D2
Cranbrook Rd HDSW B21 88 A4
Cranby St WASH/WDE B8 90 A8
Craneberry Rd
CHWD/FDBR/MGN B37 110 C2
Cranebrook Hl MGN/WHC B75 44 B8
Cranebrook La LICHS WS14 27 K7
Crane Cl WWCK CV34 205 H4
Crane Dr BNTWD WS7 26 E1
Crane Fld LICH WS13 20 E4
Crane Hollow WMBN WV5 * 64 C8
Cranehouse Rd KGSTG B44 71 L4
Cranemoor Cl VAUX/NECH B7 * 90 A7
Crane Rd BILS/COS WV14 67 K2
Craner's Rd COV CV1 9 L1
Cranesbill Cl WOLVN WV10 23 G6
Cranesbill Rd SLYOAK B29 123 L7
Cranes Park Rd
LGN/SDN/BHAMAIR B26 110 A8
Crane St KIDDW DY11 138 A7
Crane Ter DUNHL/THL/PER WV6 35 J8
Cranfield Gv
LGN/SDN/BHAMAIR B26 109 K5
Cranfield Pl DSYBK/YTR WS5 69 K1
Cranfield Rd BNTWD WS7 18 E6
Cranford Gv SOLH B91 * 149 G4
Cranford Rd BDMR/CCFT WV3 49 G5
COVW CV5 154 B1
Cranford St SMTHWK B66 88 A8
Cranford Wy SMTHWK B66 88 A8
Cranham Cl REDW B97 201 M5
Cranham Dr KGSWFD DY6 83 H8
Cranhill Cl HIA/OLT B92 127 M4
Crankhall La DARL/WED WS10 69 G3
Cranleigh Cl ALDR WS9 40 F8
SHHTH WV12 38 A4
Cranleigh Pl KGSTG B44 71 J8
Cranley Dr CDSL WV8 34 D1
Cranmer Av SHHTH WV12 38 B6
Cranmer Cl GTWY WS6 24 A4
Cranmere Av
DUNHL/THL/PER WV6 34 E7
Cranmere Ct
DUNHL/THL/PER WV6 * 34 E7
Cranmer Gv FOAKS/STRLY B74 42 D7
Cranmoor Crs HALE B63 103 L8
Cranmore Av HDSW B21 88 B6
SHLY B90 148 C5
Cranmore Bvd SHLY B90 148 B5
Cranmore Dr SHLY B90 148 C4
Cranmore Rd BDMR/CCFT WV3 49 K6
CBROM B36 92 C4
SHLY B90 148 B5
Cransley Gv SOLH B91 148 E4
Crantock Cl WNSFLD WV11 38 A4
Crantock Rd PBAR/PBCH B42 89 G1
Crantock Wy NUN CV11 99 K1
Cranwell Gn WMBN WV5 64 D8
Cranwell Gv ERDE/BCHGN B24 91 H2
Cranwell Wy CVALE B35 91 L2
Crateford La PENK ST19 14 A6
Crathie Cl COVE CV2 135 K7
Crathorne Av WOLVN WV10 36 A4
Craufurd Ct STRBR DY8 119 L2
Craven TAM/AM/WIL B77 46 F4
Craven Av COVS CV3 157 G6
Craven Rd RUGBYN/HIL CV21 186 F1
Craven St COVW CV5 154 D3
ETTPK/GDPK/PENN WV4 50 D7
Crawford Av DARL/WED WS10 52 A6
ETTPK/GDPK/PENN WV4 66 D2
SMTHWKW B67 87 J8
Crawford Cl RLSN CV32 206 F1
Crawford Rd BDMR/CCFT WV3 2 A5
WALM/CURD B76 73 K5
Crawford St WASH/WDE B8 90 A8
Crawshaws Rd CBROM B36 92 A4
Crayford Rd KGSTG B44 71 L4
Craythorne Av
BFLD/HDSWWD B20 70 C8
Crecy Cl WALM/CURD B76 73 J1
Crecy Rd COVS CV3 155 J6
Credenda Rd WBROM B70 86 E4
Crediton Cl COVS CV3 155 J8
NUN CV11 81 K8
Credon Gv EDG B15 106 D8
Creed Wy WBROM B70 86 F2
Cregoe St EDG B15 6 D8
Cremore Av WASH/WDE B8 90 C8
Cremorne Rd MGN/WHC B75 56 F3
Cremorne Wk MGN/WHC B75 * 56 F3
Crendon Cl STUD B80 203 J8
Crendon Rd
BLKHTH/ROWR B65 85 L7
Crescent Ar SOLH B91 * 149 G1
Crescent Av BRLYHL DY5 102 A3
COVS CV3 155 M3
The Crescent Grange Rd
HAG/WOL DY9 * 120 A1
Crescent Rd DARL/WED WS10 52 B7
DUDS DY2 84 F8
KIDDW DY11 138 A7
WLNHL WV13 52 A3
Crescent Studios WSNGN B18 * 88 F7
The Crescent ATHST CV9 62 A2
BILS/COS WV14 51 H7
BLKHTH/ROWR B65 103 M3
BNTWD WS7 18 D4
BRGRVE B60 191 K4
CDYHTH B64 103 L6
CHWD/FDBR/MGN B37 111 J5
DARL/WED WS10 68 E1
DUDN DY1 85 J1
DUNHL/THL/PER WV6 48 F2
GTB/HAM B43 70 E4
GTWY WS6 24 E3
HIA/OLT B92 129 M6
KIDD DY10 138 F1
KIDDW DY11 164 D5
RCOVN/BALC/EX CV7 115 K7
RRUGBY CV23 158 D1
RRUGBY CV23 185 G7
SHLY B90 147 L1
SOLH B91 148 F1
STRBR DY8 119 K8
WLNHL WV13 52 A4
WSL WS1 5 K5
WSNGN B18 88 F7
Cressage Av NFLD/LBR B31 144 E4
Cressage Rd COVE CV2 135 L7
Cressett Av BRLYHL DY5 101 M1
Cressett La BRLYHL DY5 102 A1
Cressington Dr
FOAKS/STRLY B74 56 E4
Cresswell Cl NUNW/HART CV10 81 G5
Cresswell Crs BLOX/PEL WS3 38 D3
Cresswell Gv ERDE/BCHGN B24 91 H1
Cressy Cl ALE/KHTH/YWD B14 145 M1
The Crest NFLD/LBR B31 144 F7
RLSN CV32 207 G2
Crest Vw FOAKS/STRLY B74 55 K4
Crestwood TAM/AM/WIL B77 32 E8
Crestwood Av KIDDW DY11 137 L8
Crestwood Dr KGSTG B44 71 J6
Crestwood Gln
DUNHL/THL/PER WV6 35 J6
Creswell Pl RUGBYS/DCH CV22 185 L4
Creswell Rd HLGN/YWD B28 126 F6
Creswick Gv RBRY B45 144 A6
Crewe Dr TPTN/OCK DY4 85 L3
Crew La KNWTH CV8 180 B7
Crew Rd DARL/WED WS10 68 E1
Creynolds Cl SHLY B90 174 B1
Creynolds La SHLY B90 174 C1
Cricket Cl COVW CV5 154 D2
DSYBK/YTR WS5 5 L9
Cricketers Meadow
CDYHTH B64 103 K6
Cricket La LICHS WS14 29 G1
Cricket Meadow SEDG DY3 66 C8
WOLVN WV10 36 B1
Crick La BFLD/HDSWWD B20 88 E5
Cricklewood Dr RMSLY B62 122 B2
Crigdon TAM/AM/WIL B77 47 G4
Crimmond Ri HALE B63 103 J8
Crimscote Cl SHLY B90 148 D7
Crimscote Sq
RWWCK/WEL CV35 204 B2
Cringlebrook TAM/AM/WIL B77 46 B4
Cripps Rd WSLW WS2 52 C2
Crocketts Av HDSW B21 * 88 B6
Crockett's La SMTHWK B66 87 L8
Crocketts Rd HDSW B21 88 B6
Crockett St DUDN DY1 84 E3
Crockford Dr MGN/WHC B75 56 E2
Crockford Rd HHTH/SAND B71 69 G4
Crocus Crs COVEN WV9 35 L2
Croft Av CRTAM B79 31 M7
HEDN WS12 12 E4
Croft Cl REDE B98 203 H2
RRUGBY CV23 183 K7
WWCK CV34 206 A6
YDLY B25 109 J5
Croft Ct CBROM B36 * 91 M5
Croft Crs BRWNH WS8 26 B6
Croft Down Rd HIA/OLT B92 128 B1
Croftdown Rd HRBN B17 105 K7
Crofters Cl STRBR DY8 119 M1
Crofters Ct EDG B15 106 C7
Crofters La MGN/WHC B75 57 J2
Croft Flds BDWTH CV12 116 F3
Croft La PENK ST19 14 B4
WOLVN WV10 36 D6
Croftleigh Gdns SOLH B91 * 148 C3
Croft Md NUNW/HART CV10 97 G2
Croft Pool BDWTH CV12 116 D3
Croft Rd ATHST CV9 63 H4
BDWTH CV12 116 D3
COV CV1 8 D5
LGN/SDN/BHAMAIR B26 109 J5
NUNW/HART CV10 98 D2
RWWCK/WEL CV35 197 L6
The Crofts WALM/CURD B76 73 L6
Croft St CRTAM B79 31 M7
WLNHL WV13 51 L3
WSLW WS2 53 H2
The Croft BDWTH CV12 117 M3
COVN CV6 134 D1
DSYBK/YTR WS5 54 B5
DUDS DY2 84 D7
GTWY WS6 24 C3
KIDD DY10 140 A3
KIDDW DY11 163 L2
NFLD/LBR B31 144 F2
RCOVN/BALC/EX CV7 131 G4
RUGBYN/HIL CV21 * 187 L5
SEDG DY3 66 C4
WLNHL WV13 51 L3
WMBN WV5 64 B8
The Croftway
BFLD/HDSWWD B20 70 C7
Croftwood Rd HAG/WOL DY9 120 B1
Cromarty Cl COVW CV5 132 E8
Cromdale TAM/AM/WIL B77 47 G4
Cromdale Cl NUNW/HART CV10 97 L2
Cromdale Dr HALE B63 121 H2
Cromer Gdns
DUNHL/THL/PER WV6 35 K8
Crome Rd GTB/HAM B43 71 H2
Cromer Rd BHTH/HG B12 107 K8
RLSN CV32 206 F3
Cromes Wd TLHL/CAN CV4 153 H4
Crompton Av
BFLD/HDSWWD B20 * 89 G4
Crompton Cl WSLW WS2 38 E8
Crompton Ct CDSL WV8 34 F1
Crompton Rd
BFLD/HDSWWD B20 89 G4
RBRY B45 143 H4
TPTN/OCK DY4 85 L1
VAUX/NECH B7 90 A5
Crompton St WWCK CV34 205 H7
Cromwell Cl BLKHTH/ROWR B65 85 K8
WSLW WS2 52 C1
Cromwell Dr DUDS DY2 85 K5
Cromwell La NFLD/LBR B31 123 H5
TLHL/CAN CV4 153 G7
Cromwell Rd CRTAM B79 31 J5
HEDN WS12 17 H4
RUGBYS/DCH CV22 187 G4
WOLVN WV10 36 C1
Cromwells Meadow
LICHS WS14 21 G8
Cromwell St COVN CV6 134 D7
DUDS DY2 85 J5
HHTH/SAND B71 69 G8
VAUX/NECH B7 89 M8
Crondal Pl EDG B15 106 F6
Crondal Rd
RCOVN/BALC/EX CV7 116 F6
Cronehills Linkway
WBROM B70 87 H2
Cronehills St WBROM B70 87 H1
Crookham Cl HRBN B17 105 K6
Crookhay La HHTH/SAND B71 68 E5
Crook House Yd
RRUGBY CV23 * 158 D1
Crook La ALDR WS9 54 E7
Croome Cl COVN CV6 154 D1
REDE B98 203 K3
SPARK B11 125 M2
Cropredy Rd NFLD/LBR B31 144 E5
Cropthorne Cl REDE B98 202 E6
Cropthorne Dr HLYWD B47 146 F6
Cropthorne Gdns SHLY B90 148 A2
Cropthorne Rd SHLY B90 148 A2
Crosbie Rd COVW CV5 154 C2
HRBN B17 105 M7
Crosby Cl CBHAMW B1 6 A4
DUNHL/THL/PER WV6 35 K8
Cross Cheaping COV CV1 8 F4
Cross Cl CDYHTH B64 103 K3
Cross Farm Rd HRBN B17 124 B1
Cross Farms La RBRY B45 143 K4
Crossfield TAM/AM/WIL B77 46 F4
Crossfield Rd LICH WS13 21 J5
STETCH B33 109 L2
Cross Fields Rd WWCK CV34 205 K5
Crossfield Wy BILS/COS WV14 51 J8
Crossgate Rd DUDS DY2 84 D7
REDE B98 203 G6
The Crossings LICH WS13 21 J5
Cross In Hand La LICH WS13 19 L1
Crosskey Cl STETCH B33 110 C3
Cross Keys LICH WS13 20 F5
Crossland Crs
DUNHL/THL/PER WV6 35 K7
Cross La GTB/HAM B43 70 C4
LICHS WS14 21 H7
RLSN CV32 207 J1
SEDG DY3 66 B5
Crossley St DUDS DY2 103 H1
Cross Pl SEDG DY3 66 C4
Cross Rd COVN CV6 134 D5
RCOVN/BALC/EX CV7 115 K7
RLSN CV32 206 B4
Cross St BILS/COS WV14 67 K3
BLKHTH/ROWR B65 104 A4
BLOX/PEL WS3 39 L4
BNTWD WS7 18 C5
CNCK/NC WS11 16 C8
COV CV1 9 H2
CRTAM B79 31 M8
DARL/WED WS10 68 C2
DUDN DY1 85 G4
GTWY WS6 24 B3
HALE B63 121 L2
HDSW B21 88 A5
HEDN WS12 17 J4
KGSWFD DY6 82 F5
LGLYGN/QTN B68 104 E1
NUNW/HART CV10 98 B2
RLSN CV32 206 E4
RRUGBY CV23 159 L8
RUGBYN/HIL CV21 187 G1
SMTHWK B66 87 L7
STRBR DY8 101 H2
TAM/AM/WIL B77 46 E2
WLNHL WV13 51 L4
WOLV WV1 3 M7
WWCK CV34 205 K6
Cross St South
BKHL/PFLD WV2 50 A6
Cross Wk POL/KGSB/FAZ B78 47 L7
Cross Walks Rd HAG/WOL DY9 102 C8
Crossway La KGSTG B44 71 K7
Crossway Rd COVS CV3 180 F1
Crossways Gn KGSTG B44 71 M6
Crosswells Rd
LGLYGN/QTN B68 86 F8
Crowberry Cl BRWNH WS8 26 B7
Crowberry La
POL/KGSB/FAZ B78 59 G4
Crowden Dr RLSN CV32 206 E1
Crowden Rd TAM/AM/WIL B77 46 E4
Crowesbridge Ms
BILS/COS WV14 66 F5
Crow Hl ATHST CV9 62 A4
Crowhill Rd NUN CV11 99 K3
Crowhurst Rd NFLD/LBR B31 144 C6
Crowland Av
DUNHL/THL/PER WV6 48 C1
Crowle Dr HAG/WOL DY9 102 A8
Crowmere Rd COVE CV2 135 K6
Crown Br PENK ST19 10 C4
Crown Cl BLKHTH/ROWR B65 104 B1
BRGRVW B61 191 K3
SEDG DY3 66 B4
Crown Ct DARL/WED WS10 52 A5
Crown Gn COVN CV6 134 C3
Crownhill Meadow
BRGRVW B61 168 C6
Crown La FOAKS/STRLY B74 56 C3
KIDD DY10 138 C7
STRBR DY8 101 K7
STRPT DY13 189 J5
Crown Meadow ALVE B48 170 E7
Crownmeadow Dr
TPTN/OCK DY4 68 B6
Crownoakes Dr STRBR DY8 101 J3
Crown Rd BORD B9 108 B3
BVILLE B30 145 L1
Crown St WOLV WV1 36 B8
Crown Ter RLSS CV31 206 D6
Crown Wk TPTN/OCK DY4 85 L3
Crown Wy RLSN CV32 206 F2
Crowsfurlong RRUGBY CV23 161 H4
Crows Nest Cl WALM/CURD B76 73 K2
Crowther Gdns HALE B63 103 G6
Crowther Gv
DUNHL/THL/PER WV6 49 K1
Crowther Rd
DUNHL/THL/PER WV6 35 K8
ERDW/GRVHL B23 72 B8
Crowther St KIDDW DY11 138 A7
WOLVN WV10 50 C1
Crow Thorns
RUGBYN/HIL CV21 161 G7
Croxall Dr CSHL/WTROR B46 94 E3
Croxall Wy SMTHWK B66 87 M8
Croxdene Av BLOX/PEL WS3 38 D4
Croxhall St BDWTH CV12 117 G3
Croxley Dr HEDN WS12 17 G2
Croxley Gdns WLNHL WV13 51 K5
Croxstalls Av BLOX/PEL WS3 38 E5
Croxstalls Cl BLOX/PEL WS3 38 E4
Croxstalls Pl BLOX/PEL WS3 38 E5
Croxstalls Rd BLOX/PEL WS3 38 E4
Croxton Gv STETCH B33 109 L1
Croyde Av PBAR/PBCH B42 70 E5
Croydon Cl COVS CV3 155 J7
Croydon Dr PENK ST19 10 C5
Croydon Rd ERDE/BCHGN B24 90 E4
SLYOAK B29 124 D2
Croy Dr CVALE B35 91 M1
The Crucible BILS/COS WV14 67 G3
Cruisehill La REDW B97 201 H8
Crummock Cl COVN CV6 134 B2
Crumpfields La REDW B97 201 J5
Crundalls La BEWD DY12 136 F7
Crusader Cl OLDBY B69 86 C8
Crutch La BRGRVW B61 190 A8
Crutchley Av
POL/KGSB/FAZ B78 45 L3
Crychan Cl RBRY B45 143 M3
Cryersoak Cl SHLY B90 148 E6
Cryfield Grange Rd
KNWTH CV8 180 A3
Cryfield Hts TLHL/CAN CV4 180 B3
Crystal Av STRBR DY8 101 K4
Crystal Dr SMTHWK B66 87 G5
Cubbington Rd COVN CV6 134 E2
RLSN CV32 206 E2
Cubley Rd HLGN/YWD B28 126 C4
Cuckoo Cl CNCK/NC WS11 17 G3
STETCH B33 109 K1
Cuckoo La COV CV1 9 G4
Cuckoo Rd VAUX/NECH B7 90 B5
Culn Rd SMTHWK B66 88 A8
Culey Gv STETCH B33 110 B3
Culford Dr RIDG/WDGT B32 123 G5
Culham Cl ACGN B27 127 H3
Cullwick St WOLV WV1 50 E6
Culmington Gv NFLD/LBR B31 144 D5
Culmington Rd NFLD/LBR B31 144 D5
Culmore Cl SHHTH WV12 52 B1
Culmore Rd RMSLY B62 104 C4
Culpepper Cl NUNW/HART CV10 98 C1
Culverhouse Dr BRLYHL DY5 101 L4
Culverley Crs DOR/KN B93 149 K7
Culvert Wy SMTHWK B66 87 H6
Culwell St WOLVN WV10 3 H3
Culworth Cl RLSS CV31 206 D8
RUGBYN/HIL CV21 161 J6
Culworth Rw COVN CV6 134 C5
Cumberford Av STETCH B33 110 C4
Cumberland Cl KGSWFD DY6 101 J1
Cumberland Crs BNTWD WS7 18 E5
RLSN CV32 207 G2
Cumberland Dr
NUNW/HART CV10 98 C2
POL/KGSB/FAZ B78 45 L4
Cumberland Rd BILS/COS WV14 51 H6
CNCK/NC WS11 16 E1
HHTH/SAND B71 69 H7
LGLYGN/QTN B68 104 F5
WLNHL WV13 52 B3
Cumberland St CBHAMW B1 6 B6
Cumbria Cl COV CV1 8 B4
Cumbrian Cft HALE B63 121 H3
Cumbria Wy WASH/WDE B8 90 B7
Cumming St RLSS CV31 206 E6
Cundall Cl RLSS CV31 206 F7
The Cunnery KNWTH CV8 198 E2
Cunningham Rd
DUNHL/THL/PER WV6 48 C1
WSLW WS2 52 C3
Cunningham Wy North
RUGBYS/DCH CV22 186 A3
Cupfields Av TPTN/OCK DY4 68 A5
Cupfields Crs TPTN/OCK DY4 68 A6
Curbar Rd PBAR/PBCH B42 71 G7
Curborough Rd LICH WS13 20 F2
Curdale Rd RIDG/WDGT B32 122 F5
Curdworth La WALM/CURD B76 74 D4
Curie Cl RUGBYN/HIL CV21 187 H2
Cur La REDW B97 200 F2
Curlew TAM/AM/WIL B77 46 E6
Curlew Cl KIDD DY10 164 F3
LICHS WS14 21 J6
Curlew Dr BRWNH WS8 26 C6
Curlew Hl CNCK/NC WS11 16 E2
Curlews Cl ERDW/GRVHL B23 72 A5
Curlieu Cl RWWCK/WEL CV35 204 E7
Curral Rd BLKHTH/ROWR B65 103 M2
Curriers Cl TLHL/CAN CV4 153 H6
Curslow Cottages KIDD DY10 * 165 K8
Curslow La KIDD DY10 165 K5
Curtin Dr DARL/WED WS10 67 M1
Curtis Cl SMTHWK B66 106 A1
Curtis Rd COVE CV2 135 H7
Curtiss Cl BRGRVE B60 * 192 D5
Curzon Av COVN CV6 134 C5
Curzon Circ CBHAMNE B4 7 L4
Curzon Gv RLSS CV31 207 G7
Curzon St BKHL/PFLD WV2 50 B6
CBHAMNE B4 7 K4
Cuthbert Rd WSNGN B18 106 C1
Cutlers Rough Cl
NFLD/LBR B31 123 K8
Cutler St SMTHWK B66 87 M8
Cutsdean Cl NFLD/LBR B31 123 K7
Cutshill Cl CBROM B36 92 A5
Cut Throat La HOCK/TIA B94 174 A5
The Cutting RUSH/SHEL WS4 53 K1
Cuttle Mill La
WALM/CURD B76 75 H2
Cuttle Pool La DOR/KN B93 176 D1
Cutty Sark Dr STRPT DY13 188 F3
Cutworth Cl WALM/CURD B76 73 L2
Cygnet Cl ALVE B48 170 E6
HEDN WS12 13 G6
Cygnet Ct WMBN WV5 64 D8
Cygnet Dr BRWNH WS8 26 C6
CRTAM B79 31 K8
Cygnet Gv ERDW/GRVHL B23 71 L7
Cygnet La BRLYHL DY5 84 A6
Cygnet Rd WBROM B70 68 E8
Cygnus Wy WBROM B70 68 D8
Cymbeline Wy
RUGBYS/DCH CV22 186 B7
Cypress Av SEDG DY3 66 B8
Cypress Cft COVS CV3 156 D5
Cypress Gdns
FOAKS/STRLY B74 56 E6
KGSWFD DY6 101 G1

Cypress Gv NFLD/LBR B31 144 C4
Cypress Ri HEDN WS12 13 L7
Cypress Rd DSYBK/YTR WS5 70 A1
DUDS DY2 85 K4
Cypress Sq ACGN B27 109 G8
Cypress Wy NFLD/LBR B31 144 D5
NUNW/HART CV10 80 B7
Cyprus Cl SLYOAK B29 123 L6
Cyprus St BKHL/PFLD WV2 49 M7
OLDBY B69 86 E5
Cyril Gv SMHTH B10 * 108 A5
Cyril Rd SMHTH B10 108 B5

D

Dace TAM/AM/WIL B77 46 B6
Dacer Cl BVILLE B30 124 F8
Dace Rd WOLVN WV10 50 F1
Dadford Vw BRLYHL DY5 101 M3
Dadleys Wd
RCOVN/BALC/EX CV7 * 114 D8
Dad's La MOS/BIL B13 125 G4
Daffern Av
RCOVN/BALC/EX CV7 96 E5
Daffern Rd
RCOVN/BALC/EX CV7 116 E4
Daffodil Cl SEDG DY3 66 C6
Daffodil Dr BDWTH CV12 116 B3
Daffodil Pl DSYBK/YTR WS5 54 B5
Daffodil Rd DSYBK/YTR WS5 54 B5
Daffodil Wy NFLD/LBR B31 144 C5
Dagger La HHTH/SAND B71 69 J8
Dagnall Rd ACGN B27 127 H2
Dagnell End Rd REDE B98 194 C5
Dahlia Cl WOLV WV1 51 G4
Daimler Cl CBROM B36 92 D4
Daimler Rd
ALE/KHTH/YWD B14 147 H2
COVN CV6 134 A8
Dainton Gv RIDG/WDGT B32 123 G4
Daintree Cft COVS CV3 155 G6
Daintry Dr POL/KGSB/FAZ B78 30 F6
Dairy Cl TPTN/OCK DY4 67 M8
Dairy Ct LGLYGN/QTN B68 105 H6
Dairy La REDW B97 193 L7
Daisy Bank HEDN WS12 12 D5
Daisy Bank Cl BLOX/PEL WS3 39 M3
Daisy Bank Crs
DSYBK/YTR WS5 54 B5
Daisy Cft BDWTH CV12 116 B3
Daisy Dr ERDW/GRVHL B23 71 L8
Daisy Farm Rd
ALE/KHTH/YWD B14 146 F3
Daisy Meadow TPTN/OCK DY4 68 A7
Daisy Rd LDYWD/EDGR B16 106 D3
Daisy St BILS/COS WV14 67 J3
DUNHL/THL/PER WV6 49 L1
Daisy Wk COVEN WV9 35 L2
Dalbeg Cl CDSL WV8 35 J5
Dalbury Rd HLGN/YWD B28 126 C8
Dalby Cl COVS CV3 156 C6
Dalby Rd BLOX/PEL WS3 39 K7
Dale Cl BRGRVW B61 168 D6
GTB/HAM B43 70 B4
SMTHWKW B67 105 L2
TPTN/OCK DY4 68 B8
WWCK CV34 205 L5
Dalecote Av HIA/OLT B92 128 C5
Dale Dr BNTWD WS7 18 F6
Dale End CBHAMNE B4 7 H4
DARL/WED WS10 52 B7
NUNW/HART CV10 80 C8
Dale Hl BRGRVE B60 169 K7
Dalehouse La KNWTH CV8 180 A7
Dale Meadow Cl
RCOVN/BALC/EX CV7 151 M7
Dale Rd RMSLY B62 104 D5
SLYOAK B29 124 C2
STRBR DY8 119 K3
Dales Cl DUNHL/THL/PER WV6 35 M7
Dalesman Cl KGSWFD DY6 82 F6
Dale St BDMR/CCFT WV3 2 D7
BILS/COS WV14 51 K8
DARL/WED WS10 68 C2
RLSN CV32 206 C5
RUGBYN/HIL CV21 186 E1
SMTHWK B66 105 L2
WSL WS1 4 D9
Daleswood Pk RMSLY B62 * 142 D3
Dale Ter OLDBY B69 86 A5
Daleview Rd
ALE/KHTH/YWD B14 147 G2
Daleway Rd COVS CV3 180 F2
Dalewood Cft
LGN/SDN/BHAMAIR B26 109 K7
Dalewood Rd
CHWD/FDBR/MGN B37 92 D8
Daley Cl CBHAMW B1 6 A4
Daley Rd BILS/COS WV14 67 K3
Dalkeith Av
RUGBYS/DCH CV22 186 B6
Dalkeith Rd SCFLD/BOLD B73 72 C3
Dalkeith St WSLW WS2 4 B1
Dallas Rd ERDW/GRVHL B23 90 A1
Dallimore Cl HIA/OLT B92 127 K2
Dallington Rd COVN CV6 133 J7
Dalloway Cl DIG/EDG B5 107 H7
Dalmeny Rd TLHL/CAN CV4 153 H6
Dalston Cl DUDS DY2 85 H7
Dalston Rd ACGN B27 127 G1
Dalton Cl RRUGBY CV23 158 F7
Dalton Ct WMBN WV5 64 C6
Dalton Gdns COVE CV2 156 D1
Dalton Rd BDWTH CV12 116 D3
COVW CV5 8 C9
WSLW WS2 52 E2
Dalton St BDMR/CCFT WV3 2 C9
CBHAMNE B4 7 H4
Dalton Wy CBHAMNE B4 7 G4
Dalvine Rd DUDS DY2 102 F3
Dalwood Cl BILS/COS WV14 66 F6
Daly Av RWWCK/WEL CV35 204 D7
Damar Cft
ALE/KHTH/YWD B14 146 B1
Dama Rd POL/KGSB/FAZ B78 45 K5
Dame Agnes Gv COVN CV6 134 F5
Damien Cl SMTHWKW B67 87 K8
Dam Mill Cl CDSL WV8 35 G4
Damson Cl REDW B97 201 M7
SHHTH WV12 37 L7
Damson Dr ATHST CV9 77 G1
Damson La SOLH B91 128 C8
Damson Pkwy HIA/OLT B92 128 D6
Damson Rd
RWWCK/WEL CV35 204 D7
Damson Wy BEWD DY12 162 F1
Damson Whf TPTN/OCK DY4 85 L2
Dam St LICH WS13 20 F5
Danbury Cl WALM/CURD B76 73 L5
Danbury Gdns WOLVN WV10 36 A3
Danbury Rd SHLY B90 147 M2
Danby Dr HEDN WS12 18 A1
Danby Gv ERDE/BCHGN B24 90 F3
Dando Rd DUDS DY2 85 H5
Dandy Bank Rd KGSWFD DY6 83 L5
Dandy's Wk WSL WS1 5 G6
Dane Gv BVILLE B30 125 H5
Danelagh Cl CRTAM B79 31 K6
Dane Rd COVE CV2 155 M1
Danesbury Crs KGSTG B44 71 L5
RLSS CV31 207 H7
Danes Cl WNSFLD WV11 37 K1
Danescourt Rd
DUNHL/THL/PER WV6 35 G7
Danescroft STRPT DY13 188 D1
Daneswood Dr ALDR WS9 40 D2
Daneswood Rd COVS CV3 157 J6
Dane Ter BLKHTH/ROWR B65 86 A8
Daneways Cl FOAKS/STRLY B74 55 L5
Danford Cl STRBR DY8 119 L1
Danford Gdns SMHTH B10 108 A5
Danford La SOLH B91 148 C2
Danford Rd HLYWD B47 146 D7
Danford Wy GTB/HAM B43 70 B5
Dangerfield La
DARL/WED WS10 52 A8
Daniel Av NUNW/HART CV10 98 A2
Daniel Rd ATHST CV9 63 K6
Daniels La ALDR WS9 55 G1
Daniels Rd BORD B9 108 E3
Danilo Rd CNCK/NC WS11 16 B4
Danks St TPTN/OCK DY4 85 L3
Danny Morson Wy
POL/KGSB/FAZ B78 47 J8
Danzey Cl REDE B98 202 F8
Danzey Green Rd CBROM B36 91 M4
Danzey Gv
ALE/KHTH/YWD B14 146 A2
Daphne Cl COVE CV2 135 G3
Darby Cl BILS/COS WV14 66 E3
Darby End Rd DUDS DY2 103 J1
Darby Rd DARL/WED WS10 68 F2
LGLYGN/QTN B68 87 G8
Darbys Hill Rd OLDBY B69 85 L5
Darby St BLKHTH/ROWR B65 104 A4
Darbys Wy TPTN/OCK DY4 67 M8
Darell Cft WALM/CURD B76 73 J2
Daren Cl CBROM B36 92 D5
Dare Rd ERDW/GRVHL B23 90 C1
Darfield Ct KNWTH CV8 182 A8
Darfield Wk BHTH/HG B12 * 107 K5
Darges La GTWY WS6 24 D1
Darkhouse La BILS/COS WV14 67 G3
Dark La BDWTH CV12 116 B4
BRGRVE B60 191 H7
COV CV1 8 E1
GTWY WS6 25 G4
HAG/WOL DY9 141 J6
HWK/WKHTH B38 146 B6
KINVER DY7 118 A2
LICH WS13 19 L4
POL/KGSB/FAZ B78 47 J5
RMSLY B62 142 D1
WOLVN WV10 22 B5
Darlaston La BILS/COS WV14 51 L6
Darlaston Rd DARL/WED WS10 52 B8
WSLW WS2 52 E5
Darley Av BKDE/SHDE B34 91 K7
Darleydale Av KGSTG B44 71 J4
Darley Dr DUNHL/THL/PER WV6 35 M8
Darley Green Rd DOR/KN B93 175 M4
Darley Wy FOAKS/STRLY B74 55 K6
Darlington St DARL/WED WS10 52 B8
WOLV WV1 2 E5
Darlington Yd WOLV WV1 2 E5
Darnel Cft SMHTH B10 107 M4
Darnel Hurst Rd MGN/WHC B75 57 G2
Darnford Cl COVE CV2 135 K6
CSCFLD/WYGN B72 73 H6
HLGN/YWD B28 126 E8
Darnford La LICHS WS14 21 J7
Darnford Moors LICHS WS14 21 J7
Darnford Vw LICH WS13 21 J4
Darnick Rd SCFLD/BOLD B73 72 B3
Darnley Rd LDYWD/EDGR B16 106 D3
Darrach Cl COVE CV2 135 J3
Darris Rd SLYOAK B29 124 E5
Dart TAM/AM/WIL B77 46 E8
Dartford Rd BLOX/PEL WS3 38 E8
Dartington Wy NUN CV11 99 K5
Dartmoor Cl RBRY B45 143 L3
Dartmouth Av BLOX/PEL WS3 39 J8
CNCK/NC WS11 16 A3
STRBR DY8 101 H2
WLNHL WV13 51 K3
Dartmouth Circ AST/WIT B6 89 K8
Dartmouth Cl BLOX/PEL WS3 39 J8
Dartmouth Crs BILS/COS WV14 51 L6
Dartmouth Dr ALDR WS9 40 D8
Dartmouth Pl BLOX/PEL WS3 39 J7
Dartmouth Rd CNCK/NC WS11 16 B4
COVE CV2 135 G8
SLYOAK B29 124 D3
SMTHWK B66 87 K5
Dartmouth St BKHL/PFLD WV2 3 H8
WBROM B70 86 F2
Dart St BORD B9 107 M4
Darvel Rd SHHTH WV12 52 B1
Darwall St WSL WS1 4 F3
Darwin Cl BNTWD WS7 18 F6
COVE CV2 135 L7
HEDN WS12 17 J4
Darwin Ct
DUNHL/THL/PER WV6 48 C1
Darwin Pl WSLW WS2 38 F7
Darwin Rd WSLW WS2 38 F7
Darwin St BHTH/HG B12 107 K5
Dassett Cl RWWCK/WEL CV35 204 D8
Dassett Gv BORD B9 109 G3
Dassett Rd DOR/KN B93 175 K1
Datchet Cl COVW CV5 154 A1
Datteln Rd CNCK/NC WS11 16 E1
D'Aubeny Rd TLHL/CAN CV4 153 M5
Dauntsey Covert
ALE/KHTH/YWD B14 146 B3
Davena Dr RIDG/WDGT B32 123 J3
Davena Gv BILS/COS WV14 67 H2
Davenham Rd BRGRVE B60 192 A4
Davenport Dr BRGRVE B60 191 M4
CVALE B35 92 A2
Davenport Rd
DUNHL/THL/PER WV6 34 F8
WNSFLD WV11 37 J7
Daventry Gv RIDG/WDGT B32 105 G7
Daventry Rd COVS CV3 155 G6
Davey Cl BNTWD WS7 26 D1
Davey Rd BFLD/HDSWWD B20 89 J4
WBROM B70 86 E1
David Harman Dr
HHTH/SAND B71 69 K6
David Peacock Cl
TPTN/OCK DY4 67 L8
David Rd BFLD/HDSWWD B20 88 F3
COV CV1 9 K6
RCOVN/BALC/EX CV7 116 D6
RUGBYS/DCH CV22 186 B5
TPTN/OCK DY4 67 L6
Davids Cl REDW B97 202 B3
Davidson Av RLSS CV31 206 E6
Davidson Rd LICHS WS14 20 F6
The Davids NFLD/LBR B31 124 A7
Davies Av BILS/COS WV14 67 H2
Davies Rd
RCOVN/BALC/EX CV7 116 D6
Davis Av TPTN/OCK DY4 85 J1
Davis Cl RLSN CV32 206 B3
Davis Gv YDLY B25 109 H7
Davison Rd SMTHWKW B67 105 K2
Davis Rd SHHTH WV12 38 B5
TAM/AM/WIL B77 46 D1
Davy Rd WSLW WS2 38 E8
Dawberry Cl
ALE/KHTH/YWD B14 125 H8
Dawberry Fields Rd
ALE/KHTH/YWD B14 125 G8
Dawberry Rd
ALE/KHTH/YWD B14 125 G8
Daw End RUSH/SHEL WS4 40 A7
Daw End La RUSH/SHEL WS4 39 M7
Dawes Av WBROM B70 87 G4
Dawes Cl COVE CV2 155 L1
Dawes La BRWNH WS8 26 E4
Dawley Brook Rd KGSWFD DY6 83 H6
Dawley Cl WSLW WS2 52 F6
Dawley Crs
CHWD/FDBR/MGN B37 110 F4
Dawley Rd KGSWFD DY6 83 G5
Dawlish Cl NUN CV11 81 J8
Dawlish Dr COVS CV3 155 H8
Dawlish Rd DUDN DY1 66 F8
SLYOAK B29 124 D3
SMTHWK B66 87 M8
Daw Mill Dr
POL/KGSB/FAZ B78 47 J8
Dawn Dr TPTN/OCK DY4 68 A3
Dawney Dr MGN/WHC B75 56 E1
Dawn Rd NFLD/LBR B31 123 J7
Dawson Av BILS/COS WV14 66 D3
Dawson Rd BRGRVW B61 191 J3
COVS CV3 155 L4
HDSW B21 88 C5
Dawson Sq BILS/COS WV14 * 51 G8
Dawson St BLOX/PEL WS3 39 H5
SMTHWK B66 105 L2
Day Av WNSFLD WV11 37 J6
Daybrook Cl REDW B97 193 M8
Dayhouse Bank RMSLY B62 142 F4
Daylesford Rd HIA/OLT B92 127 L2
Days Cl COV CV1 9 K3
Day's La COV CV1 9 K3
Day St WSLW WS2 4 E1
Daytona Dr COVW CV5 131 M5
Deacon Cl RUGBYS/DCH CV22 187 G4
Deacon St NUN CV11 99 G2
Deakin Av BRWNH WS8 26 D4
Deakin Rd ERDE/BCHGN B24 90 D2
MGN/WHC B75 57 J6
Deakins Rd YDLY B25 108 F6
Deal Av BNTWD WS7 18 E5
Deal Dr OLDBY B69 85 K4
Deal Gv NFLD/LBR B31 144 E1
Deanbrook Cl SHLY B90 148 E7
Dean Cl CSCFLD/WYGN B72 72 F6
KGSTG B44 71 M5
STRBR DY8 101 M7
Dean Ct DUNHL/THL/PER WV6 34 C8
Deane Pde RUGBYN/HIL CV21 187 L5
Deane Rd RUGBYN/HIL CV21 187 L5
Deanery Cl WOLVN WV10 23 G3
Deanery Rw WOLV WV1 2 F3
Dean Rd ERDW/GRVHL B23 72 D8
RUSH/SHEL WS4 40 A6
WMBN WV5 64 D8
Deans Cl REDE B98 195 H8
Deans Cft LICH WS13 21 G6
Deanscroft Dr BRGRVE B60 169 G7
Deansfield Rd WOLV WV1 50 E3
Deansford La KIDD DY10 139 K5
Deans Ga WLNHL WV13 51 H3
Deans Pl BLOX/PEL WS3 39 K7
Dean's Rd WOLV WV1 50 E2
Deans Slade Dr LICHS WS14 20 E8
Deanston Cft COVE CV2 135 K4
Dean St COVE CV2 155 L2
DIG/EDG B5 7 H7
SEDG DY3 66 B5
Deansway BRGRVW B61 191 H4
Deans Wy
RCOVN/BALC/EX CV7 116 B7
Deansway WWCK CV34 205 H4
The Deansway KIDD DY10 138 E6
Dearman Rd SPARK B11 107 M6
Dearmont Rd NFLD/LBR B31 144 C6
Dearne Ct SEDG DY3 66 E7
Deasy Rd COV CV1 9 H7
Deavall Wy CNCK/NC WS11 16 F3
Debden Cl DOR/KN B93 175 J3
Debenham Crs YDLY B25 109 H4
Debenham Rd YDLY B25 109 H4
Deblen Dr LDYWD/EDGR B16 106 B4
Deborah Cl BKHL/PFLD WV2 50 A7
De-Compton Cl
RCOVN/BALC/EX CV7 115 L6
Deedmore Rd COVE CV2 135 G5
Deegan Cl COVE CV2 134 E7
Dee Gv CNCK/NC WS11 16 B5
HWK/WKHTH B38 145 J5
Deelands Rd RBRY B45 143 K5
Deeley TAM/AM/WIL B77 46 E4
Deeley Cl CDYHTH B64 103 J6
EDG B15 107 G6
Deeley Dr TPTN/OCK DY4 68 A7
Deeley Pl BLOX/PEL WS3 38 F5
Deeley St BLOX/PEL WS3 * 38 F5
BRLYHL DY5 * 102 C4
Deepdale TAM/AM/WIL B77 47 H4
Deepdale Av
LGN/SDN/BHAMAIR B26 127 M1
Deepdale La DUDN DY1 84 C2
Deepdales WMBN WV5 64 C7
Deep La CSHL/WTROR B46 94 D7
Deeplow Cl
CSCFLD/WYGN B72 * 73 G1
Deepmoor Rd STETCH B33 109 K2
Deepmore Av WSLW WS2 52 F3
Deepmore Cl WOLVN WV10 14 B8
Deepmore Rd
RUGBYS/DCH CV22 186 B5
Deepwood Cl RUSH/SHEL WS4 39 M5
Deer Barn Hl REDE B98 202 E4
Deer Cl BLOX/PEL WS3 39 G4
CNCK/NC WS11 17 L6
HEDN WS12 12 A7
Deerdale Wy COVS CV3 156 D5
Deerfold Crs BNTWD WS7 18 D5
Deerhill TAM/AM/WIL B77 47 G4
Deerhurst Cl REDE B98 195 G6
Deerhurst Ri HEDN WS12 13 K7
Deerhurst Rd
BFLD/HDSWWD B20 70 D8
COVN CV6 133 M3
Deerings Rd
RUGBYN/HIL CV21 187 L5
The Deer Leap KNWTH CV8 179 M7
Dee Rd BLOX/PEL WS3 39 J4
Deer Pk HEDN WS12 * 13 M5
Deerpark Dr WWCK CV34 205 H5
Deer Park Rd
POL/KGSB/FAZ B78 45 J4
Deer Park Wy SOLH B91 149 G4
Defford Av RUSH/SHEL WS4 40 A4
Defford Cl REDW B97 201 J3
Defford Dr LGLYGN/QTN B68 104 F1
Dehavilland Cl NUN CV11 80 F8
De Havilland Dr CVALE B35 91 L3
Deighton Gv COVS CV3 156 A7
Deighton Rd DSYBK/YTR WS5 69 M1
Delage Cl COVN CV6 134 F1
Delamere Cl CBROM B36 92 B4
Delamere Dr DSYBK/YTR WS5 70 D2
Delamere Rd BDWTH CV12 116 D3
BEWD DY12 163 G1
HLGN/YWD B28 126 D6
SHHTH WV12 38 A6
Delamere Wy RLSN CV32 207 G1
Delancey Keep MGN/WHC B75 57 L8
Delaware Rd COVS CV3 155 G8
Delhi Av COVN CV6 134 B4
Delhurst Av
ETTPK/GDPK/PENN WV4 66 C2
Delhurst Rd KGSTG B44 71 H4
Delius St TLHL/CAN CV4 153 J2
Della Dr RIDG/WDGT B32 123 H5
Dell Cl COVS CV3 155 M8
Dell Farm Cl DOR/KN B93 149 M7
Dellow Gv ALVE B48 170 E8
Dellows Cl HWK/WKHTH B38 145 H6
Dell Rd BRLYHL DY5 83 M8
BVILLE B30 124 E8
The Dell CRTAM B79 31 M7
HEDN WS12 17 K1
HIA/OLT B92 127 L4
LDYWD/EDGR B16 * 106 D3
LICH WS13 20 D6
NFLD/LBR B31 123 H7
STRBR DY8 101 J7
STRPT DY13 188 F1
Delmore Wy WALM/CURD B76 73 M7
Delph Dr BRLYHL DY5 102 C6
Delphinium Cl BORD B9 108 D2
KIDDW DY11 138 A4
Delph La BRLYHL DY5 102 B5
Delph Rd BRLYHL DY5 102 A4
Delrene Rd HLGN/YWD B28 147 K2
Delta Wy CNCK/NC WS11 16 B7
Deltic TAM/AM/WIL B77 46 E4
Delves Crs ATHST CV9 61 H4
DSYBK/YTR WS5 53 L8
Delves Green Rd
DSYBK/YTR WS5 53 L7
Delves Rd WSL WS1 5 H9
Delville Rd DARL/WED WS10 68 D2
De Marnham Cl WBROM B70 87 J4
De Montfort Rd KNWTH CV8 179 J7
De Montfort Wy
TLHL/CAN CV4 154 A7
De Moram Gv HIA/OLT B92 128 D6
Dempster Rd BDWTH CV12 116 E1
Demuth Wy OLDBY B69 86 D7
Denaby Gv
ALE/KHTH/YWD B14 147 H1
Denbigh Cl DUDN DY1 84 D3
Denbigh Crs HHTH/SAND B71 68 F8
Denbigh Dr DARL/WED WS10 69 H1
HHTH/SAND B71 68 F7
Denbigh Rd COVN CV6 133 J7
TPTN/OCK DY4 86 A1
Denbigh St BORD B9 108 B3
Denbury Cl HEDN WS12 17 H4
Denby Buildings RLSN CV32 * 206 D5
Denby Cl RLSN CV32 207 G3
VAUX/NECH B7 89 M8
Denby Cft SHLY B90 148 F7
Dencer Cl RBRY B45 143 K5
Dencer Dr KNWTH CV8 198 A1
Dencil Cl HALE B63 103 H8
Dene Av KGSWFD DY6 101 G1
Dene Cl PENK ST19 10 D5
Dene Court Rd HIA/OLT B92 127 K4
Denefield PENK ST19 10 D5
Denegate Cl WALM/CURD B76 73 M7
Dene Hollow MOS/BIL B13 126 A7
Denehurst Cl RBRY B45 169 L4
Dene Rd
ETTPK/GDPK/PENN WV4 64 D1
STRBR DY8 119 K2
Denewood Av
BFLD/HDSWWD B20 88 E3
Denewood Wy KNWTH CV8 180 A8
Denford Gv
ALE/KHTH/YWD B14 125 H8
Dengate Dr
RCOVN/BALC/EX CV7 151 M6
Denham Av COVW CV5 153 M1
Denham Ct ATHST CV9 63 J5
Denham Gdns BDMR/CCFT WV3 48 F5
Denham Rd ACGN B27 108 F8
Denholme Gv
ALE/KHTH/YWD B14 146 E2
Denholm Rd SCFLD/BOLD B73 72 B2
Denise Dr BILS/COS WV14 66 F5
CHWD/FDBR/MGN B37 110 D1
HRBN B17 124 A1
Denleigh Rd KGSWFD DY6 101 K1
Denmark Ri HEDN WS12 13 H6
Denmark Vls LICH WS13 * 20 A8
Denmead Dr WNSFLD WV11 37 K5
Denmore Gdns WOLV WV1 50 F3
Dennett Cl WWCK CV34 205 K3
Dennfield Dr GTWY WS6 24 A3
Dennis TAM/AM/WIL B77 46 C3
Dennis Hall Rd STRBR DY8 101 L5
Dennis Rd BHTH/HG B12 125 M1
COVE CV2 134 F8
Dennis St STRBR DY8 101 K5
Denshaw Cft COVE CV2 135 L5
Denshaw Rd
ALE/KHTH/YWD B14 125 H7
Denton Cl KNWTH CV8 179 H7
Denton Cft DOR/KN B93 175 H2
Denton Gv GTB/HAM B43 70 B6
STETCH B33 109 H3
Denton Rd HAG/WOL DY9 120 E1
Dent St CRTAM B79 32 A8
Denver Rd
ALE/KHTH/YWD B14 146 E3
Denville Cl BILS/COS WV14 51 J6
Denville Crs BORD B9 108 F2
Denville Rd RLSN CV32 206 E2
Depwo Gv RIDG/WDGT B32 122 F5
Derby Av DUNHL/THL/PER WV6 35 J6
Derby Dr
CHWD/FDBR/MGN B37 110 F3
Derby La ATHST CV9 63 H5
Derby Rd LICHS WS14 30 B2
Derby St BORD B9 7 M5
WSLW WS2 53 H1
Dereham Cl WASH/WDE B8 108 A1
Dereham Ct RLSN CV32 206 E2
Dereham Wk BILS/COS WV14 67 J3
Derek Av POL/KGSB/FAZ B78 47 L7
Dereton Cl DUDN DY1 84 C6
Dering Cl COVE CV2 135 H5
Deronda Cl BDWTH CV12 116 E2
Derron Av
LGN/SDN/BHAMAIR B26 109 J8
Derry Cl HRBN B17 123 L2
KNWTH CV8 183 L2
Derrydown Cl
ERDW/GRVHL B23 90 C2
Derrydown Rd PBAR/PBCH B42 70 F8
Derry St BKHL/PFLD WV2 3 G9
BRLYHL DY5 102 A3
Dersingham Dr COVN CV6 134 F3
Derwent TAM/AM/WIL B77 46 B4
Derwent Av STRPT DY13 163 K8
Derwent Cl BRLYHL DY5 83 M7
COVW CV5 153 J1
FOAKS/STRLY B74 55 K3
RLSN CV32 206 B4
RUGBYN/HIL CV21 161 G7
WLNHL WV13 52 A3
Derwent Dr BEWD DY12 162 D1
Derwent Gv BNTWD WS7 19 H7
BVILLE B30 125 G4
CNCK/NC WS11 16 B5
Derwent Rd BDWTH CV12 116 E3
BVILLE B30 125 G5
COVN CV6 133 L3
DUNHL/THL/PER WV6 35 H5
Derwent Wy BRGRVE B60 191 M4
NUN CV11 81 K7
Desford Av PBAR/PBCH B42 71 G6
Design Cl BRGRVE B60 191 L6
Despard Rd COVW CV5 132 B8
Dettonford Rd
RIDG/WDGT B32 122 F5
Devereux Cl CBROM B36 92 A5
TLHL/CAN CV4 153 G4
Devereux Rd MGN/WHC B75 57 G4
WBROM B70 87 J4
Devey Dr TPTN/OCK DY4 68 B7
Devine Cft TPTN/OCK DY4 67 L8
Devitts Cl SHLY B90 148 D6
Devon Cl KIDDW DY11 138 A4
NUNW/HART CV10 98 D2
Devon Crs ALDR WS9 40 E4
DUDS DY2 84 D6
HHTH/SAND B71 69 G7
Devon Gv COVE CV2 134 F7
Devonport Cl REDW B97 193 M8
Devon Rd CNCK/NC WS11 16 D5
DARL/WED WS10 69 G1
RBRY B45 143 J3
SMTHWKW B67 105 J6
STRBR DY8 101 H6
WLNHL WV13 52 B4
WOLV WV1 2 D2
Devonshire Av WSNGN B18 88 D7
Devonshire Cl
RUGBYS/DCH CV22 185 M4
Devonshire Dr
POL/KGSB/FAZ B78 45 L4
WBROM B70 87 J2
Devonshire Rd
BFLD/HDSWWD B20 88 D3
SMTHWKW B67 87 J7
Devonshire St WSNGN B18 88 D7
Devon St VAUX/NECH B7 108 A1
Devoran Cl
DUNHL/THL/PER WV6 49 M1
RCOVN/BALC/EX CV7 116 F5
Dewar Gv RUGBYN/HIL CV21 187 J3
Dewberry Cl STRPT DY13 188 C1
Dewberry Dr DSYBK/YTR WS5 69 L2
Dewberry Rd STRBR DY8 101 K4
Dewhurst Cft STETCH B33 109 M2
Dewsbury Av COVS CV3 154 F8
Dewsbury Cl STRBR DY8 101 J2
Dewsbury Dr BNTWD WS7 19 G7
ETTPK/GDPK/PENN WV4 65 L2
Dewsbury Gv PBAR/PBCH B42 71 G8
Dexter La ATHST CV9 77 G2
Dexter Wy POL/KGSB/FAZ B78 47 K5
Deykin Av AST/WIT B6 89 L3
Deykin Rd LICH WS13 20 E7
D'Eyncourt Rd WOLVN WV10 36 E6
Dial Cl ALE/KHTH/YWD B14 146 C3
Dial House La COVW CV5 153 K1
Dial La STRBR DY8 101 J5
WBROM B70 68 D7
Diamond Gv CNCK/NC WS11 17 G3
Diamond Park Dr STRBR DY8 101 J4
Diana Cl ALDR WS9 40 F2
Diana Dr COVE CV2 135 J4
Diane Cl TPTN/OCK DY4 67 M3
Dibble Cl SHHTH WV12 38 B8
Dibble Rd SMTHWKW B67 87 K7
Dibdale Rd DUDN DY1 84 D2
Dibdale Rd West DUDN DY1 84 C2
Dibdale St DUDN DY1 84 D3
Dice Pleck NFLD/LBR B31 145 G3
Dickens Cl NUNW/HART CV10 97 L1
SEDG DY3 65 M8
Dickens Heath Rd SHLY B90 147 L7
SHLY B90 173 J1
Dickens Rd BILS/COS WV14 67 H3
COVN CV6 133 L5
RUGBYS/DCH CV22 186 D7
WOLVN WV10 36 E5
WWCK CV34 205 M5
Dickinson Av WOLVN WV10 36 C5
Dickinson Ct
RUGBYS/DCH CV22 186 E4
Dickinson Dr WALM/CURD B76 73 J1
WSLW WS2 53 G7
Dickinson Rd WMBN WV5 82 E1
Dick Sheppard Av
TPTN/OCK DY4 67 M5
Didcot Cl REDW B97 202 A8
Diddington Av HLGN/YWD B28 126 E8
Diddington La HIA/OLT B92 130 A5
Didgley Gv
CHWD/FDBR/MGN B37 92 E8
Didgley La
RCOVN/BALC/EX CV7 114 A1
Didsbury Rd
RCOVN/BALC/EX CV7 116 E4
Digbeth DIG/EDG B5 7 H6
WSL WS1 4 F4
Digbey Cl COVW CV5 132 F7
Digby Crs CSHL/WTROR B46 92 F2
Digby Dr
CHWD/FDBR/MGN B37 110 F7
Digby Rd CSHL/WTROR B46 93 K7
KGSWFD DY6 83 H5
SCFLD/BOLD B73 72 E2
Dilcock Wy TLHL/CAN CV4 153 K6
Dilke Rd ALDR WS9 40 D8
Dillam Cl COVN CV6 134 E1
Dillotford Av COVS CV3 155 G6
Dilloways La WLNHL WV13 51 J4
Dilwyn Cl REDE B98 203 K4

The Hill RIDG/WDGT B32 123 H3
Hilltop HAG/WOL DY9 120 C2
Hill Top ATHST CV9 61 M3
REDW B97 201 K4
WBROM B70 68 E6
Hilltop Av BEWD DY12 163 H1
Hill Top Av CRTAM B79 31 M5
RMSLY B62 104 C6
Hill Top Cl KGSTG B44 71 J7
Hilltop Cl KNWTH CV8 177 J5
Hilltop Dr CBROM B36 91 H5
Hilltop Rd DUDS DY2 85 J5
Hill Top Rd LGLYGN/QTN B68 105 G3
NFLD/LBR B31 144 D2
Hill Top Wk ALDR WS9 41 G4
Hill Vw ALDR WS9 40 F3
Hillview Cl BRGRVE B60 169 G7
HALE B63 103 J7
Hillview Rd BRGRVE B60 169 G7
RBRY B45 143 J5
Hill Village Rd MGN/WHC B75 56 E1
Hillville Gdns STRBR DY8 119 M2
Hill Wd BLOX/PEL WS3 39 K3
Hillwood Av SHLY B90 148 E7
Hillwood Cl KGSWFD DY6 101 G1
Hillwood Common Rd
MGN/WHC B75 42 F7
Hill Wood Rd MGN/WHC B75 43 G8
Hillwood Rd NFLD/LBR B31 123 J6
RMSLY B62 104 A6
Hill Wootton Rd
RWWCK/WEL CV35 197 L7
Hillyfields Rd ERDW/GRVHL B23 90 A1
Hilly Rd BILS/COS WV14 67 J3
Hilmore Wy TAM/AM/WIL B77 46 C5
Hilsea Cl CDSL WV8 35 K4
Hilston Av
ETTPK/GDPK/PENN WV4 65 G1
HALE B63 121 K1
Hilton Av HLGN/YWD B28 147 J1
NUNW/HART CV10 79 M7
Hilton Cl BLOX/PEL WS3 38 D4
Hilton Ct COVW CV5 * 154 D3
Hilton Cross WOLVN WV10 22 F8
Hilton Dr CSCFLD/WYGN B72 73 G5
Hilton La GTWY WS6 24 E3
WNSFLD WV11 23 M6
WOLVN WV10 23 H5
Hilton Pl BILS/COS WV14 51 J8
Hilton Rd BNTWD WS7 18 A5
ETTPK/GDPK/PENN WV4 66 D1
OLDBY B69 86 A5
SHHTH WV12 38 A4
WOLVN WV10 22 F6
Hilton St WBROM B70 86 E2
WOLVN WV10 3 J2
Himbleton Cl REDE B98 202 D4
Himbleton Cft SHLY B90 148 E7
Himley Av DUDN DY1 84 D3
Himley Cl GTB/HAM B43 70 A3
SHHTH WV12 37 L8
Himley Crs
ETTPK/GDPK/PENN WV4 50 A8
Himley Gdns SEDG DY3 83 K1
Himley Gv RBRY B45 143 M7
Himley La SEDG DY3 82 D3
Himley Rd BDWTH CV12 116 B3
DUDN DY1 84 C4
SEDG DY3 83 J2
Himley St DUDN DY1 84 E4
Hinbrook Rd DUDN DY1 84 C4
Hinchliffe Av BILS/COS WV14 66 F3
Hinchwick Ct DOR/KN B93 175 K2
Hinckes Rd
DUNHL/THL/PER WV6 34 F8
Hinckley Ct LGLYGN/QTN B68 * 104 F6
Hinckley La
MKTBOS/BARL/STKG CV13 81 M2
Hinckley Rd COVE CV2 135 L6
NUN CV11 81 J8
Hinckley St DIG/EDG B5 6 F7
Hincks St BKHL/PFLD WV2 50 E6
Hind Cl WWCK CV34 205 K3
Hinde Cl RUGBYN/HIL CV21 161 G6
Hindhead Rd
ALE/KHTH/YWD B14 147 G1
Hindlip Cl HALE B63 121 K3
REDE B98 203 L1
Hindlow Cl VAUX/NECH B7 107 M1
Hindon Gv ACGN B27 126 F6
Hindon Sq EDG B15 106 D5
Hingeston St WSNGN B18 6 A1
Hingley Cft ALDR WS9 55 K2
Hingley Rd HALE B63 102 E7
Hingley St CDYHTH B64 103 H4
Hinksford Gdns SEDG DY3 82 C3
Hinksford La SEDG DY3 82 C4
Hinsford Cl KGSWFD DY6 83 J5
Hinstock Cl
ETTPK/GDPK/PENN WV4 65 L1
Hinstock Rd BFLD/HDSWWD B20 88 D4
Hintlesham Av HRBN B17 106 B8
Hinton Av ALVE B48 170 E7
Hinton Flds BRGRVW B61 168 C6
Hinton Gv WNSFLD WV11 37 K6
Hintons Coppice DOR/KN B93 149 J7
Hints Ct POL/KGSB/FAZ B78 44 B3
Hints La POL/KGSB/FAZ B78 44 D2
Hints Rd POL/KGSB/FAZ B78 44 F3
Hipkins St TPTN/OCK DY4 67 J6
Hiplands Rd RMSLY B62 122 C1
Hipsley Cl CBROM B36 92 A4
Hipsley La ATHST CV9 61 J8
Hipsmoor Cl
CHWD/FDBR/MGN B37 110 D2
Hipswell Hwy COVE CV2 156 B3
Hirdemonsay SHLY B90 147 K8
Hiron Cft COVS CV3 155 G5
The Hiron COVS CV3 155 G5
Hiron Wy WWCK CV34 204 F6
Hirst Cl RRUGBY CV23 159 L8
Histons Dr CDSL WV8 34 D3
Histons Hl CDSL WV8 34 D3
Hitchcock Cl SMTHWKW B67 87 H8
Hitches La EDG B15 106 F6
Hitchman Ms RLSS CV31 206 E8
Hitchman Rd RLSS CV31 206 E7
Hither Green La REDE B98 194 D6
Hitherside SHLY B90 147 M7
Hoarestone Av NUN CV11 99 L6
Hoarstone STRBR DY8 119 K8
Hoarstone Cl BEWD DY12 137 G8
Hoarstone La BEWD DY12 137 G7
Hobacre Cl RBRY B45 143 L5
Hobart Cft VAUX/NECH B7 89 L8
Hobart Dr DSYBK/YTR WS5 54 A7
Hobart Rd HEDN WS12 17 J3
TPTN/OCK DY4 67 J4
Hobble End La GTWY WS6 24 E7
Hobgate Rd WOLVN WV10 3 L1
Hob Green Rd HAG/WOL DY9 120 C3
Hobhouse Cl PBAR/PBCH B42 70 D6
Hob La HIA/OLT B92 150 E6
KNWTH CV8 178 F2
RCOVN/BALC/EX CV7 152 C8
Hobley Cl RUGBYS/DCH CV22 186 B6
Hobley St WLNHL WV13 52 A3
Hobmoor Cft YDLY B25 109 H6
Hob Moor Rd SMHTH B10 108 E4
Hobnock Rd WNSFLD WV11 37 L1
Hobs Hole La ALDR WS9 41 H6
Hob's Meadow HIA/OLT B92 127 L3
Hob's Moat Rd HIA/OLT B92 127 M2
Hobson Cl WSNGN B18 88 E8
Hobson Rd SLYOAK B29 124 F4
Hobs Rd DARL/WED WS10 68 E1
LICH WS13 21 J4
Hobstone Hill La BNTWD WS7 19 J4
Hockett St COVS CV3 9 H9
Hocking Rd COVE CV2 156 C1
Hockley Brook Cl WSNGN B18 88 E8
Hockley Brook La
HAG/WOL DY9 167 J1
Hockley Cl LOZ/NWT B19 89 H7
Hockley Hl LOZ/NWT B19 88 F7
Hockley La COVW CV5 132 A8
DUDS DY2 102 F2
Hockley Pool Cl WSNGN B18 88 F8
Hockley Rd BILS/COS WV14 66 E6
ERDW/GRVHL B23 90 B1
TAM/AM/WIL B77 46 D6
Hockley St WSNGN B18 6 C1
Hodder Gv HHTH/SAND B71 69 K6
Hodfar Rd STRPT DY13 188 F4
Hodge Hill Av HAG/WOL DY9 120 C2
Hodge Hl Common CBROM B36 91 J6
Hodge Hill Rd BKDE/SHDE B34 91 J8
Hodge La TAM/AM/WIL B77 32 F7
Hodges Dr OLDBY B69 85 M4
Hodgetts Cl SMTHWKW B67 105 H2
Hodgetts Dr HALE B63 121 G5
Hodgett's La
RCOVN/BALC/EX CV7 152 D5
Hodgkins Cl BRWNH WS8 26 E7
Hodnell Cl CBROM B36 92 A4
Hodnet Cl BILS/COS WV14 50 F8
KNWTH CV8 179 M8
Hodnet Dr BRLYHL DY5 84 A7
Hodnet Gv DIG/EDG B5 7 G9
Hodnet Pl CNCK/NC WS11 16 F3
Hodson Av WLNHL WV13 52 A4
Hodson Cl WNSFLD WV11 37 K5
Hodson Wy CNCK/NC WS11 16 F3
Hoff Beck Ct BORD B9 107 M3
Hogarth Cl BDWTH CV12 116 E1
GTB/HAM B43 55 H8
WLNHL WV13 51 J3
Hoggs La NFLD/LBR B31 144 C1
Hogrills End La
CSHL/WTROR B46 94 D1
Holbeache La KGSWFD DY6 83 H4
Holbeache Rd KGSWFD DY6 83 G5
Holbeach Rd STETCH B33 109 M3
Holbeche Crs
RCOVN/BALC/EX CV7 114 C2
Holbeche Rd DOR/KN B93 149 L6
MGN/WHC B75 73 M1
Holbein Cl BDWTH CV12 116 E1
Holberg Gv WNSFLD WV11 37 K7
Holborn Av COVN CV6 134 A3
Holborn Hl AST/WIT B6 89 M5
Holbrook Av
RUGBYN/HIL CV21 186 E1
Holbrook Gv
CHWD/FDBR/MGN B37 110 F5
Holbrook La COVN CV6 134 A3
Holbrook Rd RRUGBY CV23 159 M8
Holbrook Wy COVN CV6 134 B4
Holbury Cl COVEN WV9 35 L3
Holcombe Rd SPARK B11 126 E2
Holcroft Leys
RUGBYS/DCH CV22 186 E6
Holcroft Rd HAG/WOL DY9 120 A1
HALE B63 103 G8
KGSWFD DY6 83 G4
Holcroft St BKHL/PFLD WV2 50 F6
TPTN/OCK DY4 85 L3
Holden Cl ERDW/GRVHL B23 90 C3
Holden Crs BLOX/PEL WS3 39 J8
Holden Cft TPTN/OCK DY4 85 M2
Holden Pl BLOX/PEL WS3 53 J1
Holden Rd DARL/WED WS10 68 A3
ETTPK/GDPK/PENN WV4 65 H2
The Holdens HLGN/YWD B28 126 C7
Holder Dr CNCK/NC WS11 15 M3
Holder Rd SPARK B11 108 A7
YDLY B25 109 G6
Holders Gdns MOS/BIL B13 125 G5
Holders La MOS/BIL B13 125 G3
Holdford Rd AST/WIT B6 89 K3
Holdgate Rd SLYOAK B29 123 M6
Hole Farm Rd NFLD/LBR B31 124 A8
Hole Farm Wy
HWK/WKHTH B38 145 K6
Hole La NFLD/LBR B31 124 A7
Holendene Wy WMBN WV5 64 C6
Holford Av WSLW WS2 53 G7
Holford Dr PBAR/PBCH B42 89 J1
Holford Wy AST/WIT B6 89 K1
Holifast Rd CSCFLD/WYGN B72 73 G6
Holioak Dr WWCK CV34 205 L7
Holland Av DOR/KN B93 149 M5
LGLYGN/QTN B68 105 G1
Holland Cft WALM/CURD B76 75 M3
Holland Rd BILS/COS WV14 51 J6
COVN CV6 133 L7
CSCFLD/WYGN B72 72 F2
GTB/HAM B43 70 B7
Holland Rd West AST/WIT B6 89 K7
Hollands Md ATHST CV9 63 J6
Hollands Pl BLOX/PEL WS3 39 H4
Hollands Rd BLOX/PEL WS3 39 H4
Holland St CBHAMNW B3 6 C4
CSCFLD/WYGN B72 72 F1
DUDN DY1 84 F5
TPTN/OCK DY4 68 A6
Hollemeadow Av
BLOX/PEL WS3 39 H6
Holliars Gv
CHWD/FDBR/MGN B37 92 D8
Hollick Crs
RCOVN/BALC/EX CV7 96 E5
Hollicombe Ter COVE CV2 135 H5
Holliday Rd ERDE/BCHGN B24 90 E1
HDSW B21 88 D6
Holliday St EDG B15 6 C7
Hollie Lucas Rd MOS/BIL B13 125 K6
Hollies Av CNCK/NC WS11 16 D4
Hollies Cft DIG/EDG B5 107 G8
Hollies Dr DARL/WED WS10 68 D2
RMSLY B62 104 B7
Hollies La KIDDW DY11 137 K2
Hollies Park Rd
CNCK/NC WS11 16 D4
Hollies Ri CDYHTH B64 103 K5
Hollies Rd OLDBY B69 85 L5
POL/KGSB/FAZ B78 47 M5
Hollies St DUDS DY2 84 B6
The Hollies AST/WIT B6 89 M5
BKHL/PFLD WV2 2 E8
RBRY B45 169 L4
RRUGBY CV23 161 K4
SMTHWK B66 * 106 A1
STRPT DY13 163 J7
Hollin Brow Cl DOR/KN B93 175 M2
Hollingberry La
WALM/CURD B76 73 K2
Hollings Gv SOLH B91 148 F5
Hollington Rd WOLV WV1 50 F5
Hollington Wy SHLY B90 149 G6
Hollinwell Cl BLOX/PEL WS3 38 E2
Hollis La KNWTH CV8 179 J5
Hollis Rd COVS CV3 155 L3
Hollister Dr RIDG/WDGT B32 123 K2
Holloway CRTAM B79 45 M1
NFLD/LBR B31 123 J7
Holloway Bank
DARL/WED WS10 68 D5
Holloway Circ Queensway
CBHAMW B1 6 F7
Holloway Dr REDE B98 202 D3
WMBN WV5 64 C8
Holloway Fld COVN CV6 133 L7
Holloway Head CBHAMW B1 6 E8
Holloway La REDE B98 202 D2
Holloway Pk REDE B98 202 E2
Holloway St BKHL/PFLD WV2 50 E6
SEDG DY3 84 B1
Holloway St West SEDG DY3 66 B8
The Holloway ALVE B48 194 A2
DUNHL/THL/PER WV6 48 F3
KIDD DY10 166 C3
SEDG DY3 82 B4
STRBR DY8 101 K6
WWCK CV34 205 H7
Hollow Crs COVN CV6 133 M8
Hollow Cft NFLD/LBR B31 144 F2
Hollow Croft Rd SHHTH WV12 37 M6
Hollowell Wy
RUGBYN/HIL CV21 161 G6
The Hollow MOS/BIL B13 125 J1
Hollowtree La BRGRVE B60 192 E2
Holly Av BHTH/HG B12 107 L8
SLYOAK B29 124 F4
Holly Bank COVW CV5 * 8 A9
Hollybank Av WNSFLD WV11 37 L2
Hollybank Cl BLOX/PEL WS3 38 E4
Hollybank Gv HALE B63 121 H4
Hollybank Rd MOS/BIL B13 125 L7
Hollyberry Av SOLH B91 148 E5
Hollyberry Cl HALE B63 121 L2
REDE B98 203 L1
Hollyberry Cft
BKDE/SHDE B34 92 A7
Hollybrow SLYOAK B29 123 L6
Holly Bush Gv RIDG/WDGT B32 105 H6
Hollybush La CDSL WV8 34 B3
COVN CV6 134 E1
ETTPK/GDPK/PENN WV4 65 H1
STRBR DY8 101 K6
Holly Cl CRTAM B79 31 M6
SHHTH WV12 38 A7
WALM/CURD B76 73 K3
Hollycot Gdns BHTH/HG B12 107 K7
Holly Ct DSYBK/YTR WS5 69 L1
Hollycroft Rd HDSW B21 88 B4
Hollydale Rd
BLKHTH/ROWR B65 104 B2
ERDE/BCHGN B24 91 G2
Holly Dell HWK/WKHTH B38 145 M3
Holly Dr ACGN B27 126 F3
ATHST CV9 77 H1
HLYWD B47 146 F6
KNWTH CV8 182 F4
Hollyfaste Rd STETCH B33 109 M4
Hollyfast La
RCOVN/BALC/EX CV7 133 G1
Hollyfast Rd COVN CV6 133 J6
Hollyfield Av SOLH B91 148 C2
Hollyfield Ct MGN/WHC B75 57 J8
Hollyfield Crs MGN/WHC B75 73 J1
Hollyfield Dr MGN/WHC B75 57 J8
RBRY B45 169 L4
Hollyfield Rd MGN/WHC B75 57 J8
Holly Gv BDMR/CCFT WV3 49 K6
BRGRVW B61 191 K2
BVILLE B30 124 D5
LOZ/NWT B19 88 F5
RRUGBY CV23 158 F8
STRBR DY8 101 K8
TLHL/CAN CV4 154 A3
Holly Grove La BNTWD WS7 18 C4
Holly Hall Rd DUDS DY2 84 E7
Hollyhedge Cl NFLD/LBR B31 123 H7
WSLW WS2 4 B2
Hollyhedge La WSLW WS2 4 B1
Hollyhedge Rd HHTH/SAND B71 69 J6
Hollyhill La LICHS WS14 42 C1
Holly Hill Rd LICHS WS14 28 D8
RBRY B45 143 L3
Hollyhock Rd ACGN B27 126 D4
DUDS DY2 85 K4
Hollyhurst BDWTH CV12 116 D4
CSHL/WTROR B46 93 G3
Hollyhurst Dr STRBR DY8 101 J2
Hollyhurst Gv
LGN/SDN/BHAMAIR B26 109 J7
SHLY B90 147 M5
Hollyhurst Rd
SCFLD/BOLD B73 71 M2
Hollyland CSHL/WTROR B46 94 D4
Holly La ALDR WS9 40 E1
ALVE B48 172 D8
ATHST CV9 63 G4
CHWD/FDBR/MGN B37 110 D5
ERDW/GRVHL B23 72 E8
FOAKS/STRLY B74 56 E2
GTWY WS6 24 D5
HEDN WS12 12 A6
KNWTH CV8 177 M3
SMTHWKW B67 87 H7
WALM/CURD B76 74 B1
Hollymoor Wy NFLD/LBR B31 143 M4
Hollymount RMSLY B62 104 E6
Hollyoak Cft NFLD/LBR B31 144 F5
Hollyoake LGLYGN/QTN B68 104 E3
Hollyoake Cl LGLYGN/QTN B68 104 E2
Hollyoak Gv SOLH B91 148 E4
Hollyoak Rd FOAKS/STRLY B74 55 K7
Hollyoak St HHTH/SAND B71 87 H1
Hollyoak Wy CNCK/NC WS11 16 D4
Holly Park Dr
ERDE/BCHGN B24 90 F1
Holly Pl AST/WIT B6 * 89 J5
SLYOAK B29 * 124 F3
Holly Rd BFLD/HDSWWD B20 88 D5
BLKHTH/ROWR B65 103 M4
BRGRVW B61 191 K1
BVILLE B30 145 L1
DARL/WED WS10 52 D8
DUDN DY1 84 E2
HHTH/SAND B71 69 J5
LDYWD/EDGR B16 106 A4
LGLYGN/QTN B68 105 G5
STRPT DY13 188 F1
Holly Stitches Rd
NUNW/HART CV10 80 C7
Holly St CNCK/NC WS11 12 D7
DUDN DY1 84 C6
RLSN CV32 206 E4
SMTHWKW B67 87 K8
Holly Wk KNWTH CV8 181 J3
NUN CV11 99 K3
RLSN CV32 206 E5
Hollywell Rd DOR/KN B93 149 L8
LGN/SDN/BHAMAIR B26 109 M7
Hollywell St BILS/COS WV14 66 E4
Holly Wd GTB/HAM B43 70 E4
Hollywood By-Pass
HLYWD B47 146 C8
Hollywood Cft PBAR/PBCH B42 70 D5
Hollywood Gdns HLYWD B47 146 E5
Hollywood La HLYWD B47 146 E5
Holman Cl WLNHL WV13 51 J3
Holman Rd WLNHL WV13 51 H3
Holman St KIDDW DY11 138 A8
Holman Wy NUN CV11 99 H2
Holmbridge Gv
RUSH/SHEL WS4 40 B3
Holmcroft COVE CV2 135 K5
Holmcroft Gdns COVEN WV9 22 A3
Holmcroft Rd KIDD DY10 138 E7
Holme Cl RUGBYN/HIL CV21 161 G7
Holme Ml WOLVN WV10 36 B1
Holme Ri PENK ST19 10 E4
Holmes Dr COVW CV5 132 B8
RBRY B45 143 K7
Holmesfield Rd
PBAR/PBCH B42 71 G6
Holmes Rd SHHTH WV12 38 B6
The Holmes WOLVN WV10 36 B2
Holme Wy RUSH/SHEL WS4 39 M6
Holmewood Cl KNWTH CV8 179 M8
Holmfield Rd COVE CV2 155 M3
Holmsdale Rd COVN CV6 134 C6
Holm View Cl LICHS WS14 28 D7
Holmwood Av KIDDW DY11 137 L7
Holmwood Dr REDW B97 202 A2
Holmwood Rd BORD B9 108 B4
Holston Cl HEDN WS12 17 K4
Holsworth Cl TAM/AM/WIL B77 46 B4
Holsworthy Cl NUN CV11 81 J8
Holt Ct North VAUX/NECH B7 * 7 K2
Holt Ct South VAUX/NECH B7 * 7 K2
Holt Crs CNCK/NC WS11 16 F3
Holte Dr MGN/WHC B75 57 H3
Holte Rd AST/WIT B6 89 L4
ATHST CV9 63 H4
SPARK B11 108 B8
Holtes Wk AST/WIT B6 * 89 M5
Holt Hl REDE B98 195 K5
Holt La RMSLY B62 142 B1
Holt Rd RMSLY B62 104 C4
Holtshill La WSL WS1 5 H3
Holt St VAUX/NECH B7 7 J1
The Holt RLSN CV32 206 F1
Holt Vls WALM/CURD B76 * 74 F6
Holwick TAM/AM/WIL B77 46 F5
Holy Cross Gn HAG/WOL DY9 141 H3
Holy Cross La HAG/WOL DY9 141 J5
Holyhead Chambers COV CV1 * 8 D4
Holyhead Rd CDSL WV8 34 B5
COV CV1 8 B3
COVW CV5 133 H8
COVW CV5 154 C1
DARL/WED WS10 68 A1
HDSW B21 88 A5
Holyhead Wy HDSW B21 88 B5
Holyoak Cl AST/WIT B6 89 K4
BDWTH CV12 116 D4
RUGBYS/DCH CV22 186 A5
Holyoakes La REDW B97 201 G1
Holy Oaks Cl REDE B98 203 J3
Holyrood Gv AST/WIT B6 * 89 J5
Holy Well Cl LDYWD/EDGR B16 106 E3
Holywell Cl TLHL/CAN CV4 153 H4
Holywell La RBRY B45 143 H7
Holywell Ri LICHS WS14 21 H7
Home Cl KNWTH CV8 182 A7
Homecroft Rd YDLY B25 109 J5
Homedene Rd NFLD/LBR B31 123 J6
Home Farm
RWWCK/WEL CV35 197 K7
Home Farm Cl ATHST CV9 63 M5
Homefield Rd CDSL WV8 34 F2
Homelands PBAR/PBCH B42 70 F6
The Homelands WOLVN WV10 * 22 A7
Homelea Rd YDLY B25 109 H5
Homemead Gv RBRY B45 143 K6
Home Meadow La REDE B98 195 J7
Home Park Rd NUN CV11 99 G2
Homer Cl WWCK CV34 206 C8
Homer Hill Rd HALE B63 102 F6
Homer Rd MGN/WHC B75 57 G3
SOLH B91 148 F2
Homers Fold BILS/COS WV14 51 H8
Homer St BHTH/HG B12 107 K8
Homerton Rd KGSTG B44 71 M4
Homestead Cl SEDG DY3 66 C8
Homestead Dr MGN/WHC B75 57 G2
Homestead Rd STETCH B33 109 M4
Homeward Wy COVS CV3 156 E4
Homewood Cl
WALM/CURD B76 73 J2
Homfray Rd KIDD DY10 138 D5
Honesty Cl BRWNH WS8 26 B6
Honeswode Cl
BFLD/HDSWWD B20 88 E5
Honeyborne Rd MGN/WHC B75 57 H6
Honeybourne
TAM/AM/WIL B77 46 B3
Honeybourne Cl COVW CV5 153 M2
HALE B63 121 L2
Honeybourne Crs WMBN WV5 64 D8
Honeybourne Rd HALE B63 122 A2
STETCH B33 110 A5
Honeybourne Wy WLNHL WV13 52 A2
Honeybrook Cl KIDDW DY11 138 B3
Honeybrook La KIDDW DY11 137 M4
Honeychurch Cl REDE B98 202 D2
Honeycomb Wy
NFLD/LBR B31 144 C2
Honeyfield Rd COV CV1 134 B8
Honeysuckle Av KGSWFD DY6 83 J6
Honeysuckle Cl
RIDG/WDGT B32 104 F8
Honeysuckle Dr COVE CV2 134 F3
DSYBK/YTR WS5 69 L2
WOLVN WV10 22 D3
Honeysuckle Gv ACGN B27 109 G8
Honeysuckle Wy GTWY WS6 24 F1
Honeytree Cl KGSWFD DY6 101 K2
Honiley Dr KGSTG B44 72 A3
Honiley Rd KNWTH CV8 177 L4
STETCH B33 109 L3
Honiley Wy COVE CV2 * 135 H4
Honington Cl
RWWCK/WEL CV35 204 D3
Honister Cl BRLYHL DY5 102 D4
Honiton Cl NFLD/LBR B31 144 C1
Honiton Crs NFLD/LBR B31 144 C1
Honiton Rd COVE CV2 134 F8
Honiton Wy ALDR WS9 40 D8
Honnington Ct SLYOAK B29 * 123 K4
Honor Av
ETTPK/GDPK/PENN WV4 50 A8
Hood Gv BVILLE B30 145 H1
Hood St COV CV1 9 J4
Hood's Wy RUGBYS/DCH CV22 186 B4
Hook Dr FOAKS/STRLY B74 56 C1
Hook La LICHS WS14 42 A2
Hooper St WSNGN B18 106 D1
Hoo Rd KIDD DY10 164 C2
Hoosen Cl RMSLY B62 104 E7
Hope Cl RCOVN/BALC/EX CV7 115 L6
Hopedale Cl COVE CV2 156 C2
Hopedale Rd RIDG/WDGT B32 105 G8
Hope Pl SLYOAK B29 * 124 D3
Hope Rd TPTN/OCK DY4 68 A7
Hope St COV CV1 8 C5
DIG/EDG B5 107 H5
DUDS DY2 85 G5
RMSLY B62 104 B5
STRBR DY8 101 H2
WBROM B70 87 J3
WSL WS1 4 F6
Hopgardens Av BRGRVE B60 191 M3
Hopkins Dr HHTH/SAND B71 69 J6
Hopkins Rd COVN CV6 8 A1
Hopkins St TPTN/OCK DY4 85 L3
Hopleys Cl TAM/AM/WIL B77 46 C1
Hop Pole La BEWD DY12 162 C2
Hopstone Gdns
ETTPK/GDPK/PENN WV4 49 K8
Hopstone Rd SLYOAK B29 123 L4
Hopton Cl COVW CV5 153 L1
DUNHL/THL/PER WV6 48 D2
TPTN/OCK DY4 68 A3
Hopton Crs WNSFLD WV11 37 J7
Hopton Crofts RLSN CV32 206 A3
Hopton Dr KIDD DY10 164 C4
Hopton Gdns DUDN DY1 84 E2
Hopton Gv MOS/BIL B13 126 A8
Hopton Meadow HEDN WS12 17 G4
Hopwas Gv
CHWD/FDBR/MGN B37 92 D8
Hopwas Hl POL/KGSB/FAZ B78 30 E7
Hopwood Cl HALE B63 121 L3
Hopwood Gv NFLD/LBR B31 144 C7
Hopyard Cl SEDG DY3 83 M2
Hopyard Gdns BILS/COS WV14 66 F2
Hopyard La REDE B98 203 H2
SEDG DY3 83 M2
Hopyard Rd WSLW WS2 52 C3
Horace Partridge Rd
DARL/WED WS10 51 L8
Horace St BILS/COS WV14 66 E5
Horatio Dr MOS/BIL B13 125 K1
Hordern Cl
DUNHL/THL/PER WV6 35 K8
Hordern Crs BRLYHL DY5 102 B5
Hordern Gv
DUNHL/THL/PER WV6 35 K8
Hordern Pk WOLVN WV10 * 22 A7
Hordern Rd
DUNHL/THL/PER WV6 49 L1
Hornbeam TAM/AM/WIL B77 46 E1
Hornbeam Cl BEWD DY12 162 C2
SLYOAK B29 123 M6
Hornbeam Crs HEDN WS12 13 L7
Hornbeam Dr TLHL/CAN CV4 153 H4
Hornbeam Gv RLSS CV31 207 G7
Hornbeam Wk BDMR/CCFT WV3 2 B6
Hornbrook Gv HIA/OLT B92 127 G6
Hornby Gv
ALE/KHTH/YWD B14 147 G1
Hornby Rd
ETTPK/GDPK/PENN WV4 66 A1
Hornchurch Cl COV CV1 8 F8
Horndean Cl COVN CV6 134 C5
Horne Cl RUGBYN/HIL CV21 187 L5
Horne Wy BKDE/SHDE B34 92 C8
Horning Dr BILS/COS WV14 67 G2
Horninghold Cl COVS CV3 156 C5
Hornsey Cl COVE CV2 135 J6
Hornsey Gv KGSTG B44 71 L3
Hornsey Rd KGSTG B44 71 L3
Hornton Cl FOAKS/STRLY B74 42 B8
Hornton Gv
RWWCK/WEL CV35 204 C3
Horobins Yd BDWTH CV12 * 116 F1
Horrell Rd
LGN/SDN/BHAMAIR B26 109 L6
SHLY B90 147 K3
Horse Bridge La KINVER DY7 118 A3
Horsecroft Dr HHTH/SAND B71 69 L5
Horse Fair KIDD DY10 138 C6
Horsehills Dr BDMR/CCFT WV3 49 J3
Horselea Cft WASH/WDE B8 109 G1
Horseley Flds WOLV WV1 3 H5
Horseley Heath TPTN/OCK DY4 85 M1
Horseley Rd TPTN/OCK DY4 67 M7
Horsepool Hollow RLSS CV31 207 G8
Horseshoe Cl WSLW WS2 52 F6
Horseshoe Dr HEDN WS12 17 K1
Horse Shoe Rd COVN CV6 134 E1
Horse Shoes La
LGN/SDN/BHAMAIR B26 109 M8
The Horseshoe
LGLYGN/QTN B68 105 G3
Horsfall Rd MGN/WHC B75 57 L8
Horsford Rd COVS CV3 155 J7
Horsham Av STRBR DY8 101 G2
Horsley La LICHS WS14 28 B5
Horsley Rd FOAKS/STRLY B74 55 M3
GTB/HAM B43 71 H1
Horton Cl CNCK/NC WS11 16 D1
DARL/WED WS10 52 B6
RCOVN/BALC/EX CV7 116 D6
SEDG DY3 66 A5
Horton Crs RUGBYS/DCH CV22 186 E3
Horton Gv SHLY B90 148 E8
Horton Pl DARL/WED WS10 52 B6
Horton Sq BHTH/HG B12 107 J6
Horton St DARL/WED WS10 52 B6
TPTN/OCK DY4 68 B8
WBROM B70 87 G4
Hosiery St BDWTH CV12 117 G3
Hoskyn Cl RUGBYN/HIL CV21 187 K5
Hospital La BDWTH CV12 115 M4
BILS/COS WV14 66 F6
GTWY WS6 23 M3
Hospital Rd BNTWD WS7 26 F1
Hospital St BKHL/PFLD WV2 3 H7
CRTAM B79 31 M8
ERDW/GRVHL B23 90 C1
LOZ/NWT B19 89 H8
WSL WS1 53 H1
Hossil La HAG/WOL DY9 140 F5
Hotchkiss Wy COVS CV3 156 E6
Hothersall Dr
SCFLD/BOLD B73 72 D5
Hothorpe Cl COVS CV3 156 D4
Hotspur Rd KGSTG B44 71 K4
Hough Pl WSLW WS2 52 F6

Hough Rd ALE/KHTH/YWD B14 125 H7
WSLW WS2 52 E6
Houghton Ct HLGN/YWD B28 147 H1
Houghton St OLDBY B69 86 D7
WBROM B70 87 H5
Houldey Rd NFLD/LBR B31 144 F4
Houldsworth Crs COVN CV6 134 A1
Houliston Cl DARL/WED WS10 52 F8
Houndel Gv WMBN WV5 64 D6
Houndsfield Cl HLYWD B47 147 G7
Houndsfield Gv HLYWD B47 146 E8
Houndsfield La HLYWD B47 146 E8
Housman Cl BRGRVE B60 191 J5
Houston Rd RUGBYN/HIL CV21 161 G7
Houting TAM/AM/WIL B77 46 B8
The Houx STRBR DY8 101 J5
Hove Av COVW CV5 153 J1
Hovelands Cl COVE CV2 135 G5
Hove Rd ACGN B27 126 F4
Hoveton Cl REDE B98 202 F4
Howard Av BRGRVW B61 191 J2
Howard Cl COVW CV5 153 K1
Howard Crs HEDN WS12 13 G6
Howard Rd
ALE/KHTH/YWD B14 125 H6
BFLD/HDSWWD B20 88 F3
BILS/COS WV14 67 K2
GTB/HAM B43 70 A5
HIA/OLT B92 127 J2
NUNW/HART CV10 98 E2
REDE B98 202 F5
WNSFLD WV11 37 K5
YDLY B25 109 G7
Howard Rd East
ALE/KHTH/YWD B14 125 J6
Howard St BKHL/PFLD WV2 3 G8
COV CV1 9 G1
LOZ/NWT B19 6 E1
TPTN/OCK DY4 67 M8
WBROM B70 68 D6
Howard Wk WWCK CV34 206 B6
Howarth Wy AST/WIT B6 89 L6
Howat Rd
RCOVN/BALC/EX CV7 115 K6
Howcotte Gn TLHL/CAN CV4 153 J6
Howden Pl BKDE/SHDE B34 91 L8
Howdle's La BRWNH WS8 26 D3
Howe Crs SHHTH WV12 38 A7
Howe Green La
RCOVN/BALC/EX CV7 115 H2
Howell Rd BKHL/PFLD WV2 50 C6
Howells Cl BDWTH CV12 116 B5
Howes Cft CVALE B35 91 L3
Howes La COVS CV3 181 G2
Howe St CBHAMNE B4 7 K3
Howford Gv VAUX/NECH B7 107 M1
Howkins Rd RUGBYN/HIL CV21 161 G7
Howland Cl COVEN WV9 35 K3
Howlette Rd TLHL/CAN CV4 153 J3
Howley Av KGSTG B44 71 J4
Howley Grange Rd RMSLY B62 104 D8
Hoylake TAM/AM/WIL B77 46 F1
Hoylake Cl BLOX/PEL WS3 38 F2
NUN CV11 99 M4
Hoylake Dr OLDBY B69 85 L6
Hoylake Rd
DUNHL/THL/PER WV6 34 B8
Hoyland Wy BVILLE B30 124 C5
Huband Cl REDE B98 194 E8
Hubert Cft SLYOAK B29 124 C3
Hubert Rd SLYOAK B29 124 D3
Hubert St AST/WIT B6 89 K8
The Hub SOLH B91 * 149 G2
Hucker Cl WSLW WS2 52 E6
Hucker Rd WSLW WS2 52 E6
Huddesford Dr
RCOVN/BALC/EX CV7 152 A5
Huddisdon Cl WWCK CV34 205 K4
Huddlestone Cl WOLVN WV10 22 E7
Huddleston Wy SLYOAK B29 124 A4
Huddocks Vw BLOX/PEL WS3 25 K8
Hudson Av CSHL/WTROR B46 93 K7
Hudson Cl CNCK/NC WS11 16 F3
Hudson Dr BNTWD WS7 19 G7
Hudson Gv
DUNHL/THL/PER WV6 34 C8
Hudson Rd BFLD/HDSWWD B20 88 E1
RUGBYS/DCH CV22 186 C4
TPTN/OCK DY4 86 A1
Hudson's Dr BVILLE B30 145 L1
Hudson V TLHL/CAN CV4 153 G2
Hudswell Dr BRLYHL DY5 102 B5
Huggins Cl
RCOVN/BALC/EX CV7 152 A6
Hughes Av BDMR/CCFT WV3 49 K5
Hughes Cl WWCK CV34 205 H3
Hughes Pl BILS/COS WV14 51 H6
Hughes Rd BILS/COS WV14 51 H6
DARL/WED WS10 51 L8
Hugh Porter Wy
DUNHL/THL/PER WV6 35 K6
Hugh Rd COVS CV3 155 L3
SMHTH B10 108 C4
SMTHWKW B67 87 H8
Hugh Vls SMHTH B10 * 108 C4
Huins Cl REDE B98 202 E1
Hulbert Dr DUDS DY2 84 F7
Hulland Pl BRLYHL DY5 102 A2
Hullbrook Rd MOS/BIL B13 126 A8
Hulme Cl COVS CV3 156 F4
Humber Av COV CV1 9 K7
COVS CV3 9 M7
WALM/CURD B76 73 L6
Humber Gdns HALE B63 102 F8
Humber Gv CBROM B36 92 D4
Humber Rd BDMR/CCFT WV3 2 B6
COVS CV3 9 M9
Humberstone Rd
ERDE/BCHGN B24 91 J1
Hume St KIDDW DY11 138 A8
Humpage Rd BORD B9 108 C3
Humphrey Av BRGRVE B60 191 J6
Humphrey Burton's Rd
COVS CV3 155 G5
Humphrey-Davy Rd
BDWTH CV12 116 B5
Humphrey Middlemore Dr
HRBN B17 124 B1
Humphrey St SEDG DY3 84 B2
Humphries Crs BILS/COS WV14 67 G7
Humphries Dr KIDD DY10 164 D3
Humphries Rd WOLVN WV10 36 B4
Humphris St WWCK CV34 205 M5
Hundred Acre Rd
FOAKS/STRLY B74 55 K6
Hungary Cl HAG/WOL DY9 102 A8
Hungary Hl HAG/WOL DY9 102 A8
Hungerfield Rd CBROM B36 92 A4
Hungerford Rd STRBR DY8 119 J3
Hungry La LICHS WS14 43 K1
Hunningham Gv SOLH B91 148 F5
Hunnington Cl
RIDG/WDGT B32 122 E4
Hunnington Crs HALE B63 121 M3
Hunscote Cl SHLY B90 147 K4
Hunslet Cl RIDG/WDGT B32 123 K1
Hunslet Rd BNTWD WS7 18 F5
RIDG/WDGT B32 123 K1
Hunstanton Av HRBN B17 105 K5
Hunstanton Cl BRLYHL DY5 102 A5
Hunt Cl RWWCK/WEL CV35 204 D7
Hunt End La REDW B97 202 A8
Hunter Av BNTWD WS7 18 F6
Hunter Cl LICHS WS14 21 H7
Hunter Crs BLOX/PEL WS3 39 K7
Hunter Rd CNCK/NC WS11 16 C5
Hunters Cl COVS CV3 156 E3
WLNHL WV13 51 L6
Hunters La RUGBYN/HIL CV21 160 E8
Hunters Pk ATHST CV9 62 A5
Hunter's Ride KINVER DY7 100 F3
Hunters Rd LOZ/NWT B19 88 F7
Hunter St DUNHL/THL/PER WV6 2 B1
RUGBYN/HIL CV21 187 G1
Hunters V LOZ/NWT B19 89 G7
Hunters Wk ATHST CV9 63 M6
Hunter Ter COVW CV5 154 A5
Huntingdon Cl
POL/KGSB/FAZ B78 45 K3
REDE B98 203 J3
Huntingdon Rd COVW CV5 8 B8
HHTH/SAND B71 68 F6
Huntingdon Wy
NUNW/HART CV10 98 C2
Huntington Rd SHHTH WV12 38 B6
Huntington Terrace Rd
CNCK/NC WS11 16 D1
Huntingtree Rd HALE B63 121 J1
Huntlands Rd HALE B63 121 J3
Hunt La ATHST CV9 63 M6
Huntley Dr SOLH B91 148 F3
Huntly Rd LDYWD/EDGR B16 106 E4
Hunton Hl ERDW/GRVHL B23 90 B2
Hunton Rd ERDW/GRVHL B23 90 C2
Hunt Paddocks KNWTH CV8 197 J4
Hunt's La SHHTH WV12 38 B7
Huntsman Cl BILS/COS WV14 67 H3
Huntsmans Ga BNTWD WS7 18 F5
Huntsmans Ri HEDN WS12 12 A5
Hunts Mill Dr BRLYHL DY5 84 A4
Hunts Ri BEWD DY12 163 G2
Hunts Rd BVILLE B30 124 E8
Hunt Ter TLHL/CAN CV4 153 M6
Hurcott La KIDD DY10 139 G4
Hurcott Rd KIDD DY10 138 D6
Hurdis Rd SHLY B90 147 L3
Hurdlow Av WSNGN B18 88 F8
Hurley Cl CSCFLD/WYGN B72 73 G3
DSYBK/YTR WS5 54 B7
RLSN CV32 206 E3
Hurley Common ATHST CV9 61 G7
Hurley Gv
CHWD/FDBR/MGN B37 92 D8
Hurley La CSHL/WTROR B46 77 J8
Hurleys Fold DUDS DY2 84 F8
Hurlingham Rd KGSTG B44 71 L4
Hurn Wy COVN CV6 134 F1
Huron Cl CNCK/NC WS11 16 F3
Hurricane Wy CVALE B35 91 L3
Hursey Dr TPTN/OCK DY4 67 L8
Hurstbourne Crs WOLV WV1 50 F4
Hurst Cl CBROM B36 92 C6
Hurstcroft Rd STETCH B33 109 M2
Hurst Green Rd DOR/KN B93 175 K1
RMSLY B62 104 C5
WALM/CURD B76 74 B7
Hurst La BKDE/SHDE B34 92 B7
BRLYHL DY5 102 D2
TPTN/OCK DY4 67 H8
Hurst La North
BKDE/SHDE B34 92 C6
Hurst Rd BDWTH CV12 116 F2
BILS/COS WV14 66 D4
COVN CV6 134 E1
SMTHWKW B67 105 H3
Hurst St DIG/EDG B5 6 F7
The Hurst HLYWD B47 146 E7
MOS/BIL B13 126 A6
The Hurstway
ERDW/GRVHL B23 72 A5
Hurstwood Rd KGSTG B44 72 A5
Huskinson Cl OLDBY B69 85 M4
Hussey Cl PENK ST19 10 D5
Hussey Rd BRWNH WS8 26 C5
CNCK/NC WS11 17 K8
Husum Wy KIDD DY10 139 G6
Hutchings La SHLY B90 147 M8
Hut Hill La GTWY WS6 24 E1
Hutton Av WASH/WDE B8 90 B8
Hutton Rd BFLD/HDSWWD B20 88 F4
WASH/WDE B8 90 B8
Huxbey Dr HIA/OLT B92 128 D5
Huxley Cl COVEN WV9 35 L2
Hyacinth Cl DSYBK/YTR WS5 69 K2
Hyatt Sq BRLYHL DY5 102 A6
Hyde Cl BRGRVE B60 191 M3
Hyde Pl RLSN CV32 206 C5
Hyde Rd COVE CV2 156 C1
KNWTH CV8 179 K8
WNSFLD WV11 37 H7
Hydes Rd DARL/WED WS10 68 E2
HHTH/SAND B71 69 G4
The Hyde HAG/WOL DY9 120 B3
Hyett Wy BILS/COS WV14 67 M3
Hylda Rd BFLD/HDSWWD B20 88 F4
Hylstone Crs WNSFLD WV11 37 H7
Hylton St WSNGN B18 89 G8
Hypericum Gdns COVE CV2 * 135 G8
Hyperion Dr
ETTPK/GDPK/PENN WV4 65 L2
Hyperion Rd CBROM B36 91 J4
KINVER DY7 101 G5
Hyron Hall Rd ACGN B27 127 G3
Hyssop Cl CNCK/NC WS11 16 F3
VAUX/NECH B7 89 L8
Hytall Rd SHLY B90 147 G3
Hythe Gv YDLY B25 109 H5

I

Ibberton Rd
ALE/KHTH/YWD B14 146 F2
Ibex Cl COVS CV3 156 D4
Ibis Cl KIDD DY10 164 F2
Ibis Gdns KGSWFD DY6 83 L7
Ibstock Cl REDE B98 203 J1
Ibstock Dr STRBR DY8 119 L1
Ibstock Rd COVN CV6 116 E8
Icknield Cl FOAKS/STRLY B74 55 L4
Icknield Port Rd
LDYWD/EDGR B16 106 C2
Icknield Sq LDYWD/EDGR B16 106 E2
Icknield St ALVE B48 194 F2
HWK/WKHTH B38 145 L8
HWK/WKHTH B38 171 M3
REDE B98 195 G6
WSNGN B18 6 A2
Icknield Street Dr REDE B98 203 H5
Ida Rd WBROM B70 87 H4
Idbury Rd KGSTG B44 71 L6
Iden Rd COV CV1 134 C8
Idmiston Cft
ALE/KHTH/YWD B14 146 D3
Idonia Rd DUNHL/THL/PER WV6 34 C8
Ilam Pk KNWTH CV8 180 A8
Ilex Ct WWCK CV34 205 L6
Ilford Cl BDWTH CV12 116 D2
Ilford Dr COVS CV3 154 F8
Ilford Rd ERDW/GRVHL B23 72 B7
Ilfracombe Gv COVS CV3 154 E8
Iliffe Wy HRBN B17 124 B1
Ilkley Gv
CHWD/FDBR/MGN B37 110 D3
Illey Cl NFLD/LBR B31 143 M4
Illey La RMSLY B62 122 A4
Illshaw COVEN WV9 35 L2
Illshaw Cl REDE B98 203 L1
Illshaw Heath Rd
HOCK/TIA B94 174 B2
Ilmer Cl RUGBYN/HIL CV21 161 J6
Ilmington Cl COVS CV3 154 F8
REDE B98 203 H4
RWWCK/WEL CV35 204 B2
Ilmington Dr SCFLD/BOLD B73 72 A2
Ilmington Rd SLYOAK B29 123 K4
Ilsham Gv NFLD/LBR B31 144 C7
Ilsley Rd ERDW/GRVHL B23 90 C1
Imber Rd KIDD DY10 164 E4
Imperial Av KIDD DY10 138 D5
Imperial Ct KIDD DY10 138 D5
Imperial Gv KIDD DY10 138 D5
Imperial Ri CSHL/WTROR B46 93 J3
Imperial Rd BORD B9 108 C4
Impney Cl REDE B98 195 H7
Impsley Cl CBROM B36 91 M5
Inca Cl COVS CV3 156 D5
Ince Rd DARL/WED WS10 52 A6
Incestre Dr GTB/HAM B43 70 A4
Inchbrook Rd KNWTH CV8 180 A6
Inchcape Av
BFLD/HDSWWD B20 88 E2
Inchford Av WWCK CV34 205 J3
Inchford Cl NUN CV11 99 K4
Inchford Rd HIA/OLT B92 128 C6
Inchlaggan Rd WOLVN WV10 36 D7
Infantry Pl MGN/WHC B75 57 L7
Ingatestone Dr STRBR DY8 101 G2
Ingestre Cl BLOX/PEL WS3 38 D2
CNCK/NC WS11 16 F4
Ingestre Dr GTB/HAM B43 70 A4
Inge St DIG/EDG B5 7 G8
Ingestre Rd HLGN/YWD B28 126 D6
WOLVN WV10 36 A4
Ingham Wy HRBN B17 105 K6
Ingleby Gdns
DUNHL/THL/PER WV6 35 L8
Ingledew Cl WSLW WS2 52 B2
Inglefield Rd STETCH B33 109 K2
Inglemere Gv SLYOAK B29 123 K6
Inglenook Dr
BFLD/HDSWWD B20 88 F3
Ingleside Vls SPARK B11 * 108 A8
Ingleton Cl NUN CV11 99 L3
Ingleton Rd WASH/WDE B8 90 E6
Inglewood Av
BDMR/CCFT WV3 49 K5
Inglewood Cl KGSWFD DY6 * 83 H8
RLSN CV32 206 E2
Inglewood Gv
FOAKS/STRLY B74 55 K3
Inglewood Rd SPARK B11 108 A8
Ingoldsby Rd NFLD/LBR B31 145 G2
Ingot Cl WSLW WS2 38 F7
Ingram Crs BEWD DY12 162 D1
Ingram Dr GTB/HAM B43 70 A5
Ingram Gv ACGN B27 126 E3
Ingram Pit La
TAM/AM/WIL B77 32 E8
Ingram Pl BLOX/PEL WS3 39 H4
Ingram Rd BLOX/PEL WS3 39 H4
COVW CV5 154 B5
Inhedge St SEDG DY3 66 C8
The Inhedge DUDN DY1 85 G4
Inkberrow Cl OLDBY B69 86 B8
Inkberrow Rd HALE B63 121 K3
Inkerman Gv WOLVN WV10 3 L4
Inkerman St VAUX/NECH B7 107 M1
WOLVN WV10 3 L2
Inland Rd ERDE/BCHGN B24 90 F3
Innage Cl RLSS CV31 206 E5
Innage Rd NFLD/LBR B31 144 F1
Innage Ter ATHST CV9 * 63 H5
The Innage HLYWD B47 146 E8
Innis Rd COVW CV5 154 C6
Inn La KIDDW DY11 189 L3
Innsworth Dr CVALE B35 91 L1
Insetton Cl REDE B98 203 H1
Inshaw Cl STETCH B33 109 J2
Institute Rd
ALE/KHTH/YWD B14 125 K5
Instone Rd COVN CV6 133 L4
HALE B63 121 K2
Instow Cl SHHTH WV12 37 M5
Insull Av ALE/KHTH/YWD B14 146 F4
Intended St HALE B63 103 G6
International Dr
LGN/SDN/BHAMAIR B26 129 G1
International Sq
CHWD/FDBR/MGN B37 * 111 G7
Intown WSL WS1 5 G3
Intown Rw WSL WS1 5 G3
Inveraray Cl KNWTH CV8 198 A1
Inverclyde Dr
ETTPK/GDPK/PENN WV4 50 C8
Inverclyde Rd
BFLD/HDSWWD B20 88 E2
Inverkip Wk
ETTPK/GDPK/PENN WV4 50 D8
Inverness Cl COVW CV5 153 L1
Inverness Rd NFLD/LBR B31 144 D2
Invicta Rd COVS CV3 156 D5
Inworth COVEN WV9 35 M2
Ipsley Church La REDE B98 203 G3
Ipsley Gv ERDW/GRVHL B23 71 L8
Ipsley La REDE B98 203 H3
Ipsley St REDW B97 202 C2
Ipstones Av STETCH B33 109 K1
Ipswich Crs PBAR/PBCH B42 70 F6
Ireland Green Rd WBROM B70 86 E2
Ireton Cl TLHL/CAN CV4 153 G4
Ireton Rd BFLD/HDSWWD B20 88 E1
WOLVN WV10 36 B2
Iris Av NUNW/HART CV10 98 E5
Iris Cl CRTAM B79 32 A7
DUDS DY2 85 K4
SLYOAK B29 123 M5
Iris Dr ALE/KHTH/YWD B14 146 B1
Irnham Rd FOAKS/STRLY B74 56 E3
Iron Bridge Wk HAG/WOL DY9 119 M5
Ironbridge Wy COVN CV6 116 F7
Iron La STETCH B33 109 H1
Ironmonger Rw COV CV1 8 F4
Ironside Cl BEWD DY12 162 D2
Ironstone Rd BNTWD WS7 18 C5
HEDN WS12 18 A1
Iron Wy BRGRVE B60 191 L6
Irvan Av WBROM B70 68 D8
Irvine Cl BLOX/PEL WS3 38 F6
Irvine Rd BLOX/PEL WS3 38 F5
Irving Cl LICH WS13 20 C3
SEDG DY3 83 L1
Irving Rd COV CV1 9 K7
HIA/OLT B92 128 C1
TPTN/OCK DY4 67 L4
Irving St CBHAMW B1 6 E8
Irwell TAM/AM/WIL B77 46 C3
Irwin Av RBRY B45 144 A7
Isaac Walton Pl WBROM B70 68 C6
Isambard Dr COVN CV6 116 D8
Isbourne Wy BORD B9 107 M2
Isis Gv CBROM B36 92 D5
WLNHL WV13 52 A3
Island Dr KIDD DY10 164 C1
Island Rd HDSW B21 88 A4
Islington HALE B63 121 L1
Islington Crs ATHST CV9 61 G4
Islington Rw EDG B15 6 A8
Ismere Rd ERDE/BCHGN B24 90 F3
Ismere Wy KIDD DY10 138 D4
Itchen Gv DUNHL/THL/PER WV6 48 C2
Ithon Gv HWK/WKHTH B38 145 J5
Ivanhoe Av NUN CV11 99 J4
Ivanhoe Rd BKHL/PFLD WV2 50 D7
GTB/HAM B43 70 F2
LICHS WS14 20 F7
Ivanhoe St DUDS DY2 84 E6
Ivatt TAM/AM/WIL B77 46 D3
Ivatt Cl RUSH/SHEL WS4 39 M6
Iverley La STRBR DY8 119 G8
Iverley Rd HALE B63 122 A2
Iverley Wk HAG/WOL DY9 119 M3
Ivor Rd ATHST CV9 63 K6
COVN CV6 134 D3
REDW B97 202 B3
SPARK B11 125 M1
Ivy Av BHTH/HG B12 107 L8
Ivy Bank ATHST CV9 * 62 B7
Ivybridge Gv PBAR/PBCH B42 89 G2
Ivybridge Rd COVS CV3 155 H8
Ivy Cl CNCK/NC WS11 16 A5
Ivy Cft COVEN WV9 35 K2
Ivydale Av
LGN/SDN/BHAMAIR B26 110 A8
Ivy Farm La TLHL/CAN CV4 154 B7
Ivyfield Rd ERDW/GRVHL B23 71 M8
Ivy Gv BRWNH WS8 40 E1
NUNW/HART CV10 80 B7
Ivyhouse La BILS/COS WV14 66 F5
Ivyhouse Rd HWK/WKHTH B38 145 G5
Ivy House Rd OLDBY B69 86 B7
Ivy La CBHAMNE B4 7 M5
RMSLY B62 121 H8
Ivy Lodge Cl
CHWD/FDBR/MGN B37 110 E5
Ivy Rd BVILLE B30 124 E7
DUDN DY1 84 E1
HDSW B21 88 E6
SCFLD/BOLD B73 72 D4
TPTN/OCK DY4 67 K6
Ivy Wy SHLY B90 147 L7
Izod Rd RUGBYN/HIL CV21 186 D1
Izod St REDW B97 202 B1
Izons La WBROM B70 86 E4
Izons Rd WBROM B70 87 G2

J

Jacamar Av STETCH B33 109 K1
Jacey Rd LDYWD/EDGR B16 106 B3
SHLY B90 147 M1
Jackdaw Cl SEDG DY3 66 A3
Jackdaw Dr CBROM B36 92 E5
Jacker's Rd COVE CV2 134 F1
Jackfield Cl REDE B98 203 J4
Jack Hayward Wy WOLV WV1 2 E2
Jack Holden Av
BILS/COS WV14 66 E3
Jacklin Dr COVS CV3 181 G1
Jackson Cl CNCK/NC WS11 25 J1
LGLYGN/QTN B68 86 F8
RCOVN/BALC/EX CV7 115 L6
RWWCK/WEL CV35 204 D7
SPARK B11 * 107 M6
TPTN/OCK DY4 67 M4
WOLVN WV10 22 E7
Jackson Crs STRPT DY13 188 C4
Jackson Dr SMTHWKW B67 87 H8
Jackson Gv KNWTH CV8 198 A1
Jackson Rd COVN CV6 134 B4
LICH WS13 20 F2
RUGBYN/HIL CV21 187 L4
WASH/WDE B8 108 D1
Jackson St DUNHL/THL/PER WV6 49 M1
HAG/WOL DY9 102 C8
LGLYGN/QTN B68 104 F1
Jackson Wy RIDG/WDGT B32 104 E8
Jacmar Crs SMTHWKW B67 87 J7
Jacob Dr TLHL/CAN CV4 154 B7
Jacobean La DOR/KN B93 149 L5
Jacob's Hall La GTWY WS6 24 E4
Jacoby Pl DIG/EDG B5 107 G8
Jacox Crs KNWTH CV8 180 A8
Jade Cl COV CV1 9 H1
Jade Gv CNCK/NC WS11 17 G3
Jaffray Crs ERDE/BCHGN B24 90 D2
Jaffray Rd ERDE/BCHGN B24 90 D2
Jaguar TAM/AM/WIL B77 46 C3
Jakeman Cl REDE B98 203 J1
Jakeman Rd BHTH/HG B12 107 J8
James Bridge Cl WSLW WS2 * 52 F6
James Cl DARL/WED WS10 52 D6
SMTHWKW B67 87 H8
Jamescroft COVS CV3 156 C7
James Dawson Dr COVW CV5 131 M5
James Dee Cl BRLYHL DY5 102 D4
James Eaton Cl
HHTH/SAND B71 69 G8
James Galloway Cl COVS CV3 156 C6
James Green Rd TLHL/CAN CV4 153 K3
Jameson Rd AST/WIT B6 90 A5
Jameson St
DUNHL/THL/PER WV6 49 M1
James Rd CSHL/WTROR B46 93 K5
GTB/HAM B43 70 C6
KIDD DY10 138 E5
SPARK B11 108 D7
James Samuel Pl
BHTH/HG B12 107 K6
James Scott Rd HALE B63 102 E7
James St BILS/COS WV14 51 J7
CBHAMNW B3 6 D3
CNCK/NC WS11 12 D8
NUN CV11 80 E8
RCOVN/BALC/EX CV7 96 E5
RUGBYN/HIL CV21 186 F2
WLNHL WV13 51 L3
James Turner St WSNGN B18 88 C7
James Watt Dr LOZ/NWT B19 88 F5
James Watt Queensway
CBHAMNE B4 7 H3
James Watt St HHTH/SAND B71 68 F5
Jane Lane Cl WSLW WS2 52 D1
Janice Gv ALE/KHTH/YWD B14 146 F1
Janine Av WNSFLD WV11 37 J6
Jaques Cl CSHL/WTROR B46 92 F3
Jardine Crs TLHL/CAN CV4 153 K3
Jardine Rd AST/WIT B6 89 K4
Jarvis Crs OLDBY B69 104 E1
Jarvis Rd ERDW/GRVHL B23 72 D7
Jarvis Wy ERDE/BCHGN B24 90 C5
Jasmin Cft
ALE/KHTH/YWD B14 146 C2
Jasmine Cl COVEN WV9 35 K2
Jasmine Gv BRGRVW B61 191 K1
CDSL WV8 34 F2
COVS CV3 156 A5
RLSN CV32 206 E3
Jasmine Pl COVS CV3 * 156 A5
Jasmine Rd DUDS DY2 85 K4
TAM/AM/WIL B77 46 E1
Jasmine Wy DARL/WED WS10 52 B6
Jason Cl TAM/AM/WIL B77 32 B8
Jason Rd HAG/WOL DY9 120 D1
Javelin Av CVALE B35 91 M2
Javelin Pk DARL/WED WS10 68 B3
Jayne Cl HHTH/SAND B71 69 J4
WNSFLD WV11 37 H6
Jay Park Crs KIDD DY10 164 E3
Jay Rd KGSWFD DY6 83 H5
Jays Av TPTN/OCK DY4 85 M1
Jays Cl REDE B98 203 L2
Jays Crs ALVE B48 170 F4
Jayshaw Av GTB/HAM B43 70 C5
Jean Dr TPTN/OCK DY4 68 B7
Jean St ATHST CV9 62 A4
Jeavons Pl BILS/COS WV14 51 G8
Jedburgh Av
DUNHL/THL/PER WV6 48 C1
Jedburgh Gv COVS CV3 180 E1
Jeddo St BKHL/PFLD WV2 2 E8
Jefferson Cl HHTH/SAND B71 68 F5
Jeffrey Av
ETTPK/GDPK/PENN WV4 50 D7
Jeffrey Cl BDWTH CV12 116 B5
Jeffrey Rd BLKHTH/ROWR B65 104 C2
Jeffs Av BKHL/PFLD WV2 3 H9
Jeliff St TLHL/CAN CV4 153 K4
Jelleyman Cl KIDDW DY11 137 M7
Jenkins Av COVW CV5 153 K1
Jenkins Cl BILS/COS WV14 51 G8
Jenkinson Rd DARL/WED WS10 68 B4
Jenkins Rd RUGBYN/HIL CV21 187 L4
Jenkins St SMHTH B10 108 A5
Jenkinstown Rd HEDN WS12 13 L7
Jenks Av WOLVN WV10 36 C5
Jenks Rd WMBN WV5 64 D8
Jennens Rd CBHAMNE B4 7 J3
Jenner Cl WSLW WS2 38 E7
Jenner Rd WSLW WS2 38 D7
Jenner St BKHL/PFLD WV2 3 J7
COV CV1 9 H1
Jennings St CDYHTH B64 103 K3
Jenny Cl BILS/COS WV14 67 J4
Jenny Walkers La
DUNHL/THL/PER WV6 48 B5
Jensen TAM/AM/WIL B77 46 C3
Jenton Rd RLSS CV31 206 F7
Jephcott Rd WASH/WDE B8 108 E2
Jephson Dr
LGN/SDN/BHAMAIR B26 109 K6
Jephson Pl RLSS CV31 * 206 F6
Jeremy Gv HIA/OLT B92 127 M1
Jeremy Rd
ETTPK/GDPK/PENN WV4 50 A8
Jerome Dr CNCK/NC WS11 17 L8
Jerome Rd CNCK/NC WS11 17 K8
CSCFLD/WYGN B72 73 H1
WSLW WS2 52 F4
Jerome Wy BNTWD WS7 18 F6
Jerrard Dr MGN/WHC B75 57 G8
Jerrard Ms MGN/WHC B75 * 57 G8
Jerry's La ERDW/GRVHL B23 72 B6
LICHS WS14 30 A5
Jersey Cl REDE B98 195 H6
Jersey Cft CBROM B36 92 F7
Jersey Rd WASH/WDE B8 108 B1
Jerusalem Wk KIDD DY10 138 C6
Jervis Cl BRLYHL DY5 84 A6
Jervis Crs FOAKS/STRLY B74 56 B2
Jervis Pk FOAKS/STRLY B74 56 A1
Jervis Rd TAM/AM/WIL B77 46 D8
Jervis Ter HDSW B21 * 88 B5
Jervoise Dr NFLD/LBR B31 124 A8
Jervoise La HHTH/SAND B71 69 J4
Jervoise Rd SLYOAK B29 123 K4
Jervoise St WBROM B70 86 E1
Jesmond Cl HEDN WS12 13 L8
Jesmond Gv ERDE/BCHGN B24 91 H1
Jesmond Rd COV CV1 9 K2
Jessel Rd WSLW WS2 4 B2
Jessie Rd ALDR WS9 40 E4
Jesson Cl WSL WS1 5 K8
Jesson Rd MGN/WHC B75 57 L8
SEDG DY3 66 E7
WSL WS1 5 H6
Jesson St WBROM B70 87 J3
Jessop Dr TAM/AM/WIL B77 32 B8
Jevons Rd SCFLD/BOLD B73 72 A2
Jevon St BILS/COS WV14 67 G5
Jew's La SEDG DY3 84 C1
Jiggins La RIDG/WDGT B32 123 G4
Jill Av GTB/HAM B43 70 A4
Jillcot Rd HIA/OLT B92 127 M2
Jim Forrest Cl COVS CV3 156 D5
Jinnah Cl BHTH/HG B12 107 K5
Jinnah Rd REDE B98 202 C3
Joanna Dr COVS CV3 181 G1
Joan St BKHL/PFLD WV2 50 C7
Joan Ward St COVS CV3 9 G9
Job's La TLHL/CAN CV4 153 L3
Jockey Fld SEDG DY3 66 C7
Jockey Hl LICHS WS14 * 21 K8
Jockey La DARL/WED WS10 68 E1
Jockey Rd SCFLD/BOLD B73 72 B3
Jodrell St NUN CV11 80 F8
Joe Obrien Cl COVS CV3 156 A7
Joe Williams Cl COVS CV3 156 D6
Joeys La CDSL WV8 35 G2
John Bright Cl TPTN/OCK DY4 67 K5
John Bright St CBHAMW B1 6 F6
Johndory TAM/AM/WIL B77 46 B7
John Fletcher Cl
DARL/WED WS10 52 F8
John Grace St COVS CV3 9 H9
John Harper St WLNHL WV13 51 M3
John Howell Dr TPTN/OCK DY4 67 L8
John Kempe Wy
BHTH/HG B12 107 L6
John Knight Rd BDWTH CV12 98 F8
John McGuire Crs COVS CV3 156 B6
John Nash Sq KNWTH CV8 197 K2

John O'Gaunt Rd KNWTH CV8 197 J2
John Padden Cl
BLKHTH/ROWR B65 103 M4
John Riley Dr SHHTH WV12 38 A5
John Rd RMSLY B62 122 D1
John Rous Av TLHL/CAN CV4 153 M6
Johns Gv GTB/HAM B43 70 A5
John Shelton Dr COVN CV6 134 A1
John Simpson Cl KNWTH CV8 183 L2
Johns La GTWY WS6 24 D2
TPTN/OCK DY4 85 M1
Johnson Av
RUGBYS/DCH CV22 186 B3
WNSFLD WV11 37 K6
Johnson Cl DARL/WED WS10 52 B8
LICH WS13 21 G4
REDE B98 194 E8
SPARK B11 108 A8
WASH/WDE B8 91 G7
Johnson Dr CVALE B35 91 K2
Johnson Pl BILS/COS WV14 51 K6
Johnson Rd BDWTH CV12 117 G2
BNTWD WS7 18 D5
CNCK/NC WS11 16 B1
COVN CV6 134 E5
DARL/WED WS10 52 B8
ERDW/GRVHL B23 72 D8
SHHTH WV12 38 B6
Johnsons Bridge Rd
HHTH/SAND B71 69 G7
Johnsons Gv LGLYGN/QTN B68 105 G5
Johnson St ATHST CV9 61 G4
BILS/COS WV14 66 D4
BKHL/PFLD WV2 3 G9
VAUX/NECH B7 90 A7
Johnstone St LOZ/NWT B19 89 H5
Johnston St WBROM B70 87 H4
John St BDWTH CV12 116 E3
BKHL/PFLD WV2 50 E7
BLKHTH/ROWR B65 104 A4
BRLYHL DY5 102 B1
CNCK/NC WS11 12 D8
HEDN WS12 17 K1
LOZ/NWT B19 88 F6
NUN CV11 99 G3
NUNW/HART CV10 98 C2
OLDBY B69 86 E6
RLSN CV32 206 D5
STRBR DY8 101 K4
TAM/AM/WIL B77 46 C2
WBROM B70 68 D8
WLNHL WV13 51 L4
WSLW WS2 4 E1
John St North HHTH/SAND B71 68 F8
John Thwaites Cl
RUGBYS/DCH CV22 186 E3
John Wesley Wy
DARL/WED WS10 68 E4
Joiners Cft HIA/OLT B92 128 C5
Joinings Bank
LGLYGN/QTN B68 104 F1
Jonathan Rd COVE CV2 135 K5
Jones Field Crs WOLV WV1 50 F3
Jones' La BNTWD WS7 19 K6
Jones Rd RCOVN/BALC/EX CV7 116 E4
SHHTH WV12 38 B4
WOLVN WV10 36 A7
Jones's La GTWY WS6 24 F4
Jones Wood Cl
WALM/CURD B76 73 K6
Jonkel Av TAM/AM/WIL B77 46 D8
Jonquil Cl ERDW/GRVHL B23 72 A6
Jordan Cl KIDDW DY11 137 L7
KNWTH CV8 197 M3
MGN/WHC B75 56 F4
SMTHWK B66 87 M8
Jordan Leys TPTN/OCK DY4 67 M8
Jordan Pl BILS/COS WV14 67 J2
Jordan Rd MGN/WHC B75 56 F4
Jordans Cl REDW B97 202 B7
The Jordans COVW CV5 154 A1
Jordan Wy ALDR WS9 40 F4
Jordan Well COV CV1 9 G5
Jorden's Wk BEWD DY12 163 G1
Joseph Creighton Cl
COVS CV3 156 C6
Joseph Dewsbury Cl
BNTWD WS7 18 C5
Joseph Luckman Rd
BDWTH CV12 116 E1
Joseph St OLDBY B69 86 D7
Joshua Cl TLHL/CAN CV4 153 L3
Josiah Houses BILS/COS WV14 * 67 G5
Josiah Rd NFLD/LBR B31 144 B3
Jowett TAM/AM/WIL B77 46 B3
Jowett's La HHTH/SAND B71 68 F5
Joyberry Dr STRBR DY8 119 K2
Joyce Pool WWCK CV34 205 J6
Joyce Wy RUGBYS/DCH CV22 185 L5
Joynson St DARL/WED WS10 52 C8
Jubilee Av HHTH/SAND B71 68 F6
REDW B97 202 B6
Jubilee Cl BLOX/PEL WS3 39 J7
GTWY WS6 24 D4
Jubilee Ct NFLD/LBR B31 144 F4
Jubilee Crs COVN CV6 133 M5
Jubilee Dr North KIDDW DY11 163 M3
Jubilee Dr South KIDDW DY11 163 M3
Jubilee Gdns ERDW/GRVHL B23 71 M6
Jubilee Rd BILS/COS WV14 67 L1
RBRY B45 143 J3
TPTN/OCK DY4 67 L6
Jubilee St HHTH/SAND B71 69 H6
RUGBYN/HIL CV21 186 C2
Jubilee Ter BDWTH CV12 * 116 F1
Judd Cl BDWTH CV12 116 D2
Judds La COVN CV6 134 C1
Judge Cl OLDBY B69 86 E6
RRUGBY CV23 159 L8
Judge Rd BRLYHL DY5 102 D6
Judith Wy RUGBYS/DCH CV22 185 L5
Juggins La HOCK/TIA B94 172 F6
Julia Av ERDE/BCHGN B24 91 K1
Julia Gdns HHTH/SAND B71 69 K5
Julian Cl BRGRVW B61 168 E5
COVE CV2 135 K5
GTWY WS6 24 E2
WOLV WV1 50 F3
Julian Rd WOLV WV1 50 F3
Julie Cft BILS/COS WV14 67 J4
Juliet Cl NUN CV11 99 L4
Juliet Dr RUGBYS/DCH CV22 186 B7
Juliet Rd RMSLY B62 122 C1
Julius Dr CSHL/WTROR B46 93 K4
Junction One
RUGBYN/HIL CV21 * 160 E7
Junction Rd BKHL/PFLD WV2 50 F6
BRGRVW B61 191 J2
HDSW B21 88 A5
STRBR DY8 101 J5
Junction St COV CV1 8 D6
DUDS DY2 84 F5
OLDBY B69 86 C4
WSL WS1 4 D8
Junction St South OLDBY B69 86 E8
The Junction STRBR DY8 101 J5
June Crs TAM/AM/WIL B77 32 C8
June Cft
LGN/SDN/BHAMAIR B26 110 B8
Junewood Cl
RUGBYN/HIL CV21 161 H6
Juniper TAM/AM/WIL B77 46 E1
Juniper Cl ACGN B27 108 F8
BDWTH CV12 116 B3
BNTWD WS7 18 E7
HEDN WS12 13 L7
WALM/CURD B76 73 K2
Juniper Dr COVW CV5 132 D8
DSYBK/YTR WS5 69 M1
WALM/CURD B76 73 L6
Juniper Ri HALE B63 103 G8
Juno Dr WWCK CV34 206 D8
Jury Rd BRLYHL DY5 102 D6
Jury St WWCK CV34 205 J7
Jutland Rd MOS/BIL B13 125 M6

K

Kalfs Dr RUGBYS/DCH CV22 185 M5
Kanzan Rd COVE CV2 135 G1
Kareen Gv COVS CV3 157 G6
Karen Cl NUNW/HART CV10 80 C6
Karen Wy BRLYHL DY5 102 B5
Karlingford Cl COVW CV5 154 B5
Katherine Rd SMTHWKW B67 105 K3
Kathleen Av BDWTH CV12 116 C4
Kathleen Rd CSCFLD/WYGN B72 73 G1
YDLY B25 109 G6
Katie Rd SLYOAK B29 124 C4
Katmandu Rd BRGRVE B60 192 A4
Katrine Cl NUNW/HART CV10 80 A8
Katrine Rd STRPT DY13 163 J7
Katsura Cl FOAKS/STRLY B74 55 K7
Kay Cl RUGBYN/HIL CV21 161 G6
Kayne Cl KGSWFD DY6 83 G6
Kaysbrook Dr RRUGBY CV23 183 L7
Kean Cl LICH WS13 20 C3
Keanscott Dr
LGLYGN/QTN B68 105 G1
Keasdon Gv WLNHL WV13 52 A2
Keating Gdns MGN/WHC B75 56 E1
Keats Av CNCK/NC WS11 12 C8
SMHTH B10 108 B6
Keats Cl CRTAM B79 31 K5
FOAKS/STRLY B74 42 D7
NUNW/HART CV10 79 L8
SEDG DY3 65 L8
STRBR DY8 101 L5
Keats Dr BILS/COS WV14 67 H3
Keats Gv ACGN B27 126 F4
WOLVN WV10 36 E5
Keats Pl KIDD DY10 138 F7
Keats Rd BLOX/PEL WS3 39 J6
COVE CV2 156 B3
SHHTH WV12 38 C6
WOLVN WV10 36 E4
Keble Cl BNTWD WS7 19 G6
CNCK/NC WS11 16 C5
Keble Gv
LGN/SDN/BHAMAIR B26 109 M7
WSL WS1 5 K9
Keble Wk CRTAM B79 31 L7
Kebull Gn TLHL/CAN CV4 153 J5
Kedleston Cl BLOX/PEL WS3 * 38 E2
Kedleston Rd HLGN/YWD B28 126 D7
Keel Dr MOS/BIL B13 126 B4
Keele Cl REDE B98 195 H7
Keeley St BORD B9 107 M3
Keeling Dr CNCK/NC WS11 15 M4
Keelinge St TPTN/OCK DY4 67 M8
Keeling Rd KNWTH CV8 179 M8
Keenan Dr BDWTH CV12 116 B4
Keen St SMTHWK B66 106 A1
Keepers Cl ALDR WS9 40 D2
BNTWD WS7 18 E7
CSHL/WTROR B46 111 L1
KGSWFD DY6 82 F5
LICHS WS14 21 J6
WSNGN B18 88 D8
Keepers Gate Cl
FOAKS/STRLY B74 57 G6
Keepers La CDSL WV8 34 E4
DUNHL/THL/PER WV6 34 E5
Keepers Rd FOAKS/STRLY B74 42 A8
Keepers Wk BDWTH CV12 * 116 B4
Keer Ct BORD B9 * 107 M2
Kegworth Cl COVN CV6 134 E1
Kegworth Rd
ERDW/GRVHL B23 90 A3
Keir Cl RLSN CV32 206 E3
Keir Pl STRBR DY8 101 J5
Keir Rd DARL/WED WS10 69 G3
Keith Rd RLSN CV32 206 F1
Keith Winter Cl BRGRVW B61 168 D7
Kelby Cl NFLD/LBR B31 144 C2
Kelby Rd NFLD/LBR B31 144 C1
Keldy Cl DUNHL/THL/PER WV6 35 K8
Kele Rd TLHL/CAN CV4 153 K6
Kelfield Av HRBN B17 123 M1
Kelia Dr SMTHWKW B67 87 K7
Kellett Rd VAUX/NECH B7 7 L1
Kelling Cl BRLYHL DY5 * 102 A5
Kellington Cl WASH/WDE B8 108 D1
Kelmarsh Dr SOLH B91 148 F4
Kelmscote Rd COVN CV6 133 K5
Kelmscott Rd HRBN B17 105 L6
Kelsall Cl WOLV WV1 50 F3
Kelsall Cft CBHAMW B1 6 A4
Kelsey Cl NUN CV11 99 J2
VAUX/NECH B7 * 107 M1
Kelsey La RCOVN/BALC/EX CV7 152 A8
Kelsey's Cl KNWTH CV8 183 K2
Kelso Gdns
DUNHL/THL/PER WV6 48 B1
Kelsull Cft
CHWD/FDBR/MGN B37 110 E3
Kelton Ct EDG B15 106 E6
Kelvedon Gv SOLH B91 149 G1
Kelverdale Gv
ALE/KHTH/YWD B14 146 A1
Kelverley Gv HHTH/SAND B71 69 L4
Kelvin Av COVE CV2 135 H8
Kelvin Cl KIDDW DY11 137 L5
Kelvin Dr CNCK/NC WS11 16 E2
Kelvin Pl WSLW WS2 38 F7
Kelvin Rd NFLD/LBR B31 144 E4
RLSN CV32 198 F8
WSLW WS2 38 E7
Kelvin Wy WBROM B70 87 G4
Kelway COVS CV3 156 E3
Kelway Av GTB/HAM B43 70 F2
Kelwood Dr HALE B63 103 K8
Kelynmead Rd STETCH B33 109 L3
Kemberton Cl BDMR/CCFT WV3 49 G4
Kemberton Rd
BDMR/CCFT WV3 49 G4
SLYOAK B29 123 L3
Kemble Cl SHHTH WV12 52 B1
Kemble Cft DIG/EDG B5 107 J6
Kemble Dr CVALE B35 91 L2
Kemelstowe Crs HALE B63 121 G5
Kemerton Wy SHLY B90 148 D8
Kemp Cl WWCK CV34 205 L6
Kempe Rd STETCH B33 109 L1
Kempley Av COVE CV2 156 A3
Kempsey Cl HALE B63 121 J1
HIA/OLT B92 127 K2
OLDBY B69 104 B1
REDE B98 202 F6
Kempsey Covert
HWK/WKHTH B38 145 J6
Kempsford Cl REDE B98 202 D7
Kemps Green Rd
RCOVN/BALC/EX CV7 151 M7
Kempson Av
CSCFLD/WYGN B72 73 G4
HHTH/SAND B71 68 F8
Kempson Rd CBROM B36 91 K5
PENK ST19 10 D4
Kempsons Gv BILS/COS WV14 66 F2
Kempthorne Av WOLVN WV10 36 C4
Kempthorne Gdns
BLOX/PEL WS3 38 E3
Kempthorne Rd
BILS/COS WV14 51 K7
Kempton Cl HEDN WS12 13 L7
Kempton Ct BRGRVW B61 168 E4
Kempton Crs RLSN CV32 207 G1
Kempton Dr GTWY WS6 24 D3
TAM/AM/WIL B77 60 B1
Kempton Park Rd CBROM B36 91 H5
Kempton Wy STRBR DY8 119 J2
Kemsey Dr BILS/COS WV14 67 K1
Kemshead Av NFLD/LBR B31 144 C5
Kemsley Rd
ALE/KHTH/YWD B14 146 D3
Kem St NUN CV11 99 J3
Kenchester Cl REDE B98 203 K3
Kendal Av CSHL/WTROR B46 93 K6
RBRY B45 143 M6
RLSN CV32 206 A3
Kendal Cl BRGRVE B60 191 M4
DUNHL/THL/PER WV6 35 K7
NUN CV11 81 L7
REDE B98 203 L2
Kendal Ct ALDR WS9 * 40 D1
CNCK/NC WS11 15 M5
Kendal Dr RBRY B45 170 B4
Kendal End Rd RBRY B45 170 A3
Kendal Gv HIA/OLT B92 128 D5
Kendall Ri KGSWFD DY6 83 K8
Kendal Ri COVW CV5 154 A1
DUNHL/THL/PER WV6 35 K7
LGLYGN/QTN B68 104 F2
Kendal Rise Rd RBRY B45 143 M6
Kendal Rd SPARK B11 107 M6
Kendlewood Rd KIDD DY10 138 F4
Kendon Av COVN CV6 133 J7
Kendrick Av BKDE/SHDE B34 110 B1
Kendrick Cl COVN CV6 134 E1
HIA/OLT B92 128 D7
Kendrick Pl BILS/COS WV14 67 L1
Kendrick Rd BILS/COS WV14 67 L1
WALM/CURD B76 73 K8
WOLVN WV10 36 C7
Kendricks Rd DARL/WED WS10 52 D6
Kendrick St DARL/WED WS10 68 E2
Kenelm Ct RMSLY B62 121 L8
Kenelm Rd BILS/COS WV14 67 G4
LGLYGN/QTN B68 104 E2
SCFLD/BOLD B73 72 F1
SMHTH B10 108 C5
Kenilworth Cl FOAKS/STRLY B74 56 E5
PENK ST19 10 E5
RCOVN/BALC/EX CV7 151 L7
REDW B97 202 B7
STRBR DY8 101 H3
TPTN/OCK DY4 85 H1
Kenilworth Ct DUDN DY1 84 D6
LDYWD/EDGR B16 * 106 D5
Kenilworth Crs
ETTPK/GDPK/PENN WV4 66 C1
WSLW WS2 52 E1
Kenilworth Dr CNCK/NC WS11 16 B1
KIDD DY10 164 C3
NUN CV11 98 E2
Kenilworth Rd
BFLD/HDSWWD B20 89 J4
COVW CV5 154 E6
DOR/KN B93 150 A7
DUNHL/THL/PER WV6 48 D1
HIA/OLT B92 151 K2
KNWTH CV8 178 C3
LGLYGN/QTN B68 105 H5
LICHS WS14 20 F7
RCOVN/BALC/EX CV7 151 L4
RLSN CV32 206 D3
TAM/AM/WIL B77 46 C1
TLHL/CAN CV4 180 A4
Kenilworth St RLSN CV32 206 D5
Kenley Gv BVILLE B30 145 L3
Kenley Wy SOLH B91 148 B1
Kenmare Wy WNSFLD WV11 51 G1
Kenmore Av HEDN WS12 12 D6
Kenmure Rd STETCH B33 110 A6
Kennan Av RLSS CV31 206 D7
Kennedy Cl KIDD DY10 164 C2
TAM/AM/WIL B77 46 A4
Kennedy Crs DARL/WED WS10 52 A6
SEDG DY3 84 B1
Kennedy Cft
LGN/SDN/BHAMAIR B26 109 L6
Kennedy Dr
RUGBYS/DCH CV22 186 A3
Kennedy Gv BVILLE B30 124 F7
Kennedy Rd WOLVN WV10 3 H3
Kennedy Sq RLSN CV32 206 E4
Kenneggy Ms SLYOAK B29 124 D3
Kennel La ATHST CV9 63 M6
Kennerley Rd YDLY B25 109 H7
Kennet TAM/AM/WIL B77 46 B4
Kennet Cl BRWNH WS8 26 A3
COVE CV2 135 G5
Kennet Gv CBROM B36 92 D5
Kenneth Gv ERDW/GRVHL B23 71 L8
Kennford Cl
BLKHTH/ROWR B65 86 A7
Kennington Rd WOLVN WV10 36 D8
Kenpas Hwy COVS CV3 154 D8
Kenrick Cft CVALE B35 91 K3
Kenrick Wy WBROM B70 87 J5
Kensington Ct
NUNW/HART CV10 80 A7
Kensington Dr CRTAM B79 31 M6
FOAKS/STRLY B74 42 D8
Kensington Gdns STRBR DY8 101 G4
Kensington Rd COVW CV5 8 A7
SHHTH WV12 37 M6
SLYOAK B29 124 E4
Kensington St LOZ/NWT B19 89 H7
Kenswick Dr HALE B63 121 L3
Kent Av POL/KGSB/FAZ B78 45 L4
WSLW WS2 52 F2
Kent Cl ALDR WS9 40 F4
COVS CV3 155 J7
HHTH/SAND B71 68 F6
KIDD DY10 164 C2
WSLW WS2 39 J8
Kenthurst Cl COVW CV5 153 G1
Kentish Rd HDSW B21 88 A5
Kentmere Cl COVE CV2 135 J3
PENK ST19 10 E4
Kentmere Rd BRGRVE B60 191 M4
Kenton Av
DUNHL/THL/PER WV6 49 K1
Kent Pl DUDS DY2 84 E7
HEDN WS12 17 K4
Kent Rd BKHL/PFLD WV2 50 C6
DARL/WED WS10 69 G2
RBRY B45 143 K4
RMSLY B62 104 C7
STRBR DY8 101 H5
WSLW WS2 52 D2
Kent's Cl HIA/OLT B92 127 K2
Kent St DIG/EDG B5 7 G9
SEDG DY3 66 C8
WSLW WS2 39 J8
Kent St North WSNGN B18 88 D8
The Kent RUGBYN/HIL CV21 187 L4
Kentwell CRTAM B79 31 H6
Kenward Cft HRBN B17 105 K6
Kenway HLYWD B47 146 E6
Kenwick Rd HRBN B17 123 M1
Kenwood Rd BORD B9 108 F2
Kenyon Cl BRGRVE B60 191 K4
STRBR DY8 101 L7
Kenyon St CBHAMNW B3 6 D2
Kepler CRTAM B79 31 J6
Keppel Cl RUGBYS/DCH CV22 186 A4
Keppel St COV CV1 134 C8
Kerby Rd ERDW/GRVHL B23 90 A1
Keresley Brook Rd COVN CV6 133 K3
Keresley Cl COVN CV6 133 K3
SOLH B91 128 A8
Keresley Green Rd COVN CV6 133 K4
Keresley Gv SLYOAK B29 123 K3
Keresley Rd COVN CV6 133 K4
Kernthorpe Rd
ALE/KHTH/YWD B14 146 A1
Kerr Dr TPTN/OCK DY4 67 J5
Kerria Rd TAM/AM/WIL B77 46 F1
Kerridge Cl COVEN WV9 35 L3
Kerr La SHLY B90 147 L7
Kerris Wy COVS CV3 156 E4
Kerry Cl BRLYHL DY5 102 A1
NFLD/LBR B31 123 K7
Kerry Croft Cl REDW B97 202 C8
Kerry Hl BRGRVE B60 191 J7
Kersley Gdns WNSFLD WV11 37 K7
Kerswell Cl REDW B97 193 M8
Kerswell Dr SHLY B90 148 E8
Kesterton Rd
FOAKS/STRLY B74 42 C8
Kesteven Cl EDG B15 106 F7
Kesteven Rd HHTH/SAND B71 69 G6
Keston Rd KGSTG B44 71 K1
Kestrel TAM/AM/WIL B77 46 E7
Kestrel Av YDLY B25 108 F5
Kestrel Cl CVALE B35 91 M2
ERDW/GRVHL B23 72 B7
KIDD DY10 164 C2
Kestrel Cft COVS CV3 156 D5
Kestrel Dr FOAKS/STRLY B74 42 D8
Kestrel Gv BVILLE B30 124 B5
HEDN WS12 17 G4
SHHTH WV12 38 A5
Kestrel Ri
DUNHL/THL/PER WV6 35 K6
Kestrel Rd DUDN DY1 84 E5
HALE B63 102 F6
LGLYGN/QTN B68 104 D3
Kestrel Vw BRGRVW B61 168 F6
Kestrel Wy GTWY WS6 24 A3
Keswick Cl NUN CV11 81 L7
Keswick Dr KGSWFD DY6 83 H7
RUGBYN/HIL CV21 161 G5
Keswick Gn RLSN CV32 206 B4
Keswick Gv FOAKS/STRLY B74 55 K3
Keswick Rd HIA/OLT B92 127 K1
Keswick Wk COVE CV2 156 D1
Ketley Cft BHTH/HG B12 107 K6
Ketley Flds KGSWFD DY6 83 L8
Ketley Hill Rd DUDN DY1 84 D5
Ketley Rd KGSWFD DY6 83 K7
Kettlebrook Rd SHLY B90 148 F7
TAM/AM/WIL B77 46 A1
Kettlehouse Rd KGSTG B44 71 K2
Kettlesbank Rd SEDG DY3 * 84 A3
Kettles Wood Dr
RIDG/WDGT B32 122 F3
Kettlewell Cl WWCK CV34 205 J4
Kettlewell Wy
CHWD/FDBR/MGN B37 110 D3
Ketton Gv STETCH B33 110 B6
Keviliok St COVS CV3 155 H7
Kew Cl CHWD/FDBR/MGN B37 110 D2
KNWTH CV8 180 A8
Kew Dr DUDN DY1 84 E3
Kew Gdns STETCH B33 109 J4
Kew Rd RUGBYN/HIL CV21 186 E1
Kewstoke Cl SHHTH WV12 37 M4
Kewstoke Cft NFLD/LBR B31 123 J7
Kewstoke Rd SHHTH WV12 38 A4
Keyes Dr KGSWFD DY6 83 H4
RUGBYS/DCH CV22 186 A3
Key Hl WSNGN B18 88 F8
Key Hill Circ WSNGN B18 88 F8
Key Hill Dr WSNGN B18 89 G8
Keynell Covert BVILLE B30 146 A3
Keynes Dr BILS/COS WV14 51 J7
Keys Cl HEDN WS12 17 G2
Keys Crs HHTH/SAND B71 69 G7
Keyse Rd MGN/WHC B75 57 K6
Keysmith Cl WLNHL WV13 52 A4
Keys Park Rd HEDN WS12 17 G2
Keyte Cl TPTN/OCK DY4 67 L8
The Keyway WLNHL WV13 51 L5
Keyworth Cl TPTN/OCK DY4 67 M8
Khyber Cl DARL/WED WS10 52 A5
Kidd Cft TPTN/OCK DY4 68 A3
Kidderminster Rd BEWD DY12 163 G1
BRGRVW B61 190 B1
KGSWFD DY6 82 E7
KIDD DY10 166 E7
STRBR DY8 119 G6
Kidderminster Rd South
KIDD DY10 140 C2
Kielder Cl DSYBK/YTR WS5 70 A2
HEDN WS12 17 J3
Kielder Dr NUNW/HART CV10 98 C3
Kielder Gdns HAG/WOL DY9 119 M4
Kier's Bridge Cl
TPTN/OCK DY4 85 L2
Kilburn Dr COVW CV5 154 D2
KGSWFD DY6 83 J4
Kilburn Gv KGSTG B44 71 K2
Kilburn Pl DUDS DY2 85 H7
Kilburn Rd KGSTG B44 71 K2
Kilby Av LDYWD/EDGR B16 106 E3
Kilbye Cl TAM/AM/WIL B77 46 D8
Kilby Gv RLSS CV31 207 G8
Kilbys Gv BFLD/HDSWWD B20 88 D3
Kilcote Rd SHLY B90 147 G3
Kildale Cl COV CV1 9 J3
Kilderkin Ct COV CV1 9 H8
Kildwick Wy WWCK CV34 205 J4
Kilmet Wk SMTHWKW B67 * 87 K8
Kilmore Cft CBROM B36 91 J4
Kilmorie Rd ACGN B27 109 G8
CNCK/NC WS11 16 A3
Kiln Cl NUNW/HART CV10 98 C2
RLSN CV32 206 E3
Kiln Cft BLKHTH/ROWR B65 103 L1
Kiln La SHLY B90 173 K1
YDLY B25 108 F7
Kilnsey Gv WWCK CV34 205 J4
Kiln Wy POL/KGSB/FAZ B78 47 K4
Kilpeck Cl REDE B98 203 K3
Kilsby Gv SOLH B91 149 G5
Kilvert Rd DARL/WED WS10 68 F3
Kilworth Rd RUGBYN/HIL CV21 187 M6
Kimberlee Av KIDD DY10 138 F1
Kimberley TAM/AM/WIL B77 46 D6
Kimberley Av WASH/WDE B8 90 C8
Kimberley Cl COVW CV5 * 153 K1
FOAKS/STRLY B74 55 L3
REDE B98 194 F6
Kimberley Pl BILS/COS WV14 66 F6
Kimberley Rd BDWTH CV12 116 F1
HIA/OLT B92 127 L3
KNWTH CV8 181 J3
RUGBYN/HIL CV21 186 F1
SMTHWK B66 87 L6
Kimberley St BDMR/CCFT WV3 2 B7
Kimble Cl COVW CV5 153 M1
Kimble Gv ERDE/BCHGN B24 91 H2
Kimbley Ri HHTH/SAND B71 68 E6
Kimbolton Dr BRGRVE B60 169 L8
Kimpton Cl
ALE/KHTH/YWD B14 146 C3
Kimsan Cft FOAKS/STRLY B74 55 L6
Kinchford Cl SOLH B91 148 F5
Kineton Cl REDE B98 203 H4
Kineton Cft RIDG/WDGT B32 123 H5
Kineton Green Rd
HIA/OLT B92 127 H5
Kineton La HOCK/TIA B94 174 C4
Kineton Ri SEDG DY3 66 A3
Kineton Rd COVE CV2 135 G7
KNWTH CV8 197 M1
RBRY B45 143 J6
SCFLD/BOLD B73 72 C4
Kinfare Dr
DUNHL/THL/PER WV6 48 F1
Kinfare Ri SEDG DY3 84 C1
King Charles Av WSLW WS2 52 C3
King Charles Cl KIDDW DY11 138 A7
King Charles Ct KGSTG B44 71 M3
King Charles Rd RMSLY B62 122 D1
King Edmund St DUDN DY1 84 F3
King Edward Av BRGRVW B61 191 K1
King Edward Rd BRGRVW B61 168 D8
COV CV1 9 K2
MOS/BIL B13 125 K2
NUN CV11 99 H1
RUGBYN/HIL CV21 186 F1
King Edwards Cl
BFLD/HDSWWD B20 * 88 F5
King Edwards Gdns
BFLD/HDSWWD B20 * 88 F6
King Edwards Rd CBHAMW B1 106 E2
King Edward's Rw
BKHL/PFLD WV2 * 2 F9
King Edward's Sq
SCFLD/BOLD B73 57 G8
King Edward St
DARL/WED WS10 52 B8
Kingfield Rd COV CV1 134 B7
SHLY B90 147 G3
Kingfisher TAM/AM/WIL B77 46 E7
Kingfisher Av
NUNW/HART CV10 80 A8
Kingfisher Cl BRWNH WS8 26 C6
LGN/SDN/BHAMAIR B26 109 L7
SEDG DY3 66 A3
Kingfisher Ct ALVE B48 170 E6
Kingfisher Dr CBROM B36 92 E5
HEDN WS12 17 G1
STRBR DY8 119 G1
Kingfisher Gv KIDD DY10 164 F2
SHHTH WV12 37 M5
Kingfisher Rd
ERDW/GRVHL B23 72 A6
Kingfisher Vw BKDE/SHDE B34 91 L8
Kingfisher Wk PENK ST19 10 D5
Kingfisher Wy BVILLE B30 124 B5
King George Av BRGRVW B61 191 K1
King George Cl BRGRVW B61 191 J1
King George Crs
RUSH/SHEL WS4 39 M7
King George Pl
RUSH/SHEL WS4 39 M7
King George's Av BDWTH CV12 98 F8
COVN CV6 134 C3
King George Vi Av WSL WS1 54 A5
Kingham Cl REDE B98 203 L1
SEDG DY3 84 A3
Kingham Covert
ALE/KHTH/YWD B14 146 B3
Kingland Dr RLSN CV32 206 A4
King Richard St COVE CV2 9 L3
Kings Arms La STRPT DY13 188 B6
Kings Av ATHST CV9 63 J5
HEDN WS12 17 G1
OLDBY B69 85 M3
Kingsbridge Rd
NUNW/HART CV10 81 H7
RIDG/WDGT B32 123 H4
Kingsbrook Dr SOLH B91 148 F5
Kingsbury Av ERDE/BCHGN B24 91 H2
Kingsbury Cl RUSH/SHEL WS4 53 M1
WALM/CURD B76 74 B8
Kingsbury Link
POL/KGSB/FAZ B78 * 60 E3
Kingsbury Rd COVN CV6 133 H7
ERDE/BCHGN B24 90 C3
TPTN/OCK DY4 67 L5
WALM/CURD B76 74 A8
Kingsclere Wk BDMR/CCFT WV3 49 G6
Kingscliff Rd SMHTH B10 108 E5
Kings Cl ALE/KHTH/YWD B14 125 G7
STUD B80 * 203 L4
Kingscote Cl REDE B98 195 H6
Kingscote Gv COVS CV3 180 E1
Kingscote Rd DOR/KN B93 175 J3
EDG B15 106 B6
King's Ct
CHWD/FDBR/MGN B37 111 J4
NUN CV11 * 98 F1
STRBR DY8 101 J8
Kings Cft CBROM B36 92 D6
HEDN WS12 17 J1
LGN/SDN/BHAMAIR B26 109 L8

Kingscroft Cl
FOAKS/STRLY B74 55 L5
Kingscroft Rd
FOAKS/STRLY B74 55 L6
Kingsdene Av KGSWFD DY6 101 G1
Kingsdown Av PBAR/PBCH B42 70 D7
Kingsdown Rd BNTWD WS7 18 C4
NFLD/LBR B31 123 J4
Kingsfield Rd
ALE/KHTH/YWD B14 125 J5
Kingsford Cl CBROM B36 92 B4
Kingsford Nouveau
KGSWFD DY6 83 L8
Kingsford Rd COVN CV6 134 A7
Kings Gdn BVILLE B30 145 J1
Kings Gdns BDWTH CV12 117 G3
Kings Green Av
HWK/WKHTH B38 145 K3
Kings Gv COVE CV2 155 M2
Kingshayes Rd ALDR WS9 40 F3
Kingshill Dr HWK/WKHTH B38 145 K3
Kings Hill Fld
DARL/WED WS10 52 C8
King's Hill La COVS CV3 180 D4
King's Hill Rd LICHS WS14 21 G7
Kingsholm Cl COVS CV3 156 F4
Kingshurst RLSS CV31 207 J7
Kingshurst Rd NFLD/LBR B31 144 E2
SHLY B90 147 K4
Kingshurst Wy
CHWD/FDBR/MGN B37 92 D8
Kingsland Av COVW CV5 154 D3
Kingsland Dr DOR/KN B93 175 J2
Kingsland Rd KGSTG B44 71 J1
WOLV WV1 2 C2
Kingslea Rd SOLH B91 148 C3
Kingsleigh Cft MGN/WHC B75 56 F3
Kingsleigh Dr CBROM B36 91 L5
Kingsleigh Rd
BFLD/HDSWWD B20 88 F3
Kingsley Av
DUNHL/THL/PER WV6 48 F1
HEDN WS12 13 G6
REDE B98 202 E2
RUGBYN/HIL CV21 187 J4
Kingsley Bank Wy
LGN/SDN/BHAMAIR B26 109 M6
Kingsley Cl CRTAM B79 31 L7
Kingsley Ct YDLY B25 * 109 J5
Kingsley Crs BDWTH CV12 117 M2
Kingsley Gdns CDSL WV8 34 C2
Kingsley Gv SEDG DY3 65 L8
Kingsley Rd BHTH/HG B12 107 L8
BVILLE B30 145 H1
KGSWFD DY6 83 G8
Kingsley St DUDS DY2 85 G8
WSLW WS2 52 F6
Kingsley Ter COVE CV2 135 J5
Kingsley Wk COVE CV2 135 K5
Kingslow Av
ETTPK/GDPK/PENN WV4 49 H7
Kingsmead Ms COVS CV3 156 A7
King's Meadow HAG/WOL DY9 141 J2
NUNW/HART CV10 97 L2
Kingsmere Cl CVALE B35 91 M3
ERDW/GRVHL B23 90 C3
Kings Mill Cl DARL/WED WS10 52 C8
Kings Newnham La
RRUGBY CV23 158 E6
Kings Newnham Rd
RRUGBY CV23 158 F7
Kingsoak Gdns DUDS DY2 85 J6
Kings Park Dr COVS CV3 156 F4
Kings Rd ALE/KHTH/YWD B14 125 G7
ERDW/GRVHL B23 90 A1
KGSTG B44 71 J2
KIDDW DY11 138 A7
RUSH/SHEL WS4 40 A6
SCFLD/BOLD B73 72 A3
SEDG DY3 66 C5
SPARK B11 108 E8
WOLVN WV10 14 E7
Kings Sq BILS/COS WV14 * 66 E5
Kings Street Prec
DARL/WED WS10 52 B7
Kingstanding Rd KGSTG B44 71 K7
Kings Ter ALE/KHTH/YWD B14 125 G7
Kingsthorpe Rd
ALE/KHTH/YWD B14 146 E2
Kingston Cl CRTAM B79 32 A6
Kingston Ms RLSS CV31 207 G7
Kingston Rd BORD B9 107 M4
COVW CV5 154 D3
MGN/WHC B75 57 K7
Kingston Rw CBHAMW B1 6 C5
Kingston Wy KGSWFD DY6 83 G6
King St ALDR WS9 40 D3
BDWTH CV12 117 G3
BILS/COS WV14 66 E5
BNTWD WS7 18 D8
BRLYHL DY5 102 D5
CRTAM B79 45 M1
DARL/WED WS10 68 C3
DUDS DY2 85 G4
HAG/WOL DY9 120 D1
RLSN CV32 206 E4
RUGBYN/HIL CV21 186 E1
SMTHWK B66 87 M6
SPARK B11 107 L7
STRBR DY8 101 J7
WLNHL WV13 51 M3
WOLV WV1 2 F5
WSL WS1 4 D9
King Street Pas BRLYHL DY5 102 E5
DUDS DY2 85 G4
Kingsway CNCK/NC WS11 16 E1
LGLYGN/QTN B68 104 F6
NUN CV11 98 F1
POL/KGSB/FAZ B78 60 A7
RLSS CV31 206 D7
RUGBYS/DCH CV22 186 E4
STRBR DY8 101 H5
STRPT DY13 163 J6
WOLVN WV10 36 E7
Kingsway Av TPTN/OCK DY4 67 L5
Kingsway Dr
HWK/WKHTH B38 145 K3
Kingsway North ALDR WS9 * 40 C7
Kingsway Rd WOLVN WV10 36 E7
Kingsway South ALDR WS9 * 40 C7
Kingsway Ter WNSFLD WV11 * 37 L1
Kingswear Av
DUNHL/THL/PER WV6 48 D2
Kingswinford Rd DUDN DY1 84 C6
Kingswood Av CNCK/NC WS11 16 A6
RCOVN/BALC/EX CV7 114 F5
Kingswood Cl BVILLE B30 146 C2
COVN CV6 134 B4
HOCK/TIA B94 176 C8
SHLY B90 148 B4
Kingswood Cft VAUX/NECH B7 90 A6
Kingswood Dr BVILLE B30 146 A2
CNCK/NC WS11 17 K8
FOAKS/STRLY B74 71 K1
GTWY WS6 24 E1
Kingswood Gdns
ETTPK/GDPK/PENN WV4 49 K7
Kingswood Rd KGSWFD DY6 101 G1
MOS/BIL B13 125 L1
NFLD/LBR B31 144 D7
NUNW/HART CV10 97 M2
Kingswood Ter YDLY B25 * 108 F6
Kington Cl SHHTH WV12 37 M5
Kington Gdns
CHWD/FDBR/MGN B37 110 D3
Kington Wy STETCH B33 109 J4
King William St COV CV1 9 J2
STRBR DY8 101 K5
Kiniths Crs HHTH/SAND B71 87 J1
Kiniths Wy HHTH/SAND B71 87 J1
RMSLY B62 104 C4
Kinlet Cl BDMR/CCFT WV3 48 E5
COVN CV6 134 A6
REDE B98 203 J2
Kinlet Gv NFLD/LBR B31 145 G3
Kinloch Dr DUDN DY1 84 D2
Kinman Wy RUGBYN/HIL CV21 161 G7
Kinnerley St WSL WS1 5 J5
Kinnersley Cl REDE B98 203 J2
Kinnersley Crs OLDBY B69 86 B8
Kinnerton Crs SLYOAK B29 123 K3
Kinross Av HEDN WS12 12 D6
Kinross Cl NUNW/HART CV10 98 D3
Kinross Crs GTB/HAM B43 70 F1
Kinross Rd RLSN CV32 206 F1
Kinsall Gn TAM/AM/WIL B77 47 G7
Kinsey Gv ALE/KHTH/YWD B14 146 D1
Kinsham Dr SOLH B91 148 F5
Kintore Cft RIDG/WDGT B32 122 F6
Kintyre Cl RBRY B45 143 J4
The Kintyre COVE CV2 135 M6
Kinver Av KIDDW DY11 163 L4
SHHTH WV12 37 M8
Kinver Cl COVE CV2 135 J4
Kinver Crs ALDR WS9 41 G4
Kinver Cft BHTH/HG B12 107 J7
WALM/CURD B76 73 K5
Kinver Dr
ETTPK/GDPK/PENN WV4 49 G8
HAG/WOL DY9 120 A6
Kinver Rd NFLD/LBR B31 145 H3
Kinver St STRBR DY8 101 H4
Kinwalsey La
RCOVN/BALC/EX CV7 113 J7
Kinwarton Cl YDLY B25 109 H7
Kipling Av BILS/COS WV14 66 F4
Kipling Cl NUNW/HART CV10 79 L8
TPTN/OCK DY4 67 L5
Kipling Ri CRTAM B79 31 K5
Kipling Rd COVN CV6 133 K5
NFLD/LBR B31 145 G1
SEDG DY3 65 L8
SHHTH WV12 38 C6
WOLVN WV10 36 B3
Kirby Av WWCK CV34 205 K4
Kirby Cl BILS/COS WV14 67 J2
COV CV1 134 B7
KNWTH CV8 157 K8
Kirby Corner Rd
TLHL/CAN CV4 153 M8
Kirby Dr DUDN DY1 84 C2
Kirby Rd COVW CV5 154 D3
WSNGN B18 88 C7
Kirkby Cl RUGBYN/HIL CV21 161 J7
Kirkby Gn SCFLD/BOLD B73 72 E2
Kirkby Rd RUGBYN/HIL CV21 187 K5
Kirkdale Av COVN CV6 134 B2
Kirkham Gdns BRLYHL DY5 84 A7
Kirkham Gv STETCH B33 109 K1
Kirkham Wy TPTN/OCK DY4 67 L8
Kirkland Wy
POL/KGSB/FAZ B78 44 F5
Kirkside Gv BRWNH WS8 26 D6
Kirkstall Cl BLOX/PEL WS3 38 D3
Kirkstall Crs BLOX/PEL WS3 38 D3
Kirkstone RUGBYN/HIL CV21 161 H6
Kirkstone Ct BRLYHL DY5 101 M5
Kirkstone Crs GTB/HAM B43 70 D7
WMBN WV5 64 D7
Kirkstone Rd BDWTH CV12 116 E3
Kirkstone Wy BRLYHL DY5 101 M5
Kirkwall Rd RIDG/WDGT B32 123 H4
Kirkwood Av ERDW/GRVHL B23 72 D6
Kirstead Gdns
DUNHL/THL/PER WV6 48 F2
Kirtley TAM/AM/WIL B77 46 C3
Kirton Cl COVN CV6 133 K4
Kirton Gv DUNHL/THL/PER WV6 49 G1
SOLH B91 148 E4
STETCH B33 109 L1
Kitchener Rd COVN CV6 134 C4
DUDS DY2 85 K4
SLYOAK B29 124 F4
Kitchener St WSNGN B18 88 B7
Kitchen La WNSFLD WV11 37 J5
Kitebrook Cl REDE B98 203 J1
SHLY B90 148 E6
Kitegreen Cl
CHWD/FDBR/MGN B37 111 H1
Kite La REDW B97 193 L8
Kites Cl WWCK CV34 205 J3
Kites Nest La
RWWCK/WEL CV35 196 A4
Kitsland Rd BKDE/SHDE B34 92 C7
Kitswell Gdns RIDG/WDGT B32 122 E5
Kittermaster Rd
RCOVN/BALC/EX CV7 130 F3
Kittiwake Dr BRLYHL DY5 102 A6
KIDD DY10 164 F2
Kittoe Rd FOAKS/STRLY B74 56 D2
Kitt's Green Rd STETCH B33 109 M2
Kitwell La RIDG/WDGT B32 122 E5
Kitwood Av POL/KGSB/FAZ B78 47 K7
Kitwood Dr HIA/OLT B92 128 B6
Kixley La DOR/KN B93 150 A7
Klevedon Cl NUN CV11 99 L4
Knaresdale Cl BRLYHL DY5 102 A5
Knaves Castle Av BRWNH WS8 26 D3
Knebley Crs NUNW/HART CV10 99 G4
Knebworth Cl KGSTG B44 71 J5
The Knibbs WWCK CV34 * 205 J6
Knight Av COV CV1 9 K7
Knightcote Dr SOLH B91 148 F5
Knightley Cl RLSN CV32 199 J8
Knightley Rd SOLH B91 148 D3
Knightlow Av COVS CV3 156 A8
Knightlow Cl KNWTH CV8 198 A2
Knightlow Rd HRBN B17 105 M5
Knighton Cl FOAKS/STRLY B74 56 D2
Knighton Dr FOAKS/STRLY B74 56 D3
Knighton Rd DUDS DY2 103 H1
FOAKS/STRLY B74 42 B8
HEDN WS12 17 J2
NFLD/LBR B31 145 G1
Knight Rd BNTWD WS7 18 C4
KIDDW DY11 138 A2
Knights Av
DUNHL/THL/PER WV6 35 J7
Knightsbridge Av
BDWTH CV12 98 F8
Knightsbridge Cl
FOAKS/STRLY B74 56 D1
Knightsbridge La SHHTH WV12 37 M7
Knightsbridge Rd
HIA/OLT B92 127 K4
Knights Cl ERDW/GRVHL B23 90 C3
PENK ST19 10 D6
WLNHL WV13 51 M3
Knights Ct
CHWD/FDBR/MGN B37 111 J5
CNCK/NC WS11 25 L1
Knights Crs
DUNHL/THL/PER WV6 35 J6
Knightsfield Cl
SCFLD/BOLD B73 72 A2
Knightsford Cl REDW B97 201 K3
Knights Hl ALDR WS9 54 F2
Knights Rd SPARK B11 126 E1
Knights Templar Wy
TLHL/CAN CV4 153 L4
Knightstone Av WSNGN B18 106 E1
Knights Wood Cl
MGN/WHC B75 57 H6
Knightwick Crs
ERDW/GRVHL B23 72 A8
Knipersley Rd
ERDW/GRVHL B23 72 E7
Knob Hl RRUGBY CV23 183 K7
Knoll Cl BNTWD WS7 18 E8
Knoll Cft ALDR WS9 41 G4
COVS CV3 155 G7
LDYWD/EDGR B16 * 106 E3
SHLY B90 174 B1
Knoll Dr COVS CV3 155 G7
WWCK CV34 205 J3
The Knoll KGSWFD DY6 83 J8
RIDG/WDGT B32 123 G4
Knotting Wy COVS CV3 156 A4
Knottsall La LGLYGN/QTN B68 104 F2
Knotts Farm Rd KGSWFD DY6 101 L1
Knowesley Cl BRGRVE B60 191 M3
Knowlands Rd SHLY B90 148 E6
Knowle Cl RBRY B45 144 B6
REDE B98 195 G7
Knowle Hl ATHST CV9 77 G1
KNWTH CV8 180 A7
Knowle Hill Rd DUDS DY2 102 F1
Knowle La LICHS WS14 28 F3
Knowle Rd
BLKHTH/ROWR B65 103 K1
HIA/OLT B92 150 C3
SPARK B11 126 B2
Knowles Av NUNW/HART CV10 98 A1
Knowles Dr FOAKS/STRLY B74 56 E6
Knowles Rd WOLV WV1 3 L6
Knowles St DARL/WED WS10 68 E2
Knowle Wood Rd DOR/KN B93 175 M3
Knox Crs NUN CV11 81 K6
Knox Rd BKHL/PFLD WV2 50 A7
Knox's Grave La LICHS WS14 29 M6
Knutswood Cl MOS/BIL B13 * 126 B6
Kohima Dr STRBR DY8 101 J8
Kossuth Rd BILS/COS WV14 66 E4
Kurtus TAM/AM/WIL B77 46 B7
Kyle Cl WOLVN WV10 35 M4
Kylemilne Wy STRPT DY13 189 G2
Kyles Wy RIDG/WDGT B32 122 F6
Kynaston Crs CDSL WV8 34 F3
Kyngsford Rd STETCH B33 110 B2
Kynner Wy COVS CV3 156 F5
Kyotts Lake Rd SPARK B11 107 L6
Kyrwicks La SPARK B11 107 L7
Kyter La CBROM B36 91 M5

L

Laburnham Rd KGSWFD DY6 83 J7
Laburnum Av
CHWD/FDBR/MGN B37 92 D7
CNCK/NC WS11 16 B6
COVN CV6 133 K8
CRTAM B79 31 M5
KNWTH CV8 197 L1
SMTHWKW B67 105 J1
Laburnum Cl BDWTH CV12 116 C3
BLOX/PEL WS3 39 K3
CHWD/FDBR/MGN B37 92 D7
CNCK/NC WS11 16 C6
HLYWD B47 146 E8
POL/KGSB/FAZ B78 60 B7
Laburnum Cft OLDBY B69 85 M3
Laburnum Dr WALM/CURD B76 73 L2
Laburnum Gv BNTWD WS7 18 D7
BRGRVW B61 191 K1
KIDDW DY11 137 L5
MOS/BIL B13 * 125 K2
NUNW/HART CV10 80 B7
RUGBYS/DCH CV22 186 C5
WSLW WS2 52 D2
WWCK CV34 205 M4
Laburnum Rd ALDR WS9 40 E2
BVILLE B30 124 D6
DARL/WED WS10 68 F2
DSYBK/YTR WS5 54 A8
DUDN DY1 84 F1
ETTPK/GDPK/PENN WV4 66 C2
TPTN/OCK DY4 67 K6
WOLV WV1 50 F5
Laburnum St BDMR/CCFT WV3 2 B7
STRBR DY8 101 J6
Laburnum Vls SPARK B11 * 108 A8
Laburnum Wy NFLD/LBR B31 144 E4
Lacell Cl WWCK CV34 205 H4
Laches Cl WOLVN WV10 14 B8
Laches La WOLVN WV10 22 C3
Ladbroke Dr WALM/CURD B76 73 K3
Ladbroke Gv ACGN B27 127 G5
Ladbroke Pk WWCK CV34 * 205 J5
Ladbrook Cl REDE B98 202 C6
Ladbrook Gv SEDG DY3 83 L2
Ladbrook Rd COVW CV5 153 L1
SOLH B91 149 G2
Ladbury Gv DSYBK/YTR WS5 69 L1
Ladbury Rd DSYBK/YTR WS5 69 L1
Ladeler Gv STETCH B33 110 B3
Ladies Wk SEDG DY3 66 B5
Lady Bank CRTAM B79 * 45 M1
RIDG/WDGT B32 122 F6
Lady Br CRTAM B79 45 L1
Lady Bracknell Ms
NFLD/LBR B31 145 G1
Lady Byron La DOR/KN B93 149 K6
Ladycroft RLSN CV32 199 J8
Ladyfields Wy COVN CV6 133 M1
Lady Grey's Wk STRBR DY8 101 H8
Ladygrove Cl REDE B98 202 E5
Lady Harriet's La REDE B98 202 D1
Lady La COVN CV6 134 D1
HOCK/TIA B94 173 L3
Ladymead Dr COVN CV6 133 M3
Lady Meadow Cl
POL/KGSB/FAZ B78 45 L2
Ladymoor Rd BILS/COS WV14 67 G3
Ladypool Av SPARK B11 * 107 M7
Ladypool Cl RMSLY B62 122 A1
RUSH/SHEL WS4 39 L8
Ladypool Rd BHTH/HG B12 107 L8
Ladysmith Rd HALE B63 103 G7
Ladysmock RRUGBY CV23 161 H5
Lady Warwick Av
BDWTH CV12 117 G3
Ladywell Cl WMBN WV5 64 E5
Ladywell Wk DIG/EDG B5 7 G7
Ladywood Circ
LDYWD/EDGR B16 106 E3
Ladywood Cl BRLYHL DY5 102 D3
Ladywood Middleway
LDYWD/EDGR B16 106 E3
Ladywood Rd
FOAKS/STRLY B74 56 E5
LDYWD/EDGR B16 106 D4
Laggan Cl NUNW/HART CV10 80 A8
Lagonda TAM/AM/WIL B77 46 B2
Lagoon Rd TAM/AM/WIL B77 46 C7
Lagrange CRTAM B79 31 J7
The Lair POL/KGSB/FAZ B78 47 K5
Lake Av DSYBK/YTR WS5 5 M9
Lake Cl DSYBK/YTR WS5 54 A6
Lakedown Cl
ALE/KHTH/YWD B14 146 C4
Lakefield Cl HLGN/YWD B28 126 F6
Lakefield Rd WNSFLD WV11 37 J8
Lakehouse Gv
HWK/WKHTH B38 145 H2
Lakehouse Rd SCFLD/BOLD B73 72 C5
Lakeland Dr TAM/AM/WIL B77 46 E6
Lakenheath CRTAM B79 32 A6
Laker Cl STRBR DY8 101 L6
Lakes Cl KIDDW DY11 138 A6
Lakes Ct BEWD DY12 162 D2
Lakeside BDWTH CV12 116 E3
CHWD/FDBR/MGN B37 111 J5
FOAKS/STRLY B74 41 M8
REDW B97 193 H6
Lakeside Cl WLNHL WV13 51 J2
Lakeside Ct BRLYHL DY5 101 M5
Lakeside Dr CNCK/NC WS11 17 L7
ERDW/GRVHL B23 71 M8
SHLY B90 148 D6
Lakeside Rd WBROM B70 68 E7
Lakes Rd ERDW/GRVHL B23 71 L7
The Lakes Rd BEWD DY12 162 D2
Lake St SEDG DY3 84 B2
Lake View Cl BVILLE B30 124 C8
Lake View Rd COVW CV5 154 D1
Lakewood Dr RBRY B45 143 M4
Lakey La HLGN/YWD B28 126 E5
Lakin Ct WWCK CV34 205 K5
Lakin Rd WWCK CV34 205 K5
Lambah Cl BILS/COS WV14 51 J6
Lamb Cl BKDE/SHDE B34 92 C8
Lamb Crs WMBN WV5 64 D8
Lambert Cl ERDW/GRVHL B23 72 B7
Lambert Ct KGSWFD DY6 83 H5
Lambert Dr BNTWD WS7 18 E6
Lambert End WBROM B70 86 F2
Lambert Fold DUDS DY2 85 J5
Lambert Rd WOLVN WV10 36 D7
Lambert St WBROM B70 86 F2
Lambeth Cl
CHWD/FDBR/MGN B37 110 F1
COVE CV2 135 J6
Lambeth Rd BILS/COS WV14 50 F6
KGSTG B44 71 J2
Lambourn Crs RLSS CV31 207 G7
Lambourne Cl COVW CV5 153 L1
GTWY WS6 24 D2
LICHS WS14 21 J5
Lambourne Gv
CHWD/FDBR/MGN B37 110 C3
Lambourne Wy BRLYHL DY5 101 M5
CNCK/NC WS11 17 L8
Lambourn Rd
ERDW/GRVHL B23 90 B1
WLNHL WV13 52 B4
Lambscote Cl SHLY B90 147 G3
Lamb St COV CV1 8 E3
Lamerton Cl COVE CV2 135 G7
Lamintone Dr RLSN CV32 206 A3
Lammas Cl HIA/OLT B92 128 A4
Lammas Ct KNWTH CV8 183 L2
Lammas House COVN CV6 * 8 A2
Lammas Rd COVN CV6 154 D1
STRBR DY8 101 G2
Lammermoor Av GTB/HAM B43 70 D3
Lamont Av RIDG/WDGT B32 123 K2
Lamorna Cl BDMR/CCFT WV3 48 F5
NUN CV11 99 K1
Lamp La RCOVN/BALC/EX CV7 96 D7
Lamprey TAM/AM/WIL B77 46 B7
Lanark Cl KGSWFD DY6 83 K8
Lanark Cft CVALE B35 91 K2
Lancaster Av ALDR WS9 40 F5
DARL/WED WS10 69 G2
RBRY B45 143 L5
Lancaster Circ Queensway
CBHAMNE B4 7 H2
Lancaster Cl ATHST CV9 63 J4
BVILLE B30 124 E7
Lancaster Dr CVALE B35 91 M3
Lancaster Gdns
ETTPK/GDPK/PENN WV4 49 J8
Lancaster Pl BLOX/PEL WS3 39 G3
KNWTH CV8 197 J3
Lancaster Rd BEWD DY12 162 D2
BRLYHL DY5 102 A3
RUGBYN/HIL CV21 186 E1
Lancaster St CBHAMNE B4 7 H1
Lance Dr BNTWD WS7 18 C4
Lancelot Cl WASH/WDE B8 108 C2
Lanchester Cl CRTAM B79 31 J6
Lanchester Rd COVN CV6 133 M7
HWK/WKHTH B38 145 L4
Lanchester Wy CBROM B36 92 C4
Lancia Cl COVN CV6 134 F1
Lancut Hl RRUGBY CV23 161 H4
Lander Cl RBRY B45 143 L7
Landgate Rd HDSW B21 88 A3
Land La
CHWD/FDBR/MGN B37 110 E6
Land Oak Dr KIDD DY10 138 F6
Landor Rd DOR/KN B93 149 L7
REDE B98 202 E4
WWCK CV34 205 H5
Landor St BORD B9 107 M2
Landport Rd BKHL/PFLD WV2 3 L8
Landrake Rd KGSWFD DY6 83 K8
Landsdown Pl WSNGN B18 88 E8
Landseer Cl RUGBYN/HIL CV21 187 M5
Landseer Gv GTB/HAM B43 71 H1
Landsgate STRBR DY8 119 L4
Landswood Cl KGSTG B44 71 L4
Landswood Rd
LGLYGN/QTN B68 105 G1
Landywood Gn GTWY WS6 24 C3
Landywood La GTWY WS6 24 B3
Lane Av WSLW WS2 52 F2
Lane Cl WSLW WS2 52 F2
Lane Cft WALM/CURD B76 73 L5
Lane Green Av CDSL WV8 35 G4
Lane Green Rd CDSL WV8 35 G3
Lane Rd
ETTPK/GDPK/PENN WV4 66 E2
Lanes Cl WMBN WV5 64 B8
Lanesfield Dr
ETTPK/GDPK/PENN WV4 66 E1
Laneside COVS CV3 156 C7
Laneside Av FOAKS/STRLY B74 55 K6
Laneside Gdns WSLW WS2 52 E3
Lane St BILS/COS WV14 67 H2
Langbank Av COVS CV3 156 A5
Langcliffe Av WWCK CV34 205 K4
Langcomb Rd SHLY B90 147 L5
Langdale Av COVN CV6 134 B2
Langdale Cl BRWNH WS8 26 C7
RLSN CV32 207 H2
RUGBYN/HIL CV21 161 G6
Langdale Ct TAM/AM/WIL B77 32 E7
Langdale Cft HDSW B21 88 C6
Langdale Dr BILS/COS WV14 51 H6
CNCK/NC WS11 15 M6
NUN CV11 81 L7
Langdale Rd GTB/HAM B43 70 D6
STRPT DY13 188 B4
Langdale Wy HAG/WOL DY9 120 B1
Langdon St BORD B9 107 M3
Langfield Rd DOR/KN B93 149 L6
Langford Av GTB/HAM B43 70 C5
Langford Cl WSL WS1 5 H5
Langford Cft SOLH B91 149 G3
Langford Gv HRBN B17 124 A2
Langham Cl
LGN/SDN/BHAMAIR B26 109 L6
Langham Gn FOAKS/STRLY B74 55 K4
Langholm Dr HEDN WS12 17 J3
KGSTG B44 72 B4
Langland Dr SEDG DY3 66 A5
Langley Av BILS/COS WV14 67 G5
Langley Cl ALDR WS9 40 E2
REDE B98 203 H4
Langley Crs LGLYGN/QTN B68 104 F1
Langley Cft TLHL/CAN CV4 153 K3
Langley Dr CVALE B35 91 L4
Langley Gdns
BDMR/CCFT WV3 49 H6
Langley Green Rd OLDBY B69 104 E1
Langley Gv SMTHTH B10 * 108 B5
Langley Hall Dr MGN/WHC B75 57 M7
Langley Hall Rd HIA/OLT B92 127 G6
MGN/WHC B75 57 M8
Langley Heath Dr
WALM/CURD B76 73 K2
Langley High St OLDBY B69 86 E8
Langley Pkwy MGN/WHC B75 57 K7
Langley Ri HIA/OLT B92 128 B2
Langley Rd
ETTPK/GDPK/PENN WV4 48 C7
LGLYGN/QTN B68 104 E1
SMHTH B10 108 B5
Langleys Rd SLYOAK B29 124 C4
Langlodge Rd COVN CV6 133 M3
Langmead Cl WSLW WS2 52 B2
Langnor Rd COVE CV2 135 G6
Langsett Rd WOLVN WV10 3 J1
Langstone Rd
ALE/KHTH/YWD B14 146 F3
DUDN DY1 84 C4
Langton Cl CBROM B36 92 F7
COVS CV3 156 C5
Langton Pl BILS/COS WV14 51 L7
Langton Rd RUGBYN/HIL CV21 187 J4
WASH/WDE B8 108 C1
Langtree Av SOLH B91 148 F4
Langtree Cl HEDN WS12 17 H4
Langwood Cl TLHL/CAN CV4 153 M6
Langwood Ct CBROM B36 91 M5
Langworth Av ACGN B27 109 G8
Lannacombe Rd
NFLD/LBR B31 144 C7
Lansbury Av DARL/WED WS10 68 A1
Lansbury Dr CNCK/NC WS11 16 C1
Lansbury Gn CDYHTH B64 103 M5
Lansbury Rd CDYHTH B64 103 M5
Lansdale Av HIA/OLT B92 128 D5
Lansdowne Av CDSL WV8 34 C3
Lansdowne Circ RLSN CV32 206 E4
Lansdowne Cl BDWTH CV12 116 E2
BILS/COS WV14 66 E6
DUDS DY2 85 K7
Lansdowne Crs RLSN CV32 * 206 E4
TAM/AM/WIL B77 46 B4
Lansdowne Pl
RUGBYN/HIL CV21 187 H3
Lansdowne Rd BILS/COS WV14 51 J6
ERDW/GRVHL B23 90 D2
HALE B63 121 H3
HDSW B21 88 E6
RLSN CV32 206 E4
RMSLY B62 104 D5
WOLV WV1 2 D3
Lansdowne St COVE CV2 9 L4
RLSN CV32 206 E4
WSNGN B18 106 D1
Lansdown Gn KIDDW DY11 137 M8
Lansdown Pl WSNGN B18 * 88 E8
Lant Cl TLHL/CAN CV4 152 F6
Lantern Rd DUDS DY2 103 G3
Lanthorn Cl LICH WS13 20 E6
Lanton Cl BLOX/PEL WS3 38 E3
Lapal La North RMSLY B62 122 C2
Lapal La South RMSLY B62 122 C2
Lapley Cl WOLV WV1 50 F3
Lapper Av
ETTPK/GDPK/PENN WV4 66 D3
Lapwing TAM/AM/WIL B77 46 E7
Lapwing Cl BRWNH WS8 26 C6
GTWY WS6 24 A4
KIDD DY10 164 F4
Lapwing Cft ERDW/GRVHL B23 72 A6
Lapwing Dr HIA/OLT B92 129 M6
Lapwood Av KGSWFD DY6 83 L8
Lapworth Cl REDE B98 202 D6
Lapworth Dr SCFLD/BOLD B73 72 A2
Lapworth Gv BHTH/HG B12 107 K7
Lapworth Rd COVE CV2 135 G4
Lara Cl HRBN B17 105 M5
Lara Gv TPTN/OCK DY4 85 L3
Larch Av HDSW B21 88 B3
Larch Cl KINVER DY7 118 A2
LICHS WS14 21 J6
RUGBYS/DCH CV22 185 M3
Larch Cft
CHWD/FDBR/MGN B37 110 F3
OLDBY B69 85 M3
Larch Dr NFLD/LBR B31 144 A4
Larches Cottage Gdns
KIDDW DY11 * 164 B2
Larches La BDMR/CCFT WV3 2 A5
Larches Rd KIDDW DY11 164 B2
Larches St SPARK B11 107 L7
The Larches
POL/KGSB/FAZ B78 60 B6
RCOVN/BALC/EX CV7 116 E5

Rainsbrook Av
RUGBYS/DCH CV22 187 J5
Rainsbrook Dr NUN CV11 99 L4
SHLY B90 148 D7
Rainscar TAM/AM/WIL B77 46 F6
Raison Av NUN CV11 81 K5
Rake Hl BNTWD WS7 18 F5
Rake Wy EDG B15 6 B8
Raleigh Cl HDSW B21 87 M4
Raleigh Cft GTB/HAM B43 70 C2
Raleigh Rd BILS/COS WV14 67 K2
BORD B9 108 B3
COVE CV2 155 M2
Raleigh St HHTH/SAND B71 87 G1
WSLW WS2 4 A2
Ralph Crs POL/KGSB/FAZ B78 60 A7
Ralph Rd COVN CV6 133 K8
SHLY B90 148 A1
WASH/WDE B8 108 B1
Ralphs Meadow
RIDG/WDGT B32 123 H3
Ralston Cl BLOX/PEL WS3 38 E1
Ramillies Crs GTWY WS6 24 D4
Ramp Rd
CHWD/FDBR/MGN B37 111 G8
Ramsay Cl HHTH/SAND B71 69 K5
Ramsay Crs COVW CV5 132 F6
Ramsay Rd LGLYGN/QTN B68 105 G4
TPTN/OCK DY4 67 J6
WSLW WS2 38 E8
Ramsden Av NUNW/HART CV10 80 A6
Ramsden Cl SLYOAK B29 123 M6
Ramsden Ct
NUNW/HART CV10 * 80 A6
Ramsden Rd ATHST CV9 63 L6
Ramsey Cl RBRY B45 143 J4
Ramsey Rd RLSS CV31 206 F7
VAUX/NECH B7 90 A6
Ranby Rd COVE CV2 9 L2
Randall Av ALVE B48 170 E7
Randall Cl KGSWFD DY6 101 K1
Randall Rd KNWTH CV8 197 K2
Randle Dr MGN/WHC B75 57 G2
Randle Rd HAG/WOL DY9 120 A1
NUNW/HART CV10 98 B1
Randle St COVN CV6 133 M8
Randolph Cl RLSS CV31 207 G7
Randwick Gv KGSTG B44 71 H4
Ranelagh Rd BKHL/PFLD WV2 50 A7
Ranelagh St RLSS CV31 206 E7
Ranelagh Ter RLSS CV31 206 D7
Range Meadow Cl RLSN CV32 206 A2
Rangeview Cl
FOAKS/STRLY B74 55 K7
Range Wy POL/KGSB/FAZ B78 60 B8
Rangeways Rd KGSWFD DY6 101 K2
KIDDW DY11 137 L5
Rangeworthy Cl REDW B97 202 A6
Rangifer Rd
POL/KGSB/FAZ B78 45 K4
Rangoon Rd HIA/OLT B92 128 C1
Rankine Cl RUGBYN/HIL CV21 160 B6
Ranleigh Av KGSWFD DY6 101 K1
Rann Cl LDYWD/EDGR B16 106 E4
Rannoch Cl BRLYHL DY5 101 M5
STRPT DY13 163 J6
Rannoch Dr NUNW/HART CV10 80 A8
Ranscombe Dr SEDG DY3 84 A3
Ransome Rd
RCOVN/BALC/EX CV7 96 E5
Ransom Rd COVN CV6 134 C5
ERDW/GRVHL B23 90 A1
Ranulf Cft COVS CV3 155 G6
Ranworth Ri
ETTPK/GDPK/PENN WV4 66 B1
Raphael Cl COVW CV5 154 A2
Rashwood Cl HOCK/TIA B94 174 F6
Ratcliffe Av BVILLE B30 146 B2
Ratcliffe Br ATHST CV9 63 K3
Ratcliffe Cl SEDG DY3 66 D6
Ratcliffe Dr WLNHL WV13 51 L5
Ratcliffe La ATHST CV9 63 K1
Ratcliffe Rd ATHST CV9 63 J4
SOLH B91 128 A6
WNSFLD WV11 37 L7
Ratcliffe St ATHST CV9 63 H5
Ratcliff Wk OLDBY B69 * 86 D6
Ratcliff Wy TPTN/OCK DY4 68 A7
Rathbone Cl BILS/COS WV14 51 H8
DIG/EDG B5 107 J6
RCOVN/BALC/EX CV7 115 L7
RUGBYN/HIL CV21 187 L5
Rathbone Rd SMTHWKW B67 105 K3
Rathlin Cl COVEN WV9 35 L2
Rathlin Cft CBROM B36 92 F8
Rathmore Cl STRBR DY8 119 J3
Rathwell Cl COVEN WV9 35 L3
Ratliffe Rd RUGBYS/DCH CV22 186 D6
Rattle Cft STETCH B33 109 J2
Raveloe Dr NUN CV11 99 H4
Ravenall Cl BKDE/SHDE B34 91 M6
Raven Cl GTWY WS6 24 B3
HEDN WS12 12 A6
HEDN WS12 17 J1
Raven Cragg Rd COVW CV5 154 C5
Raven Crs WNSFLD WV11 37 K5
Ravenfield Cl WASH/WDE B8 90 D8
Ravenglass RUGBYN/HIL CV21 161 H6
Ravenhayes La
RIDG/WDGT B32 122 E7
Raven Hays Rd NFLD/LBR B31 144 A3
Ravenhill Dr CDSL WV8 34 E2
Ravenhurst Dr GTB/HAM B43 70 C2
Ravenhurst Ms
ERDW/GRVHL B23 90 C2
Ravenhurst Rd HRBN B17 106 A6
Ravenhurst St BHTH/HG B12 7 L9
Raven Rd DSYBK/YTR WS5 53 M7
Ravens Bank Dr REDE B98 195 H6
Ravensbourne Gv
WLNHL WV13 52 A3
Ravenscroft STRBR DY8 101 G7
Ravenscroft Rd HIA/OLT B92 127 L5
SHHTH WV12 37 M8
Ravensdale Av RLSN CV32 206 A3
Ravensdale Cl DSYBK/YTR WS5 5 L9
Ravensdale Gdns
DSYBK/YTR WS5 53 M7
Ravensdale Rd COVE CV2 156 A2
SMHTH B10 108 D6
Ravenshaw La SOLH B91 149 L1
Ravenshaw Rd
LDYWD/EDGR B16 106 A3
Ravenshaw Wy DOR/KN B93 149 L3
Ravenshill Rd
ALE/KHTH/YWD B14 147 G1
Ravensholme
DUNHL/THL/PER WV6 48 D3
Ravensholst TLHL/CAN CV4 * 154 B7
Ravensitch Wk BRLYHL DY5 102 C4
Ravensmere Rd REDE B98 202 F4
Ravensthorpe Cl COVS CV3 156 C5
Ravenstone TAM/AM/WIL B77 46 F5
Raven St STRPT DY13 188 D2
Ravenswood EDG B15 106 C5
Ravenswood Cl
FOAKS/STRLY B74 56 F5
Ravenswood Dr SOLH B91 148 C4
Ravenswood Hl
CSHL/WTROR B46 93 K6
Raven Wy NUN CV11 99 K3
Rawdon Gv KGSTG B44 71 M5
Rawlings Rd SMTHWKW B67 105 L3
Rawlins Cft CVALE B35 91 M2
Rawlinson Rd RLSN CV32 206 F3
Rawlins St LDYWD/EDGR B16 106 E4
Rawnsley Dr KNWTH CV8 180 A7
Rawnsley Rd HEDN WS12 13 J6
Rawn Vw ATHST CV9 63 K7
Raybolds Bridge Rd WSLW WS2 53 G1
Raybolds Bridge St WSLW WS2 53 G1
Raybon Cft RBRY B45 * 143 L7
Raybould's Fold DUDS DY2 85 G8
Rayford Dr HHTH/SAND B71 69 K3
Raygill TAM/AM/WIL B77 46 F5
Ray Hall La GTB/HAM B43 69 L4
Rayleigh Rd BDMR/CCFT WV3 2 A9
Ray Mercer Wy KIDD DY10 138 D8
Raymond Av PBAR/PBCH B42 70 F7
Raymond Cl COVN CV6 116 D8
WSLW WS2 39 H8
Raymond Gdns WNSFLD WV11 37 J8
Raymond Rd WASH/WDE B8 108 C1
Raymont Gv GTB/HAM B43 70 F1
Rayners Cft
LGN/SDN/BHAMAIR B26 109 K3
Raynor Crs BDWTH CV12 116 B4
Raynor Rd WOLVN WV10 36 D7
Raynsford Wk WWCK CV34 205 H4
Rayson Cl LICH WS13 21 L4
The Raywoods
NUNW/HART CV10 98 D2
Rea Av RBRY B45 143 J5
Reabrook Rd NFLD/LBR B31 144 D5
Rea Cl NFLD/LBR B31 144 E6
Readers Wk GTB/HAM B43 70 D4
Reading Av NUN CV11 81 K5
Reading Cl COVE CV2 134 F2
Read St COV CV1 9 K4
Rea Fordway RBRY B45 143 K4
Reansway Sq
DUNHL/THL/PER WV6 49 L1
Reapers Cl SHHTH WV12 38 B8
Reardon Ct WWCK CV34 205 J4
Reaside Crs
ALE/KHTH/YWD B14 124 F8
Reaside Cft BHTH/HG B12 * 107 J7
Reaside Dr RBRY B45 143 M4
Rea St DIG/EDG B5 7 J8
Rea St South DIG/EDG B5 7 H9
Rea Ter DIG/EDG B5 7 K6
Rea Valley Dr NFLD/LBR B31 144 F3
Reaview Dr SLYOAK B29 124 F3
Reaymer Cl WSLW WS2 38 F7
Reay Nadin Dr SCFLD/BOLD B73 71 M1
Rebecca Dr SLYOAK B29 124 C3
Rebecca Gdns
ETTPK/GDPK/PENN WV4 65 K1
Recreation Rd BRGRVW B61 191 K2
COVN CV6 134 E2
Recreation St DUDS DY2 85 H8
Rectory Av DARL/WED WS10 52 B7
Rectory Cl COVW CV5 133 G7
POL/KGSB/FAZ B78 45 J8
RCOVN/BALC/EX CV7 116 E4
STRBR DY8 119 M2
Rectory Cottages
RCOVN/BALC/EX CV7 * 96 C4
Rectory Dr
RCOVN/BALC/EX CV7 116 E4
Rectory Gdns KIDDW DY11 189 L2
SOLH B91 149 H2
STRBR DY8 119 M2
Rectory Gv WSNGN B18 88 C7
Rectory La CBROM B36 91 L5
COVW CV5 133 G7
KIDDW DY11 189 L2
STRPT DY13 188 B3
Rectory Park Av
MGN/WHC B75 73 J1
Rectory Park Cl MGN/WHC B75 73 J1
Rectory Park Rd
LGN/SDN/BHAMAIR B26 110 A8
Rectory Rd MGN/WHC B75 57 G8
NFLD/LBR B31 144 F2
RCOVN/BALC/EX CV7 96 C4
REDW B97 202 A4
SOLH B91 149 G2
STRBR DY8 119 M2
Rectory St STRBR DY8 101 H2
Redacre Rd SCFLD/BOLD B73 72 D3
Redacres DUNHL/THL/PER WV6 35 J7
Redbank Av ERDW/GRVHL B23 90 A2
Redbourn Rd BLOX/PEL WS3 38 E1
Red Brick Cl CDYHTH B64 103 H6
Redbrook Cl HEDN WS12 17 H4
Redbrook Covert
HWK/WKHTH B38 145 J6
Red Brook Rd WSLW WS2 38 E8
Redbrooks Cl SOLH B91 148 E4
Redburn Dr
ALE/KHTH/YWD B14 146 B3
Redcap Cft COVN CV6 * 134 B1
Redcar Cl BRGRVW B61 168 E4
RLSN CV32 206 F1
Redcar Cft CBROM B36 91 G5
Redcar Rd WOLVN WV10 36 B1
Redcliff TAM/AM/WIL B77 32 D8
Redcliffe Dr WMBN WV5 64 F7
Redcotts Cl WOLVN WV10 36 E6
Redcroft Dr ERDE/BCHGN B24 73 G8
Redcroft Rd DUDS DY2 85 J7
Reddal Hill Rd CDYHTH B64 103 J4
Red Deeps NUN CV11 99 H5
Reddicap Heath Rd
MGN/WHC B75 73 K1
Reddicap Hl WALM/CURD B76 73 H1
Reddicroft SCFLD/BOLD B73 57 G8
Reddings La CSHL/WTROR B46 76 E8
HLGN/YWD B28 126 C3
Reddings Rd MOS/BIL B13 125 H3
The Reddings HLYWD B47 146 E8
Redditch Ringway REDW B97 202 B2
Redditch Rd ALVE B48 170 F5
ALVE B48 194 A3
BRGRVE B60 191 H7
NFLD/LBR B31 145 G7
STUD B80 203 H7
Redesdale Av COVN CV6 133 K8
Redfern Av KNWTH CV8 179 L7
Redfern Cl HIA/OLT B92 127 M4
Redfern Dr BNTWD WS7 18 F8
Redfern Park Wy SPARK B11 108 E8
Redfern Rd SPARK B11 108 E8
Redfly La BRLYHL DY5 84 A7
Redford Cl MOS/BIL B13 125 M3
Redgate Cl HWK/WKHTH B38 145 H3
Redgrave Cl COVE CV2 135 M5
Redhall Rd RIDG/WDGT B32 105 J6
SEDG DY3 84 A3
Red Hl BEWD DY12 162 F3
REDE B98 202 D3
STRBR DY8 119 M1
Redhill Av WMBN WV5 64 E7
Redhill Cl CRTAM B79 31 L6
STRBR DY8 119 M1
Red Hill Cl STUD B80 203 J7
Redhill Furrows RLSS CV31 207 G8
Redhill Gdns NFLD/LBR B31 145 G6
Red Hill Gv HWK/WKHTH B38 145 K6
Redhill La BRGRVW B61 143 G8
Red Hill Pl RMSLY B62 121 L6
Redhill Rd CNCK/NC WS11 16 D1
HWK/WKHTH B38 145 H6
NFLD/LBR B31 144 F5
RRUGBY CV23 185 M1
YDLY B25 108 E7
Red Hill St WOLV WV1 2 F2
Red House Av DARL/WED WS10 68 F2
Red House Cl DOR/KN B93 149 J8
Redhouse La ALDR WS9 40 C8
Red House Park Rd
GTB/HAM B43 70 C3
Redhouse Rd
DUNHL/THL/PER WV6 34 F8
Red House Rd STETCH B33 109 J2
STRPT DY13 188 B5
Redhouse St WSL WS1 4 F9
Redhurst Dr WOLVN WV10 35 M2
Redlake TAM/AM/WIL B77 46 C5
Redlake Dr HAG/WOL DY9 119 M5
Redlake Rd HAG/WOL DY9 119 M4
Redland Cl BRGRVE B60 169 G4
COVE CV2 135 H3
Redland La KNWTH CV8 182 E2
Redland Rd RLSS CV31 206 F8
Redlands Cl SOLH B91 128 B8
Redlands Rd SOLH B91 128 A8
Redlands Wy FOAKS/STRLY B74 55 L4
Red La COVN CV6 134 C8
KNWTH CV8 178 F1
NUNW/HART CV10 97 J6
SEDG DY3 65 M5
WNSFLD WV11 38 A3
Red Leasowes Rd HALE B63 121 K2
Redliff Av CBROM B36 92 B4
Red Lion Av CNCK/NC WS11 25 L1
Red Lion Cl OLDBY B69 85 L4
Red Lion Crs CNCK/NC WS11 25 L1
Red Lion La CNCK/NC WS11 25 L1
Red Lion St ALVE B48 170 F7
REDE B98 202 C1
WOLV WV1 2 E4
Redlock Fld LICHS WS14 20 E8
Red Lodge Dr
RUGBYS/DCH CV22 186 C5
Redmead Cl NFLD/LBR B31 145 G1
Redmoor Gdns
ETTPK/GDPK/PENN WV4 49 L8
Redmoor Rd RUGE WS15 18 D2
Redmoor Wy WALM/CURD B76 74 B7
Rednal Hill La RBRY B45 143 L7
Rednall Dr MGN/WHC B75 57 G2
Rednal Mill Dr RBRY B45 144 A6
Rednal Rd HWK/WKHTH B38 145 G5
Redpine Crest SHHTH WV12 52 B1
Red River Rd WSLW WS2 38 E8
Red Rock Dr CDSL WV8 34 D3
Redruth Cl COVN CV6 134 E5
DSYBK/YTR WS5 54 B6
KGSWFD DY6 83 H5
NUN CV11 99 K1
Redruth Rd DSYBK/YTR WS5 54 B6
Red Sands Rd KIDD DY10 138 C5
Redstart Av KIDD DY10 164 F3
Redstone Cl REDE B98 195 G7
Redstone Dr WNSFLD WV11 37 K8
Redstone Farm Rd
HLGN/YWD B28 126 F7
Redstone La STRPT DY13 188 C5
Redthorne Gv KNWTH CV8 179 M5
Redthorn Gv STETCH B33 109 H2
Redvers Rd BORD B9 108 C4
Redwell Cl TAM/AM/WIL B77 32 B8
Redwing TAM/AM/WIL B77 46 F2
Redwing Cl BNTWD WS7 19 H8
Redwing Ct KIDD DY10 164 E4
Redwing Dr HEDN WS12 12 A6
Redwing Gv ERDW/GRVHL B23 71 M6
Redwood Av DUDN DY1 66 D8
Redwood Cl BVILLE B30 145 J1
FOAKS/STRLY B74 55 K3
Redwood Cft
ALE/KHTH/YWD B14 125 J6
NUNW/HART CV10 98 E3
Redwood Dr BNTWD WS7 18 D5
CNCK/NC WS11 16 D2
OLDBY B69 85 M3
POL/KGSB/FAZ B78 60 B6
Redwood Gdns ACGN B27 108 F8
Redwood Rd BILS/COS WV14 67 H3
BVILLE B30 145 J1
DSYBK/YTR WS5 69 M1
KINVER DY7 118 A2
Redwood Wy SHHTH WV12 37 M5
Reedham Gdns
ETTPK/GDPK/PENN WV4 49 H7
Reedly Rd SHHTH WV12 38 A4
Reedmace TAM/AM/WIL B77 46 A3
Reedmace Cl
HWK/WKHTH B38 145 K5
Reed Mace Dr BRGRVW B61 168 E8
Reedswood Cl WSLW WS2 53 G2
Reedswood Gdns WSLW WS2 53 G2
Reedswood La WSLW WS2 53 G2
Reedswood Wy WSLW WS2 52 E1
Rees Dr COVS CV3 181 G1
WMBN WV5 64 F6
Reeve Ct KIDD DY10 164 E4
Reeve Dr KNWTH CV8 197 L1
Reeve La LICH WS13 20 F5
Reeves Cl TPTN/OCK DY4 85 M3
Reeves Gdns CDSL WV8 34 E1
Reeves Rd
ALE/KHTH/YWD B14 125 G7
Reeves St BLOX/PEL WS3 38 F5
Reform St WBROM B70 87 H2
Regal Cl TAM/AM/WIL B77 46 A5
Regal Cft CBROM B36 90 F5
Regal Dr WSLW WS2 4 B7
Regan Av SHLY B90 147 L4
Regan Crs ERDW/GRVHL B23 72 C7
Regan Dr OLDBY B69 86 B5
Regency Cl BORD B9 108 B4
NUNW/HART CV10 81 H7
Regency Ct COVW CV5 154 D5
WSL WS1 5 K8
Regency Dr COVS CV3 154 D8
HWK/WKHTH B38 145 J3
KNWTH CV8 197 K2
Regency Gdns
ALE/KHTH/YWD B14 147 G2
Regency Ms RLSN CV32 * 206 E5
Regency Wk FOAKS/STRLY B74 42 B8
Regent Av OLDBY B69 85 L4
Regent Cl DIG/EDG B5 107 H7
HALE B63 121 L1
KGSWFD DY6 83 G7
OLDBY B69 85 L5
Regent Ct SMTHWK B66 87 L8
Regent Dr OLDBY B69 85 L4
Regent Gv RLSN CV32 206 D5
Regent Ms BRGRVW B61 * 191 J5
Regent Pde CBHAMW B1 6 C2
Regent Park Rd SMHTH B10 108 A5
Regent Pl CBHAMW B1 6 C2
OLDBY B69 85 M3
RLSS CV31 206 E6
RUGBYN/HIL CV21 186 E1
Regent Rd
ETTPK/GDPK/PENN WV4 49 J8
HDSW B21 88 B5
HRBN B17 106 A7
OLDBY B69 85 L4
Regents Ct BKHL/PFLD WV2 * 2 F7
Regents Park Rd BRGRVE B60 192 A3
Regent St BDWTH CV12 117 G1
BILS/COS WV14 51 H7
BVILLE B30 124 E6
CBHAMW B1 6 C2
CDYHTH B64 103 K3
COV CV1 8 C7
DUDN DY1 67 G7
NUN CV11 99 H1
RLSN CV32 206 C5
RUGBYN/HIL CV21 186 E2
SMTHWK B66 87 L7
TPTN/OCK DY4 67 J5
WLNHL WV13 51 L2
Regents Wy MGN/WHC B75 57 K7
Regiment Ct COVN CV6 133 L4
Regina Av KGSTG B44 71 H5
Regina Cl RBRY B45 143 J4
Regina Crs COVE CV2 135 L6
DUNHL/THL/PER WV6 48 F1
Regina Dr PBAR/PBCH B42 89 H2
RUSH/SHEL WS4 53 L1
Reginald Rd SMTHWKW B67 105 K3
WASH/WDE B8 108 B1
Regis Beeches
DUNHL/THL/PER WV6 * 35 G8
Regis Gdns BLKHTH/ROWR B65 104 A4
Regis Heath Rd
BLKHTH/ROWR B65 104 A3
Regis Rd BLKHTH/ROWR B65 104 A3
DUNHL/THL/PER WV6 34 F8
Regis Wk COVE CV2 135 K6
Reid Av SHHTH WV12 38 B7
Reid Cl BNTWD WS7 19 H7
Reid Rd LGLYGN/QTN B68 105 G4
Reigate Av WASH/WDE B8 109 G1
Reindeer Rd
POL/KGSB/FAZ B78 45 J4
Relay Dr TAM/AM/WIL B77 47 G6
Relko Dr CBROM B36 91 G6
Rembrandt Cl CNCK/NC WS11 17 H3
COVW CV5 154 A2
Remburn Gdns WWCK CV34 205 K5
Remembrance Rd COVS CV3 156 B7
DARL/WED WS10 69 G2
Remington Dr CNCK/NC WS11 16 D5
Remington Pl WSLW WS2 39 G8
Remington Rd WSLW WS2 38 F7
Renaissance Ct COVS CV3 154 E8
Rendermore Cl PENK ST19 10 C6
Rene Rd TAM/AM/WIL B77 32 C8
Renfrew Cl STRBR DY8 101 G2
Renfrew Gdns KIDDW DY11 138 A8
Renfrew Sq CVALE B35 91 M1
Renison Rd BDWTH CV12 116 C4
Rennie Gv RIDG/WDGT B32 105 H8
Rennison Dr WMBN WV5 64 E7
Renolds Cl COVW CV5 154 A3
Renown Av COVW CV5 154 A4
Renown Cl BRLYHL DY5 83 M6
Renton Gv WOLVN WV10 35 L4
Renton Rd WOLVN WV10 35 L4
Repington Av ATHST CV9 63 H3
Repington Rd North
TAM/AM/WIL B77 32 E8
Repington Rd South
TAM/AM/WIL B77 32 E8
Repington Wy MGN/WHC B75 57 M7
Repton Av
DUNHL/THL/PER WV6 48 B2
Repton Cl CNCK/NC WS11 15 M5
Repton Dr COVN CV6 134 F3
Repton Gv BORD B9 108 F2
Repton Rd BORD B9 108 F2
Reservoir Cl WSLW WS2 52 F5
Reservoir Dr CSHL/WTROR B46 94 D3
Reservoir Pas DARL/WED WS10 68 D2
Reservoir Pl WSLW WS2 52 F5
Reservoir Retreat
LDYWD/EDGR B16 106 D4
Reservoir Rd
BLKHTH/ROWR B65 104 B2
ERDW/GRVHL B23 90 B1
HEDN WS12 17 H1
HIA/OLT B92 127 K5
KIDDW DY11 164 A2
LGLYGN/QTN B68 105 G1
RBRY B45 170 A2
RUGBYN/HIL CV21 161 G7
SLYOAK B29 124 A2
Reservoir St WSLW WS2 52 F5
Resolution Wy STRPT DY13 188 F3
Retallack Cl SMTHWK B66 87 M5
Retford Dr WALM/CURD B76 73 J1
Retford Gv YDLY B25 109 G7
Retreat Gdns SEDG DY3 66 C6
The Retreat CDYHTH B64 103 J6
Reuben Av NUNW/HART CV10 79 M7
Revesby Wk VAUX/NECH B7 7 M2
Revival St BLOX/PEL WS3 38 F4
Rex Cl TLHL/CAN CV4 153 H5
Reyde Cl REDW B97 201 K3
Reynard Cl REDW B97 201 K2
Reynards Cl REDW B97 201 K2
SEDG DY3 66 E6
Reynolds Cl LICH WS13 20 F3
RUGBYN/HIL CV21 187 M5
SEDG DY3 82 C3
Reynolds Gv
DUNHL/THL/PER WV6 34 D8
Reynolds Rd BDWTH CV12 116 E1
HDSW B21 88 C6
Reynoldstown Rd CBROM B36 91 G5
Reynolds Wk WNSFLD WV11 37 L5
Rhayader Rd NFLD/LBR B31 123 J8
Rhodes Cl SEDG DY3 83 L1
Rhone Cl SPARK B11 126 A2
Rhoose Cft CVALE B35 91 M3
Rhuddlan Wy KIDD DY10 164 C4
Rhys Thomas Cl SHHTH WV12 52 B1
Rian Ct CDYHTH B64 103 H5
Ribbesford Av WOLVN WV10 35 M5
Ribbesford Cl HALE B63 103 H8
Ribbesford Crs
BILS/COS WV14 67 H4
Ribbesford Dr STRPT DY13 188 C1
Ribbesford Rd STRPT DY13 188 B3
Ribble Cl BDWTH CV12 117 L3
Ribble Rd COVS CV3 9 M6
Ribblesdale TAM/AM/WIL B77 46 F6
Ribblesdale Rd BVILLE B30 124 E6
Ribbonfields NUN CV11 99 H2
Richard Cooper Rd
LICHS WS14 28 D8
Richard Joy Cl COVN CV6 134 A3
Richard Pl DSYBK/YTR WS5 54 A5
Richard Rd DSYBK/YTR WS5 54 A5
Richards Cl
BLKHTH/ROWR B65 104 C1
KNWTH CV8 179 K8
NFLD/LBR B31 144 D7
Richards Gv RLSS CV31 206 E8
Richardson Cl WWCK CV34 205 K4
Richardson Dr STRBR DY8 101 J5
Richardson Wy COVE CV2 135 M5
Richards Rd TPTN/OCK DY4 67 K4
Richards St DARL/WED WS10 52 B6
Richard St VAUX/NECH B7 89 K8
WBROM B70 86 F2
Richard St West WBROM B70 86 F3
Richard Watts Dr
DARL/WED WS10 52 D8
Richard Williams Rd
DARL/WED WS10 68 F3
Richborough Dr DUDN DY1 84 C2
Rich Cl WWCK CV34 205 L6
Riches St DUNHL/THL/PER WV6 49 K2
Richford Gv STETCH B33 110 B3
Richmond Aston Dr
TPTN/OCK DY4 67 L8
Richmond Av BDMR/CCFT WV3 49 K4
BHTH/HG B12 * 107 K8
Richmond Cl
BFLD/HDSWWD B20 88 E3
CNCK/NC WS11 12 E8
CRTAM B79 31 L8
Richmond Cft PBAR/PBCH B42 70 D7
Richmond Dr BDMR/CCFT WV3 49 J4
DUNHL/THL/PER WV6 48 D2
LICHS WS14 21 H6
MGN/WHC B75 57 K7
Richmond Gdns WMBN WV5 64 E8
Richmond Gv STRBR DY8 101 J5
Richmond Hl LGLYGN/QTN B68 87 G8
Richmond Hill Gdns EDG B15 106 C7
Richmond Hl Rd EDG B15 106 C7
Richmond Pk KGSWFD DY6 83 G5
Richmond Pl
ALE/KHTH/YWD B14 125 K5
Richmond Rd ATHST CV9 63 H6
BDMR/CCFT WV3 49 J4
BEWD DY12 162 D2
DUDN DY1 84 F5
HIA/OLT B92 127 J3
HLYWD B47 147 G6
NUN CV11 98 E2
RBRY B45 143 J6
RUGBYN/HIL CV21 187 G3
SCFLD/BOLD B73 56 F7
SEDG DY3 66 C6
SMTHWK B66 105 L3
STETCH B33 109 H3
WSNGN B18 88 F7
Richmond St COVE CV2 155 L2
HALE B63 121 L1
WBROM B70 68 C8
WSL WS1 5 H5
Richmond St South
WBROM B70 68 C8
Richmond Wy
CHWD/FDBR/MGN B37 111 G2
Rickard Cl DOR/KN B93 149 J8
Rickets Cl KIDDW DY11 163 M6
Ricketts Pl BEWD DY12 162 F2
Rickman Dr EDG B15 107 H5
Rickyard Cl
POL/KGSB/FAZ B78 47 L3
SLYOAK B29 123 L7
YDLY B25 109 H4
Rickyard La REDE B98 195 H8
Rickyard Piece
RIDG/WDGT B32 123 J1
The Rickyard RRUGBY CV23 159 K1
Riddfield Rd CBROM B36 91 J5
Ridding Gdns
POL/KGSB/FAZ B78 47 L5
Ridding La DARL/WED WS10 68 D3
Riddings Cl BEWD DY12 137 G8
Riddings Crs BLOX/PEL WS3 39 K1
Riddings Hl
RCOVN/BALC/EX CV7 152 A5
Riddings La ATHST CV9 62 A2
The Riddings ATHST CV9 62 A3
COVW CV5 154 B6
HAG/WOL DY9 120 B3
STETCH B33 109 J1
TAM/AM/WIL B77 32 C8
WALM/CURD B76 73 M5
WOLVN WV10 36 E6
Ridgacre La RIDG/WDGT B32 105 G8
Ridgacre Rd HHTH/SAND B71 68 F7
RIDG/WDGT B32 104 F7
Ridgacre Rd West
RIDG/WDGT B32 104 E7
Ridge Cl MOS/BIL B13 126 A7
WSLW WS2 52 B2
Ridge Ct COVW CV5 132 E7
Ridge Dr RUGBYN/HIL CV21 187 H1
Ridgefield Rd RMSLY B62 104 A5
Ridge Gv HAG/WOL DY9 102 A8
Ridge La NUNW/HART CV10 78 E3
WNSFLD WV11 36 H6
Ridgeley Cl WWCK CV34 205 H3
Ridgemount Dr
HWK/WKHTH B38 145 H6
Ridge Rd KGSWFD DY6 83 G8
Ridge St STRBR DY8 101 G7
Ridgethorpe COVS CV3 156 C8
Ridgewater Cl RBRY B45 143 M7
Ridge Wy ALDR WS9 54 F1
Ridgeway HRBN B17 105 M3
RIDG/WDGT B32 104 E8
SEDG DY3 66 B6
Ridgeway Av COVS CV3 155 G7
RMSLY B62 104 F7
Ridgeway Ct WSLW WS2 52 D4
Ridgeway Dr
ETTPK/GDPK/PENN WV4 65 K2
Ridgeway Rd STRBR DY8 101 K3
TPTN/OCK DY4 67 L5
The Ridgeway BNTWD WS7 18 E8
ERDW/GRVHL B23 71 L8
STRPT DY13 163 K8
WWCK CV34 205 L4
Ridgewood BKDE/SHDE B34 91 M7
Ridgewood Av STRBR DY8 101 G7
Ridgewood Cl RLSN CV32 206 A4
WSL WS1 5 G6
Ridgewood Dr MGN/WHC B75 56 F4
Ridgewood Gdns KGSTG B44 71 K6

Ridgewood Ri
TAM/AM/WIL B77 32 E8
Ridgley Rd TLHL/CAN CV4 153 J5
Ridgmont Cft RIDG/WDGT B32 105 J8
Riding Cl HHTH/SAND B71 69 K6
Ridings Brook Dr
CNCK/NC WS11 16 E3
Ridings La REDE B98 194 F6
Ridings Pk CNCK/NC WS11 * 16 E3
The Ridings CNCK/NC WS11 16 D5
Riding Wy SHHTH WV12 38 B7
Ridley La CSHL/WTROR B46 76 E8
Ridleys Cross STRPT DY13 188 C7
Ridley St CBHAMW B1 6 D8
Ridpool Rd STETCH B33 109 M2
Rifle Range Rd KIDDW DY11 163 M2
Rifle St BILS/COS WV14 66 E5
Rigby Dr CNCK/NC WS11 16 C1
Rigby La BRGRVE B60 191 M5
Rigby St DARL/WED WS10 68 D4
Rigdale Cl COVE CV2 156 C3
Riland Rd MGN/WHC B75 57 H8
Riley TAM/AM/WIL B77 46 C2
Riley Cl KNWTH CV8 198 A1
Riley Crs BDMR/CCFT WV3 49 K7
Riley Dr CBROM B36 92 E4
Riley Rd ALE/KHTH/YWD B14 147 H2
Riley St WLNHL WV13 51 M3
Rilstone Rd RIDG/WDGT B32 105 K8
Rindleford Av
ETTPK/GDPK/PENN WV4 49 G7
Ringhills Rd CDSL WV8 34 F3
Ringinglow Rd KGSTG B44 71 G3
Ringmere Av CBROM B36 91 M5
Ring Rd BNTWD WS7 18 B6
Ring Rd North EDG B15 124 D1
Ring Road St Andrews
WOLV WV1 2 D5
Ring Road St Davids
WOLV WV1 3 H4
Ring Road St Georges
BKHL/PFLD WV2 3 G7
Ring Road St Johns
BKHL/PFLD WV2 2 E7
Ring Road St Marks
BDMR/CCFT WV3 2 D6
Ring Road St Patricks
WOLV WV1 3 G3
Ring Rd South EDG B15 124 D2
Ringswood Rd HIA/OLT B92 127 J1
The Ring YDLY B25 109 G5
Ringway CNCK/NC WS11 16 C4
Ringway Hill Cross COV CV1 8 D3
Ringway Queens COV CV1 8 D6
Ringway Rudge COV CV1 8 D5
Ringway St Johns COV CV1 9 G6
Ringway St Nicholas COV CV1 8 F3
Ringway St Patricks COV CV1 8 E7
Ringway Swanswell COV CV1 9 G2
The Ringway KIDD DY10 138 C7
Ringway Whitefriars COV CV1 9 H4
Ringwood Av ALDR WS9 40 F8
Ringwood Dr RBRY B45 143 L4
Ringwood Hwy COVE CV2 135 J3
Ringwood Rd WOLVN WV10 36 B4
Ripley Cl OLDBY B69 85 K5
Ripley Gv ERDW/GRVHL B23 71 M8
Ripon Cl COVW CV5 132 E5
Ripon Dr HHTH/SAND B71 69 H4
Ripon Rd ALE/KHTH/YWD B14 147 G1
WOLVN WV10 36 A6
WSLW WS2 52 F3
Rippingille Rd GTB/HAM B43 71 G1
Ripple Rd BVILLE B30 124 F6
Risborough Cl COVW CV5 154 A2
Rischale Wy RUSH/SHEL WS4 40 A5
Risdale Cl RLSN CV32 206 A3
Rise Av RBRY B45 143 L6
Riseley Crs DIG/EDG B5 107 H7
The Rise ALVE B48 170 F1
CHWD/FDBR/MGN B37 110 E6
KGSWFD DY6 83 J8
PBAR/PBCH B42 70 E5
Rising Brook
DUNHL/THL/PER WV6 48 F1
Rising La HOCK/TIA B94 176 C8
Rising Rd HOCK/TIA B94 176 A8
Rissington Av SLYOAK B29 124 E5
Ritchie Cl MOS/BIL B13 125 L4
Rivendell Gdns
DUNHL/THL/PER WV6 34 F8
Riverbank Rd WLNHL WV13 52 B3
River Brook Dr BVILLE B30 124 F6
River Cl BDWTH CV12 116 D4
RLSN CV32 206 A5
River Ct COV CV1 * 8 C4
River Dr ATHST CV9 63 H3
Riverdrive CRTAM B79 45 M2
Riverfield Gv TAM/AM/WIL B77 32 B8
Riverford Cft TLHL/CAN CV4 180 B2
River Lee Rd SPARK B11 * 108 C8
Rivermead NUN CV11 98 E1
Rivermead Pk BKDE/SHDE B34 91 L8
Riversdale Rd
ALE/KHTH/YWD B14 147 H2
ATHST CV9 63 K5
Riverside ATHST CV9 63 L6
RLSN CV32 206 C5
Riverside Cl BRGRVE B60 169 G7
COVS CV3 155 K7
Riverside Ct HWK/WKHTH B38 145 H2
Riverside Crs HLGN/YWD B28 147 H1
Riverside Dr SOLH B91 149 J3
STETCH B33 109 H1
Riverside North BEWD DY12 162 F1
Riverslea Rd COVS CV3 156 A4
Riversleigh Dr STRBR DY8 101 J5
Riversley Rd NUN CV11 99 G2
River St DIG/EDG B5 7 L6
River Wk DARL/WED WS10 68 E4
Riverway DARL/WED WS10 68 F3
Riverway Dr BEWD DY12 162 F1
Rivington Cl STRBR DY8 119 J1
Rivington Crs KGSTG B44 72 A4
Roach TAM/AM/WIL B77 46 B7
Roach Cl BRLYHL DY5 84 B8
CHWD/FDBR/MGN B37 111 G2
Roach Crs WNSFLD WV11 * 37 K5
Roach Pool Cft
LDYWD/EDGR B16 106 A3
Road No 1 KIDD DY10 164 C3
Road No 2 KIDD DY10 164 C2
Road No 3 KIDD DY10 164 C3
Roanne Ringway NUN CV11 98 F1
Robbins Ct RUGBYS/DCH CV22 187 K5
Robert Av ERDW/GRVHL B23 72 C7
Robert Cl COVS CV3 182 A1
CRTAM B79 31 K6
Robert Cramb Av
TLHL/CAN CV4 153 K5
Robert Hill Cl
RUGBYN/HIL CV21 187 L4
Robert Rd BFLD/HDSWWD B20 88 F4
RCOVN/BALC/EX CV7 116 D5
TPTN/OCK DY4 67 K7
Roberts Cl ALDR WS9 40 D3
RRUGBY CV23 183 K7
Roberts Green Rd SEDG DY3 84 C1
Roberts La HAG/WOL DY9 119 M5
Robertson Cl RRUGBY CV23 161 L8
Robertson Knoll CBROM B36 91 K6
Robertsons Gdns
VAUX/NECH B7 90 A6
Roberts Rd ACGN B27 127 G2
BLOX/PEL WS3 39 K8
DARL/WED WS10 69 J2
Robert St SEDG DY3 84 C1
Robert Wynd BILS/COS WV14 66 D4
Robeson Cl TPTN/OCK DY4 67 H8
Robey's La POL/KGSB/FAZ B78 33 H8
Robin Cl CBROM B36 92 E5
HEDN WS12 12 A6
KGSWFD DY6 83 L7
Robin Ct KIDD DY10 164 E3
Robin Gv WNSFLD WV11 37 G6
Robin Hood Crs
HLGN/YWD B28 126 C6
Robin Hood Cft
HLGN/YWD B28 126 D8
Robin Hood La
HLGN/YWD B28 126 C6
Robin Hood Rd BRLYHL DY5 102 D3
COVS CV3 156 A7
Robinia TAM/AM/WIL B77 46 E1
Robinia Cl RLSN CV32 206 F3
Robin Rd ERDW/GRVHL B23 90 C1
Robins Cl GTWY WS6 24 B3
STRBR DY8 119 L2
Robins Cft CNCK/NC WS11 16 E4
Robinsfield Dr NFLD/LBR B31 144 E6
Robins La REDW B97 194 A7
Robinson Cl CRTAM B79 31 J6
Robinson Rd BDWTH CV12 116 B5
BNTWD WS7 18 D5
Robinson's Wy
WALM/CURD B76 74 B8
Robins Rd BNTWD WS7 18 B7
Robins Wy NUNW/HART CV10 97 L2
Robotham Cl
RUGBYN/HIL CV21 160 D7
Robottom Cl WSLW WS2 38 F7
Rocester Av WNSFLD WV11 37 J6
Rochdale Wk SMHTH B10 108 A6
Rocheberie Wy
RUGBYS/DCH CV22 186 D5
Roche Rd BLOX/PEL WS3 38 D4
Rochester Av BNTWD WS7 18 E5
Rochester Cl NUN CV11 98 F2
REDW B97 202 A5
Rochester Cft WSLW WS2 52 E1
Rochester Rd COVW CV5 154 C5
NFLD/LBR B31 144 E1
Rochester Wy HEDN WS12 17 G4
The Roche LICH WS13 19 L5
Roche Wy BLOX/PEL WS3 38 D4
Rochford Cl HALE B63 121 K3
RBRY B45 143 J6
WALM/CURD B76 73 L5
WSLW WS2 4 A8
Rochford Ct SHLY B90 148 E7
Rochford Gv
ETTPK/GDPK/PENN WV4 49 H8
Rock Av RBRY B45 144 A6
Rock Cl COVN CV6 134 F4
NUNW/HART CV10 97 K1
Rocken End COVN CV6 134 B5
Rocket Pool Dr
BILS/COS WV14 67 K3
Rockford Cl REDE B98 202 D8
Rockford Rd PBAR/PBCH B42 70 E6
Rock Gv HIA/OLT B92 127 J2
Rock Hl BRGRVW B61 191 H6
LICHS WS14 44 A1
Rockingham Cl
BLOX/PEL WS3 * 38 F4
DOR/KN B93 175 H3
SEDG DY3 83 M2
Rockingham Dr
DUNHL/THL/PER WV6 48 C2
NUN CV11 99 K6
Rockingham Gdns
FOAKS/STRLY B74 56 F7
Rockingham Hall Gdns
HAG/WOL DY9 120 B6
Rockingham Rd YDLY B25 109 H5
Rockland Dr STETCH B33 109 J1
Rockland Gdns WLNHL WV13 51 K5
Rocklands Crs LICH WS13 21 H4
Rocklands Dr MGN/WHC B75 56 F5
Rock La RCOVN/BALC/EX CV7 115 G6
Rockley Gv RBRY B45 143 M6
Rockley Rd BLKHTH/ROWR B65 85 L7
Rockmead Av KGSTG B44 71 K3
Rock Mill La WWCK CV34 206 A5
Rockmoor Cl
CHWD/FDBR/MGN B37 110 C2
Rock Rd BILS/COS WV14 66 D5
HIA/OLT B92 127 J2
Rockrose Gdns WOLVN WV10 22 E6
Rock St SEDG DY3 66 C8
The Rock DUNHL/THL/PER WV6 35 H8
Rockville Rd WASH/WDE B8 108 E1
Rockwell La ALVE B48 194 C1
Rockwood Rd ACGN B27 126 F1
Rocky La AST/WIT B6 89 L7
BRGRVW B61 168 C5
KNWTH CV8 198 B2
PBAR/PBCH B42 70 D7
Rodbaston Dr PENK ST19 10 C8
Rodborough Rd DOR/KN B93 175 J3
LGN/SDN/BHAMAIR B26 109 M7
Rodbourne Rd HRBN B17 124 A2
Roddis Cl ERDW/GRVHL B23 72 B5
Roden Av KIDD DY10 138 D6
Roderick Dr WNSFLD WV11 37 H6
Roderick Rd SPARK B11 108 A8
Rodhouse Cl TLHL/CAN CV4 153 H4
Rodlington Av KGSTG B44 71 K4
Rodman Cl EDG B15 106 B5
Rodney Cl HIA/OLT B92 * 127 M4
LDYWD/EDGR B16 106 E3
RUGBYS/DCH CV22 186 A4
Rodney Rd HIA/OLT B92 127 M4
Rodway Cl BRLYHL DY5 102 B6
ETTPK/GDPK/PENN WV4 66 B2
LOZ/NWT B19 89 H6
Rodway Dr COVW CV5 153 H1
Rodwell Gv KGSTG B44 71 K5
Rodyard Wy COV CV1 9 H8
Roebuck Cl BKDE/SHDE B34 110 C1
Roebuck Gld SHHTH WV12 52 C1
Roebuck La WBROM B70 87 J4
Roebuck Pl BLOX/PEL WS3 39 J7
Roebuck Rd BLOX/PEL WS3 39 J7
Roebuck St WBROM B70 87 K4
Roe Cl WWCK CV34 205 K5
Roedean Cl KGSTG B44 71 M6
Roford Ct SEDG DY3 66 C8
Rogerfield Rd
ERDW/GRVHL B23 72 E7
Rogers Cl WNSFLD WV11 37 L4
Rogers Rd WASH/WDE B8 90 F8
Rokeby Cl WALM/CURD B76 73 J1
Rokeby Rd GTB/HAM B43 70 D3
Rokeby St RUGBYN/HIL CV21 187 G2
Rokewood Cl KGSWFD DY6 83 H4
Rokholt Crs CNCK/NC WS11 16 A4
Roland Av COVN CV6 133 M2
Roland Mt COVN CV6 134 A2
Rolan Dr SHLY B90 147 J5
Roland Rd LOZ/NWT B19 89 G5
Roland Vernon Wy
TPTN/OCK DY4 68 A6
Rolfe St SMTHWK B66 87 L7
Rollason Cl COVN CV6 134 A5
Rollason Rd COVN CV6 133 M5
DUDS DY2 85 H5
ERDE/BCHGN B24 90 E2
Rollasons Yd COVN CV6 * 134 E2
Rollesby Dr WLNHL WV13 51 K5
Rolling Mill Cl DIG/EDG B5 * 107 J6
Rolling Mill Rd
CNCK/NC WS11 25 K2
Rollingmill St WSLW WS2 4 B5
Rollswood Dr SOLH B91 148 D1
Roman Cl BRWNH WS8 26 C3
Roman Ct TAM/AM/WIL B77 46 C6
Roman Gra FOAKS/STRLY B74 42 A8
Roman La FOAKS/STRLY B74 55 M1
Roman Pk FOAKS/STRLY B74 55 M1
Roman Rd COVE CV2 155 M2
FOAKS/STRLY B74 56 A2
LICHS WS14 29 G6
STRBR DY8 119 H1
Roman Vw CNCK/NC WS11 16 D8
Roman Wy
BLKHTH/ROWR B65 104 A2
BRGRVW B61 191 M1
COVS CV3 181 H2
CRTAM B79 31 J6
CSHL/WTROR B46 93 J3
EDG B15 124 B2
LICHS WS14 21 H6
POL/KGSB/FAZ B78 47 L7
RUGBYN/HIL CV21 160 E6
Romany Rd RBRY B45 143 H4
Romany Wy STRBR DY8 119 G2
Roma Rd SPARK B11 108 C8
Romford Cl
LGN/SDN/BHAMAIR B26 109 M7
Romford Rd COVN CV6 133 M3
Romilly Av BFLD/HDSWWD B20 88 F3
Romilly Cl STRBR DY8 101 J7
WALM/CURD B76 73 L1
Romney TAM/AM/WIL B77 46 D5
Romney Cl HLGN/YWD B28 126 D5
Romney Pl RUGBYS/DCH CV22 186 D6
Romney Wy GTB/HAM B43 71 H1
Romsey Av NUNW/HART CV10 81 H5
Romsey Gv WOLVN WV10 36 A2
Romsey Rd WOLVN WV10 36 A2
Romsey Wy BLOX/PEL WS3 38 D2
Romsley Cl HALE B63 121 M3
RBRY B45 143 J5
REDE B98 203 K2
RUSH/SHEL WS4 40 A3
Romsley Rd COVN CV6 134 A7
HAG/WOL DY9 102 A8
LGLYGN/QTN B68 104 F3
RIDG/WDGT B32 122 F5
Romulus Cl BFLD/HDSWWD B20 88 F2
Ronald Gv CBROM B36 92 B4
Ronald Pl BORD B9 108 C3
Ronald Rd BORD B9 108 B3
Ron Davis Cl SMTHWK B66 * 87 M8
Ro-Oak Rd COVN CV6 133 K8
Rood End Rd LGLYGN/QTN B68 87 G7
Rooker Av BKHL/PFLD WV2 50 C7
Rooker Crs BKHL/PFLD WV2 50 D7
Rookery Av BRLYHL DY5 101 L3
ETTPK/GDPK/PENN WV4 66 E2
Rookery Cl REDW B97 202 B4
Rookery La BKHL/PFLD WV2 49 L7
COVN CV6 133 M2
POL/KGSB/FAZ B78 44 A3
Rookery Pk BRLYHL DY5 83 M8
Rookery Ri WMBN WV5 64 F7
Rookery Rd
ETTPK/GDPK/PENN WV4 66 E2
HDSW B21 88 C4
SLYOAK B29 124 D3
WMBN WV5 64 F7
Rookery St WNSFLD WV11 37 G8
The Rookery NUNW/HART CV10 78 D3
RMSLY B62 122 E3
Rooks Meadow HAG/WOL DY9 119 M7
Rooks Nest RRUGBY CV23 158 C2
Rookwood Dr
DUNHL/THL/PER WV6 48 D4
Roosevelt Dr TLHL/CAN CV4 153 J3
Rooth St DARL/WED WS10 68 F1
Roper Cl RUGBYN/HIL CV21 187 L5
Roper Wy SEDG DY3 66 D7
Rosafield Av RMSLY B62 104 D7
Rosalind Av DUDN DY1 66 F7
Rosalind Gv WNSFLD WV11 37 L8
Rosamond St WSL WS1 4 C8
Rosary Rd ERDW/GRVHL B23 90 B2
Rosary Vls SPARK B11 * 108 A8
Rosaville Crs COVW CV5 132 E7
Rose Av ALVE B48 170 E8
COVN CV6 133 K8
KGSWFD DY6 83 K8
LGLYGN/QTN B68 105 G6
Rose Bank Dr BLOX/PEL WS3 * 53 J1
Rosebay Av HWK/WKHTH B38 145 K5
Rose Bay Meadow
CNCK/NC WS11 17 G3
Roseberry Av COVE CV2 134 F4
Roseberry Gdns KIDD DY10 139 G2
Rosebery Rd SMTHWK B66 106 A1
TAM/AM/WIL B77 60 A1
Rosebery St BDMR/CCFT WV3 2 C7
WSNGN B18 106 E1
Rosebury Gv WMBN WV5 64 C7
Rose Cl SMTHWK B66 88 A8
Rose Cottage Dr STRBR DY8 101 H2
Rose Cottages
RUGBYN/HIL CV21 * 186 C2
SLYOAK B29 * 124 D3
Rose Cft KNWTH CV8 179 J7
Rosecroft Rd
LGN/SDN/BHAMAIR B26 110 A7
Rosedale Av ERDW/GRVHL B23 90 C2
SMTHWK B66 88 A8
Rosedale Cl REDW B97 201 L1
Rosedale Gv YDLY B25 109 G5
Rosedale Pl WLNHL WV13 51 L5
Rose Dene STRPT DY13 188 C1
Rosedene Dr
BFLD/HDSWWD B20 88 D3
Rose Dr BRWNH WS8 26 C8
Rosefield Cft AST/WIT B6 89 K6
Rosefield Pl RLSN CV32 206 D5
Rosefield Rd SMTHWKW B67 105 L1
Rosefield St RLSN CV32 206 E5
Rosegreen Cl COVS CV3 155 J7
Rosehall Cl REDE B98 202 C7
SOLH B91 148 D4
Rose Hl ATHST CV9 63 J6
BRLYHL DY5 102 E4
Rosehill HEDN WS12 12 D5
Rose Hl RBRY B45 169 L1
WLNHL WV13 51 L4
Rose Hill Cl CBROM B36 91 M5
Rose Hill Gdns WLNHL WV13 51 L1
Rose Hill Rd HDSW B21 88 E6
Rosehip Cl DSYBK/YTR WS5 69 L2
Rosehip Dr COVE CV2 134 F7
Roseland Av DUDS DY2 85 K4
Roseland Rd KNWTH CV8 197 K3
Roselands Av COVE CV2 135 H5
Roseland Wy EDG B15 6 B8
Rose La BNTWD WS7 19 G6
BRGRVW B61 167 L7
NUN CV11 99 G2
Roseleigh Rd RBRY B45 143 M7
Rosemary Av BILS/COS WV14 51 K7
ETTPK/GDPK/PENN WV4 50 A7
GTWY WS6 24 B2
Rosemary Cl BRWNH WS8 26 B7
TLHL/CAN CV4 153 J2
Rosemary Ct WNSFLD WV11 37 K6
Rosemary Crs DUDN DY1 66 D7
ETTPK/GDPK/PENN WV4 50 A8
Rosemary Crs West
ETTPK/GDPK/PENN WV4 49 M8
Rosemary Dr FOAKS/STRLY B74 56 A2
HEDN WS12 12 B8
Rosemary Hill Rd
FOAKS/STRLY B74 56 A2
Rosemary La STRBR DY8 119 H2
Rosemary Nook
FOAKS/STRLY B74 42 B8
Rosemary Rd GTWY WS6 24 B2
HALE B63 121 H3
KIDD DY10 138 F6
STETCH B33 109 K3
TAM/AM/WIL B77 46 C1
TPTN/OCK DY4 67 L8
Rosemary Wy
NUNW/HART CV10 98 E5
Rosemoor Dr BRLYHL DY5 101 M6
Rosemount Cl COVE CV2 135 J6
Rosemullion Cl
RCOVN/BALC/EX CV7 116 F5
Rosenhurst Dr BEWD DY12 162 E2
Rose Rd CSHL/WTROR B46 93 K5
HRBN B17 106 B7
Rose St BILS/COS WV14 67 K3
Rosetti Cl KIDD DY10 139 G7
Rose Vls YDLY B25 * 108 E6
Roseville Gdns CDSL WV8 34 D1
Roseville Prec
BILS/COS WV14 * 67 G5
Rosewood NUN CV11 99 K4
Rosewood Av
RUGBYS/DCH CV22 186 D5
Rosewood Cl TAM/AM/WIL B77 46 B1
Rosewood Ct TAM/AM/WIL B77 46 B1
Rosewood Crs RLSN CV32 206 F3
Rosewood Dr
ERDW/GRVHL B23 90 B3
RBRY B45 170 A6
SHHTH WV12 37 M5
Rosewood Gdns WNSFLD WV11 37 M2
Rosewood Pk GTWY WS6 24 B3
Rosewood Rd DUDN DY1 66 F8
Roshven Rd BHTH/HG B12 125 L1
Roslin Cl BRGRVE B60 191 M4
Roslin Gv LOZ/NWT B19 89 G6
Roslyn Cl SMTHWK B66 87 L7
Ross BLKHTH/ROWR B65 103 M3
Ross Cl BDMR/CCFT WV3 49 J3
COVW CV5 132 E8
Ross Dr KGSWFD DY6 83 G6
Rosse Ct HIA/OLT B92 128 D5
Rossendale Cl HALE B63 103 H7
Rossendale Wy
NUNW/HART CV10 98 B3
Ross Hts BLKHTH/ROWR B65 103 M2
Rosslyn Av COVN CV6 133 J7
Rosslyn Rd WALM/CURD B76 73 K7
Ross Rd BLOX/PEL WS3 39 K7
Ross Wy NUN CV11 99 M6
Rostrevor Rd SMHTH B10 108 D4
Rosy Cross CRTAM B79 31 M8
Rothay TAM/AM/WIL B77 46 D5
Rothbury Gn HEDN WS12 17 J3
Rotherby Gv
CHWD/FDBR/MGN B37 110 F6
Rotherfield Cl RLSS CV31 206 F6
Rotherfield Rd
LGN/SDN/BHAMAIR B26 109 M5
Rotherham Rd COVN CV6 133 M3
Rotherhams Hl ATHST CV9 61 M5
Rotherhams Oak La
HOCK/TIA B94 174 D7
Rothesay Av TLHL/CAN CV4 153 M3
Rothesay Cl NUNW/HART CV10 98 E3
Rothesay Cft RIDG/WDGT B32 122 F6
Rothesay Dr STRBR DY8 101 G2
Rothesay Gdns
ETTPK/GDPK/PENN WV4 50 C8
Rothesay Wy SHHTH WV12 37 M7
Rothley Dr RUGBYN/HIL CV21 161 J6
Rothwell Dr SOLH B91 127 H8
Rothwell Rd WWCK CV34 205 G4
Rotten Rw LICH WS13 21 G5
Rotton Park Rd
LDYWD/EDGR B16 106 B4
Rotton Park St
LDYWD/EDGR B16 106 D2
Rough Hay Pl DARL/WED WS10 52 A6
Rough Hay Rd
DARL/WED WS10 52 A6
Rough Hill Dr
BLKHTH/ROWR B65 85 K7
REDE B98 202 C8
Rough Hills Rd
BKHL/PFLD WV2 50 D7
Roughknowles Rd
TLHL/CAN CV4 153 H7
Roughlea Av CBROM B36 91 K6
Roughley Dr MGN/WHC B75 57 G3
Roughley Farm Rd
MGN/WHC B75 57 J2
Rough Rd KGSTG B44 71 L2
The Rough REDW B97 202 B5
Rouncil Cl HIA/OLT B92 128 B6
Rouncil La RWWCK/WEL CV35 196 C3
The Roundabout
NFLD/LBR B31 144 B4
Round Av RRUGBY CV23 159 L8
Round Cft WLNHL WV13 51 K3
Round Hl SEDG DY3 66 B3
Round Hill Av HAG/WOL DY9 120 A4
Roundhill Cl WALM/CURD B76 73 J1
Roundhills Rd RMSLY B62 104 D5
Roundhill Ter RMSLY B62 104 C4
Roundhill Wy BRWNH WS8 26 E3
Roundhill Whf KIDDW DY11 164 B1
Round House Rd COVS CV3 155 L5
SEDG DY3 84 C1
Roundlea Cl SHHTH WV12 37 M6
Roundlea Rd NFLD/LBR B31 123 J6
Round Rd ERDE/BCHGN B24 90 F3
Round Saw Cft RBRY B45 143 K5
Rounds Gdns
RUGBYN/HIL CV21 186 D2
Rounds Green Rd OLDBY B69 86 C6
Rounds Hl KNWTH CV8 197 J3
Rounds Hill Rd
BILS/COS WV14 67 H5
Rounds Rd BILS/COS WV14 67 H2
Round St DUDS DY2 85 G7
RUGBYN/HIL CV21 186 D2
Roundway Down
DUNHL/THL/PER WV6 48 C2
Rounton Cl FOAKS/STRLY B74 56 B1
Rousay Cl RBRY B45 143 K4
Rousdon Gv GTB/HAM B43 70 B5
Rover Dr ACGN B27 127 H1
CBROM B36 92 D4
Rover Rd COV CV1 * 8 E5
Rowallan Rd MGN/WHC B75 57 H3
Rowanberry Cl STRPT DY13 188 C1
Rowan Cl BRGRVW B61 191 J3
COVS CV3 157 H6
HLYWD B47 146 F8
LICH WS13 21 H5
POL/KGSB/FAZ B78 60 B7
WALM/CURD B76 73 K3
Rowan Ct BVILLE B30 145 L3
Rowan Crs BDMR/CCFT WV3 49 J6
BILS/COS WV14 66 F4
REDW B97 201 L1
Rowan Dr HLGN/YWD B28 126 E8
RUGBYS/DCH CV22 185 M3
WNSFLD WV11 37 M2
WWCK CV34 205 K5
Rowan Gdns
POL/KGSB/FAZ B78 47 M5
Rowan Gv BNTWD WS7 18 D6
COVE CV2 135 J3
Rowan Ri KGSWFD DY6 83 J7
Rowan Rd CNCK/NC WS11 16 A3
CSCFLD/WYGN B72 73 G3
DSYBK/YTR WS5 69 K1
NUNW/HART CV10 80 A7
REDW B97 201 L1
SEDG DY3 66 C4
The Rowans BDWTH CV12 116 C3
Rowantrees RBRY B45 143 M8
Rowan Wy
CHWD/FDBR/MGN B37 111 G4
NFLD/LBR B31 144 D4
NUNW/HART CV10 79 K5
Roway La OLDBY B69 86 C4
Rowborough Cl
RWWCK/WEL CV35 204 C3
Rowbrook Cl SHLY B90 147 J5
Rowchester Ct CBHAMNE B4 * 7 G3
Rowcroft Covert
ALE/KHTH/YWD B14 146 A2
Rowcroft Rd COVE CV2 135 L7
Rowdale Rd PBAR/PBCH B42 71 G6
Rowden Dr ERDW/GRVHL B23 72 E7
SOLH B91 148 C3
Rowe Cl RUGBYN/HIL CV21 187 M5
Rowena Gdns SEDG DY3 66 A3
Rowheath Rd BVILLE B30 145 K1
Rowington Av
BLKHTH/ROWR B65 104 B2
Rowington Cl COVN CV6 133 H7
Rowington Rd BKDE/SHDE B34 92 C7
Rowington Ter YDLY B25 * 108 F6
Rowland Av POL/KGSB/FAZ B78 47 L2
Rowland Ct
RCOVN/BALC/EX CV7 96 C4
Rowland Gdns WSLW WS2 4 A1
Rowland Hill Av KIDDW DY11 137 M8
Rowland Hill Dr
TPTN/OCK DY4 * 86 A1
Rowlands Av WOLV WV1 50 F3
WSLW WS2 52 C2
Rowlands Cl WSLW WS2 52 C1
Rowlands Crs SOLH B91 127 M5
Rowlands Rd
LGN/SDN/BHAMAIR B26 109 J6
Rowland St RUGBYN/HIL CV21 186 D2
WSLW WS2 4 A1
Rowland Wy ATHST CV9 63 G3
KIDDW DY11 164 C4
Rowley Cl HEDN WS12 12 F5
Rowley Dr COVS CV3 181 L1
Rowley Gv STETCH B33 110 B2
Rowley Hall Av
BLKHTH/ROWR B65 104 A2
Rowley Hill Vw CDYHTH B64 103 K5
Rowley La COVS CV3 182 B1
Rowley Pl RUSH/SHEL WS4 39 M6
Rowley Rd KNWTH CV8 181 K2
Rowley's Green La COVN CV6 134 C1
Rowley St WSL WS1 5 H3
Rowley Vw WBROM B70 86 F2
Rowley Village
BLKHTH/ROWR B65 104 A2
Rowney Cft HLGN/YWD B28 147 J1
Rowney Green La ALVE B48 194 B2
Rowood Dr HIA/OLT B92 128 A6
Rowse Cl RUGBYN/HIL CV21 161 G6
The Row KNWTH CV8 * 181 K3
Rowthorn Cl FOAKS/STRLY B74 55 L6
Rowthorn Dr SHLY B90 148 E7
Rowton Av
DUNHL/THL/PER WV6 48 C2
Rowton Dr FOAKS/STRLY B74 55 K8
Roxall Cl KIDD DY10 140 A3
Roxburgh Cft RLSN CV32 198 F8
Roxburgh Gv GTB/HAM B43 71 G1
Roxburgh Rd NUN CV11 99 J4
SCFLD/BOLD B73 72 E2
Roxby Gdns
DUNHL/THL/PER WV6 35 L8
Royal Cl BLKHTH/ROWR B65 86 A8
BRLYHL DY5 102 A5
Royal Ct RUGBYN/HIL CV21 * 186 D2
Royal Crs COVS CV3 156 A8
Royal Gv ERDW/GRVHL B23 71 M6
Royal Mail St CBHAMW B1 6 E6
Royal Meadow Dr ATHST CV9 63 J3
Royal Oak La BDWTH CV12 116 A6
Royal Oak Rd
BLKHTH/ROWR B65 85 K8
RMSLY B62 122 D1
Royal Oak Yd BDWTH CV12 * 116 F1
Royal Priors RLSN CV32 * 206 D4
Royal Rd CSCFLD/WYGN B72 57 G8
Royal Scot Gv WSL WS1 53 H8
Royal Star Cl STETCH B33 110 A3
Royal Wy TPTN/OCK DY4 85 L3
Royal Worcester Crs
BRGRVE B60 192 A4
Roydon Rd ACGN B27 127 G5

Roylesden Crs
SCFLD/BOLD B73 72 A3
Royston Cha FOAKS/STRLY B74 55 L2
Royston Cl COVS CV3 156 E2
Royston Cft BHTH/HG B12 107 K7
Royston Wy SEDG DY3 66 A5
Rozel Av KIDD DY10 138 F4
Rubens Cl COVW CV5 154 A2
SEDG DY3 66 B8
Rubery Farm Gv RBRY B45 143 K5
Rubery Field Cl RBRY B45 143 L4
Rubery La RBRY B45 143 K4
Rubery La South RBRY B45 143 K4
Rubery St DARL/WED WS10 52 B5
Ruckley Av LOZ/NWT B19 * 89 G6
Ruckley Rd SLYOAK B29 123 L5
Rudd Gdns WOLVN WV10 50 F1
Ruddington Wy LOZ/NWT B19 89 J8
Rudgard Rd COVN CV6 134 E1
Rudge Av WOLV WV1 50 F2
Rudge Cl SHHTH WV12 52 A1
Rudge Cft STETCH B33 109 L1
Rudge Wk WSNGN B18 * 106 E2
Rudgewick Cft AST/WIT B6 89 K7
Rudyard Cl WOLVN WV10 36 C1
Rudyard Gv STETCH B33 109 M2
Rudyngfield Dr STETCH B33 109 K2
Rufford CRTAM B79 31 J7
Rufford Cl ERDW/GRVHL B23 72 B5
Rufford Rd HAG/WOL DY9 120 A1
Rufford St HAG/WOL DY9 102 B7
Rufford Wy ALDR WS9 40 C6
Rugby La RRUGBY CV23 183 L7
Rugby Rd COVS CV3 157 G5
RLSN CV32 199 G8
RLSN CV32 206 B4
RRUGBY CV23 161 K8
RRUGBY CV23 185 M1
STRBR DY8 101 H6
Rugby St WOLV WV1 2 C2
Rugeley Av SHHTH WV12 38 B5
Rugeley Cl TPTN/OCK DY4 67 J8
Rugeley Rd BNTWD WS7 18 D5
HEDN WS12 13 G7
Ruislip Cl CVALE B35 91 L1
Ruiton St SEDG DY3 84 B1
Rumbow HALE B63 121 M1
Rumbow La RMSLY B62 142 B1
Rumbush La HOCK/TIA B94 173 H4
SHLY B90 147 L7
Rumer Hill Rd CNCK/NC WS11 16 C6
Runcorn Cl
CHWD/FDBR/MGN B37 111 G1
REDE B98 202 D5
Runcorn Rd BHTH/HG B12 107 K8
Runnymede Gdns
NUNW/HART CV10 98 D2
Runnymede Dr
RCOVN/BALC/EX CV7 152 A8
Runnymede Rd SPARK B11 126 C2
Rupert Brooke Rd
RUGBYS/DCH CV22 186 C6
Rupert Rd COVN CV6 133 M5
Rupert St BDMR/CCFT WV3 2 A4
VAUX/NECH B7 89 L8
Rushall Cl RUSH/SHEL WS4 53 M1
STRBR DY8 101 J5
Rushall Manor Cl
RUSH/SHEL WS4 53 M1
Rushall Manor Rd
RUSH/SHEL WS4 53 M1
Rushall Rd WOLVN WV10 36 C3
Rushbrook Cl BRWNH WS8 26 C7
HIA/OLT B92 127 J3
Rushbrooke Cl MOS/BIL B13 125 K1
Rushbrooke Dr
SCFLD/BOLD B73 72 A1
Rushbrook Gv
ALE/KHTH/YWD B14 146 A2
Rushbury Cl BILS/COS WV14 50 F8
SHLY B90 148 B1
Rushden Cft KGSTG B44 71 K4
Rushes Ml BLOX/PEL WS3 39 J2
Rushey La SPARK B11 108 E8
Rushford Av WMBN WV5 64 E7
Rushford Cl SHLY B90 148 E6
Rush Gn RIDG/WDGT B32 123 J3
Rush La POL/KGSB/FAZ B78 60 C2
REDE B98 194 F7
TAM/AM/WIL B77 60 B2
Rushleigh Rd SHLY B90 147 J5
Rushmead Gv RBRY B45 143 L6
Rushmere Rd TPTN/OCK DY4 67 L5
Rushmoor Cl FOAKS/STRLY B74 56 F7
Rushmoor Dr COVW CV5 8 A4
Rushmore St RLSS CV31 206 F6
Rushmore Ter RLSS CV31 206 F7
Rushock Cl REDE B98 203 G7
Rushton Cl
RCOVN/BALC/EX CV7 152 A6
Rushwater Cl WMBN WV5 64 C7
Rushwick Gv SHLY B90 148 E7
Rushwood Cl RUSH/SHEL WS4 53 L2
Rushy Piece RIDG/WDGT B32 123 H2
Rusina Ct RLSS CV31 * 206 D7
Ruskin Av BLKHTH/ROWR B65 104 B3
ETTPK/GDPK/PENN WV4 66 D1
KIDD DY10 139 G7
SEDG DY3 65 L8
Ruskin Cl AST/WIT B6 89 K6
NUNW/HART CV10 79 L8
RUGBYS/DCH CV22 186 D7
Ruskin Gv ACGN B27 126 F3
Ruskin Hall Gv AST/WIT B6 89 K6
Ruskin Rd WOLVN WV10 36 D5
Ruskin St HHTH/SAND B71 69 G8
Russell Cft BRGRVE B60 191 L6
Russell Bank Rd
FOAKS/STRLY B74 56 C1
Russell Cl OLDBY B69 86 B3
TAM/AM/WIL B77 46 C7
TPTN/OCK DY4 68 A4
WNSFLD WV11 37 K4
Russell Rd BILS/COS WV14 51 K6
HLGN/YWD B28 126 C3
KIDD DY10 164 D1
MOS/BIL B13 125 H2
Russell's Hall Rd DUDN DY1 84 C4
The Russells MOS/BIL B13 125 H2
Russell St BDMR/CCFT WV3 2 D7
COV CV1 9 G2
DARL/WED WS10 68 D3
DUDN DY1 84 F4
RLSN CV32 206 D4
WLNHL WV13 51 M3
Russell St North COV CV1 * 9 G1
Russell Ter RLSS CV31 206 E6
Russelsheim Wy
RUGBYS/DCH CV22 186 E3
Russet Gv TLHL/CAN CV4 * 180 B2
Russett Cl BNTWD WS7 18 E7
DSYBK/YTR WS5 54 B5
Russett Wy BEWD DY12 162 D1
BRLYHL DY5 83 L6
Russet Wy NFLD/LBR B31 123 J7
Ruston St LDYWD/EDGR B16 106 E4
Ruthall Cl SLYOAK B29 124 A6
Ruth Cl TPTN/OCK DY4 68 A3
Rutherford Gln NUN CV11 99 K4
Rutherford Rd BRGRVE B60 191 M7
ERDW/GRVHL B23 72 C6
WSLW WS2 38 E7
Rutherglen Av COVS CV3 155 L7
Rutland Av
ETTPK/GDPK/PENN WV4 65 H1
NUNW/HART CV10 98 D1
Rutland Cl RUGBYN/HIL CV21 187 J3
Rutland Crs ALDR WS9 40 F4
BILS/COS WV14 51 H6
Rutland Cft COVS CV3 156 D5
Rutland Dr BRGRVE B60 191 L5
LGN/SDN/BHAMAIR B26 109 J6
POL/KGSB/FAZ B78 45 L4
Rutland Pl STRBR DY8 101 H5
Rutland Rd DARL/WED WS10 69 G1
HEDN WS12 17 J4
HHTH/SAND B71 69 G6
SMTHWK B66 105 L4
Rutland St BLOX/PEL WS3 39 J8
Rutland Ter WSNGN B18 * 88 E8
Rutley Gv RIDG/WDGT B32 123 K1
Rutters Meadow
RIDG/WDGT B32 122 F1
Rutter St WSL WS1 4 E8
Ryan Av WNSFLD WV11 37 L6
Ryan Pl DUDS DY2 85 G7
Rycroft Gv STETCH B33 110 A3
Rydal TAM/AM/WIL B77 46 E6
Rydal Av NUN CV11 81 L7
Rydal Cl COVW CV5 132 F5
FOAKS/STRLY B74 55 K3
HEDN WS12 12 E5
RUGBYN/HIL CV21 161 H7
STRPT DY13 163 K7
WNSFLD WV11 37 G6
Rydal Dr DUNHL/THL/PER WV6 48 D1
Rydding La HHTH/SAND B71 69 G5
Rydding Sq HHTH/SAND B71 68 F5
Ryde Av NUNW/HART CV10 81 H7
Ryde Gv ACGN B27 126 E4
Ryde Park Rd RBRY B45 144 A7
Ryder Cl RWWCK/WEL CV35 204 D7
Ryder Rw RCOVN/BALC/EX CV7 96 E5
Ryders Green Rd WBROM B70 86 C1
Ryders Hayes La
BLOX/PEL WS3 39 L1
Ryders Hill Crs
NUNW/HART CV10 80 A6
Ryder St CBHAMNE B4 * 7 H3
STRBR DY8 101 H3
WBROM B70 68 D8
Ryebank Cl BVILLE B30 124 A8
Ryeclose Cft
CHWD/FDBR/MGN B37 111 H2
Rye Cft ACGN B27 109 G8
HAG/WOL DY9 120 C3
HLYWD B47 146 E8
Ryecroft Av
ETTPK/GDPK/PENN WV4 49 M8
Ryecroft Cl SEDG DY3 66 A5
Ryecroft Dr BNTWD WS7 18 E5
Ryecroft Pk WSLW WS2 53 J2
Ryecroft Pl BLOX/PEL WS3 39 K7
Ryecroft St WSLW WS2 53 J2
Ryefield CDSL WV8 35 J4
Ryefield Cl HAG/WOL DY9 140 E1
SOLH B91 127 J8
Ryefield La WALM/CURD B76 74 E2
Ryefield Wy KGSWFD DY6 83 G7
Ryegrass La REDW B97 202 A7
Rye Grass Wk CVALE B35 91 M2
Rye Gv SPARK B11 126 D1
Rye Hl COVW CV5 132 E7
The Ryelands RRUGBY CV23 185 G6
Rye Meadow KNWTH CV8 179 J3
Rye Piece Ringway
BDWTH CV12 116 F2
Ryhope Cl BDWTH CV12 116 A4
Ryknild Cl FOAKS/STRLY B74 42 C7
Ryknild Dr FOAKS/STRLY B74 55 L6
Ryknild St LICHS WS14 21 J7
Ryland Cl HALE B63 121 J3
RLSS CV31 206 F7
TPTN/OCK DY4 67 M8
Ryland Rd EDG B15 107 G6
ERDE/BCHGN B24 90 D4
SPARK B11 126 B1
Rylands Dr
ETTPK/GDPK/PENN WV4 65 L1
Ryland St LDYWD/EDGR B16 6 A7
Ryle St BLOX/PEL WS3 39 H3
Rylston Av COVN CV6 133 L4
Rylstone Wy WWCK CV34 * 205 J4
Rymond Rd BKDE/SHDE B34 91 J7
Ryton TAM/AM/WIL B77 46 D5
Ryton Br KNWTH CV8 182 B2
Ryton Cl REDE B98 203 H4
SCFLD/BOLD B73 56 F8
TLHL/CAN CV4 153 M5
WNSFLD WV11 36 E8
Ryton Gv BKDE/SHDE B34 92 B6
Ryvere Cl STRPT DY13 188 D3

S

Sabell Rd SMTHWKW B67 87 K7
Sabrina Dr BEWD DY12 162 E1
Sabrina Rd
DUNHL/THL/PER WV6 48 C4
Saddington Rd COVS CV3 156 C5
Saddlers Cl HALE B63 102 F8
LICHS WS14 21 J5
Saddlers Ms SOLH B91 149 G4
The Saddlestones
DUNHL/THL/PER WV6 48 B1
Saddleworth Rd BLOX/PEL WS3 38 E1
Sadler Gdns BDWTH CV12 117 G3
Sadler Rd BRWNH WS8 26 E5
COVN CV6 133 L4
MGN/WHC B75 57 K6
Sadlers Ct WSLW WS2 52 F6
Sadlers Meadow
CSHL/WTROR B46 95 L3
Sadlers Ml BRWNH WS8 * 26 E6
Sadlers Wk LDYWD/EDGR B16 106 E4
Sadlerswell La HOCK/TIA B94 174 F7
Saffron TAM/AM/WIL B77 46 F1
Saffron Cl RRUGBY CV23 161 J5
Saffron Gdns
ETTPK/GDPK/PENN WV4 65 L1
Sage Cft NFLD/LBR B31 123 K8
St Agatha's Rd COVE CV2 155 L2
WASH/WDE B8 90 F8
St Agnes Cl MOS/BIL B13 125 M3
St Agnes La COV CV1 * 8 F3
St Agnes Rd MOS/BIL B13 125 M3
St Agnes Wy NUN CV11 99 K1
St Aidan's Rd CNCK/NC WS11 16 C1
St Aidans Wk SMTHWK B10 * 108 A5
St Alban's Av KIDDW DY11 137 L6
St Albans Cl RLSN CV32 206 A3
SMTHWKW B67 * 87 J7
WNSFLD WV11 37 L5
St Albans Rd MOS/BIL B13 125 L1
SMTHWKW B67 87 J7
St Alphege Cl SOLH B91 * 149 G2
St Ambrose Cl RMSLY B62 103 M5
St Andrew Cl HEDN WS12 13 L8
St Andrews TAM/AM/WIL B77 46 F1
St Andrews Av BLOX/PEL WS3 25 L8
St Andrews Cl
RIDG/WDGT B32 123 L2
SEDG DY3 83 L2
STRBR DY8 119 K3
St Andrews Crs
RUGBYS/DCH CV22 186 E5
St Andrews Dr
DUNHL/THL/PER WV6 34 B8
NUN CV11 99 M4
OLDBY B69 85 M6
St Andrews Gn KIDD DY10 164 C1
St Andrew's Rd BORD B9 107 M3
COVW CV5 154 D5
MGN/WHC B75 57 G6
RLSN CV32 198 F8
St Andrew's St BORD B9 107 M3
DUDS DY2 85 G8
St Andrews Wy BRGRVW B61 191 H5
St Annes Cl BFLD/HDSWWD B20 88 D1
BNTWD WS7 26 C1
St Anne's Ct MOS/BIL B13 125 J1
St Annes Gv DOR/KN B93 149 L7
St Anne's Rd DUDS DY2 103 G4
LICH WS13 20 F2
RUGBYS/DCH CV22 186 C4
WLNHL WV13 51 M2
WOLVN WV10 35 M4
St Annes Wy KGSTG B44 71 L6
St Ann's Rd COVE CV2 155 L2
St Anthonys Dr BLOX/PEL WS3 25 M8
St Athan Cft CVALE B35 91 M2
St Augustine's Rd
LDYWD/EDGR B16 106 B4
St Augustine's Wk COVN CV6 133 L6
St Augustus Cl WBROM B70 87 K2
St Austell Cl CRTAM B79 31 L7
NUN CV11 81 L8
St Austell Rd COVE CV2 156 C2
DSYBK/YTR WS5 54 B6
St Bartholemews Cl COVS CV3 156 E3
St Bartholomew's Rd
STRPT DY13 188 C3
St Bartholomew Ter
DARL/WED WS10 68 D2
St Benedicts Cl ATHST CV9 63 H5
WBROM B70 87 K3
St Benedict's Rd BNTWD WS7 18 F7
SMTHH B10 108 D5
Saint Benedicts Rd WMBN WV5 64 E6
St Bernards Cl HEDN WS12 18 A1
St Bernards Rd
CSCFLD/WYGN B72 73 G3
HIA/OLT B92 127 H8
St Blaise Av CSHL/WTROR B46 92 F3
St Blaise Rd MGN/WHC B75 57 H2
St Brades Cl OLDBY B69 86 A6
St Brides Cl SEDG DY3 66 A5
WMBN WV5 64 D7
St Buryan Cl NUN CV11 81 L8
Saintbury Dr SOLH B91 149 G6
St Caroline Cl WBROM B70 87 K2
St Catharines Cl WSL WS1 5 J9
St Catherines Cl BRGRVE B60 169 L7
COVS CV3 155 M5
DUDS DY2 * 85 L4
MGN/WHC B75 57 K6
St Catherine's Crs
ETTPK/GDPK/PENN WV4 65 K1
St Catherine's Rd
BRGRVE B60 169 K7
LICH WS13 20 F2
St Cecilia Cl KIDD DY10 164 C3
St Chad Ct TAM/AM/WIL B77 46 D3
St Chad's Circ CBHAMNW B3 6 F3
St Chad's Cl CNCK/NC WS11 16 E1
LICH WS13 20 F4
SEDG DY3 83 M2
St Chads Queensway
CBHAMNE B4 7 G2
St Chads Rd BILS/COS WV14 51 K6
LICH WS13 20 F4
MGN/WHC B75 57 J8
RBRY B45 143 K6
WOLVN WV10 36 D5
St Christian's Cft COVS CV3 9 H9
St Christian's Rd COVS CV3 9 J9
St Christopher Cl HEDN WS12 13 L8
WBROM B70 87 J3
St Christophers
BFLD/HDSWWD B20 88 D1
St Christopher's Cl
WWCK CV34 205 H5
St Christopher's Dr
TAM/AM/WIL B77 46 A4
St Clement's Av
BLOX/PEL WS3 39 G6
St Clement's La
HHTH/SAND B71 87 H1
St Clements Rd VAUX/NECH B7 90 A7
St Columba's Cl COV CV1 8 E2
St Columbas Dr RBRY B45 144 B6
St Cuthbert's Cl WBROM B70 87 K3
St David Cl HEDN WS12 13 L7
St Davids Cl BLOX/PEL WS3 25 M8
KIDDW DY11 137 K6
STRPT DY13 163 J7
WBROM B70 87 K3
St Davids Dr RIDG/WDGT B32 104 F8
St Davids Gv
BFLD/HDSWWD B20 88 D1
St Davids Orch COVS CV3 156 D6
St Davids Pl BLOX/PEL WS3 39 H3
St Davids Wy
NUNW/HART CV10 98 E7
St Denis Rd SLYOAK B29 123 L7
St Dominic's Rd
ERDE/BCHGN B24 90 C4
St Edburghs Rd YDLY B25 109 J4
St Editha's Cl CRTAM B79 31 M8
St Edithas Rd
POL/KGSB/FAZ B78 47 L5
St Ediths Gn WWCK CV34 * 205 M5
St Edmonds Rd ATHST CV9 61 G8
St Edmund's Cl
DUNHL/THL/PER WV6 * 49 K2
WBROM B70 87 K3
St Edward's Rd SLYOAK B29 124 D3
St Eleanor Cl WBROM B70 87 K2
St Elizabeth's Rd COVN CV6 134 C6
St Francis Av SOLH B91 127 J7
St Francis Cl BLOX/PEL WS3 25 M8
HEDN WS12 13 L8
St Francis Dr BVILLE B30 146 B2
St Fremund Wy RLSS CV31 207 G8
St George Dr HEDN WS12 13 L8
SMTHWK B66 * 87 L6
St Georges Av
ERDW/GRVHL B23 72 E8
RUGBYS/DCH CV22 186 D5
St Georges Cl DARL/WED WS10 52 B6
EDG B15 106 E6
MGN/WHC B75 57 K7
St Georges Ct
FOAKS/STRLY B74 42 C8
St George's Pde
BKHL/PFLD WV2 3 G6
St Georges Pl WBROM B70 87 G1
St George's Rd ATHST CV9 63 H3
COV CV1 9 L5
DUDS DY2 85 H7
REDE B98 202 D1
RLSS CV31 206 D7
SHLY B90 148 B5
STRBR DY8 119 H3
St Georges St DARL/WED WS10 52 B6
LOZ/NWT B19 6 E1
St George's Ter KIDD DY10 138 D7
St Georges Wy
NUNW/HART CV10 98 F5
TAM/AM/WIL B77 46 C1
St Gerards Rd SOLH B91 148 C3
St Giles Av BLKHTH/ROWR B65 103 M1
St Giles Cl BLKHTH/ROWR B65 103 M1
St Giles Crs WOLV WV1 50 E3
St Giles Rd BNTWD WS7 18 F7
RCOVN/BALC/EX CV7 116 B7
STETCH B33 110 B3
WLNHL WV13 51 M4
WOLV WV1 50 E3
St Giles Rw STRBR DY8 * 101 L7
St Giles St DUDS DY2 85 G8
St Godwald's Crs BRGRVE B60 191 M5
St Godwald's Rd BRGRVE B60 191 M6
St Helens Av TPTN/OCK DY4 68 A8
St Helens Rd LICH WS13 20 F2
RLSS CV31 206 D8
SOLH B91 127 L7
St Helen's Wy COVW CV5 132 F5
St Heliers Rd NFLD/LBR B31 144 C1
St Ives Cl CRTAM B79 31 M7
St Ives Rd COVE CV2 156 B2
DSYBK/YTR WS5 54 B6
St Ives Wy NUN CV11 99 K1
St James Av
BLKHTH/ROWR B65 103 L1
St James Cl BLOX/PEL WS3 * 25 M8
WBROM B70 87 K3
St James' La COVS CV3 156 A8
St James Meadow Rd
RLSN CV32 206 A4
St James Pk WOLVN WV10 * 22 D4
St James Pl SHLY B90 147 M3
VAUX/NECH B7 7 M3
St James Rd CNCK/NC WS11 16 A4
CNCK/NC WS11 17 M8
EDG B15 6 A9
HDSW B21 88 B5
MGN/WHC B75 57 G3
OLDBY B69 86 B5
St James's Rd DUDN DY1 84 F3
St James's Ter DUDN DY1 84 E3
St James St DARL/WED WS10 68 C3
SEDG DY3 84 B2
WOLV WV1 3 J6
Saint James Wk BRWNH WS8 26 D6
St John Bosco Cl
HHTH/SAND B71 68 F6
St John Cl MGN/WHC B75 57 H1
St Johns WWCK CV34 205 K6
St Johns Av
BLKHTH/ROWR B65 103 M1
KIDDW DY11 137 L7
KNWTH CV8 197 L2
RUGBYS/DCH CV22 187 J5
St John's Cl ALDR WS9 40 D2
BNTWD WS7 18 C4
CNCK/NC WS11 16 B5
DOR/KN B93 149 M7
LICH WS13 * 20 F7
SEDG DY3 82 B3
WBROM B70 87 K3
St John's Ct HEDN WS12 17 J4
LICHS WS14 * 20 F6
NFLD/LBR B31 144 F4
St John's Dr LICHS WS14 28 D8
St Johns Gv
CHWD/FDBR/MGN B37 110 D2
St John's Hl LICHS WS14 28 D8
St John's La RRUGBY CV23 159 L8
St Johns Rd BLOX/PEL WS3 25 M8
BRWNH WS8 26 E6
CNCK/NC WS11 16 B5
DARL/WED WS10 52 A8
DUDS DY2 85 H5
HALE B63 121 J1
HRBN B17 106 B7
LGLYGN/QTN B68 87 G8
NUNW/HART CV10 79 J5
RLSS CV31 206 E7
SPARK B11 108 A8
STRBR DY8 101 L7
STRPT DY13 163 L8
TPTN/OCK DY4 67 K6
WNSFLD WV11 37 L2
WSLW WS2 52 F5
St John's Sq BKHL/PFLD WV2 2 F7
St Johns St COV CV1 9 G6
DUDS DY2 85 G8
KIDDW DY11 138 A7
KNWTH CV8 197 K2
St Johns Ter RLSS CV31 * 206 E7
St John St BRGRVW B61 191 K3
CRTAM B79 31 M8
RUGBYN/HIL CV21 186 E1
St Johns Wk PBAR/PBCH B42 89 H1
St Johns Wd LICHS WS14 28 E8
RBRY B45 143 M8
St Josephs Av NFLD/LBR B31 123 M8
St Josephs Cl BLOX/PEL WS3 39 L1
St Josephs Rd WASH/WDE B8 90 F8
St Joseph St DUDS DY2 85 H4
St Judes Cl
ALE/KHTH/YWD B14 146 D3
MGN/WHC B75 57 K7
St Jude's Crs COVS CV3 156 B6
St Jude's Pas DIG/EDG B5 * 6 F7
St Jude's Rd
DUNHL/THL/PER WV6 49 K2
St Jude's Rd West
DUNHL/THL/PER WV6 49 K2
St Katherine's Rd
LGLYGN/QTN B68 105 G3
St Kenelms Av HALE B63 121 H4
St Kenelm's Cl WBROM B70 87 K3
St Kenelm's Rd RMSLY B62 121 H8
St Kilda's Rd WASH/WDE B8 * 90 C8
St Laurence Av WWCK CV34 205 H8
St Laurence Cl ALVE B48 170 F7
St Laurence Rd NFLD/LBR B31 123 L8
St Lawrence Cl DIG/EDG B5 107 H6
DOR/KN B93 149 M8
St Lawrence Dr CNCK/NC WS11 16 F3
St Lawrence Rd
NUNW/HART CV10 96 F1
St Lawrence's Rd COVN CV6 134 D4
St Lawrence Wy
DARL/WED WS10 52 B7
St Leonards Cl
CHWD/FDBR/MGN B37 110 E6
St Leonards Vw
POL/KGSB/FAZ B78 47 K5
St Leonard's Wk KNWTH CV8 182 E4
St Loye's Cl RMSLY B62 104 B6
St Lukes Cl BLKHTH/ROWR B65 103 M1
CNCK/NC WS11 16 A5
St Luke's Rd BNTWD WS7 19 G7
COVN CV6 134 B3
DARL/WED WS10 68 E3
DIG/EDG B5 107 J6
St Lukes St CDYHTH B64 103 H4
St Lukes Wy NUNW/HART CV10 98 A2
St Margaret Rd COV CV1 9 L6
St Margaret's
FOAKS/STRLY B74 56 A2
St Margarets Av KNWTH CV8 183 L1
WASH/WDE B8 90 F7
St Margarets Dr HALE B63 121 K3
St Margarets Rd
BLOX/PEL WS3 39 K1
CRTAM B79 31 M6
GTB/HAM B43 70 D3
HIA/OLT B92 127 J4
LICH WS13 20 F2
RLSS CV31 206 E8
WASH/WDE B8 90 E7
St Mark's Av
RUGBYS/DCH CV22 186 A6
St Marks Cl GTWY WS6 24 D1
NUNW/HART CV10 98 A1
St Marks Ct CBHAMW B1 106 E2
St Mark's Ms RLSN CV32 206 C4
St Mark's Rd BDMR/CCFT WV3 2 B6
BLOX/PEL WS3 39 L1
BNTWD WS7 19 G7
BRWNH WS8 26 E8
DUDS DY2 85 K3
HAG/WOL DY9 102 B8
RLSN CV32 206 B4
SMTHWKW B67 105 H2
TPTN/OCK DY4 67 L5
St Mark's St BDMR/CCFT WV3 2 D6
CBHAMW B1 6 A3
St Martin's Cl
BKHL/PFLD WV2 50 C7
WBROM B70 87 K3
St Martin's Dr TPTN/OCK DY4 67 L8
St Martin's Queensway (Below)
DIG/EDG B5 7 G6
St Martin's Rd COVS CV3 180 F2
MGN/WHC B75 57 K8
St Martin's St EDG B15 6 B8
St Martin's Ter
BILS/COS WV14 67 J2
St Marys Cl ACGN B27 126 F2
ERDE/BCHGN B24 91 H1
SEDG DY3 66 D5
WOLVN WV10 23 G3
WWCK CV34 205 H5
St Mary's Ct KNWTH CV8 197 K2
WLNHL WV13 * 51 L3
St Mary's Crs RLSS CV31 206 F6
St Mary's La STRBR DY8 119 M2
St Marys Ringway KIDD DY10 138 B7
St Mary's Rd ATHST CV9 63 J5
DARL/WED WS10 68 D2
HRBN B17 106 A8
LICH WS13 20 F2
NUN CV11 80 F8
RCOVN/BALC/EX CV7 114 C1
RLSS CV31 206 F6
St Mary's Rw CBHAMNE B4 7 G2
MOS/BIL B13 125 K2
St Mary's Ter RLSS CV31 206 F6
St Mary St COV CV1 9 G5
St Marys Vw
ERDW/GRVHL B23 72 B5
St Mary's Wy ALDR WS9 40 E8
TAM/AM/WIL B77 46 C1
St Matthew Cl HEDN WS12 13 L8
St Matthew's Av BNTWD WS7 19 K6
St Matthews Cl
BLOX/PEL WS3 * 25 M8
WSL WS1 5 G5
St Matthew's Rd BNTWD WS7 19 K6
LGLYGN/QTN B68 104 E3
SMTHWK B66 88 A8
St Matthew St WOLV WV1 3 M6
St Matthews Wy
NUNW/HART CV10 98 A1
St Mawes Rd
DUNHL/THL/PER WV6 48 D2
St Mawgen Cl CVALE B35 92 A1
St Michael Rd LICH WS13 21 G4
St Michaels Cl ATHST CV9 63 K4
ATHST CV9 61 G4
BLOX/PEL WS3 39 K3
PENK ST19 10 C5
RCOVN/BALC/EX CV7 96 D5
STRPT DY13 188 E1
St Michael's Ct
DUNHL/THL/PER WV6 35 J8
St Michael's Crs OLDBY B69 104 D1
St Michaels Dr HEDN WS12 13 L8
St Michael's Gv DUDS DY2 85 K4
St Michael's Rd COVE CV2 155 L2
PENK ST19 10 C5
SCFLD/BOLD B73 72 D5
SEDG DY3 65 K8
WSNGN B18 89 G6
WWCK CV34 205 H5
St Michael's Sq PENK ST19 10 C4
St Michael St WSL WS1 4 F7
St Michael St West
WBROM B70 87 G2
St Michael's Wy
NUNW/HART CV10 98 A1
TPTN/OCK DY4 85 L2
St Modwena Wy PENK ST19 10 D6
St Nicholas Av KNWTH CV8 197 K2
St Nicholas Cl BLOX/PEL WS3 39 L1
St Nicholas Ct WWCK CV34 * 205 K7
St Nicholas Est ATHST CV9 61 M3
St Nicholas St COV CV1 8 E1
St Nicholas Wk
WALM/CURD B76 74 F7
St Nicolas Gdns
HWK/WKHTH B38 145 K3
St Nicolas Park Dr NUN CV11 81 J6
St Nicolas Rd NUN CV11 81 H8
St Osburg's Rd COVE CV2 155 L2
St Oswalds Cl KIDD DY10 138 D5
St Oswalds Rd SMHTH B10 108 C5
St Patrick Cl HEDN WS12 13 L8

St Patricks Cl
ALE/KHTH/YWD B14 125 J7
St Paul's Av BHTH/HG B12 107 L8
KIDDW DY11 137 L7
St Paul's Cl CNCK/NC WS11 16 F4
COVEN WV9 22 A3
WWCK CV34 205 H7
St Paul's Ct TAM/AM/WIL B77 * 60 A1
St Pauls Crs BLOX/PEL WS3 25 M8
CSHL/WTROR B46 93 L6
WBROM B70 68 C6
St Pauls Dr RMSLY B62 104 B4
TPTN/OCK DY4 85 M1
St Paul's Rd BHTH/HG B12 107 K7
BNTWD WS7 19 G7
COVN CV6 134 C7
DARL/WED WS10 52 F8
DUDS DY2 85 H8
HEDN WS12 17 J2
NUNW/HART CV10 98 A2
SMTHWK B66 87 H6
St Paul's Sq CBHAMNW B3 6 D3
St Paul's St WSL WS1 4 E2
St Pauls Ter WWCK CV34 * 205 H7
St Peter Cft DARL/WED WS10 69 J2
St Peter's Av ATHST CV9 63 M6
St Peter's Cl ALDR WS9 41 J1
ATHST CV9 63 M6
BRGRVW B61 191 J4
CSCFLD/WYGN B72 72 F2
CSHL/WTROR B46 92 F3
HLGN/YWD B28 126 B7
KIDD DY10 164 C3
REDW B97 202 B8
TAM/AM/WIL B77 46 A4
TPTN/OCK DY4 86 B1
St Peters Ct BLOX/PEL WS3 38 F4
COV CV1 * 9 J2
St Peters Cft
SCFLD/BOLD B73 * 72 F2
St Peters Dr BLOX/PEL WS3 39 L1
NUNW/HART CV10 97 K1
St Peters La HIA/OLT B92 129 H5
St Peter's Pl
POL/KGSB/FAZ B78 60 B8
St Peters Rd ATHST CV9 63 L6
BFLD/HDSWWD B20 89 G4
BNTWD WS7 19 G7
DUDS DY2 85 H7
HAG/WOL DY9 120 A3
HEDN WS12 17 H1
HRBN B17 105 M8
RUGBYN/HIL CV21 187 G3
St Peters Sq WOLV WV1 2 F4
St Peters Ter WSLW WS2 53 J1
St Philips Av BDMR/CCFT WV3 49 L6
St Phillips Av
BDMR/CCFT WV3 49 K6
St Phillips Gv
BDMR/CCFT WV3 49 K6
St Quentin St WSLW WS2 4 A8
St Saviour's Cl
BKHL/PFLD WV2 50 D7
St Saviour's Rd WASH/WDE B8 108 B1
St Silas' Sq LOZ/NWT B19 88 F6
St Simons Cl MGN/WHC B75 57 K7
St Stephen's Av WLNHL WV13 51 K3
St Stephens Ct HEDN WS12 * 17 G1
St Stephens Gdns REDE B98 194 D8
WLNHL WV13 * 51 L4
St Stephen's Rd BNTWD WS7 18 F7
HHTH/SAND B71 87 M5
SLYOAK B29 124 F5
St Stephens St AST/WIT B6 89 J7
Saints Wy NUNW/HART CV10 81 H8
St Thomas' Cl ALDR WS9 40 F4
BLOX/PEL WS3 39 J7
MGN/WHC B75 57 K8
St Thomas Ct COV CV1 * 8 C6
St Thomas Dr HEDN WS12 13 L8
St Thomas' Rd COVN CV6 134 D2
ERDW/GRVHL B23 90 B3
St Thomass Cl
NUNW/HART CV10 98 A2
St Thomas's Ct COV CV1 8 C6
St Thomas St DUDS DY2 85 G8
St Valentines Cl WBROM B70 87 K3
St Vincent Crs WBROM B70 68 D7
St Vincent St
LDYWD/EDGR B16 6 A5
St Vincent St West
LDYWD/EDGR B16 106 E3
St Wilfreds Cottages
RCOVN/BALC/EX CV7 * 96 C3
Saladin Av OLDBY B69 86 C8
Salcombe Av
LGN/SDN/BHAMAIR B26 110 A8
Salcombe Cl CNCK/NC WS11 15 M5
COVS CV3 156 B7
NUN CV11 81 K8
Salcombe Dr BRLYHL DY5 102 A5
Salcombe Gv BILS/COS WV14 67 H4
Salcombe Rd SMTHWK B66 87 M8
Salemorton Ct
RUGBYS/DCH CV22 185 M7
Salem St TPTN/OCK DY4 68 B8
Salford Cl COVE CV2 134 E8
REDE B98 202 F7
Salford St AST/WIT B6 90 A5
Salisbury Av COVS CV3 155 G7
Salisbury Chambers
MOS/BIL B13 * 125 K1
Salisbury Cl DUDN DY1 84 D2
KNWTH CV8 183 K2
LICH WS13 21 G2
MOS/BIL B13 125 J2
Salisbury Dr CSHL/WTROR B46 93 G2
HEDN WS12 16 F4
KIDDW DY11 137 K7
NUNW/HART CV10 79 M6
Salisbury Gv
CSCFLD/WYGN B72 73 G6
Salisbury Rd LOZ/NWT B19 89 H5
MOS/BIL B13 125 J2
SMTHWK B66 105 M1
WASH/WDE B8 90 C8
WBROM B70 87 J4
Salisbury St BDMR/CCFT WV3 2 C7
DARL/WED WS10 52 C6
Sallow Gv BRWNH WS8 26 D4
Sally Ward Dr ALDR WS9 40 E1
Salop Cl HHTH/SAND B71 68 F6
Salop Dr CNCK/NC WS11 16 D5
LGLYGN/QTN B68 105 G3
Salop Rd LGLYGN/QTN B68 105 G2
REDW B97 202 B3
Salop St BHTH/HG B12 107 K5
BILS/COS WV14 67 J1
DUDN DY1 84 E3
OLDBY B69 86 C4
WOLV WV1 2 E6
Salstar Cl AST/WIT B6 89 J7
Saltash Gv YDLY B25 109 G4
Saltbrook Rd HALE B63 102 E6
Salter Rd TPTN/OCK DY4 67 K6
Salter's La CRTAM B79 31 M7
HHTH/SAND B71 87 J1
REDW B97 201 L1
Salter's Rd ALDR WS9 40 E2
Salter St HOCK/TIA B94 174 A4
Salters V WBROM B70 87 J4
Saltisford WWCK CV34 205 H6
Saltisford Gdns WWCK CV34 205 H5
Salt La COV CV1 8 F5
Saltley Cottages
ERDE/BCHGN B24 * 90 D5
Saltley Rd VAUX/NECH B7 89 M8
Saltley Viad VAUX/NECH B7 90 A8
Saltney Cl ERDE/BCHGN B24 73 H8
Salts La POL/KGSB/FAZ B78 59 K1
Saltwells La BRLYHL DY5 102 E3
Saltwells Rd DUDS DY2 102 F3
Salwarpe Gv SLYOAK B29 123 K3
Salwarpe Rd BRGRVE B60 191 J6
Sam Barber Ct HEDN WS12 * 17 J3
Sambar Rd POL/KGSB/FAZ B78 45 H6
Sambourn Cl SOLH B91 128 C7
Sambourne Dr BKDE/SHDE B34 92 B6
Sambrook Rd WOLVN WV10 36 E7
Sam Gault Cl COVS CV3 156 C6
Sammons Wy TLHL/CAN CV4 153 H4
Sampson Cl COVE CV2 135 G4
HDSW B21 88 A4
OLDBY B69 86 A6
Sampson Rd SPARK B11 107 M6
Sampson Rd West SPARK B11 107 L5
Sampson St DARL/WED WS10 68 F2
Samsara Rd BRGRVE B60 192 A4
Sams La WBROM B70 87 G3
Sam Spencer Ct KIDD DY10 165 L4
Samuel Cl LICH WS13 21 G3
Samuels Rd RIDG/WDGT B32 104 E8
Samuel St BLOX/PEL WS3 38 F4
Sanby Cl BDWTH CV12 116 E1
Sanda Cft CBROM B36 92 F7
Sandalls Cl NFLD/LBR B31 144 B4
Sandal Ri SOLH B91 149 J2
Sandals Ri RMSLY B62 122 B2
Sandalwood Cl SHHTH WV12 37 M5
Sand Bank BLOX/PEL WS3 38 E4
Sandbarn Cl SHLY B90 148 D7
Sandbeds Rd SHHTH WV12 52 A1
Sandbourne Dr BEWD DY12 163 G2
Sandbourne Rd
WASH/WDE B8 108 E1
Sanderling Cl WOLVN WV10 22 F6
Sanderling Ct KIDD DY10 164 E4
Sanderling Ri BNTWD WS7 18 F5
KGSWFD DY6 83 L7
Sanders Cl ATHST CV9 63 J4
DUDS DY2 85 J6
REDW B97 201 L1
Sanders Crs TPTN/OCK DY4 67 M8
Sanders Rd BRGRVW B61 191 J4
COVN CV6 116 F7
Sandfield Br BRLYHL DY5 83 M4
Sandfield Cl LICH WS13 20 E7
SHLY B90 147 L5
Sandfield Farm Home Pk
BRWNH WS8 * 26 F4
Sandfield Gv SEDG DY3 83 M3
Sandfield Meadow LICH WS13 20 E7
Sandfield Rd HHTH/SAND B71 69 J4
STRBR DY8 101 K3
Sandfields Av SMHTH B10 107 M5
Sandfields Rd
LGLYGN/QTN B68 105 G3
Sandford Av
BLKHTH/ROWR B65 104 A2
Sandford Cl COVE CV2 135 H2
Sandford Ri
DUNHL/THL/PER WV6 35 J7
Sandford Rd DUDN DY1 84 C4
MOS/BIL B13 125 L2
Sandford St LICH WS13 20 E6
Sandgate Crs COVE CV2 156 B3
Sandgate Rd HLGN/YWD B28 147 K1
TPTN/OCK DY4 67 L5
Sandhampton STRPT DY13 188 C7
Sandhills Crs SOLH B91 148 F5
Sandhills Gn ALVE B48 170 C6
Sandhills La RBRY B45 170 B6
Sandhills Rd RBRY B45 170 B5
Sandhill St BLOX/PEL WS3 38 E4
Sandhurst Av CBROM B36 91 H7
HAG/WOL DY9 120 B3
Sandhurst Cl REDE B98 195 G7
Sandhurst Dr
ETTPK/GDPK/PENN WV4 65 L1
Sandhurst Gv COVN CV6 133 M8
STRBR DY8 101 J2
Sandhurst Rd
FOAKS/STRLY B74 42 D8
KGSWFD DY6 101 L1
MOS/BIL B13 125 J3
Sandicliffe Cl KIDDW DY11 138 A5
Sandilands Cl COVE CV2 156 C1
Sandland Cl BILS/COS WV14 51 K7
Sandland Rd SHHTH WV12 38 A5
Sandmartin Cl DUDS DY2 103 G3
Sandmartin Wy KIDD DY10 164 E3
Sandmeadow Pl KGSWFD DY6 83 G8
Sandmere Gv
ALE/KHTH/YWD B14 147 H2
Sandmere Ri WOLVN WV10 36 C4
Sandmere Rd
ALE/KHTH/YWD B14 147 H2
Sandon Cl REDE B98 202 E2
Sandon Gv ERDE/BCHGN B24 90 E1
Sandon Rd HAG/WOL DY9 120 D1
NUN CV11 80 F8
SMTHWK B66 105 L4
WOLVN WV10 35 M3
Sandown TAM/AM/WIL B77 32 D8
Sandown Av COVN CV6 134 C3
Sandown Cl BNTWD WS7 18 D4
HEDN WS12 13 L7
RLSN CV32 207 G1
Sandown Dr BRGRVW B61 * 168 F4
DUNHL/THL/PER WV6 48 D1
Sandown Rd CBROM B36 91 H5
RUGBYN/HIL CV21 187 G1
Sandpiper TAM/AM/WIL B77 46 E8
Sandpiper Cl HAG/WOL DY9 102 D8
HEDN WS12 13 G6
KIDD DY10 164 F3
RRUGBY CV23 161 G4
Sandpiper Gdns
HWK/WKHTH B38 145 K6
Sandpiper Rd COVE CV2 134 F2
Sandpiper Wy
ERDW/GRVHL B23 72 A7
Sandpit BVILLE B30 * 124 C5
Sandpits Cl WALM/CURD B76 74 F7
Sandpits La
RCOVN/BALC/EX CV7 133 J3
Sand Pits Pde CBHAMW B1 6 B4
The Sandpits BVILLE B30 124 C5
Sandra Cl ALDR WS9 40 F8
Sandringham Av SHHTH WV12 37 M7
Sandringham Cl BNTWD WS7 18 C4
TLHL/CAN CV4 153 K8
Sandringham Dr ALDR WS9 40 F4
BLKHTH/ROWR B65 104 A1
Sandringham Pl STRBR DY8 101 H4
Sandringham Rd
ETTPK/GDPK/PENN WV4 65 L1
PBAR/PBCH B42 70 F7
RMSLY B62 103 M6
STRBR DY8 101 G4
WMBN WV5 64 D7
Sandringham Wy BRLYHL DY5 102 A5
Sandstone Av RBRY B45 143 L5
Sandstone Cl SEDG DY3 84 B1
Sandstone Ct TAM/AM/WIL B77 46 E6
Sandstone Rd BEWD DY12 163 G2
Sand St WBROM B70 86 C1
Sandway Gdns WASH/WDE B8 90 B7
Sandway Gv MOS/BIL B13 126 A6
Sandwell Av DARL/WED WS10 51 M8
Sandwell Pl SHHTH WV12 38 B6
Sandwell Rd HDSW B21 88 B4
WBROM B70 87 G1
WOLVN WV10 35 M4
Sandwell Rd North
HHTH/SAND B71 87 H1
Sandwell St WSL WS1 5 G8
Sandwell Wk WSL WS1 5 G7
Sandwick Cl COVS CV3 156 D5
Sandwood Dr KGSTG B44 71 K5
Sandyacre Wy STRBR DY8 101 M8
Sandy Bank BEWD DY12 162 E2
Sandy Crs WNSFLD WV11 37 L5
Sandy Cft CSCFLD/WYGN B72 73 G2
MOS/BIL B13 126 A6
Sandyfields Rd SEDG DY3 65 K8
Sandygate Cl REDW B97 201 K3
Sandy Gv BRWNH WS8 26 D4
Sandy Hill Ri SHLY B90 126 E8
Sandy Hill Rd SHLY B90 147 L1
Sandy Hollow
DUNHL/THL/PER WV6 49 G3
Sandy La AST/WIT B6 89 L6
BRGRVW B61 142 D8
CDSL WV8 34 D1
CNCK/NC WS11 15 L4
COVN CV6 134 A8
CSHL/WTROR B46 95 J1
DSYBK/YTR WS5 69 J1
DUNHL/THL/PER WV6 35 J7
KIDD DY10 140 B7
KIDDW DY11 137 L4
LICHS WS14 30 A1
PBAR/PBCH B42 71 H5
RCOVN/BALC/EX CV7 114 C1
RLSN CV32 206 A2
RUGBYN/HIL CV21 186 C2
STRPT DY13 188 F4
WOLVN WV10 36 C4
Sandy Mt WMBN WV5 64 F6
Sandy Mount Rd WSL WS1 5 H7
Sandy Rd STRBR DY8 119 H4
Sandys Gv TPTN/OCK DY4 67 J8
Sandy Wy EDG B15 6 B7
TAM/AM/WIL B77 46 E2
Sangwin Rd BILS/COS WV14 67 G6
Sankey Rd CNCK/NC WS11 16 D2
Sansome Ri SHLY B90 147 K3
Sansome Rd SHLY B90 147 K3
Sanstone Cl BLOX/PEL WS3 39 G2
Sanstone Rd BLOX/PEL WS3 38 F2
Santa Maria Wy STRPT DY13 188 F2
Santolina Dr DSYBK/YTR WS5 69 L2
Santos Cl COVS CV3 156 D5
Santridge La BRGRVW B61 191 L1
Sant Rd NFLD/LBR B31 144 F6
Sapcote Gv COVN CV6 134 F1
The Saplings PENK ST19 10 D4
WALM/CURD B76 73 L5
Sapphire Ct COVE CV2 * 135 M4
Sapphire Dr CNCK/NC WS11 17 G2
RLSS CV31 206 D8
Sapphire Ga COVE CV2 156 A3
Saracen Dr MGN/WHC B75 57 K7
RCOVN/BALC/EX CV7 151 J7
Sara Cl FOAKS/STRLY B74 56 F2
Sarah Cl BILS/COS WV14 67 J4
Sarah Gdns DSYBK/YTR WS5 69 K1
Sarah Seager Cl STRPT DY13 * 163 J7
Sarah St BORD B9 107 M3
Sarawak Pl RUGBYS/DCH CV22 185 M5
Saredon Cl BLOX/PEL WS3 39 L4
Saredon Rd CNCK/NC WS11 23 M1
WOLVN WV10 23 H3
Sarehole Rd HLGN/YWD B28 126 B6
Sargeaunt St RLSS CV31 206 D6
Sargent Cl GTB/HAM B43 71 H1
Sark Dr CBROM B36 92 F7
Satchwell Ct RLSN CV32 206 D5
Satchwell Pl RLSS CV31 * 206 E6
Saturn Rd CNCK/NC WS11 12 E8
Saumur Wy WWCK CV34 206 A7
Saunders Av BDWTH CV12 116 F3
Saunders Cl HEDN WS12 13 K7
Saunton Cl COVW CV5 132 F4
Saunton Rd
RUGBYS/DCH CV22 186 D4
Saunton Wy SLYOAK B29 124 A4
Savannah Cl TLHL/CAN CV4 153 G2
Saveker Dr WALM/CURD B76 73 J1
Savernake Cl RBRY B45 143 L3
Saville Cl RBRY B45 143 M6
Saville Gv KNWTH CV8 180 A7
Savoy Cl RIDG/WDGT B32 105 H5
Saw Mill Cl RUSH/SHEL WS4 4 F1
Saxelby Cl
ALE/KHTH/YWD B14 146 C3
Saxifrage Pl KIDD DY10 164 D2
Saxilby Pl STRPT DY13 188 F1
Saxon Cl COVS CV3 157 H6
GTWY WS6 24 E3
POL/KGSB/FAZ B78 47 K4
RUGBYS/DCH CV22 185 L5
STUD B80 203 J8
TAM/AM/WIL B77 46 D7
Saxoncourt
DUNHL/THL/PER WV6 35 G8
Saxondale Av
LGN/SDN/BHAMAIR B26 109 K7
Saxon Dr BLKHTH/ROWR B65 104 A1
CRTAM B79 46 A1
Saxonfields
DUNHL/THL/PER WV6 35 G8
Saxon Mill La CRTAM B79 46 A1
Saxon Rd COVE CV2 155 M1
PENK ST19 10 D5
Saxons Wy
ALE/KHTH/YWD B14 146 E3
Saxon Wk LICH WS13 20 C7
Saxon Wy
CHWD/FDBR/MGN B37 110 D2
Saxon Wood Cl NFLD/LBR B31 144 E1
Saxon Wood Rd SHLY B90 148 B8
Saxton Dr FOAKS/STRLY B74 42 D7
Scafell RUGBYN/HIL CV21 161 H6
Scafell Cl COVW CV5 153 L1
Scafell Dr BILS/COS WV14 51 K6
ERDW/GRVHL B23 72 A8
Scafell Rd STRBR DY8 101 M7
Scaife Rd BRGRVE B60 191 M6
Scammerton TAM/AM/WIL B77 46 F6
Scampton Cl
DUNHL/THL/PER WV6 34 C8
Scampton Wy CRTAM B79 32 A5
Scar Bank WWCK CV34 205 J4
Scarborough Rd WSLW WS2 4 A6
Scarborough Wy
TLHL/CAN CV4 153 K6
Scarecrow La MGN/WHC B75 57 J1
Scarfield Hl ALVE B48 170 B8
Scarman Rd TLHL/CAN CV4 153 M8
Scarsdale Rd PBAR/PBCH B42 71 H5
Schofield Av HHTH/SAND B71 68 F5
Schofield Rd
CHWD/FDBR/MGN B37 92 D8
Scholars Ct KIDD DY10 164 C1
Scholars Dr
RUGBYS/DCH CV22 185 M5
Scholars Ga BNTWD WS7 19 H7
STETCH B33 109 M3
Scholars Rd HDSW B21 88 D6
Scholfield Rd
RCOVN/BALC/EX CV7 115 L7
Schoolacre Ri
FOAKS/STRLY B74 55 J4
Schoolacre Rd BKDE/SHDE B34 91 M7
School Av BRWNH WS8 26 D5
School Bell Ms KNWTH CV8 * 180 F7
School Cl BDMR/CCFT WV3 48 F6
BNTWD WS7 18 B5
CDSL WV8 34 E1
CHWD/FDBR/MGN B37 92 E7
CNCK/NC WS11 17 L7
COVS CV3 9 M6
CVALE B35 91 M2
NFLD/LBR B31 144 C3
OLDBY B69 86 A6
WMBN WV5 64 A4
School Cottages
WOLVN WV10 * 35 M3
School Crs CNCK/NC WS11 17 L7
School Dr BILS/COS WV14 * 67 G4
BKDE/SHDE B34 92 C8
BRGRVE B60 191 L3
HLYWD B47 172 E2
STRBR DY8 101 K5
The School Dr DUDS DY2 85 H6
Schoolfield Gv
RUGBYN/HIL CV21 186 D2
Schoolfields Rd LICHS WS14 28 E8
School Gdns
RUGBYN/HIL CV21 187 L4
Schoolgate Cl RUSH/SHEL WS4 40 B4
WASH/WDE B8 90 E7
School Gn BILS/COS WV14 51 G5
School Hl BTACH/HAR CV33 207 M5
NUNW/HART CV10 79 L6
Schoolhouse Cl
HWK/WKHTH B38 145 M3
School House La COVE CV2 135 L7
School La ALVE B48 170 F8
BKDE/SHDE B34 91 M6
BLOX/PEL WS3 39 K1
BNTWD WS7 18 B5
BRGRVE B60 168 F7
BRLYHL DY5 101 M1
COVEN WV9 22 A1
CRTAM B79 33 K6
HAG/WOL DY9 120 B7
KNWTH CV8 179 K8
NUNW/HART CV10 79 J8
POL/KGSB/FAZ B78 44 B2
RCOVN/BALC/EX CV7 112 B6
RCOVN/BALC/EX CV7 116 C6
RLSS CV31 207 J8
RRUGBY CV23 183 K7
RWWCK/WEL CV35 177 J8
SOLH B91 149 H1
STETCH B33 109 K4
TAM/AM/WIL B77 46 B8
WALM/CURD B76 75 L6
WOLVN WV10 23 H3
WOLVN WV10 36 B3
School Rd ALE/KHTH/YWD B14 146 F1
BRLYHL DY5 102 E3
CNCK/NC WS11 17 L7
DARL/WED WS10 69 H3
DUNHL/THL/PER WV6 48 E1
HLGN/YWD B28 126 D5
HOCK/TIA B94 174 C4
MOS/BIL B13 125 K4
RBRY B45 143 J7
SEDG DY3 82 F2
SHLY B90 147 M3
WMBN WV5 64 A4
WNSFLD WV11 36 F7
School St BDMR/CCFT WV3 2 E6
BRLYHL DY5 84 B6
CDYHTH B64 103 H4
DARL/WED WS10 52 A7
DUDN DY1 84 F4
KNWTH CV8 183 L1
RRUGBY CV23 158 F8
RUGBYN/HIL CV21 187 L4
RUSH/SHEL WS4 40 B4
SEDG DY3 66 C5
STRBR DY8 * 101 K7
TAM/AM/WIL B77 46 C1
WLNHL WV13 51 K3
School St West
BILS/COS WV14 67 G5
School Ter SLYOAK B29 * 124 D3
School Wk BILS/COS WV14 51 G5
BNTWD WS7 18 B5
CRTAM B79 31 M7
NUN CV11 99 J3
Scimitar Cl CRTAM B79 31 J6
Scorers Cl SHLY B90 126 F7
The Scotchill COVN CV6 133 K4
The Scotchings CBROM B36 91 J5
Scotch Orch LICH WS13 21 H4
Scotia Rd CNCK/NC WS11 16 B2
Scotland La RIDG/WDGT B32 122 F7
Scotland St CBHAMW B1 6 C4
Scots Cl RUGBYS/DCH CV22 186 A6
Scots La COVN CV6 133 K7
STRPT DY13 188 D8
Scott Av DARL/WED WS10 68 F3
ETTPK/GDPK/PENN WV4 65 J1
NUNW/HART CV10 81 H5
Scott Cl LICHS WS14 20 F7
Scott Gv HIA/OLT B92 127 J2
Scott Rd DSYBK/YTR WS5 54 B7
GTB/HAM B43 70 D3
HIA/OLT B92 127 J3
KNWTH CV8 197 J2
REDW B97 202 A5
RLSS CV31 206 F7
TAM/AM/WIL B77 46 C1
Scott's Green Cl DUDN DY1 84 D5
Scott's Rd STRBR DY8 101 K7
Scott St HEDN WS12 17 K2
TPTN/OCK DY4 68 A8
Scotwell Cl
BLKHTH/ROWR B65 103 M2
Scout Cl STETCH B33 110 A3
Scribbans Cl SMTHWK B66 105 M1
Scribers La HLGN/YWD B28 147 H1
Scribers Meadow
HLGN/YWD B28 147 J1
Sculthorpe Rd KIDD DY10 139 M3
Seabroke Av
RUGBYS/DCH CV22 186 D2
Seacroft Av YDLY B25 109 J4
Seafield TAM/AM/WIL B77 32 D8
Seafield Cl KGSWFD DY6 101 J1
Seafield La ALVE B48 172 C7
REDE B98 195 K2
Seaford Cl COVN CV6 134 F1
Seaforth Gv SHHTH WV12 37 M4
Seagar St HHTH/SAND B71 87 H1
Seager's La BRLYHL DY5 102 B3
Seagrave Rd COV CV1 9 J6
Seagull Bay Dr
BILS/COS WV14 67 H4
Sealand Dr BDWTH CV12 116 D2
Seal Cl WALM/CURD B76 73 J2
Seals Gn HWK/WKHTH B38 145 H6
Seamless Dr WNSFLD WV11 51 H1
Sear Hills Cl
RCOVN/BALC/EX CV7 151 M7
Seathwaite RUGBYN/HIL CV21 161 G6
Seaton TAM/AM/WIL B77 46 D5
Seaton Cl NUN CV11 81 K8
WNSFLD WV11 37 K8
Seaton Gv MOS/BIL B13 125 H4
Seaton Pl STRBR DY8 101 G3
Seaton Rd SMTHWK B66 87 M8
Sebastian Cl COVS CV3 155 M8
Sebright Gn KIDDW DY11 138 A2
Sebright Rd KIDDW DY11 138 A2
Second Av BORD B9 108 C4
BRWNH WS8 26 E4
COVS CV3 156 A4
KGSWFD DY6 83 K6
SLYOAK B29 124 F2
WOLVN WV10 36 C6
Second Exhibition Av
BHAMNEC B40 129 H1
Sedge Av HWK/WKHTH B38 145 K2
Sedgeberrow Covert
HWK/WKHTH B38 145 J5
Sedgeberrow Rd HALE B63 121 L3
Sedgebourne Wy
NFLD/LBR B31 144 A4
Sedge Dr BRGRVW B61 168 E7
Sedgefield Cl DUDN DY1 84 C2
Sedgefield Gv
DUNHL/THL/PER WV6 48 D1
Sedgefield Wk BRGRVW B61 * 168 F4
Sedgefield Wy CNCK/NC WS11 25 L1
Sedgeford Cl BRLYHL DY5 102 B5
Sedgehill Av HRBN B17 123 M1
Sedgemere Gv
RCOVN/BALC/EX CV7 152 A8
RUSH/SHEL WS4 40 A5
Sedgemere Rd
LGN/SDN/BHAMAIR B26 109 K4
Sedgemoor Av BNTWD WS7 18 F8
Sedgemoor Rd COVS CV3 155 M8
Sedgley Cl REDE B98 202 D1
Sedgley Gv BFLD/HDSWWD B20 88 C1
Sedgley Hall Av SEDG DY3 66 A5
Sedgley Rd
ETTPK/GDPK/PENN WV4 65 K3
Sedgley Rd East TPTN/OCK DY4 85 L1
Sedgley Rd West
TPTN/OCK DY4 67 G7
Sedgley St BKHL/PFLD WV2 50 A6
Sedlescombe Pk
RUGBYS/DCH CV22 186 D5
Seed Field Cft COVS CV3 155 H6
Seedgreen Cl STRPT DY13 188 C5
Seedhouse Ct CDYHTH B64 103 L5
Seeds La BRWNH WS8 26 D5
Seekings Dr KNWTH CV8 197 M1
Seeleys Rd SPARK B11 126 B1
Seeney La WALM/CURD B76 75 M2
Seeswood Cl NUNW/HART CV10 98 A3
Sefton Dr BLKHTH/ROWR B65 85 K7
Sefton Gv TPTN/OCK DY4 68 A3
Sefton Rd LDYWD/EDGR B16 106 D3
TAM/AM/WIL B77 60 B1
TLHL/CAN CV4 154 C7
Segbourne Rd RBRY B45 143 J5
Segundo Cl DSYBK/YTR WS5 69 J1
Segundo Rd DSYBK/YTR WS5 69 K1
Selba Dr KIDDW DY11 137 K7
Selborne Cl WSL WS1 * 5 J4
Selborne Gv MOS/BIL B13 126 A8
Selborne Rd
BFLD/HDSWWD B20 88 E3
DUDS DY2 85 H6
RUGBYS/DCH CV22 186 B5
Selborne St WSL WS1 5 J4
Selbourne Crs WOLV WV1 50 F4
Selby Cl LGN/SDN/BHAMAIR B26 109 K4
Selby Gv MOS/BIL B13 126 A8
Selby Wy BLOX/PEL WS3 38 C3
NUNW/HART CV10 79 M8
Selcombe Wy
HWK/WKHTH B38 145 K6
Selco Wy WALM/CURD B76 73 L8
Selcroft Av RIDG/WDGT B32 105 K8
Selecta Av KGSTG B44 71 H3
Selker Dr TAM/AM/WIL B77 32 C8
Selkirk Cl HHTH/SAND B71 69 G7
Selly Av SLYOAK B29 124 E3
Selly Cl SLYOAK B29 124 E3
Selly Hall Cft BVILLE B30 124 D7
Selly Hill Rd SLYOAK B29 124 D3
Selly Oak Rd BVILLE B30 124 C8
Selly Park Rd SLYOAK B29 124 E3
Selly Whf SLYOAK B29 124 C4
Selly Wick Dr SLYOAK B29 124 F3
Selly Wick Rd SLYOAK B29 124 E3
Sellywood Rd BVILLE B30 124 C6
Selma Gv ALE/KHTH/YWD B14 126 B8
Selmans Hl BLOX/PEL WS3 39 G2
Selmans Pde BLOX/PEL WS3 * 39 G3
Selsdon Cl HLYWD B47 147 G8
KIDDW DY11 137 M8
Selsdon Rd BLOX/PEL WS3 38 D2
Selsey Av HRBN B17 105 M2
Selsey Cl COVS CV3 182 A1
Selsey Rd HRBN B17 105 M2
Selside RUGBYN/HIL CV21 161 H6
Selston Rd AST/WIT B6 89 J6
Selvey Av GTB/HAM B43 70 F2
Selworthy Rd CBROM B36 92 D6
COVN CV6 134 B2
Selwyn Cl BKHL/PFLD WV2 50 A6
Selwyn Rd BILS/COS WV14 51 K7
BNTWD WS7 19 K6
LDYWD/EDGR B16 106 B2

Bentley West Primary School *WSLW* WS2 52 C2
Beoley First School *REDE* B98 195 J5
Berkswell CE Primary School *RCOVN/BALC/EX* CV7 152 A2
Berkswell Windmill *RCOVN/BALC/EX* CV7 178 B1
Bermuda Business Park *NUNW/HART* CV10 98 E6
Bermuda Park Industrial Estate *NUNW/HART* CV10 98 D4
Berrybrook Primary School *WOLVN* WV10 36 F4
Bescot Industrial Estate *DARL/WED* WS10 68 B2
Best Western Abbey Hotel Golf & Country Club *REDE* B98 194 D6
Best Western Falstaff Hotel *RLSN* CV32 206 B5
Best Western Premier Moor Hall Hotel & Spa *MGN/WHC* B75 57 H4
Best Western The Fairlawns at Aldridge *ALDR* WS9 41 J7
Best Western Lea Marston Hotel *WALM/CURD* B76 75 L4
Best Western Westley Hotel *ACGN* B27 126 F2
Best Western Weston Hall Hotel *BDWTH* CV12 117 M2
Bevan Industrial Estate *BRLYHL* DY5 101 L3
Beverley Hotel *RUSH/SHEL* WS4 53 L1
Bewdley CC *BEWD* DY12 162 F3
Bewdley High School *BEWD* DY12 163 G3
Bewdley Medical Centre *BEWD* DY12 162 F2
Bewdley Museum *BEWD* DY12 162 F2
Bewdley Pines Golf Club *BEWD* DY12 137 J7
Bewdley Rowing Club *BEWD* DY12 162 F1
Bewdley St Annes CE First School *BEWD* DY12 162 D3
Bewdley Tennis Club *BEWD* DY12 163 G2
BGW Business Park *BRGRVE* B60 191 K7
Bhylls Acre Primary School *BDMR/CCFT* WV3 48 F6
Bickenhill Trading Estate *CHWD/FDBR/MGN* B37 111 H8
Bickford Road Industrial Estate *AST/WIT* B6 89 L4
Big Apple Bowling *RUGBYN/HIL* CV21 160 F7
Bilbrook CE Middle School *CDSL* WV8 34 F2
Bilbrook Medical Centre *CDSL* WV8 34 F2
Billesley Primary School *MOS/BIL* B13 126 A7
Bilston Cemetery *BILS/COS* WV14 51 G6
Bilston Central Industrial Estate *BILS/COS* WV14 51 J8
Bilston CE Primary School *BKHL/PFLD* WV2 50 F7
Bilston Health Centre *BILS/COS* WV14 51 H7
Bilston High School *BILS/COS* WV14 51 H8
Bilston Industrial Estate *BILS/COS* WV14 67 L1
Bilston Key Industrial Estate *BILS/COS* WV14 51 L8
Bilston Leisure Centre *BILS/COS* WV14 51 H7
Bilston Public Library & Art Gallery *BILS/COS* WV14 51 J7
Bilston Town FC *BILS/COS* WV14 51 K7
Bilton CE Junior School *RUGBYS/DCH* CV22 186 B7
Bilton High School *RUGBYS/DCH* CV22 185 M4
Bilton Industrial Estate *COV* CV1 9 M7
HWK/WKHTH B38 145 J5
Bilton Infant School *RUGBYS/DCH* CV22 186 A5
Bingley Primary School *BDMR/CCFT* WV3 2 B9
Binley Business Park *COVS* CV3 156 E4
Binley Industrial Estate *COVS* CV3 156 E6
Binley Woods Primary School *COVS* CV3 157 J6
Binswood Hall Sixth Form *RLSN* CV32 206 D3
Birchbrook Industrial Park *LICHS* WS14 28 C7
Birch Business Park *CNCK/NC* WS11 16 D7
Birch Coppice Industrial Estate *POL/KGSB/FAZ* B78 47 J8
Birchen Coppice First & Middle School *KIDDW* DY11 163 L3
Birchensale Middle School *REDW* B97 202 A1
Birches First School *CDSL* WV8 34 F4
Birches Green J & I School *ERDE/BCHGN* B24 90 F2
Birchfield Independent Girls School *AST/WIT* B6 89 J5
Birchfield Primary School *AST/WIT* B6 89 H4
Birchills CE Primary School *WSLW* WS2 4 C2
Birchills Health Centre *WSLW* WS2 4 B1
Birchley Industrial Estate *OLDBY* B69 86 C8
Birch Road East Industrial Estate *AST/WIT* B6 89 M3
Birchwood Primary School *POL/KGSB/FAZ* B78 47 K6
Birds Bush Primary School *TAM/AM/WIL* B77 46 C5
Birmingham Alexander Stadium *PBAR/PBCH* B42 71 G7
The Birmingham & Midland Hospital for Woman *SPARK* B11 126 A2
Birmingham Area Civil Service Sports Club *HIA/OLT* B92 128 E3
Birmingham Botanical Gardens & Glasshouses *EDG* B15 106 D6
Birmingham Business Centre *WBROM* B70 87 K3
Birmingham Business Park *CHWD/FDBR/MGN* B37 111 J5
Birmingham Christian Centre *CBHAMNW* B3 6 F4
Birmingham City College *BORD* B9 108 E2
Birmingham City FC (St Andrews Stadium) *BORD* B9 107 M4
Birmingham College of Food, Tourism & Creative Studies *CBHAMNW* B3 6 D4
Birmingham Community College *CSCFLD/WYGN* B72 57 G8
Birmingham Conservatoire (University of Central England) *CBHAMNW* B3 6 D5
The Birmingham Crematorium *PBAR/PBCH* B42 71 G8
Birmingham Crown Court *CBHAMNE* B4 7 G3
Birmingham Heartlands Hospital *BORD* B9 108 F3
Birmingham Hebrew Congregation Cemetery *TAM/AM/WIL* B77 46 B1
Birmingham International Airport *CHWD/FDBR/MGN* B37 110 E8
LGN/SDN/BHAMAIR B26 129 G1
The Birmingham Mint *WSNGN* B18 6 B1
Birmingham Museum & Art Gallery *CBHAMNW* B3 6 E5
The Birmingham Nuffield Hospital *EDG* B15 106 D8
Birmingham One Industrial Estate *CBHAMW* B1 6 B4
Birmingham Repertory Theatre *CBHAMW* B1 6 D5
Birmingham Wheels Adventure Park *BORD* B9 108 A3
Birmingham Womens Hospital *HRBN* B17 106 B8
Birmingham (Yardley) Crematorium *YDLY* B25 109 H8
Bishop Ashbury's Cottage *GTB/HAM* B43 69 M4
The Bishop Challoner RC School *ALE/KHTH/YWD* B14 125 J5
Bishopgate Business Park *COV* CV1 134 B8
Bishop Milner RC Secondary School *DUDN* DY1 84 E2
Bishop Ullathorne RC Comprehensive School *TLHL/CAN* CV4 180 C1
Bishop Veseys Grammar School *FOAKS/STRLY* B74 57 G7
Bishop Walsh Catholic School *WALM/CURD* B76 73 H3
Bishop Wilson CE Primary School *CHWD/FDBR/MGN* B37 111 G2
Bishop Wulstan RC High School *RUGBYS/DCH* CV22 186 E3
Bi-Tec Industrial Park *WOLV* WV1 3 M6
Black Boy Hotel *BEWD* DY12 162 F2
Blackbrook Valley Industrial Estate *DUDS* DY2 84 E7
Blackbrook Valley Industrial Park *BRLYHL* DY5 84 E8
Black Country Living Museum *DUDN* DY1 85 H2
Blackheath Primary School *BLKHTH/ROWR* B65 103 M4
Blackheath Trading Estate *BLKHTH/ROWR* B65 104 C3
Black Lake Industrial Estate *WBROM* B70 68 E7
The Blackwell Golf Club *BRGRVE* B60 169 M8
Blackwood School *FOAKS/STRLY* B74 55 J4
Blakebrook Special School *KIDDW* DY11 138 A7
Blakedown CE First School *KIDD* DY10 140 A4
Blake High School *HEDN* WS12 12 E7
Blakeley Heath Primary School *WMBN* WV5 64 E8
Blakenall FC *BLOX/PEL* WS3 39 G6
Blakenall Heath Junior School *BLOX/PEL* WS3 39 G5
Blakenhale Infant School *STETCH* B33 109 M4
Blakenhale Junior School *STETCH* B33 109 M4
Blakenhall Industrial Estate *BDMR/CCFT* WV3 49 M6
Blakesley Hall *YDLY* B25 109 J4
Blakesley Hall Primary School *STETCH* B33 109 H4
Blanford Mere Primary School *KGSWFD* DY6 83 J6
Bleakhouse Clinic *LGLYGN/QTN* B68 105 G4
Bleakhouse Junior School *LGLYGN/QTN* B68 105 G4
Blossomfield Infant School *SHLY* B90 148 B2
Blowers Green Primary School *DUDS* DY2 84 F5
Bloxwich Business Park *WSLW* WS2 38 F6
Bloxwich CE Primary School *BLOX/PEL* WS3 38 F4
Bloxwich Golf Club *BLOX/PEL* WS3 38 F1
Bloxwich Hospital *BLOX/PEL* WS3 38 F5
Bloxwich Lane Industrial Estate *WSLW* WS2 52 E2
Bloxwich Leisure Centre *BLOX/PEL* WS3 39 G5
Blue Coat CE Comprehensive School *WSL* WS1 5 G5
Blue Coat CE Infant School *WSL* WS1 5 G6
Blue Coat CE Junior School *WSL* WS1 5 H5
Blue Coat CE School *COV* CV1 9 L8
The Blue Coat School *HRBN* B17 106 C7
Blythe Business Park *SHLY* B90 174 D2
Blythe Special School *CSHL/WTROR* B46 111 L1
BMI Meriden Hospital *COVE* CV2 135 L7
BMI Priory Hospital *DIG/EDG* B5 106 F8
Boddis Industrial Park *CDYHTH* B64 103 L3
Bodmin Road Industrial Estate *COVE* CV2 135 J8
Boldmere Clinic *SCFLD/BOLD* B73 72 D4
Boldmere Golf Club *SCFLD/BOLD* B73 72 C2
Boldmere J & I School *SCFLD/BOLD* B73 72 D4
Boldmere St Michaels FC *SCFLD/BOLD* B73 72 D5
Bond's Hospital & Bablake Old School *COV* CV1 8 D4
Bonehill Industrial Estate *POL/KGSB/FAZ* B78 45 K4
Boney Hay Primary School *BNTWD* WS7 18 E4
Bordesley Green Girls School *WASH/WDE* B8 108 C2
Bordesley Green Primary School *BORD* B9 108 E3
Bordesley Green Trading Estate *WASH/WDE* B8 108 B2
Borough Cemetery *DUDS* DY2 84 F5
Borough Of Redditch Cemeteries & Crematorium *REDW* B97 194 C7
Boscomoor Industrial Estate *PENK* ST19 10 C6
Boscomoor Shopping Centre *PENK* ST19 10 B6
Boswells Monument *LICH* WS13 20 F5
Bosworth Wood Primary School *CBROM* B36 92 D4
Boughton Leigh County Junior School *RUGBYN/HIL* CV21 161 G6
Boughton Leigh Infant School *RUGBYN/HIL* CV21 161 H6
Boughton Road Industrial Estate *RUGBYN/HIL* CV21 160 F7
Boulton Industrial Centre *WSNGN* B18 88 F8
The Boundary Hotel *WSL* WS1 5 L9
Boundary Industrial Estate *WOLVN* WV10 22 A8
Bournebrook CE Primary School *RCOVN/BALC/EX* CV7 114 B2
Bourneville Infant School *BVILLE* B30 124 C6
Bourneville Junior School *BVILLE* B30 124 C6
Bournville College of Further Education *SLYOAK* B29 124 A6
Bournville School of Art & Craft *BVILLE* B30 124 C6
Bournville School & Sixth Form Centre *NFLD/LBR* B31 124 A7
Bowlplex *LDYWD/EDGR* B16 106 E4
Brackendale Shopping Centre *SHHTH* WV12 52 B1
Bradford Street Clinic *WSL* WS1 4 E5
Braidwood School for Deaf Children *ERDW/GRVHL* B23 71 M7
Bramford Primary School *BILS/COS* WV14 66 E7
Brandhall Clinic *LGLYGN/QTN* B68 104 F5
Brandhall Golf Club *LGLYGN/QTN* B68 104 E3
Brandhall Primary School *LGLYGN/QTN* B68 104 F4
Brandon Court Leofric Business Park *COVS* CV3 156 E6
Brandon Way Industrial Estate *WBROM* B70 86 D2
Brandwood End Cemetery *ALE/KHTH/YWD* B14 146 C1
Brasshouse Infant School *SMTHWK* B66 87 L6
Brasshouse Language Centre *LDYWD/EDGR* B16 6 B7
Brays Special School *LGN/SDN/BHAMAIR* B26 109 L7
Breener Industrial Estate *BRLYHL* DY5 101 M4
Briars Country Club *KIDDW* DY11 137 L6
Brickhouse J & I School *BLKHTH/ROWR* B65 103 L2
Bridge Industrial Estate *SOLH* B91 128 A5
The Bridge Medical Centre *STRPT* DY13 188 D3
Bridgeside Industrial Estate *TAM/AM/WIL* B77 46 B3
Bridgeside Trading Estate *TAM/AM/WIL* B77 46 A3
Bridge Special School *ERDW/GRVHL* B23 90 C1
Bridge Street Industrial Estate *DARL/WED* WS10 68 D4
The Bridge Trading Estate *SMTHWK* B66 87 M6
Bridgtown Business Centre *CNCK/NC* WS11 16 C7
Bridgtown CP School *CNCK/NC* WS11 16 C7
Brierley Hill Cemetery *BRLYHL* DY5 101 M3
The Brierley Hill Health Centre *BRLYHL* DY5 102 B2
Brierley Hill Primary School *BRLYHL* DY5 102 B3
The Brierley Trading Estate *BRLYHL* DY5 102 A2
Brierly Hill Leisure Centre *BRLYHL* DY5 102 C3
The Brier Special School *BRLYHL* DY5 102 C2
Brindley Business Park *CNCK/NC* WS11 16 F2
Brineton Industrial Estate *WSLW* WS2 4 B6
Brinklow CE First School *RRUGBY* CV23 158 D1
Bristnall Hall High School *LGLYGN/QTN* B68 105 H2
Broadcott Industrial Estate *CDYHTH* B64 103 L4
Broadfield House Glass Museum *KGSWFD* DY6 83 H8
Broad Heath Community Primary School *COVN* CV6 134 C7
Broad Heath School *COVN* CV6 134 C6
Broad Lane Trading Estate *TLHL/CAN* CV4 153 G1
Broadmeadow J & I School *BVILLE* B30 145 M3
Broad Street Health Centre *COVN* CV6 134 D6
Broad Street Old Boys RFC *COVS* CV3 156 F5
Broad Street RFC *COVE* CV2 135 G5
Broadwalk Retail Park *WSL* WS1 53 H7
Broadway Medical Centre *WSL* WS1 53 K7
Broadway Plaza *LDYWD/EDGR* B16 106 E4
Broadway School *BFLD/HDSWWD* B20 89 J3
Broadwell Industrial Park *OLDBY* B69 86 D5
Broadwyn Trading Estate *CDYHTH* B64 103 L4
Brockencote Hall Country House Hotel *KIDD* DY10 166 B6
Brockmoor Industrial Estate *KGSWFD* DY6 101 L2
Brockmoor Primary School *BRLYHL* DY5 102 A2
Bromford Road Industrial Estate *OLDBY* B69 86 E4
Bromley Hills Primary School *KGSWFD* DY6 101 K1
Bromley Primary School *BRLYHL* DY5 83 M8
Bromsgrove Business Centre *BRGRVW* B61 191 K3
Bromsgrove Cemetery *BRGRVW* B61 191 K3
Bromsgrove Clinic *BRGRVW* B61 191 K2
Bromsgrove Golf Centre *BRGRVE* B60 192 A3
The Bromsgrove Hotel *BRGRVW* B61 191 H3
Bromsgrove Lower School *BRGRVE* B60 191 K4
Bromsgrove Museum *BRGRVW* B61 191 L2
Bromsgrove Pre Preparatory School *BRGRVE* B60 191 J8
Bromsgrove Private Hospital *BRGRVE* B60 192 F4
Bromsgrove RFC *BRGRVE* B60 192 A5
Bromsgrove Rovers FC *BRGRVW* B61 191 L2
Bromsgrove Upper School *BRGRVE* B60 191 K4
Brooke Special School *RUGBYS/DCH* CV22 186 D4
Brook Farm Industrial Estate *HOCK/TIA* B94 173 M3
Brookfields Primary School *WSNGN* B18 6 A1
Brookhurst Primary School *RLSN* CV32 206 B4
Brooklands Grange Hotel *COVW* CV5 133 H8
Brooklands Hospital *CHWD/FDBR/MGN* B37 110 F5
The Brook Primary School *STRBR* DY8 101 K4
Brookside Industrial Estate *DARL/WED* WS10 68 F2
Brook Street Business Centre *TPTN/OCK* DY4 67 J7
Brookvale Primary School *ERDW/GRVHL* B23 89 M1
Brookvale Trading Estate *AST/WIT* B6 89 L2
Brownhills Business Park *BRWNH* WS8 26 D8
Brownhills Clinic *BRWNH* WS8 26 D6
Brownhills Comprehensive School *BRWNH* WS8 26 D4
Brownhills West JMI School *BRWNH* WS8 26 A3
Brownhills West Station *BRWNH* WS8 26 A2
Browning Street Industrial Estate *LDYWD/EDGR* B16 6 A6
Brownmead Primary School *BKDE/SHDE* B34 91 M7
Brownsover Community School *RRUGBY* CV23 161 H5
Brownsover Hall Hotel *RUGBYN/HIL* CV21 160 F5
Brunswick Park Trading Estate *DARL/WED* WS10 68 F1
Brymill Industrial Estate *TPTN/OCK* DY4 67 J6
BSA Business Park *SPARK* B11 108 B7
BT Tower *CBHAMNW* B3 6 E3
Budbrooke Industrial Estate *WWCK* CV34 205 G5
Budbrooke Medical Centre *RWWCK/WEL* CV35 204 D6
Budbrooke Primary School *RWWCK/WEL* CV35 204 D7
Bullring Shopping Centre *DIG/EDG* B5 7 H6
Bull Ring Trading Estate *BHTH/HG* B12 7 K7
Bull Street Trading Estate *BRLYHL* DY5 101 M4
Buntsford Hill Business Park *BRGRVE* B60 191 K7
Burlish Middle School *STRPT* DY13 163 K7
The Burlish Park First School *STRPT* DY13 163 K8
Burman Infant School *SHLY* B90 147 L3
Burnsall Road Industrial Estate *COVW* CV5 154 A5
Burnt Tree Industrial Estate *TPTN/OCK* DY4 85 M3
Burnt Tree J & I School *OLDBY* B69 85 L3
Burntwood Baths *BNTWD* WS7 18 D7
Burntwood Health Centre *BNTWD* WS7 19 G7
Burntwood Town Shopping Centre *BNTWD* WS7 18 C6
Burton Green CE Primary *KNWTH* CV8 178 F2
Burton Industrial Estate *CDYHTH* B64 103 J5
Bushbury Baths *WOLVN* WV10 36 C4
Bushbury Cemetery *WOLVN* WV10 36 D3
Bushbury Health Centre *WOLVN* WV10 36 C3
Bushbury Hill J & I School *WOLVN* WV10 36 D4
Busill Jones JMI School *BLOX/PEL* WS3 38 D5
The Business Centre *SPARK* B11 108 D7
Butlers Leap Industrial Estate *RUGBYN/HIL* CV21 187 H1
Butts JMI School *RUSH/SHEL* WS4 5 G1
Butts Park Arena *COVW* CV5 8 B5
Cadbury College *HWK/WKHTH* B38 145 K4
Cadbury World *BVILLE* B30 124 D6
Calderfields Golf Club & Academy *RUSH/SHEL* WS4 54 A3
Caldmore JMI School *WSL* WS1 4 F7
Caldmore Medical Centre *WSL* WS1 4 F7
Calthorpe Special School *BHTH/HG* B12 107 L5
Caludon Castle School *COVE* CV2 156 C1
Caludon Centre *COVE* CV2 135 K7
Cambrian Wharf *CBHAMW* B1 6 C5
Cambridge Tutorial College *SMHTH* B10 108 B5
Campanile Hotel *COVE* CV2 135 L5
REDE B98 195 L8
VAUX/NECH B7 89 K8
Camp Hill Clinic *NUNW/HART* CV10 80 B7
Camp Hill Old Edwardians RFC *SHLY* B90 147 M2
Camp Hill Primary School *NUNW/HART* CV10 80 C7
Campion School *RLSS* CV31 207 G8
Canal View Industrial Estate *STRBR* DY8 101 L4
Canley Garden Cemetery *TLHL/CAN* CV4 154 B7
Canley Gardens Crematorium *TLHL/CAN* CV4 154 B7
Canning Wharf *CBHAMNW* B3 6 D4
Cannock Centre *CNCK/NC* WS11 16 C4
Cannock Chase Country Park *HEDN* WS12 13 H3
Cannock Chase FC *HEDN* WS12 12 F5
Cannock Chase High School *CNCK/NC* WS11 16 C3
Cannock Chase Hospital *CNCK/NC* WS11 16 C3
Cannock Chase Technical College *CNCK/NC* WS11 16 B4
CNCK/NC WS11 16 C6
HEDN WS12 12 B5
Cannock Industrial Centre *CNCK/NC* WS11 16 B8
Cannock Motor Racing Stadium *HEDN* WS12 13 K8
Cannock Park Golf Club *CNCK/NC* WS11 16 B3
Cannock & Rugeley CC *HEDN* WS12 13 L8
Cannock Sports Stadium *CNCK/NC* WS11 12 D8
Cannon Business Park *BILS/COS* WV14 67 G4
Cannon Park Primary School *TLHL/CAN* CV4 154 B8
Canon Evans CE Infant School *BDWTH* CV12 116 E3
Canon Maggs CE Junior School *BDWTH* CV12 116 F3
Canterbury Cross Primary NC School *BFLD/HDSWWD* B20 89 H3
Cape Hill Medical Centre *SMTHWK* B66 106 A1
Cape Industrial Estate *WWCK* CV34 205 J6

Cape Primary School
SMTHWK B66 ...... 106 A1
Cardinal Griffin RC School
CNCK/NC WS11 ...... 16 B2
Cardinal Newman RC School & Community College
COVN CV6 ...... 133 K3
Cardinal Wiseman Catholic School
KGSTG B44 ...... 71 K3
Cardinal Wiseman RC School
COVE CV2 ...... 135 J4
Carlton Business Centre
VAUX/NECH B7 ...... 90 A8
Carlyle Business Park
WBROM B70 ...... 68 D8
Carlyon Road Industrial Estate
ATHST CV9 ...... 63 K4
Carters Green Medical Centre
WBROM B70 ...... 87 G1
Cash's Business Centre
COV CV1 ...... 134 B8
Caslon Primary School
HALE B63 ...... 120 F1
Castle Bromwich Business Park
CVALE B35 ...... 91 K4
Castle Bromwich CC
CBROM B36 ...... 92 A5
Castle Bromwich Hall Gardens
CBROM B36 ...... 91 L5
Castle Bromwich Infant School
CBROM B36 ...... 92 C5
Castle Bromwich Junior School
CBROM B36 ...... 92 B6
Castlecroft J & I School
BDMR/CCFT WV3 ...... 48 F4
Castlefort JMI School
ALDR WS9 ...... 40 F2
Castle High School
DUDN DY1 ...... 84 F3
Castle Hills
RCOVN/BALC/EX CV7 ...... 114 D1
Castle Museum
CRTAM B79 ...... 45 L1
Castle Place Industrial Estate
COV CV1 ...... 9 J2
Castle Pleasure Grounds
CRTAM B79 ...... 45 M1
The Castle Pool & Adventure Play Centre
CVALE B35 ...... 92 A3
Castle Sixth Form Centre
KNWTH CV8 ...... 197 K3
Castle Special School
BLOX/PEL WS3 ...... 38 F6
Castle Vale Health Centre
CVALE B35 ...... 91 K2
Castle Vale Industrial Estate
WALM/CURD B76 ...... 73 L8
Castle Vale Shopping Centre
CVALE B35 ...... 91 K2
Castle View Industrial Estate
TPTN/OCK DY4 ...... 85 K2
Cathedral Lanes Shopping Centre
COV CV1 ...... 8 F4
Catshill Clinic
BRGRVW B61 ...... 168 E5
Catshill First School
BRGRVW B61 ...... 168 E5
Catshill Middle School
BRGRVW B61 ...... 168 D5
Causeway Green Primary School
LGLYGN/QTN B68 ...... 104 D2
Cawston Grange Primary School
RUGBYS/DCH CV22 ...... 185 L4
Cedars Business Centre
CNCK/NC WS11 ...... 16 A6
Cedars Hotel
KIDDW DY11 ...... 138 A7
Centech Business Park
REDE B98 ...... 195 K7
Centenary Business Centre
NUN CV11 ...... 99 J2
Central Business Park
STETCH B33 ...... 110 B4
Central City Industrial Estate
COVN CV6 ...... 134 D8
Central Clinic
DUDS DY2 ...... 85 H4
Central Hall
CBHAMNE B4 ...... 7 H3
Central Industrial Estate
BKHL/PFLD WV2 ...... 50 D6
Central Park Industrial Estate
DUDS DY2 ...... 103 J2
Central Six Retail Park
COVS CV3 ...... 8 D7
Central Trading Estate
KGSWFD DY6 ...... 83 K4
Centre Link Industrial Estate
VAUX/NECH B7 ...... 89 M7
Centrovell Industrial Estate
NUN CV11 ...... 99 G3
Century Industrial Estate
KGSTG B44 ...... 71 J2
The Chace Hotel
COVS CV3 ...... 155 M8
Chace Primary School
COVS CV3 ...... 156 A7
Chaddesley Corbett Endowed First School
KIDD DY10 ...... 166 C5
Chaddesley Woods National Nature Reserve
BRGRVW B61 ...... 167 G6
Chadsgrove Special School
BRGRVW B61 ...... 168 D5
Chadsmead Primary School & IT Centre
LICH WS13 ...... 20 E4
Chadsmoor CE Junior School
CNCK/NC WS11 ...... 16 E1
Chadsmoor Infants School
CNCK/NC WS11 ...... 16 E1
Chad Vale Primary School
EDG B15 ...... 106 B6
Chadwick Bank Industrial Estate
STRPT DY13 ...... 189 H5
Chadwick Business Park
STRPT DY13 ...... 189 H5
Chadwick Industrial Estate
STRPT DY13 ...... 189 H5
Challenge Business Park
COV CV1 ...... 134 B8
Chamber of Commerce
WSL WS1 ...... 5 H2
Chamber of Commerce & Industry
BDMR/CCFT WV3 ...... 2 A4
Chancel Industrial Estate
DARL/WED WS10 ...... 52 B8
KGSWFD DY6 ...... 83 H4
WLNHL WV13 ...... 51 M3
Chancel Way Industrial Estate
AST/WIT B6 ...... 71 K8
Chandos Primary School
DIG/EDG B5 ...... 107 J6
Chantry Industrial Estate
WALM/CURD B76 ...... 74 F6
Chapel Fields Junior School
HIA/OLT B92 ...... 127 K2
Chapel House Hotel
ATHST CV9 ...... 63 H5
Chapel Street Industrial Estate
DUDS DY2 ...... 103 H1
Charford First School
BRGRVE B60 ...... 191 K6
Charlemont Primary School
HHTH/SAND B71 ...... 69 J5
Charles Street Industrial Estate
TPTN/OCK DY4 ...... 68 C8
Charnwood Business Park
BILS/COS WV14 ...... 51 G8
Charnwood CP School
LICH WS13 ...... 21 G2
Charterfield Shopping Centre
KGSWFD DY6 ...... 83 H5
Chase Academy
CNCK/NC WS11 ...... 16 C5
The Chase Golf Club
PENK ST19 ...... 11 L5
Chase Leisure Centre
CNCK/NC WS11 ...... 16 B3
Chase Park Industrial Estate
BNTWD WS7 ...... 18 B6
Chaseside Industrial Estate
CNCK/NC WS11 ...... 16 F2
Chase Terrace High School
BNTWD WS7 ...... 18 C5
BNTWD WS7 ...... 18 E6
Chase Terrace Primary School
BNTWD WS7 ...... 18 D5
Chase Terrace Technology College
BNTWD WS7 ...... 18 D5
Chasetown Community Special School
BNTWD WS7 ...... 18 C8
Chase Town High School
BNTWD WS7 ...... 26 C1
Chasetown Industrial Estate
BNTWD WS7 ...... 18 C6
Chasewater Country Park
CNCK/NC WS11 ...... 18 A8
Chasewater Heaths Business Park
BNTWD WS7 ...... 18 A6
Chasewater Heaths Station
BNTWD WS7 ...... 18 B7
Chasewater Industrial Estate
BNTWD WS7 ...... 18 C7
Chase Watersports Centre
BRWNH WS8 ...... 26 A2
Chasewood Park Business Centre
HEDN WS12 ...... 17 J4
Cheapside Industrial Estate
BHTH/HG B12 ...... 7 K8
Chelmsley Wood Industrial Estate
CHWD/FDBR/MGN B37 ...... 92 E8
Chelmsley Wood Shopping Centre
CHWD/FDBR/MGN B37 ...... 110 F3
Chelsea Trading Estate
AST/WIT B6 ...... 89 L7
Cherry Oak Special School
SLYOAK B29 ...... 124 B3
Cherry Orchard Primary School
BFLD/HDSWWD B20 ...... 88 E2
Cherry Tree Sports Club
COVN CV6 ...... 134 C3
Cherry Trees Special School
WMBN WV5 ...... 64 D7
Cherrywood Industrial Estate
WASH/WDE B8 ...... 108 B2
Chesford Grange Hotel
KNWTH CV8 ...... 198 A5
Cheshunt Pre Preparatory School
COV CV1 ...... 8 F7
Cheslyn Hay Primary School
GTWY WS6 ...... 23 M2
Cheslyn Hay Sport & Community High School
GTWY WS6 ...... 23 M2
Cheston Industrial Estate
AST/WIT B6 ...... 89 M6
Cheswick Green Primary School
SHLY B90 ...... 148 C8
Chetwynd Junior School
NUN CV11 ...... 99 K6
Cheylesmore Welfare Clinic
COVS CV3 ...... 155 J7
Chilcote Primary School
HLGN/YWD B28 ...... 147 K1
Chilvers Coton Community Infant School
NUNW/HART CV10 ...... 98 F2
Chinese Quarter
DIG/EDG B5 ...... 7 G7
The Chiropody Surgery
YDLY B25 ...... 109 H4
Chivenor Primary School
CVALE B35 ...... 91 L3
Christ Church CE Infant School
DUNHL/THL/PER WV6 ...... 2 D1
Christ Church CE Junior School
DUNHL/THL/PER WV6 ...... 49 G1
Christ Church CE Primary School
BLOX/PEL WS3 ...... 39 H6
LICH WS13 ...... 20 D6
OLDBY B69 ...... 86 E5
SPARK B11 ...... 107 M6
Christ Church Infant School
DUNHL/THL/PER WV6 ...... 48 E2
Christ Church Primary School
BILS/COS WV14 ...... 67 H4
Christ Church School
PENK ST19 ...... 14 A3
Christ the King Catholic Infant School
COVN CV6 ...... 133 K7
Christ the King RC Junior School
COVN CV6 ...... 133 K6
Christ the King RC Primary School
KGSTG B44 ...... 71 L4
Chrystie School of Theatre Dance
GTWY WS6 ...... 24 A3
Chuckery Primary School
WSL WS1 ...... 5 J4
Churchbridge Industrial Estate
OLDBY B69 ...... 86 D7
Churchfield Industrial Estate
DUDS DY2 ...... 85 G5
Church Hill Middle School
REDE B98 ...... 195 H7
Churchill & Blakedown Golf Club
KIDD DY10 ...... 139 L3
Churchill Precinct
DUDN DY1 ...... 85 H4
Church Lane Health Centre
STETCH B33 ...... 109 K2
Church Lane Industrial Estate
HHTH/SAND B71 ...... 69 G7
Church Lawford Business Centre
RRUGBY CV23 ...... 158 E8
Church of Ascension CE Primary School
KGSWFD DY6 ...... 82 F5
Cineworld
DIG/EDG B5 ...... 7 G8
EDG B15 ...... 6 B8
SOLH B91 ...... 149 G2
RUGBYN/HIL CV21 ...... 160 F7
City Arcade
COV CV1 ...... 8 E5
City College
ACGN B27 ...... 127 G2
City College Birmingham
BKDE/SHDE B34 ...... 92 B7
HDSW B21 ...... 88 E6
HRBN B17 ...... 106 B7
STETCH B33 ...... 109 M5
City College Coventry
COV CV1 ...... 8 B6
KNWTH CV8 ...... 197 K1
TLHL/CAN CV4 ...... 153 K4
City Estate
CDYHTH B64 ...... 103 H5
City Farm
COV CV1 ...... 9 J2
City of Coventry-Brandon Wood Golf Club
KNWTH CV8 ...... 157 G8
City of Wolverhampton College
BDMR/CCFT WV3 ...... 49 J2
BKHL/PFLD WV2 ...... 3 G6
City Plaza Shopping Centre
CBHAM B2 ...... 6 F5
City Road Primary School
LDYWD/EDGR B16 ...... 106 B2
The City Technology College
CHWD/FDBR/MGN B37 ...... 110 E1
City Trading Estate
LDYWD/EDGR B16 ...... 106 D2
City Walls & Gate
COV CV1 ...... 9 G3
Clapham Terrace CP School
RLSS CV31 ...... 206 E6
Claregate Primary School
DUNHL/THL/PER WV6 ...... 35 K6
Clarendon House Hotel
KNWTH CV8 ...... 179 K7
Clarkes Industrial Estate
SCFLD/BOLD B73 ...... 72 E4
Clearwater Industrial Estate
BKHL/PFLD WV2 ...... 50 D6
Clent Hills C&CC Site
RMSLY B62 ...... 142 C1
Clent Hills Country Park (NT)
HAG/WOL DY9 ...... 141 L1
Clent Parochial First School
HAG/WOL DY9 ...... 141 K3
Cleton Street Business Park
TPTN/OCK DY4 ...... 85 M2
Clifford Bridge Primary School
COVS CV3 ...... 156 E2
Clifton Infant School
BHTH/HG B12 ...... 107 L8
Clifton Junior School
BHTH/HG B12 ...... 107 L8
Clifton Road Cemetery
RUGBYN/HIL CV21 ...... 187 G2
Clifton Road Industrial Estate
BHTH/HG B12 ...... 107 K8
Clifton upon Dunsmore CE Primary School
RRUGBY CV23 ...... 161 K8
Clinton Combined School
KNWTH CV8 ...... 197 J2
The Clock Towers Shopping Centre
RUGBYN/HIL CV21 ...... 186 E2
Closers Business Centre
NUN CV11 ...... 99 H3
Clothier Street Primary School
WLNHL WV13 ...... 51 L2
CMT Industrial Estate
OLDBY B69 ...... 86 E5
Coach House Special School
BRGRVE B60 ...... 191 G8
Coalpool Clinic
BLOX/PEL WS3 ...... 39 K7
Coal Pool Lane Cemetery
BLOX/PEL WS3 ...... 39 K8
Cobham Business Centre
WASH/WDE B8 ...... 108 B2
Cockshut Hill Technology College
LGN/SDN/BHAMAIR B26 ...... 109 L5
Cocks Moors Woods Leisure Centre
ALE/KHTH/YWD B14 ...... 146 D1
Codsall Clinic
CDSL WV8 ...... 34 E2
Codsall Middle School
CDSL WV8 ...... 34 E2
Cofton Medical Centre
NFLD/LBR B31 ...... 144 E6
Cofton Primary School
NFLD/LBR B31 ...... 144 E7
Coldland Colts FC
SOLH B91 ...... 128 D7
Colebourne Primary School
BKDE/SHDE B34 ...... 91 J8
Coleshill CE Primary School
CSHL/WTROR B46 ...... 93 K7
Coleshill Clinic
CSHL/WTROR B46 ...... 93 L7
Coleshill Heath Primary School
CHWD/FDBR/MGN B37 ...... 111 G4
Coleshill Hotel
CSHL/WTROR B46 ...... 93 L7
Coleshill Industrial Estate
CSHL/WTROR B46 ...... 93 K3
Coleshill Leisure Centre
CSHL/WTROR B46 ...... 93 K7
Coleshill School
CSHL/WTROR B46 ...... 111 L2
Coleshill Town FC
CSHL/WTROR B46 ...... 111 L2
The College High School
KGSTG B44 ...... 71 L7
College of Continuing Education
WSL WS1 ...... 4 F9
College of Traditional Acupuncture
WWCK CV34 ...... 206 C7
Colley Lane Health Clinic
HALE B63 ...... 103 G7
Colley Lane Primary School
HALE B63 ...... 102 F7
Collingwood Primary School
WOLVN WV10 ...... 36 C3
Colmers Farm J & I School
RBRY B45 ...... 143 M5
Colmers Farm Secondary School
RBRY B45 ...... 143 M5
Colmore J & I School
ALE/KHTH/YWD B14 ...... 125 H6
Colonial Industrial Park
CDYHTH B64 ...... 103 H6
Colton Hills School
ETTPK/GDPK/PENN WV4 ...... 65 M1
Combe Abbey Country Park
COVS CV3 ...... 156 F2
Comberton First & Middle School
KIDD DY10 ...... 164 F1
Combined Courts
WOLV WV1 ...... 3 H5
Comfort Inn
LDYWD/EDGR B16 ...... 106 B4
Common Lane Industrial Estate
KNWTH CV8 ...... 180 A6
Community High School
CDSL WV8 ...... 34 E1
Community Leisure Centre
TPTN/OCK DY4 ...... 67 H7
Conduit Road Industrial Estate
CNCK/NC WS11 ...... 25 L1
Coneygre Industrial Estate
TPTN/OCK DY4 ...... 85 K2
Connect Business Park
WASH/WDE B8 ...... 108 A3
Conway Primary School
SPARK B11 ...... 107 M7
Cookley Wharf Industrial Estate
BRLYHL DY5 ...... 101 L2
Cooper & Jordan CE J & I School
ALDR WS9 ...... 41 G7
Copperfield House Hotel
SLYOAK B29 ...... 124 E2
Coppice High Community School
WNSFLD WV11 ...... 37 M5
Coppice Junior School
HIA/OLT B92 ...... 128 C6
Coppice Primary School
HLYWD B47 ...... 146 E7
MGN/WHC B75 ...... 57 G4
Coppice Side Industrial Estate
BRWNH WS8 ...... 26 B6
Coppice Trading Estate
KIDDW DY11 ...... 163 M5
Copsewood School
COVN CV6 ...... 133 M2
Copt Heath Golf Club
DOR/KN B93 ...... 149 L5
Copthorne Hotel
BRLYHL DY5 ...... 102 C1
CBHAMNW B3 ...... 6 D5
Corbett Hospital
STRBR DY8 ...... 101 L6
Corbett Industrial Estate
DUDS DY2 ...... 85 G7
Corley CC
RCOVN/BALC/EX CV7 ...... 115 G7
Corley School
RCOVN/BALC/EX CV7 ...... 114 F7
Corngreaves Hall Golf Club
CDYHTH B64 ...... 103 K5
Corngreaves J & I School
CDYHTH B64 ...... 103 H4
Corngreaves Trading Estate
CDYHTH B64 ...... 103 H6
Cornwall Industrial Estate
SMTHWK B66 ...... 88 A6
WASH/WDE B8 ...... 108 A1
Cornwall Road Industrial Estate
SMTHWK B66 ...... 88 A6
Corpus Christi RC Primary School
COVS CV3 ...... 156 B6
STETCH B33 ...... 109 H3
WNSFLD WV11 ...... 37 L5
Corus Hotel Solihull
SHLY B90 ...... 148 C6
Coseley Medical Centre
BILS/COS WV14 ...... 67 G5
The Coseley School
BILS/COS WV14 ...... 66 F4
Coseley Swimming Pool
BILS/COS WV14 ...... 67 G5
Coten End Primary School
WWCK CV34 ...... 205 K6
Coton Green Primary School
CRTAM B79 ...... 31 K6
Cotteridge Primary School
BVILLE B30 ...... 124 E8
Cottesbrooke Infant School
ACGN B27 ...... 127 H1
Cottesbrooke Junior School
ACGN B27 ...... 127 G1
Cotwall End Primary School
SEDG DY3 ...... 66 A6
Coundon Court School & Community College
COVN CV6 ...... 133 J6
COVN CV6 ...... 134 C6
Coundon Primary School
COVN CV6 ...... 133 J8
County Bridge Primary School
WLNHL WV13 ...... 52 C4
Courtfarm Primary School
ERDW/GRVHL B23 ...... 72 C7
Courthouse Green Primary School
COVN CV6 ...... 134 E5
Courtyard by Marriott
KNWTH CV8 ...... 182 B2
WWCK CV34 ...... 206 B8
Coventry Airport
COVS CV3 ...... 181 L4
Coventry Athletics Track
TLHL/CAN CV4 ...... 153 M7
Coventry Business Park
COVW CV5 ...... 154 B4
COVW CV5 ...... 154 D4
TLHL/CAN CV4 ...... 154 A3
Coventry Cathedral & Visitor Centre
COV CV1 ...... 9 G4
Coventry City FC (Jaguar Arena)
COVN CV6 ...... 134 C2
Coventry Golf Club
COVS CV3 ...... 181 H3
Coventry Grammar School
COVW CV5 ...... 154 D4
Coventry Hearsall Golf Club
COVW CV5 ...... 154 D5
Coventry Muslim School
COVN CV6 ...... 134 C5
Coventry RFC
COVN CV6 ...... 8 B2
Coventry Sports Centre
COV CV1 ...... 9 H4
The Coventry Toy Museum
COV CV1 ...... 9 H6
Coventry Trading Estate
COVS CV3 ...... 182 A4
Coventry Transport Museum
COV CV1 ...... 8 F3
Coventry University
COV CV1 ...... 9 G4
Coventry University Technocentre
COV CV1 ...... 9 H7
Coventry Welsh RFC
COVN CV6 ...... 134 B1
Crabbs Cross Medical Centre
REDW B97 ...... 202 C7
Crabtree Clinic
CHWD/FDBR/MGN B37 ...... 110 D3
Cradley CE Primary School
HALE B63 ...... 103 G6
Cradley Heath Community Recreation Centre
DUDS DY2 ...... 103 J3
Cradley High School
HALE B63 ...... 102 F7
Cradley Town FC
HALE B63 ...... 121 G1
Craig Croft Child Health Clinic
CHWD/FDBR/MGN B37 ...... 111 G3
Craig Croft Medical Centre
CHWD/FDBR/MGN B37 ...... 111 G3
Cranmore Industrial Estate
SHLY B90 ...... 148 C5
Cranmore Infant School
SOLH B91 ...... 148 C4
Crescent Industrial Park
DUDS DY2 ...... 84 F6
The Crescent School
RUGBYS/DCH CV22 ...... 186 B5
Crescent Theatre
LDYWD/EDGR B16 ...... 6 B6
Crestwood Park Primary School
KGSWFD DY6 ...... 83 L8
The Crestwood Secondary School
KGSWFD DY6 ...... 83 K8
Criterion Theatre
COVW CV5 ...... 8 A9
Crocketts Lane Primary School
SMTHWK B66 ...... 87 L8
Croft Foundry Industrial Estate
WLNHL WV13 ...... 51 L3
Croft Industrial Estate
CHWD/FDBR/MGN B37 ...... 110 F3
CHWD/FDBR/MGN B37 ...... 111 H3
Croft Junior School
NUNW/HART CV10 ...... 98 C2
Croft Medical Centre
RLSS CV31 ...... 207 G8
Croft Street JMI School
WSLW WS2 ...... 53 H1
Cromwell Primary School
VAUX/NECH B7 ...... 89 L7
Cronehill Primary School
WBROM B70 ...... 87 G1
Cronehills Health Centre
WBROM B70 ...... 87 H2
Croop Hill Cemetery
RUGBYS/DCH CV22 ...... 186 B3
Crossfield Industrial Estate
LICH WS13 ...... 21 J5
Crossings Industrial Estate
BLOX/PEL WS3 ...... 38 E5
Crossley Retail Park
KIDDW DY11 ...... 138 B6
Cross Quays Business Park
OLDBY B69 ...... 86 A3
Cross Road Industrial Estate
COVN CV6 ...... 134 D6
Cross Street Health Centre
DUDN DY1 ...... 85 G4
Crossways Shopping Centre
WOLVN WV10 ...... 50 E2
Crown Meadow First School
ALVE B48 ...... 170 E7
Crown Wharf Shopping Centre
WSLW WS2 ...... 4 D2
Crown Wharf Shopping Park
WSLW WS2 ...... 53 G1
Crystal Leisure Centre
STRBR DY8 ...... 101 K8
Cubbington CE Primary School
RLSN CV32 ...... 199 K8
Culwell Industrial Park
WOLVN WV10 ...... 3 J3
Culwell Trading Estate
WOLVN WV10 ...... 3 L1
Curdworth Primary School
WALM/CURD B76 ...... 75 G7
Dadsford Bridge Industrial Estate
STRBR DY8 ...... 101 J3
Dalehouse Lane Industrial Estate *KNWTH* CV8 ...... 180 A6
The Dales Community Junior School
TAM/AM/WIL B77 ...... 46 F5
Dame Elizabeth Cadbury School
BVILLE B30 ...... 124 C6
Dame Ellen Pinsent School
HRBN B17 ...... 105 M3
Damson Wood Infant School
HIA/OLT B92 ...... 128 B6
Danescourt Crematorium & Cemetery
DUNHL/THL/PER WV6 ...... 34 F7
Danesmore Park Primary School
WNSFLD WV11 ...... 37 K4
Darlaston Central Trading Estate
DARL/WED WS10 ...... 52 C6

Darlaston Clinic DARL/WED WS10 52 B7
Darlaston Community School DARL/WED WS10 51 M7
Darlaston FC DARL/WED WS10 52 B7
Darlaston Road Industrial Estate DARL/WED WS10 52 B8
Dartmouth Golf Club HHTH/SAND B71 69 J7
Dartmouth High School GTB/HAM B43 70 B2
Dartmouth Special School COVE CV2 135 H7
Davenport Lodge School COVW CV5 8 C9
David Lloyd Birmingham KGSTG B44 71 J2
Daw End School RUSH/SHEL WS4 39 M7
Dawley Brook Primary School KGSWFD DY6 83 G6
Dawley Trading Estate KGSWFD DY6 83 H5
Daylesford Infant School HIA/OLT B92 127 L2
Days Inn NUNW/HART CV10 98 F6
SPARK B11 108 A6
Deanery CE Primary School WALM/CURD B76 73 K5
Deansfield High School WOLV WV1 51 G3
Deedmore Special School COVE CV2 135 G5
Deeleys Industrial Estate WSLW WS2 38 F7
Deepdale Industrial Estate DUDN DY1 84 C2
The Dell Stadium BRLYHL DY5 83 M8
Delph Road Industrial Estate BRLYHL DY5 102 A4
Delph Road Industrial Park BRLYHL DY5 102 B4
Delta Business Centre CNCK/NC WS11 16 B7
Delta Trading Estate BKHL/PFLD WV2 3 L8
Delves J & I School DSYBK/YTR WS5 53 L8
Dental Health Centre KGSTG B44 71 K3
Dental Hospital CBHAMNE B4 7 G2
The Dentists Surgery WWCK CV34 205 J4
Department of Art (University of Central England) CBHAMNW B3 6 E4
The De Vere Belfry WALM/CURD B76 75 G2
Devonshire J & I School SMTHWKW B67 87 J8
Deykin Avenue J & I School AST/WIT B6 89 L3
D'Eyncourt Primary School WOLVN WV10 36 F6
Diana Princess of Wales Childrens Hospital CBHAMNE B4 7 G3
Dickens Heath Primary School SHLY B90 147 K7
Digbeth Coach Station DIG/EDG B5 7 J7
Dingle Primary School KGSWFD DY6 101 L1
Dingleside Middle School REDE B98 202 F5
Dock Lane Industrial Estate DUDN DY1 84 F4
Dock Meadow Drive Industrial Estate ETTPK/GDPK/PENN WV4 66 E1
Dodford First School BRGRVW B61 167 L8
Dolphin Sports Centre BRGRVE B60 191 L3
Doranda Way Industrial Park HHTH/SAND B71 87 K4
Dordon Primary School POL/KGSB/FAZ B78 47 L7
Dormston Secondary School SEDG DY3 66 C5
Dormston Trading Estate DUDN DY1 84 D1
Dorothy Pattison Hospital WSLW WS2 52 F4
Dorothy Purcell Junior School BILS/COS WV14 67 M2
Dorridge CC DOR/KN B93 175 J4
Dorridge J & I School DOR/KN B93 175 L2
Dorrington Primary School PBAR/PBCH B42 70 E7
Dosthill Primary School TAM/AM/WIL B77 46 A8
Doulton Trading Estate BLKHTH/ROWR B65 103 K1
Dovecote J & I School CDSL WV8 35 J4
The Dovecote Surgery LGLYGN/QTN B68 105 H6
Downing Close Health Clinic DOR/KN B93 175 L1
Drayton Court Hotel POL/KGSB/FAZ B78 45 L5
Drayton Manor Theme Park POL/KGSB/FAZ B78 45 K5
Drayton Park Golf Club POL/KGSB/FAZ B78 45 K6
Dreamwell Industrial Estate SPARK B11 108 D7
Driving Test Centre LICH WS13 20 E6
Droicon Industrial Estate BLKHTH/ROWR B65 85 M8
Droicon Trading Estate BLKHTH/ROWR B65 85 M8
The Dr Phillips Shopping Centre COVE CV2 135 H4
Druids Heath Golf Club ALDR WS9 41 G5
Duddeston Mill Trading Estate WASH/WDE B8 108 A1
Dudley Castle & Zoological Gardens DUDN DY1 85 H3
Dudley Central Trading Estate DUDS DY2 84 F5
Dudley College BRLYHL DY5 102 A2
BRLYHL DY5 102 C1
DUDN DY1 84 F3
Dudley College (Mons Hill Campus) DUDN DY1 84 F1
Dudley County Court BRLYHL DY5 102 C1
Dudley Golf Club BLKHTH/ROWR B65 85 L7
Dudley Kingswinford RFC KGSWFD DY6 82 E6
Dudley Leisure Centre DUDN DY1 84 F4
Dudley Metropolitan Borough Council DUDS DY2 103 H1
SEDG DY3 66 B4
Dudley Museum & Art Gallery DUDN DY1 85 G4
Dudley Town Hall DUDN DY1 85 G3
Dudley Water Sports Centre DUDS DY2 102 F2
Dudley Wood Primary School DUDS DY2 103 G3
Dunstall Hill Industrial Estate DUNHL/THL/PER WV6 36 A8
Dunton Trading Estate VAUX/NECH B7 90 B6
Durbar Avenue Industrial Estate COVN CV6 134 B5
Durberville Road Industrial Estate BKHL/PFLD WV2 50 D6
Eagle Industrial Estate TPTN/OCK DY4 68 B6
Eagle Trading Estate HALE B63 121 L1
Earl Place Business Park TLHL/CAN CV4 153 M4
Earlsdon Business Centre COVW CV5 154 D5
Earlsdon Primary School COVW CV5 8 A8
Earls High School HALE B63 121 M1
Earlswood Trading Estate HOCK/TIA B94 173 G7
Eastbourne House School ACGN B27 127 G1
East Cannock Industrial Estate HEDN WS12 16 F2
Eastern Green Junior School COVW CV5 132 B8
Eastfield Primary School WOLV WV1 3 M5
Eastlands CP School RUGBYN/HIL CV21 187 H3
Eastlands Court Business Centre RUGBYN/HIL CV21 187 G2
East Park J & I School WOLV WV1 50 F5
East Park Trading Estate BKHL/PFLD WV2 3 M8
Eastwood Business Village COVS CV3 156 D4
Eaton Wood Medical Centre ERDE/BCHGN B24 91 H2
Ebrook Adult Training Centre CSCFLD/WYGN B72 73 H2
Eclipse Industrial Estate TPTN/OCK DY4 67 J8
Eclipse Trading Estate TPTN/OCK DY4 67 J8
Edgar Stammers Primary School BLOX/PEL WS3 39 K6
Edgbaston Golf Club EDG B15 106 F7
Edgbaston Health Clinic EDG B15 106 C8
SOLH B91 127 K7
Edgbaston High School for Girls & Preparatory Department EDG B15 106 D6
Edgbaston Shopping Centre LDYWD/EDGR B16 106 E5
Edgewick Community Primary School COVN CV6 134 C5
Edgewood Road Clinic RBRY B45 143 M7
Edgwick Park Industrial Estate COVN CV6 134 D5
Edmondscote Track RLSN CV32 206 B6
Edward Street Hospital WBROM B70 87 G2
Electra Park Industrial Estate AST/WIT B6 89 M4
Electric Cinema DIG/EDG B5 6 F6
Electric Wharf COV CV1 134 A8
Elgar House Surgery REDW B97 202 C1
Elliott's Field Retail Park RUGBYN/HIL CV21 160 F6
The Ellowes Hall School SEDG DY3 66 A8
Elmdon Trading Estate CHWD/FDBR/MGN B37 111 G7
Elmore Green JMI School BLOX/PEL WS3 38 E4
Elms Farm Primary School STETCH B33 110 A6
Elms Health Centre HALE B63 102 F7
Elm Terrace Clinic OLDBY B69 85 M4
Elston Hall Primary School WOLVN WV10 36 B3
Embassy Industrial Estate HAG/WOL DY9 102 D8
Emmanuel School WSL WS1 4 F5
Empire Industrial Park ALDR WS9 40 D5
Emscote County Infant School WWCK CV34 205 M5
Emscote House School RLSN CV32 206 B5
Enfield Industrial Estate REDW B97 194 B8
English Martyrs RC Primary School RUGBYS/DCH CV22 187 K6
SPARK B11 126 A1
Ensign Business Centre TLHL/CAN CV4 153 K7
Enterprise Industrial Park LICHS WS14 21 K5
Enterprise Trading Estate BRLYHL DY5 102 D2
Episode - Leamington RLSN CV32 206 E4
Erasmus Darwin House LICH WS13 20 E5
Erdington Hall Primary School ERDE/BCHGN B24 90 D3
Erdington Industrial Park ERDE/BCHGN B24 91 K1
Erdington Medical Centre ERDW/GRVHL B23 90 C3
Erdington Pool & Turkish Suite ERDW/GRVHL B23 90 E1
Ernesford Grange Primary School COVS CV3 156 C4
Ernesford Grange School & Community School COVS CV3 156 B5
Essington Light Industrial Estate WNSFLD WV11 37 K1
Etone Community School NUN CV11 81 H8
Etone Sports Centre NUN CV11 81 H8
Ettingshall Primary School BKHL/PFLD WV2 50 F6
Euro Business Park OLDBY B69 86 C4
European Business Park OLDBY B69 86 C6
Eversfield Preparatory School SOLH B91 149 G1
Exchange Industrial Estate CNCK/NC WS11 16 C7
Exhall Business Park RCOVN/BALC/EX CV7 116 F5
Exhall Cedars Infant School RCOVN/BALC/EX CV7 116 F5
Exhall Grange Special School RCOVN/BALC/EX CV7 116 B8
Express by Holiday Inn COVS CV3 180 F1
Expressway Industrial Estate AST/WIT B6 89 J7
Eye Infirmary BDMR/CCFT WV3 2 B5
Fairey Industrial Estate TAM/AM/WIL B77 46 B5
Fairfax School MGN/WHC B75 57 K8
Fairfield First School BRGRVW B61 168 B2
Fairfield Villa FC BRGRVW B61 168 B2
Fairhaven Primary School STRBR DY8 101 H2
Fair View Industrial Estate WALM/CURD B76 74 F6
Fairway Primary School NFLD/LBR B31 145 H3
Falcon Lodge Clinic MGN/WHC B75 57 L8
Fallings Heath Cemetery DARL/WED WS10 52 D5
Fallings Park Industrial Estate WOLVN WV10 36 D8
Fallings Park Primary School WOLVN WV10 36 E6
Fazeley Health Centre POL/KGSB/FAZ B78 45 L5
Fazeley Industrial Estate DIG/EDG B5 7 K5
Featherstone Health Centre WOLVN WV10 22 F6
Featherstone Primary School ERDW/GRVHL B23 90 C1
Feldon Lane Clinic RMSLY B62 104 C6
Fernbank Medical Centre WASH/WDE B8 108 E1
Ferndale Primary School GTB/HAM B43 70 C5
Field Road Cemetery BLOX/PEL WS3 39 G4
Field Road Industrial Estate BLOX/PEL WS3 39 G5
Finham Park School COVS CV3 180 E1
Finham Primary School COVS CV3 180 F2
Finstall First School BRGRVE B60 191 M4
Firs Industrial Estate KIDDW DY11 164 A6
Firs Primary School CBROM B36 91 J5
Fir Tree Primary School DSYBK/YTR WS5 69 L1
Five Ways Primary School HEDN WS12 17 H3
Five Ways Shopping Centre EDG B15 6 A8
Flax Hill Junior School CRTAM B79 31 M6
Fletchamstead Highway Industrial Estate COVW CV5 154 B6
Fletchworth Gate Industrial Estate COVW CV5 154 A5
Florendine Primary School TAM/AM/WIL B77 32 D8
Foleshill Cemetery COVN CV6 134 E3
Foleshill CE Primary School COVN CV6 134 E3
Foleshill Leisure Centre COVN CV6 134 B6
Foley Business Park KIDDW DY11 163 M5
Foley Industrial Estate KIDDW DY11 164 A3
Foley Industrial Park KIDDW DY11 164 A4
Foley Park First School KIDDW DY11 164 A2
The Foot Clinic CBHAMNW B3 6 E4
Fordhouse Road Industrial Estate WOLVN WV10 36 A5
Fordhouses CC WOLVN WV10 36 B1
Fords Hospital COV CV1 8 E5
Forest Glades Leisure Centre KIDD DY10 138 C7
Forest Oak School CBROM B36 92 C4
Forge Mill Needle Museum & Bordesley Abbey REDE B98 194 D7
Forge Trading Estate RMSLY B62 104 A8
Formans Trading Estate SPARK B11 126 B2
Fort Industrial Park CVALE B35 91 K4
The Fort Shopping Park ERDE/BCHGN B24 91 G4
Forum Health Centre COVE CV2 156 B1
Fosse Wayside Industrial Estate RUGBYN/HIL CV21 187 H1
Foundry Primary School WSNGN B18 88 B7
Fountain Court Hotel LDYWD/EDGR B16 106 A4
Four Dwellings High School RIDG/WDGT B32 104 F8
Four Dwellings Infant School RIDG/WDGT B32 104 F8
Four Oaks J & I School FOAKS/STRLY B74 56 C1
Four Oaks Medical Centre MGN/WHC B75 56 F3
Four Oaks Saints CC FOAKS/STRLY B74 42 C8
Four Seasons Art Gallery ERDE/BCHGN B24 72 E8
Foxford School & Community Arts College COVN CV6 116 E8
Fox & Goose Shopping Centre WASH/WDE B8 91 G7
The Fox Hollies Leisure Centre HLGN/YWD B28 126 E4
Fox Hollies Special School ACGN B27 126 E4
Foxmill Estate SPARK B11 126 B3
Foxyards Primary School TPTN/OCK DY4 67 G8
Franche Clinic KIDDW DY11 137 M5
Franche First School KIDDW DY11 137 M5
Franche Middle School KIDDW DY11 137 M5
Frank F Harrison Comprehensive School SHHTH WV12 38 D6
Frank Halfpenny Hall LICH WS13 21 G5
Frankley Community High School RBRY B45 143 K3
Frankley Health Centre RBRY B45 143 L4
Frankley Industrial Park RBRY B45 143 M4
Frank Whittle Primary School COVE CV2 135 K5
Frederick Bird Primary School COVE CV2 134 D8
Friar Park Clinic DARL/WED WS10 69 H2
Friary Grange Sports Centre LICH WS13 20 D3
The Friary School LICH WS13 20 C3
Frogmill Junior School RBRY B45 143 M3
Fulfen Primary School BNTWD WS7 19 H6
Fulford Heath Golf Club HLYWD B47 172 F3
Gainsborough House Hotel KIDDW DY11 137 M8
Gainsborough Trading Estate STRBR DY8 119 M1
Gallagher Business Park COVN CV6 134 C1
Gallagher Retail Park COVN CV6 134 D5
Galley Common Infant School NUNW/HART CV10 79 K8
Galley Common Medical Centre NUNW/HART CV10 97 K1
Garden Organic Ryton KNWTH CV8 183 J3
Garretts Green Trading Estate STETCH B33 110 A4
Gas Street Basin CBHAMW B1 6 C6
Gatehouse Trading Estate BRWNH WS8 26 E4
Gate Medical Centre WASH/WDE B8 90 B7
Gay Hill Golf Club HLYWD B47 146 E5
George Auden School NFLD/LBR B31 123 K8
George Betts Primary School SMTHWK B66 87 G6
George Dixon School & Sixth Form HRBN B17 106 A3
The George Eliot Hospital NUNW/HART CV10 98 F3
George Eliot School NUN CV11 99 H4
George Fentham Endowed Primary School HIA/OLT B92 129 L7
The George Hotel BEWD DY12 162 E2
LICH WS13 20 F5
George Salter High School WBROM B70 86 E1
German Cemetery HEDN WS12 12 D1
Gibbons Industrial Park KGSWFD DY6 83 L6
The Giffard RC Primary School DUNHL/THL/PER WV6 35 K8
Gig Mill Primary School STRBR DY8 119 J2
Gilbertstone Primary School LGN/SDN/BHAMAIR B26 109 H8
GK Davies Industrial Estate HALE B63 102 E7
Glascote Health Centre TAM/AM/WIL B77 46 D3
Glascote Heath Primary School TAM/AM/WIL B77 46 D3
Glebe Farm Industrial Estate RUGBYN/HIL CV21 160 D6
Glebefields Health Centre TPTN/OCK DY4 67 L5
Glebe Fields Primary School TPTN/OCK DY4 67 L4
Glendale Infant School NUNW/HART CV10 98 D3
Glenmead J & I School KGSTG B44 71 H5
Glenthorne CP School GTWY WS6 24 C2
Glynne Primary School KGSWFD DY6 101 G1
Godiva Trading Estate COVN CV6 134 D5
Golden Hillock School SPARK B11 108 B7
The Golden Lion Hotel RRUGBY CV23 159 J1
Goldtel Industrial Estate ETTPK/GDPK/PENN WV4 50 E8
Goldthorne Medical Centre BKHL/PFLD WV2 50 A7
Goldthorn Park Primary School ETTPK/GDPK/PENN WV4 50 B8
Good Hope Hospital MGN/WHC B75 57 H7
Good Shepherd RC Primary School COVN CV6 134 D4
Goodyers End Primary School BDWTH CV12 116 C5
Gornal Wood Cemetery SEDG DY3 83 M4
Gorsemoor Primary School HEDN WS12 17 H4
Goscote Hospital BLOX/PEL WS3 39 K5
Goscote Industrial Estate BLOX/PEL WS3 39 J4
Gosford Industrial Estate COV CV1 9 K5
Gosford Park Primary School COV CV1 9 M6
Gossey Lane J & I School STETCH B33 110 A3
The GPT Golf Club COVS CV3 156 B4
Gracechurch Shopping Centre CSCFLD/WYGN B72 56 F8
Grace Mary Primary School OLDBY B69 86 A6
Grafton Manor House BRGRVW B61 190 F6
Graiseley Primary School BKHL/PFLD WV2 2 E9
Granada Industrial Estate OLDBY B69 86 D7
The Granary Hotel KIDD DY10 165 H5
Granby Business Park STETCH B33 110 B4
Grand Theatre WOLV WV1 3 G5
The Grange Arts & Media Centre WSL WS1 4 F2
Grange Farm Primary School COVS CV3 154 F8
Grangehurst Primary School COVE CV2 134 F1
The Grange Playhouse WSL WS1 5 M4
The Grange School HAG/WOL DY9 120 B1
Gravel Hill Surgery WMBN WV5 64 F7
Gravelly Industrial Park ERDE/BCHGN B24 90 C5
Grazebrook Industrial Estate DUDS DY2 84 E7
Grazebrook Industrial Park DUDS DY2 84 F7
Great Barr Business Park PBAR/PBCH B42 70 E8
Great Barr Golf Club GTB/HAM B43 70 D1
Great Barr Hotel & Conference Centre GTB/HAM B43 69 M4
Great Bridge Industrial Estate TPTN/OCK DY4 68 A6
Great Bridge Primary School TPTN/OCK DY4 68 A7
Great Central Way Industrial Estate RUGBYN/HIL CV21 187 H1
Great Western Industrial Estate WSNGN B18 88 C7
Great Wyrley High School GTWY WS6 24 D1
Green Acres Primary School BILS/COS WV14 51 K7
Greenacres Primary School TAM/AM/WIL B77 32 F8
Greenfield Primary School RUSH/SHEL WS4 40 A5
STRBR DY8 101 K8
Greenfield Surgery STRBR DY8 101 K8
Greenhill Health Centre LICH WS13 21 G5
Greenhill Industrial Estate KIDD DY10 138 E6
Greenholm J & I School KGSTG B44 71 J6
Green Industrial Estate HEDN WS12 13 G6
Greenlands Business Centre REDE B98 202 F4
Green Lane Industrial Estate BORD B9 108 C3
Green Meadow Primary School SLYOAK B29 123 K6
Green Rock J & I School BLOX/PEL WS3 39 J4
Green Street Trading Estate KIDD DY10 138 C8
Greet Primary School SPARK B11 126 B1
Greets Green Road Industrial Estate WBROM B70 86 D1
Gregston Industrial Estate OLDBY B69 86 F5
Grendon Primary School ALE/KHTH/YWD B14 146 E2
Grestone Primary School BFLD/HDSWWD B20 88 C1
Greswold Primary School SOLH B91 127 M7
Greysbrooke CP School LICHS WS14 28 E7
Griff Clara Industrial Estate NUNW/HART CV10 98 D6
Griffin Business Park CHWD/FDBR/MGN B37 111 G2
Griffin Industrial Estate BLKHTH/ROWR B65 104 D2

Griffins Brook Medical Centre *SLYOAK* B29 ... 124 A6
Grimstock Country House Hotel *CSHL/WTROR* B46 ... 93 J4
The Grinnall Business Centre *STRPT* DY13 ... 188 F4
Grosvenor Hotel *RUGBYN/HIL* CV21 ... 186 F2
Grosvenor Shopping Centre *NFLD/LBR* B31 ... 144 E1
Grovelands Industrial Estate *RCOVN/BALC/EX* CV7 ... 116 E7
Grove Medical Centre *BKHL/PFLD* WV2 ... 3 J9
Grove Park Industrial Estate *CNCK/NC* WS11 ... 16 C7
Grove Primary School *BKHL/PFLD* WV2 ... 3 J9
Grove School *HDSW* B21 ... 88 D5
Grove Vale Primary School *GTB/HAM* B43 ... 70 B4
Guardian Angels RC Primary School *BKDE/SHDE* B34 ... 92 B7
Guest Hospital *DUDN* DY1 ... 85 J2
Gulson Road Clinic *COV* CV1 ... 9 J5
Gun Barrel Industrial Centre *CDYHTH* B64 ... 103 L7
Gun Hill Infant School *RCOVN/BALC/EX* CV7 ... 96 E5
Guns Village Primary School *WBROM* B70 ... 86 E2
Gunter Primary School *ERDE/BCHGN* B24 ... 91 J1
Gupta Trading Estate *OLDBY* B69 ... 86 D4
Guy Motors Industrial Park *WOLVN* WV10 ... 36 C8
GWS Industrial Estate *DARL/WED* WS10 ... 68 B4
GWS Trading Estate *TPTN/OCK* DY4 ... 68 B4
Habberley Golf Club *KIDDW* DY11 ... 137 J4
Haden Hill Leisure Centre *CDYHTH* B64 ... 103 K5
Hadley Stadium *SMTHWK* B66 ... 105 L2
Hagley Cemetery *HAG/WOL* DY9 ... 119 M8
Hagley Golf & Country Club *HAG/WOL* DY9 ... 120 E5
Hagley Hall *HAG/WOL* DY9 ... 120 B7
Hagley RC High School *STRBR* DY8 ... 119 K7
Haigs Hotel *RCOVN/BALC/EX* CV7 ... 151 M6
Halas Industrial Estate *HALE* B63 ... 103 M8
Halcyon Gallery *CBHAM* B2 ... 6 F6
Halesbury Special School *RMSLY* B62 ... 104 C5
Hales Industrial Park *COVN* CV6 ... 134 C1
Halesowen CC *HALE* B63 ... 121 M3
Halesowen CE Primary School *HALE* B63 ... 121 L1
Halesowen College *HALE* B63 ... 103 M8
Halesowen FC (The Grove Recreation Ground) *HALE* B63 ... 103 L8
Halesowen Golf Club *RMSLY* B62 ... 104 B8
Halesowen Harriers FC *HALE* B63 ... 102 F8
Halesowen Health Centre *HALE* B63 ... 121 M2
Halesowen Industrial Park *RMSLY* B62 ... 103 M7
Halesowen Leisure Centre *HALE* B63 ... 121 M2
Halesowen Magistrates Court *HALE* B63 ... 121 M2
Hale Trading Estate *TPTN/OCK* DY4 ... 67 M8
Hallfield School *EDG* B15 ... 106 E6
Hall Green J & I School *HHTH/SAND* B71 ... 69 G4
HLGN/YWD B28 ... 126 C6
Hall Green Little Theatre *ACGN* B27 ... 126 E3
Hall Green Secondary School *HLGN/YWD* B28 ... 126 C5
Hall Green Stadium *HLGN/YWD* B28 ... 126 D4
Hallmoor Special School *STETCH* B33 ... 109 M2
Hall of Memory *CBHAMW* B1 ... 6 D5
Hamd House School *SMHTH* B10 ... 108 C5
Ham Dingle Primary School *HAG/WOL* DY9 ... 120 A3
Hamilton Special School *HDSW* B21 ... 88 B5
Hammerwich Hospital *BNTWD* WS7 ... 18 F8
Hammond Business Centre *NUN* CV11 ... 99 J2
Hams Hall International Freight Terminal *CSHL/WTROR* B46 ... 93 L2
Hams Hall National Distribution Park *CSHL/WTROR* B46 ... 93 M1
Hamstead Hall School *BFLD/HDSWWD* B20 ... 70 C7
Hamstead J & I School *GTB/HAM* B43 ... 70 B6
Hanburys Farm Community Primary School *TAM/AM/WIL* B77 ... 46 B4
Handsworth Boys Grammar School *HDSW* B21 ... 88 C5
Handsworth Cemetery *HDSW* B21 ... 87 M3
Handsworth Golf Club *BFLD/HDSWWD* B20 ... 88 B1
Handsworth Leisure Centre *BFLD/HDSWWD* B20 ... 88 D5
Handsworth RFC *GTB/HAM* B43 ... 70 B1
Handsworth Wood Girls School & Sixth Form Centre *BFLD/HDSWWD* B20 ... 88 D3
Hanford Close Industrial Estate *COVN* CV6 ... 134 C7
Harborne Church Farm Golf Club *HRBN* B17 ... 123 M1
Harborne Golf Club *RIDG/WDGT* B32 ... 105 L8
Harborne Hill School *EDG* B15 ... 106 C7
Harborne Pool & Fitness Centre *HRBN* B17 ... 105 M8
Harborne Primary School *HRBN* B17 ... 106 A7
Harden Primary School *BLOX/PEL* WS3 ... 39 J6
Hargate Primary School *HHTH/SAND* B71 ... 87 G1
Harnall Lane Industrial Estate *COV* CV1 ... 9 H1
Harnall Lane Medical Centre *COV* CV1 ... 9 H1
Harriers Industrial Estate *KIDD* DY10 ... 138 D8
Harris CE High School *RUGBYS/DCH* CV22 ... 186 D4
Harrisons Institute & Sports Club *GTWY* WS6 ... 24 E4
Harry Mitchell Leisure Centre *SMTHWKW* B67 ... 87 K8
The Harry Taylor First School *REDW* B97 ... 202 C7
Hartlebury Castle *KIDDW* DY11 ... 189 K2
Hartlebury CE School *KIDDW* DY11 ... 189 K2
Hartshill Hayes Country Park *NUNW/HART* CV10 ... 79 L4
Hartshill School *NUNW/HART* CV10 ... 79 M5
Harvey Road Health Centre *LGN/SDN/BHAMAIR* B26 ... 109 J6
Harvills Hawthorn Primary School *WBROM* B70 ... 68 D6
Harvington Hall *KIDD* DY10 ... 165 M4
Hasbury CE Primary School *HALE* B63 ... 121 K3
Haslucks Green Junior School *SHLY* B90 ... 147 L2
Hastingwood Industrial Park *ERDE/BCHGN* B24 ... 90 F4
Hatchford Brook Golf Club *LGN/SDN/BHAMAIR* B26 ... 128 C1
Hatchford Brook Primary School *HIA/OLT* B92 ... 128 A2
Hatchford GM Primary School *CHWD/FDBR/MGN* B37 ... 110 D3
Hateley Heath Primary School *HHTH/SAND* B71 ... 68 F6
Hatherton Lane Primary School *WSLW* WS2 ... 38 D7
Haunchwood Park Industrial Estate *NUNW/HART* CV10 ... 97 J1
Havergal CE Primary School *WOLVN* WV10 ... 23 G3
Hawbush Primary School *BRLYHL* DY5 ... 101 M3
Hawkesbury Field School *COVE* CV2 ... 135 G2
Hawkes Green Medical Centre *HEDN* WS12 ... 17 G3
Hawkesley Church Primary School *HWK/WKHTH* B38 ... 145 J6
Hawkesley Health Centre *HWK/WKHTH* B38 ... 145 J6
Hawkins Colliery Sports Club *GTWY* WS6 ... 24 B1
Hawkins Sports Club *GTWY* WS6 ... 24 B1
Hawksmill Industrial Estate *SMHTH* B10 ... 108 A4
Hawthorne Primary School *KGSTG* B44 ... 71 L6
Hawthorns Business Centre *SMTHWK* B66 ... 87 L5
Hawthorns Industrial Estate *SMTHWK* B66 ... 87 M5
Haybridge High School & Sixth Form *STRBR* DY8 ... 119 K7
Hayes Trading Estate *HAG/WOL* DY9 ... 102 E7
Hayley Green Hospital *HALE* B63 ... 121 H5
Hayward Industrial Park *ALDR* WS9 ... 40 E6
Hazelhead Industrial Estate *COV* CV1 ... 9 L6
Hazell Way Industrial Estate *NUNW/HART* CV10 ... 98 D4
Hazel Oak School *SHLY* B90 ... 147 L3
Hazel Slade Primary School *HEDN* WS12 ... 13 L7
Healthcare Clinic *CSCFLD/WYGN* B72 ... 72 F5
Hearsall Primary School *COVW* CV5 ... 8 A6
The Heartlands High School *VAUX/NECH* B7 ... 7 M1
Heart of England Crematorium *NUN* CV11 ... 99 K2
Heart of England School *RCOVN/BALC/EX* CV7 ... 151 M7
Heath Business Park *KNWTH* CV8 ... 184 B4
Heath Clinic *SOLH* B91 ... 128 B8
Heathcote Industrial Estate *WWCK* CV34 ... 206 B8
Heathfield Foundation Technology College *CDYHTH* B64 ... 103 K3
Heathfield Primary School *LOZ/NWT* B19 ... 89 G5
Heathfield School *KIDD* DY10 ... 138 D3
Heathfields Infant School *TAM/AM/WIL* B77 ... 46 D7
Heath Hayes Clinic *HEDN* WS12 ... 17 J4
Heath Hayes Primary School *HEDN* WS12 ... 17 K3
Heathlands Primary (NC) School *BKDE/SHDE* B34 ... 91 K6
Heath Lane Cemetery *HHTH/SAND* B71 ... 69 H6
Heath Lane Hospital *HHTH/SAND* B71 ... 69 H6
Heath Lodge Hotel *CHWD/FDBR/MGN* B37 ... 111 H5
Heath Mount Primary School *BHTH/HG* B12 ... 107 J7
Heath Park High School *WOLVN* WV10 ... 36 E8
Heath Street Industrial Estate *SMTHWK* B66 ... 88 B8
Heath Town Leisure Centre *WOLVN* WV10 ... 50 E1
Hebrew Congregation *CBHAMW* B1 ... 6 E7
Hedging Lane Industrial Estate *TAM/AM/WIL* B77 ... 46 B8
Hednesford Town FC (Keys Park) *HEDN* WS12 ... 17 H2
Hemdale Business Park *NUN* CV11 ... 99 K2
Henley College Coventry *COVE* CV2 ... 155 M2
COVN CV6 ... 134 F4
Henley College ECDL Centre *COVN* CV6 ... 133 L6
Henley Industrial Park *COVE* CV2 ... 135 J6
Henry Bellairs CE Junior School *BDWTH* CV12 ... 117 H2
Henry Hinde Infant School *RUGBYS/DCH* CV22 ... 186 A4
Henry Hinde Junior School *RUGBYS/DCH* CV22 ... 185 M3
Henry Parkes Primary School *TLHL/CAN* CV4 ... 154 A5
Herald Business Park *COVS* CV3 ... 156 D6
Herbert Art Gallery & Museum *COV* CV1 ... 9 G5
Herbert Fowler Junior School *RCOVN/BALC/EX* CV7 ... 96 D3
Hereford & Worcester County Museum *KIDDW* DY11 ... 189 K2
Hereward College *TLHL/CAN* CV4 ... 153 K4
Hewell Road Swimming Pool *REDW* B97 ... 194 A8
Higham Lane School *NUNW/HART* CV10 ... 81 J7
Higham on the Hill Primary School *MKTBOS/BARL/STKG* CV13 ... 81 L1
The High Arcal Secondary School *SEDG* DY3 ... 66 D7
Highclare St Paul's School *FOAKS/STRLY* B74 ... 56 F6
Highclare School *CSCFLD/WYGN* B72 ... 73 G4
Highclare the Abbey School *ERDW/GRVHL* B23 ... 72 E8
Highcroft Hospital *ERDW/GRVHL* B23 ... 90 B2
Highfield Primary School *WASH/WDE* B8 ... 90 C8
Highfields Primary School *BILS/COS* WV14 ... 67 G3
BLKHTH/ROWR B65 ... 104 A5
BNTWD WS7 ... 19 G6
Highfields School *ETTPK/GDPK/PENN* WV4 ... 48 F8
Highgate Business Centre *BHTH/HG* B12 ... 107 M7
Highgate Medical Centre *BHTH/HG* B12 ... 107 K6
Highgate Primary School *DUDS* DY2 ... 84 D7
Highgate Retail Park *BHTH/HG* B12 ... 107 K6
Highgate Trading Estate *BHTH/HG* B12 ... 107 L6
Highgate United FC *SHLY* B90 ... 147 J7
High Meadow Infant School *CSHL/WTROR* B46 ... 93 K5
Highters Heath J & I School *ALE/KHTH/YWD* B14 ... 146 F2
Hillary Primary School *WSLW* WS2 ... 4 A9
Hill Avenue Primary School *ETTPK/GDPK/PENN* WV4 ... 66 D2
Hillcrest Business Park *DUDS* DY2 ... 85 G6
Hillcrest Industrial Estate *CDYHTH* B64 ... 103 H5
Hillcrest School & Community College *DUDS* DY2 ... 84 F8
Hillcrest School & Sixth Form Centre *RIDG/WDGT* B32 ... 123 J2
Hill Farm Primary School *COVN* CV6 ... 133 M6
Hillfields Health Centre *COV* CV1 ... 9 H2
Hillmeads Health Centre *HWK/WKHTH* B38 ... 145 L4
Hillmorton Primary School *RUGBYN/HIL* CV21 ... 187 M5
Hillstone Primary School *BKDE/SHDE* B34 ... 92 B8
Hill Top Industrial Estate *WBROM* B70 ... 68 D5
Hilltop Medical Centre *LGLYGN/QTN* B68 ... 105 G3
Hilltop Public Golf Course *HDSW* B21 ... 88 A1
Hilton Cross Business Park *WOLVN* WV10 ... 22 F7
Hilton Main Industrial Estate *WNSFLD* WV11 ... 23 G8
Hilton Trading Estate *ETTPK/GDPK/PENN* WV4 ... 66 D1
Himley Country Hotel *SEDG* DY3 ... 82 F2
Himley Hall Golf Centre *SEDG* DY3 ... 83 J1
Himley Hall & Park *SEDG* DY3 ... 83 H1
Himley House Hotel *SEDG* DY3 ... 83 G2
Hingley Industrial Park *DUDS* DY2 ... 103 G4
Hippodrome Theatre *CBHAMW* B1 ... 6 F8
Hive Industrial Centre *WSNGN* B18 ... 88 E7
HM Prison *WOLVN* WV10 ... 22 D6
WSNGN B18 ... 88 C8
Hob Green Primary School *HAG/WOL* DY9 ... 120 C3
Hobmoor Primary School *YDLY* B25 ... 109 H5
Hobs Moat Medical Centre *HIA/OLT* B92 ... 127 L3
Hockley Brook Trading Estate *WSNGN* B18 ... 88 E7
Hockley Heath Pavilion (Sports Centre) *HOCK/TIA* B94 ... 175 G7
Hockley Heath Primary School *HOCK/TIA* B94 ... 174 F7
Hockley Hill Industrial Estate *WSNGN* B18 ... 88 F8
Hodge Hill Girls School *CBROM* B36 ... 91 G6
Hodge Hill School *CBROM* B36 ... 91 G6
Holbrook Park Industrial Estate *COVN* CV6 ... 134 B5
Holbrook Primary School *COVN* CV6 ... 134 C4
Holiday Inn *SOLH* B91 ... 148 F2
Holland House Infant School *CSCFLD/WYGN* B72 ... 73 G1
Holland Industrial Park *DARL/WED* WS10 ... 52 B5
Holliday Wharf *CBHAMW* B1 ... 6 D7
Hollies Business Park *CNCK/NC* WS11 ... 16 D5
The Hollies Clinic *LGLYGN/QTN* B68 ... 104 F1
Hollies Industrial Estate *BDMR/CCFT* WV3 ... 2 D8
Holloway Bank Trading Estate *DARL/WED* WS10 ... 68 D4
Holly Bush Medical Centre *RIDG/WDGT* B32 ... 105 H6
Holly Farm Business Park *KNWTH* CV8 ... 177 M6
Hollyfast Primary School *COVN* CV6 ... 133 J6
Hollyfield Primary School *MGN/WHC* B75 ... 73 K1
Holly Grove Primary School *BNTWD* WS7 ... 18 C4
Holly Hall Clinic *DUDN* DY1 ... 84 D6
Hollyhedge Primary School *HHTH/SAND* B71 ... 69 J5
Holly Hill Infant School *RBRY* B45 ... 143 K3
Holly Lane Cemetery *SMTHWKW* B67 ... 87 H8
Holly Lodge High School *SMTHWKW* B67 ... 87 H6
Holly Park Industrial Estate *ERDE/BCHGN* B24 ... 91 G3
Hollywalk Clinic *RLSN* CV32 ... 206 E5
Hollywood Primary School *ALE/KHTH/YWD* B14 ... 146 E4
Holte School *LOZ/NWT* B19 ... 89 H6
Holt Farm Primary School *RMSLY* B62 ... 104 C4
Holy Child School *EDG* B15 ... 106 F7
Holy Cross Catholic Primary School *WALM/CURD* B76 ... 73 L2
Holy Family RC J & I School *COVN* CV6 ... 133 M2
Holy Family RC Primary School *SMHTH* B10 ... 108 C6
Holyhead Primary School *DARL/WED* WS10 ... 68 B2
Holyhead School *HDSW* B21 ... 88 B5
Holy Name RC Primary School *GTB/HAM* B43 ... 70 C4
Holyoakes Field First School *REDW* B97 ... 202 B1
Holy Rosary RC Primary School *WOLV* WV1 ... 50 E4
Holy Souls RC Primary School *ACGN* B27 ... 127 G2
Holy Trinity Catholic Primary School *BILS/COS* WV14 ... 51 J7
Holy Trinity CE Primary School *BFLD/HDSWWD* B20 ... 89 G3
BRWNH WS8 ... 26 B7
WBROM B70 ... 87 H4
Holy Trinity RC School *SMHTH* B10 ... 108 A5
Holy Trinity School *KIDD* DY10 ... 138 D6
Holywell Primary School *RBRY* B45 ... 143 H6
Honiley Court Hotel & Conference Centre *KNWTH* CV8 ... 177 M8
Hoobrook Industrial Estate *KIDD* DY10 ... 164 B1
Hood Street Industrial Estate *COV* CV1 ... 9 J4
Hoo Farm Industrial Estate *KIDD* DY10 ... 164 C4
Hope Aldridge Business Centre *NUNW/HART* CV10 ... 81 G7
Horeston Grange Shopping Centre *NUN* CV11 ... 81 L8
Hornchurch Close Industrial Estate *COV* CV1 ... 8 F8
Horrell Road Health Centre *LGN/SDN/BHAMAIR* B26 ... 109 L6
Horse Shoe Associated FC *SHLY* B90 ... 147 K7
Hospital of St Cross *RUGBYS/DCH* CV22 ... 186 F4
Hotel Clarine *LDYWD/EDGR* B16 ... 106 C4
Hotel du Vin & Bistro *CBHAMNW* B3 ... 6 F4
Hotel Ibis *CBHAMW* B1 ... 6 E8
COV CV1 ... 9 G7
COVS CV3 ... 155 K7
DIG/EDG B5 ... 7 G7
SMHTH B10 ... 107 M4
Howard Street Industrial Estate *WBROM* B70 ... 68 D6
Howes Primary School *COVS* CV3 ... 155 H8
Howley Grange Primary School *RMSLY* B62 ... 104 E8
HRS Business Park *STETCH* B33 ... 109 M4
HRS Industrial Estate *STETCH* B33 ... 110 A4
Hudson Industrial Estate *BKHL/PFLD* WV2 ... 50 D6
Hulbert Industrial Estate *DUDS* DY2 ... 84 F7
Hunt End Industrial Estate *REDW* B97 ... 202 A8
Hunters Hill School *BRGRVE* B60 ... 169 K8
Hunters Lane Industrial Estate *RUGBYN/HIL* CV21 ... 160 E8
Huntingtree Primary School *HALE* B63 ... 121 J1
Hurley Primary School *ATHST* CV9 ... 77 H1
Hurst Business Park *BRLYHL* DY5 ... 102 D1
Hurstgreen Primary School *RMSLY* B62 ... 104 C5
Hurst Hill Primary School *BILS/COS* WV14 ... 66 E5
Hydesville Tower School *WSL* WS1 ... 5 J2
Hylands Hotel *COVS* CV3 ... 8 E9
IKEA Store Coventry *COV* CV1 ... 8 D5
IKEA Store Wednesbury *DARL/WED* WS10 ... 52 E7
Ikon Gallery *CBHAMW* B1 ... 6 C6
Ikon Industrial Estate *KIDD* DY10 ... 165 H8
IMAX Cinema *DIG/EDG* B5 ... 7 K4
Imex Business Park *BKHL/PFLD* WV2 ... 50 A6
BORD B9 ... 108 B3
SPARK B11 ... 108 D7
STETCH B33 ... 91 H8
TPTN/OCK DY4 ... 85 L2
Imex Industrial Estate *WSNGN* B18 ... 106 E1
Indian High Commission *WSNGN* B18 ... 6 C1
Industrial Training Centre *TLHL/CAN* CV4 ... 153 J5
Infant Welfare Clinic *GTB/HAM* B43 ... 70 C3
Innkeeper's Lodge *BRGRVW* B61 ... 168 F4
DOR/KN B93 ... 176 B2
HIA/OLT B92 ... 127 M1
KGSWFD DY6 ... 83 G7
LICH WS13 ... 20 C3
RCOVN/BALC/EX CV7 ... 131 G4
RIDG/WDGT B32 ... 105 G6
SCFLD/BOLD B73 ... 55 L8
International Convention Centre *CBHAMW* B1 ... 6 C5
International School & Community College *STETCH* B33 ... 110 B2
Ipsley CE Middle School *REDE* B98 ... 203 J3
Izons Lane Industrial Estate *WBROM* B70 ... 86 D4
Jack o'Watton Business Park *CSHL/WTROR* B46 ... 93 H2
Jack o'Watton Industrial Estate *CSHL/WTROR* B46 ... 93 H2
Jaguar Daimler Heritage Centre *COVW* CV5 ... 132 F5
James Watt Industrial Park *SMTHWK* B66 ... 88 A7
Jane Lane Special School *WSLW* WS2 ... 52 D2
Janet Shaw Clinic *CHWD/FDBR/MGN* B37 ... 110 E5
JAS Industrial Park *BLKHTH/ROWR* B65 ... 104 C1
Jerome Primary School *CNCK/NC* WS11 ... 17 K8
Jerome Retail Park *WSL* WS1 ... 4 D5
Jervoise J & I School *SLYOAK* B29 ... 123 L4
Jessons CE First & Middle School *DUDN* DY1 ... 84 E4
Jewellery Quarter *WSNGN* B18 ... 6 C1
The Jewellery Quarter Discovery Centre *WSNGN* B18 ... 88 F8
Jewish Cemetery *AST/WIT* B6 ... 71 L8
JFK Memorial *CBHAMNE* B4 ... 6 F3
John Black Day Hospital *CHWD/FDBR/MGN* B37 ... 110 F5
John Gulson Primary School *COV* CV1 ... 134 B8
John Shelton Primary School *COVN* CV6 ... 134 B1
John Willmott School *WALM/CURD* B76 ... 73 K1
John Wood CE Infant School *CNCK/NC* WS11 ... 16 B5
Joseph Cash JMI School *COVN* CV6 ... 134 A6
Joseph Chamberlain Sixth Form College *BHTH/HG* B12 ... 107 K6
Joseph Leckie Comprehensive School *WSL* WS1 ... 53 J8
Joseph Turner Primary School *TPTN/OCK* DY4 ... 67 M6
Josiah Mason College *CVALE* B35 ... 91 M2
DUDN DY1 ... 84 D5
KGSTG B44 ... 71 H4
MOS/BIL B13 ... 125 J3
Jubilee Business Park *HAG/WOL* DY9 ... 102 D8
Jubilee Park Primary School *TPTN/OCK* DY4 ... 67 M5
Jubilee Sports Centre *NUNW/HART* CV10 ... 98 E2
Junction 2 Industrial Estate *OLDBY* B69 ... 86 D7
Junction 6 Industrial Park *AST/WIT* B6 ... 89 M3
Junction Industrial Estate *SMTHWK* B66 ... 87 K5
Junction One Retail Park *RUGBYN/HIL* CV21 ... 160 F7
Jurys Inn *CBHAMW* B1 ... 6 C6
Karis Medical Centre *LDYWD/EDGR* B16 ... 106 D4

INTRODUCTION

In the early days of the National Literacy Strategy, schools found it necessary to make best use of their existing collections of texts because of financial constraints. There was also limited understanding on the part of many publishers about the type of texts needed to enable children to make use of different sources of 'searchlight' information in a balanced way. We were very reluctant to include many reading scheme books that were written from a different pedagogical approach, but felt obliged to make our listings inclusive during that initial period.

Over the past five years, however, there has been an explosion in educational publishing, and publishers, working closely with educational advisers, have produced a greater proportion of high quality guided reading materials. More funding has been available in schools for books, and teachers have become more skilled at choosing sets of books that offer a range of experience, particularly in the earliest bands.

In this edition, therefore, we have been selective. We have omitted, as before, out-of-print materials, texts that lack punctuation, those marketed as 'phonic' texts, and those we feel to be too expensive for most schools to afford in multiple sets. Also absent from the bandings are 'reading schemes' published prior to the NLS that offer, in our view, limited opportunities for children to learn and for teachers to teach. In their place, we have listed over 1,500 new titles, including a higher proportion of non-fiction texts, and a richer choice at the lowest and highest bands.

We need to keep the third edition hard copy a manageable size. We are currently working on an interactive CD *Book Bands* that will be fully inclusive and as informative as we can make it. The greatly enhanced capacity of a CD will enable us to offer more information and enable you to add new titles as they are published, and create your own auditing lists.

Book Bands is still not a list of recommended titles. Many schools do get in touch to ask our advice, and we do not hesitate to recommend a range of resources we feel to be of high quality. Too often, schools still offer children little choice of non-fiction guided reading texts across Key Stage 1, and a limited range of high quality band 1 and 2 texts.

Again we would like to emphasise that the banding is not infallible. Publishers are increasingly providing new 'book banded' series, mostly with but sometimes without our involvement! Don't be afraid to make your own decisions. Remember: no handbook can take the place of an individual teacher's experience and knowledge about the choice of book for a particular group of children.

March 2003

USING THE NATIONAL LITERACY STRATEGY FRAMEWORK FOR TEACHING

The intellectual challenge for children learning to read:

Reading, like thinking, is very complex. When you think, all you have to do is produce responses from within you. When you read you have to produce responses which interpret what the author wrote: you have to try to match your thinking to his.

Marie M. Clay, 1991
(*Becoming Literate*, p. 320)

Inexperienced readers must develop their knowledge of books and reading behaviours, their understanding of the world and control over oral language together with growing expertise in all aspects of print information in order to re-create an author's message in their own minds.

A balanced class-reading programme consists of a variety of reading experiences, levels of support and methods of instruction to foster these skills:

- Shared reading, in which the whole class joins in the collaborative act of fluent, expressive text reading and re-reading. The teacher takes the lead, orchestrating responses, and drawing attention to reading strategies and features at text, sentence and word levels appropriate to the age, experience and ability of the majority. Sensitive questioning and prompting of individual children helps to ensure maximum participation and understanding.

- Guided reading, where children put into practice their developing expertise at an appropriate level in a structured situation. The teacher differentiates the instructional reading programme and guides children who have reached a similar level of skill to develop independent reading strategies on new and increasingly challenging texts.

- Reading independently, when children return to familiar texts and read a variety of new easy texts. Re-reading strengthens the novice reader's control over the reading process. Access to a broad range of supplementary reading materials is important through class, school and neighbourhood libraries. Children also carry out activities during the literacy hour designed to direct their attention more closely to specific aspects of reading and writing.

SOME IMPORTANT DISTINCTIONS BETWEEN SHARED, GUIDED AND INDEPENDENT READING

	SHARED READING	GUIDED READING	INDEPENDENT READING
Grouping of pupils	WHOLE CLASS: mixed ability.	SMALL GROUP: usually 3–8 selected pupils at a similar stage of acquisition.	INDIVIDUALLY, in pairs or in small groups.
Text	LARGE PRINT: One text for whole group (or copy of text per child). Text re-read aloud repeatedly until familiar.	SETS of texts with one copy for each group member. Lesson consists of unfamiliar text or section of text.	VARIETY of texts from shared and guided reading, library books, games, activities, book-tapes, environmental print, instructions, recipes, etc.
Text level	RICH, CHALLENGING text beyond the current ability of most of the class.	INSTRUCTIONAL LEVEL: i.e. each member of group able to read and readily comprehend text at or above 90 per cent accuracy.	EASY LEVEL: i.e. each child able to read and readily comprehend texts at or above 95 per cent accuracy.
Performance	HIGH LEVEL OF SUPPORT within a collaborative social framework of explicit teaching and oral response.	LOWER LEVEL OF SUPPORT: Teacher structures the task and then calls for individuals to apply strategies already introduced and practised in shared reading.	LITTLE/NO TEACHER SUPPORT: Pupils work independently or with others to practise reading in a variety of contexts, or respond to reading. Adults may organise and supervise certain activities.
Teaching style	TEACHER-LED, with formal, pre-planned teaching objectives.	PUPILS expected to take the initiative and read to themselves following an introduction, with TEACHER facilitating.	PUPILS monitor their own activities, assist and work with others within classroom organisation where expectations are clear and routines well established.
Focus	INTRODUCING AND PRACTISING planned objectives at the word, sentence and/or text levels.	REINFORCING AND EXTENDING strategies and/or objectives already taught in shared reading.	ACHIEVING FLUENCY AND FLEXIBILITY at current level of control. RESPONDING personally to text.

SEARCHLIGHTS IN ACTION

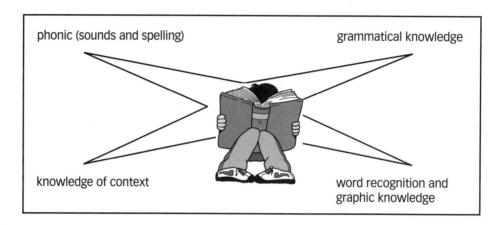

phonic (sounds and spelling)

grammatical knowledge

knowledge of context

word recognition and
graphic knowledge

**ATTENDING TO
MEANING
(knowledge of
context)**

Illustrations, titles, discussion and book introductions provide a context for the reader's thinking before reading begins. Bright covers, photographs and lively pictures throughout books, magazines and newspapers help the reader to bring relevant ideas and predictions to the text by activating memories and prior experiences. This receptive frame of mind is particularly important where the learner reader cannot yet attend to all the print detail. Pictures of dogs together with some letter knowledge will support a beginner reader to attempt 'puppy', whereas a photo of flowers is more likely to produce 'poppy'. Taking risks and making informed guesses is a crucial part of learning.

Illustrations can most easily indicate key nouns, adjectives and some verbs in a text. They can show objects in relation to one another, establish a setting and sequence of events, and create atmosphere. What they cannot do is indicate exactly how an author's thinking orders these into a story with a distinctive voice. A young child from any culture may open a new picture book, scan the illustrations carefully and proceed to tell a unique story to match the pictures. This is attending to meaning but it is not reading.

Teachers have traditionally checked comprehension through oral or written questions following text reading. Guided reading offers opportunities to **teach** for comprehension by alerting children **beforehand** to search for information or examples, impressions or evidence as they read, so that they learn to be active and discerning and in control of their reading.

**ATTENDING TO PRINT
(word recognition/
graphic knowledge;
phonic sounds/
spelling)**

There are no rules for looking at most scenes or even most illustrations. Precise scanning conventions **do** apply when reading words on a page. In English, the sequence of speech is represented by a left-to-right, top-to-bottom, linear progression of grouped letters, left page before right. Breaks between written words do not necessarily exist in oral language, e.g. 'bread'n'butter', 'Humpty Dumpty satona wall'. The novice reader has to be persuaded to relinquish for a while the marvellous fluency and flexibility of seeing and speaking developed since babyhood in order to grapple with the conventions of the printed page.

For many children, getting to grips with print conventions comes more easily through writing. With the message secure in their minds, they slow down their speech to listen to the dominant sounds of their own spoken words and represent what they hear using their developing knowledge of letter–sound relationships. In this way, they

CHILDREN'S PROGRESS THROUGH READING LEVELS AT KEY STAGE 1

SCHOOL: CLASS: YEAR:

Names	Sept	Oct	Nov	Dec	Jan	Feb	Mar	Apr	May	Jun	Jul

NATIONAL CURRICULUM READING LEVELS: Colour key

PINK	RED	YELLOW	BLUE	GREEN	ORANGE
Working towards Level 1	Working towards Level 1	Level 1	Level 1	Level 1	Level 1

TURQUOISE	PURPLE	GOLD	WHITE
Working towards Level 2	Level 2C	Level 2B	Level 2A–3

PROFESSIONAL DEVELOPMENT AND SCHOOL MANAGEMENT

Book Bands for Guided Reading can be used to inform and stimulate professional development. Individual teachers and school teams may find the suggestions below helpful as they review their organisation and practice in teaching literacy, and reflect upon children's learning and the effectiveness of class teaching.

1 REVIEWING AND ENHANCING THE EFFECTIVENESS OF GUIDED READING

Each colour band listing is introduced by an exemplar lesson. These lessons are intended to be used as a basis for staff development, and show how the support or 'scaffolding' provided by the teacher changes as the proficiency of the group increases. It is particularly important to note:

- A brief, carefully worded overview, of fiction in particular, orients children to the verb tense used and the main thrust of a book, enabling them to make full use of the more detailed introduction;
- A rich page-by-page introduction at the earliest bands enables children to use the structures and vocabulary of the text, and enjoy the illustrations fully **before** they grapple with the text on their own. Try not to let the discussion stray from the text and mislead novices; they will quickly learn to attend carefully to skilled introductions and make good use of them.
- Once children are able to decode some unfamiliar vocabulary for themselves, introductions should be briefer and prompts for problem-solving more demanding.
- Along with the focus on comprehension and other curriculum areas at the text and sentence levels, it is important to direct children's attention back to relevant spelling features of words they may have read correctly but not fully attened to.

2 TRACKING THE PROGRESS OF INDIVIDUAL KEY STAGE 1 PUPILS IN TEXT READING

OBSERVING AND ASSESSING READING PROGRESS

The combination of *Book Bands for Guided Reading* as a reliable gradient of difficulty, and running records as an objective record of children's control of the reading process, can enable schools and individual teachers to organise, carry out and monitor children's progress very effectively.

Learning how to take and interpret running records of text reading should enable teachers to be more accurate and detailed observers.
(See Clay, M.M. (2002) *An Observation Survey of Early Literacy Achievement*, 2nd edition, Heinemann.)

For children in the early stages of learning to read, a more comprehensive assessment including letter knowledge and high frequency word reading and writing, may help to identify children for special support. These are also fully described in *An Observation Survey of Early Literacy Achievement*.

MONITORING AT CLASS AND SCHOOL LEVELS

The gradient of difficulty in *Book Bands for Guided Reading* can provide a baseline for identifying the starting point of individuals or groups of pupils at the beginning of each school year. Children's progress can be tracked throughout KS1 using the form on page 13 to provide formative assessment of the effectiveness of classroom teaching and school policies.

3 EXTENDING STAFF KNOWLEDGE OF KEY STAGE 1 TEXTS

USING THE BANDING RATIONALE

- Descriptions introducing each band can be used as a starting point to explore ways in which texts vary as their challenge increases and new opportunities for learning are introduced.
- Enhanced judgement may be applied to new materials to enable teachers to select and use the most appropriate texts to achieve specific learning goals.

ORGANISING AND AUDITING KEY STAGE 1 TEXTS

- *Book Bands for Guided Reading* forms an effective basis for organising texts throughout KS1, ensuring continuity and consistency across years and classes.
- It can be used as an auditing tool towards ensuring the range of text type, variety of appeal, satisfactory representation of race and gender, replacement of battered books and incomplete sets, and an injection of attractive up-to-date materials.
- Schools may also use it to identify themes within different bands in order to support class topic work through guided reading.

4 EMPOWERING CHILDREN TO READ INDEPENDENTLY

DEEPENING UNDERSTANDING OF SEARCHLIGHTS MODEL

- *Book Bands for Guided Reading* can provide a stimulus and a context for discussion about the challenges children face when they learn to read.
- Learning how to take running records of children reading text and how to analyse errors and self-corrections enhances awareness of different types of information used and neglected, according to the searchlights model.
- Examples of teaching at each band can stimulate reflection about how to praise a child's attempts to read a new text attending to certain cues, and prompts to alert a child to use neglected information at particular points in the reading, in order to foster balanced, independent problem-solving. Self-monitoring and self-correction are significant evidence of this independence.

5 INVESTIGATING DISAPPOINTING PROGRESS IN TEXT READING

There are many reasons why children may not make satisfactory progress in reading; the following points provide a springboard for reflection, discussion with colleagues and further classroom observation.

TEXTS

Poor-quality texts; limited quantity and variety; poor choice of texts for a particular group – too easy or too hard; known rather than new texts.

GROUPING

Range of ability within the group too wide so that some children become bored and others frustrated; little challenge, variety or breadth offered to high-progress readers.

LESSON FREQUENCY

Too few guided reading sessions, particularly at the early stages (a minimum of three lessons per week is recommended for Year R, EAL pupils, and slow-progress children).

SERIES	PUBLISHER	SET (OR AUTHOR)	TITLE	BAND
PM Storybook Starters	Nelson Thornes	Set 2	Looking Down	1
			My Accident	1
			My Little Dog	1
			Out in the Weather	1
			Packing My Bag	1
			Pencil, The	1
			Rock Pools, The	1
			Sally's New Shoes	1
			Stop!	1
			We Can Run	1
			We Like Fish!	1
			Where are the Babies?	1
Rigby Star	Rigby	Pink Level	At the Seaside	1
			Catch It!	1
			Dog Show, The	1
			Fancy Dress	1
			Goodnight Josie	1
			Home for Curly, A	1
			Josie and the Junk Box	1
			Juggling	1
			Moving Day	1
			Ned's Noise Machine	1
			New Pet, The	1
			Play, The	1
			Scaredy Cat	1
			That's Mine!	1
			Where is Patch?	1
			Who Can Curly See?	1
		Red Level	Animal Presents	1
			Guess Who?	1
Story Chest	Kingscourt	Get-ready Set A	Ghost, The	1
			Go, Go, Go	1
			If You Meet a Dragon	1
			In the Mirror	1
			Painting	1
			Storm, The	1
		Get-ready Set AA	Brenda's Birthday	1
			Escalator, The	1
			Snowman	1
			Swing	1
			Waiting	1
		Get-ready Set B	On a Chair	1
		Get-ready Set BB	Fishing	1
			Green Grass	1
			Rat's Funny Story	1
		Get-ready Set C	Clown and Elephant	1
			Going to School	1
			Hello	1
		Get-ready Set CC	Jump, Jump, Kangaroo	1
			My Picture	1
		Large Read-tog Set 2	Farm Concert, The	1

SERIES	PUBLISHER	SET (OR AUTHOR)	TITLE	BAND
Story Chest	Kingscourt	Ready-set-go Set AA	Bears' Picnic, The	1
Story Steps	Kingscourt	Level 1 Benchmark Bk	My Place	1
		Level 1 Collection	Two Little Birds	1
		Level 1 Little Books	I Spy	1
			Patterns	1
			Who Lives on a Farm?	1
		Level 2 Benchmark Bk	Snowman, The	1
		Level 2 Collection	Bake a Cake	1
		Level 2 Little Books	Birthday Bug, The	1
			Off to School	1
			Patterns are Fun!	1
Story Street	Longman	Step 1	Go Away!	1
			Goose Chase, The	1
			New Football Kit, The	1
			Playing with Pip	1
			Teatime for Sam	1
			Where is Pip Going?	1
Storyteller	Kingscourt	Set 1	Big and Little	1
			Chalk Talk	1
			Fun With Fruit	1
			Helping Dad	1
			I Made a Picture	1
			Look at the Ball	1
			My Special Book	1
			Nest, The	1
			Our Week	1
			Puzzle, The	1
			Things I Like	1
			We Ski	1
			What Can I See?	1
Storyworlds	Heinemann	Stage 2 Animal World	Bingo and the Bone	1
Individual Titles	Collins Pict Lions	Aruego, Jose	Look What I Can Do	1
	Picture Puffin	Carle, Eric	Do You Want to Be My Friend?	1
	Picture Puffin	Pienkowski, Jan	Colours	1
	Picture Puffin	Pienkowski, Jan	Sizes	1
	Scholastic	Sharratt, Nick	Ketchup on Your Cornflakes	1
	Walker	Sharratt, Nick	Monday, Run Day	1

Band 2 RED

Reading Recovery Levels 3–5

FOUNDATION STAGE

WORKING TOWARDS LEVEL 1: LEARNING OPPORTUNITIES

- Locate title

- Locate and recall title

- Consolidate secure control of one-to-one matching

- Use known words to check and confirm reading

- Start to read more rhythmically or use phrasing while maintaining track of the print

- Repeat words, phrases or sentences to check, confirm or modify own reading

- Predict from meaning, syntax and print to solve new words.

TEXT CHARACTERISTICS

- slightly longer, highly predictable text involving familiar objects and actions

- repetitive sentence/phrase patterns including high frequency words

- sentences short, clear and straightforward following children's speech patterns

- illustrations provide full and direct support for the text

- simple story development (fiction text)

- non-fiction texts may have more than one type of print format

- reasonably large print with obvious spaces between words

- full range of punctuation

SERIES	PUBLISHER	SET (OR AUTHOR)	TITLE	BAND
Literacy Plus Topic	Kingscourt	Emergent B	Who Ate the Lettuce?	2
		Emergent C	Going to Work	2
			Hiding	2
			In a Minute	2
			Jump into Bed	2
			Our Shadows	2
			Piece of Paper, A	2
		Emergent D	Buzz Off, Bee	2
			I am a Cat	2
			Let Me in	2
			My Little Dog	2
			Wanda's New Bed	2
National Geographic	Rigby	Red Level	Up, Down and Around	2
			Weather in the City	2
		Yellow Level	This is an Island	2
Oxford Literacy Web	OUP	First Non-fiction: Pack B	Which Animals Lay Eggs?	2
		Stage 1 (Duck Green)	Oh No, Jo, No!	2
			Poppy's Pot	2
			Two the Same	2
		Stage 1 (Variety)	Animals at the Zoo	2
			Can I Have a Pet?	2
			Magic Paintbrush, The	2
			Nama's Hats	2
			Nelly Paints a Monster	2
		Stage 2 (Duck Green)	Box, The	2
			Lost and Found	2
		Stage 2 (Variety)	Big Bear's Bad Day	2
			Big Bear's Party	2
			Where's Daddy Bear?	2
		Stage 3 (Duck Green)	Big Puddle, The	2
			Choose the Shoes	2
			Pets	2
			String's the Thing	2
		Stage 3 (Variety)	Hermit Crab's New Shell	2
Oxford Reading Tree	OUP	Stage 1+ First Sentences	Big Feet	2
			Go Away, Floppy	2
			Reds and Blues	2
		Stage 1+ More First Sentences	Go Away, Cat	2
			Go on, Mum!	2
			Look After Me	2
			Presents for Dad	2
			Top Dog	2
			What Dogs Like	2
		Stage 2 More Wrens	Goal!	2
			Shopping	2
			What a Mess!	2
			Who Did That?	2
		Stage 2 Storybooks	New Dog, A	2
			Toy's Party, The	2
		Stage 2 Wrens	At the Park	2
			Good Old Mum!	2

SERIES	PUBLISHER	SET (OR AUTHOR)	TITLE	BAND
Oxford Reading Tree	OUP	Stage 2 Wrens	Push!	2
		Stage 3 More Wrens	Band, The	2
			Little Dragon, The	2
			Lost Puppy, The	2
			New Trees	2
			Up and Down	2
			What is it?	2
		Stage 3 Storybooks	Nobody Wanted to Play	2
		Stage 3 Wrens	Creepy Crawly	2
			Hey Presto!	2
			It's the Weather	2
			Monkey Tricks	2
			Naughty Children	2
			Sinking Feeling, A	2
Pathways	Collins	Year 1	Monsters	2
			What's There?	2
PM Maths	Nelson Thornes	Stage A	Five Birds and Five Mice	2
			Four Cars	2
			Game with Shapes, A	2
			Long and Short	2
			Making a Butterfly	2
			Red Block, Blue Block	2
			Sorting Leaves	2
			We Can See Three	2
PM Storybooks	Nelson Thornes	Red Set A	Baby Lamb's First Drink	2
			Ben's Teddy Bear	2
			Ben's Treasure Hunt	2
			Big Kick, The	2
			Father Bear Goes Fishing	2
			Hedgehog is Hungry	2
			Lazy Pig, The	2
			Lizard Loses His Tail	2
			Merry Go Round, The	2
			Photo Book, The	2
			Pussy and the Birds	2
			Sally and the Daisy	2
			Sausages	2
			Tiger, Tiger	2
			Tom is Brave	2
			Wake Up, Dad!	2
		Red Set B	Baby Owls, The	2
			Birthday Cake for Ben, A	2
			Bumper Cars, The	2
			Flower Girl, The	2
			Hide and Seek	2
			Home for Little Teddy, A	2
			Little Snowman, The	2
			Where is Hannah?	2
Rigby Star	Rigby	Red Level	Curly is Hungry	2
			Den, The	2
			Elephant Walk	2

SERIES	PUBLISHER	SET (OR AUTHOR)	TITLE	BAND
Rigby Star	Rigby	Red Level	I Like to Jump	2
			Josie and the Parade	2
			Max Gets Ready	2
			Monster Meal	2
			My Camera	2
			Nature Trail	2
			New Hat, The	2
			Next Door Pets	2
			Shopping	2
			Snake is Going Away!	2
			What is He?	2
		Yellow Level	Grandpa	2
			Josie and the Baby	2
Star Quest	Rigby	Blue Level	What's it Made of?	2
		Yellow Level	Baby Animals	2
			Funny Ears	2
Story Chest	Kingscourt	Get-ready Set A	Party, The	2
			Tree-house, The	2
		Get-ready Set AA	New Pants	2
			Shoo, Fly!	2
			Surprise, The	2
		Get-ready Set B	Bicycle, The	2
			Big Hill, The	2
			Feet	2
			Houses	2
			Monster Sandwich, A	2
			Mouse	2
			Night-time	2
		Get-ready Set BB	Bridge, The	2
			Chick's Walk	2
			Gotcha Box, The	2
			Mrs Wishy-Washy's Tub	2
			Salad	2
		Get-ready Set C	I am Frightened	2
			Little Brother	2
			One, One is the Sun	2
			Silly Old Possum	2
			What's for Lunch?	2
		Get-ready Set CC	Dan Gets Dressed	2
			Halloween	2
			Look Out, Dan!	2
			Mouse Train	2
			Nest, The	2
			What Can Jigarees do?	2
		Get-ready Set DD	Boogie-Woogie Man, The	2
			Gifts, The	2
			Happy Birthday, Frog	2
			How to Make a Hot Dog	2
			Microscope	2
		Ready-set-go Set A	Come With Me	2
			I Want an Ice-Cream	2

SERIES	PUBLISHER	SET (OR AUTHOR)	TITLE	BAND
Alphakids Plus	Horwitz Gardner	Early Level 7	Fishing	3
			Gymnastics	3
			My Brother's Birthday	3
			Working with Dad	3
		Early Level 8	Lizard's Tail	3
			Mammals	3
		Early Level 11	Picnic, The	3
		Emergent Level 4	Dinosaurs	3
		Emergent Level 5	Best Pizza in the World, The	3
			Riding My Bike	3
AlphaWorld	Horwitz Gardner	Band 3: Yellow	Favourite Places	3
			Hurry Up!	3
			Ice and Snow	3
			One Step, Two Steps	3
			Pets	3
			When I Was Sick	3
Beginner Books	Collins	Eastman, P D	Go, Dog, Go!	3
Book Project Fiction 1	Longman	Cluster B: Animals	Come into the Garden	3
			Garden Friends	3
		Cluster B: Animals	Who's There?	3
		Cluster C: Mai Ling	Late Again, Mai Ling?	3
			Where's Mai Ling?	3
		Cluster D: Teddy	Freddy's Teddy	3
			Teddy Goes Swimming	3
			Teddy in the Garden	3
		Cluster E: Ben Biggins	Ben Biggins' Box	3
			Ben Biggins' Week	3
		Cluster F: Webster	Fetch the Stick, Webster!	3
			Stop it, Webster!	3
			Wake Up, Webster!	3
			Webster's Week	3
			What Webster Wants	3
Book Project Fiction 2	Longman	Cluster B: Bean	Jumping Beans	3
		Cluster C: Little Frog	Little Frog and the Dog	3
		Cluster E: Family	Lisa's Letter	3
Bright and Early Books	Collins	Berenstain, Stan & Jan	Bears on Wheels	3
			Inside, Outside, Upside Down	3
		Le Seig, Theo	Eye Book, The	3
Discovery World	Heinemann	Stage C	Materials	3
Genre Range	Longman	Beginner Comics	Cats and Dogs	3
			Looking for Lucky	3
			Nuts	3
		Beginner Trad Tales	Mouse and the Bull, The	3
Hotlinks	Kingscourt	9	Rainy Days	3
Info Trail	Longman	Beginner Geography	Addressing a Letter	3
			What Shall We Have for Tea Tonight?	3
		Beginner History	Emma's Photo Album	3
			It's Best to be Five!	3
			When Grandad Was at School	3
		Emergent History	How to Dress a Knight	3
Lighthouse	Ginn	Yellow: 1	Cecil the Caterpillar	3

SERIES	PUBLISHER	SET (OR AUTHOR)	TITLE	BAND
Lighthouse	Ginn	Yellow: 2	Jenny in Bed	3
		Yellow: 3	Charlie's PE Kit	3
		Yellow: 4	What Do You Want That For?	3
		Yellow: 5	Our Camping Trip	3
		Yellow: 6	Bear Hunt	3
		Yellow: 7	Carnivals Around The World	3
		Yellow: 8	Meg's Cat	3
Literacy Links Plus	Kingscourt	Contemporary Stories	Wake Up, Isabel!	3
		Early A	At Night	3
			Bruno's Birthday	3
			Screech!	3
			Trucks	3
		Early B	Roll Over	3
			Sleeping	3
		Emergent B	Dad's Garden	3
			Don't Leave Anything Behind	3
			Hungry Horse	3
			I Can Do it Myself	3
		Emergent C	Ben the Bold	3
			Camping	3
			Train Ride, The	3
			When I was Sick	3
		Emergent D	Boogly, The	3
			Circus Clown, The	3
			Go Back to Sleep	3
			Grandpa Snored	3
			Green Footprints	3
			Hands	3
			Henry the Helicopter	3
			Pets	3
			Shadows	3
			Storm, The	3
			Timmy	3
			Visitors	3
			Wedding, The	3
Literacy Plus Topic	Kingscourt	Early A	Amy Goes to School	3
			Carrot Soup	3
			Lost	3
			Lunchtime	3
			Names and Games	3
			Our Soccer Team	3
			Sarah's Seed	3
		Early B	Don't Forget	3
			Stop, Look and Listen	3
		Emergent D	Look Out For Bears	3
			Pirate and the Parrot, The	3
National Geographic	Rigby	Yellow Level	Baby Shark, The	3
			New Clothes	3
			Now and Then	3
Oxford Literacy Web	OUP	First Non-fiction: Pack A	Make a Milkshake	3
		First Non-fiction: Pack B	Growing Mr Greenhead	3

SERIES	PUBLISHER	SET (OR AUTHOR)	TITLE	BAND
Oxford Literacy Web	OUP	Stage 1 (Variety)	Anansi Traps a Snake	3
		Stage 2 (Duck Green)	Baby Bird, The	3
			Big Books and Little Books	3
			Poppy's Puppets	3
			What's in Your Lunchbox?	3
		Stage 2 (Variety)	Lunch for Tig	3
			Tig	3
			Tig's Pet	3
		Stage 2 First Words NF	Festivals	3
			My Pet	3
			What Do You Want to Be?	3
		Stage 3 (Duck Green)	Best Fish, The	3
			Little Angels	3
		Stage 3 (Variety)	At the Fair	3
			Late for School	3
			Octopus's Legs	3
			Shark's Tooth	3
			Who Made This Mess?	3
		Stage 4 (Duck Green)	Fly Away, Cheep	3
			Mr Jelly's Surprise	3
			That Cat!	3
		Stage 4 (Variety)	Billy Beetle	3
			Ned the Fighting Donkey	3
			Rabbit's Trick	3
Oxford Reading Tree	OUP	Stage 2 More Stories A	Baby-sitter, The	3
			Floppy's Bath	3
			Kipper's Balloon	3
			Kipper's Birthday	3
			Spots	3
			Water Fight, The	3
		Stage 2 More Stories B	Biff's Aeroplane	3
			Chase, The	3
			Foggy Day, The	3
		Stage 2 Storybooks	Go-kart, The	3
			New Trainers	3
			What a Bad Dog!	3
		Stage 3 More Stories A	At the Seaside	3
			Jumble Sale, The	3
			Kipper the Clown	3
			Snowman, The	3
			Strawberry Jam	3
		Stage 3 More Stories B	At the Pool	3
			Book Week	3
			Bull's-eye	3
		Stage 3 Sparrows	Jan and the Anorak	3
			Jan and the Chocolate	3
			Joe and the Bike	3
			Midge in Hospital	3
			Roy and the Budgie	3
		Stage 3 Storybooks	By the Stream	3
			Dolphin Pool, The	3

SERIES	PUBLISHER	SET (OR AUTHOR)	TITLE	BAND
AlphaWorld	Horwitz Gardner	Band 4: Blue	Using Rocks	4
Book Project Fiction 2	Longman	Cluster B: Bean	Magic Bean	4
		Cluster C: Little Frog	Little Frog and the Frog Olympics	4
			Little Frog and the Tadpoles	4
		Cluster D: Cat	Pudding	4
			Snowflake	4
			Tiger	4
		Cluster F: Harry	Go Away, Harry	4
			Look Out, Harry!	4
Book Project Fiction 3	Longman	Cluster A: Minnie	Minnie Meets a Monkey	4
			Minnie's Bike	4
		Cluster B: Doodling Daniel	Doodledragon	4
			Doodlemaze	4
Book Project Fiction 4	Longman	Cluster A: Poems	Wake Up!	4
			Water, Water	4
		Cluster B: Monster	Monster Who Loved Telephones, The	4
Bright and Early Books	Collins	Berenstain, Stan & Jan	Spooky Old Tree, The	4
		Perkins, Al	Ear Book, The	4
Cambridge Reading	CUP	Y1 A: Fantasy Worlds	Lucy's Box	4
			Wayne's Box	4
		Y1 A: Narrative Recount	Going Fishing	4
			Not Yet, Nathan!	4
		Y1 A: Poetry	Five Little Monkeys	4
			One Blue Hen	4
		Y1 A: Range of Cultures	Gingerbread Man, The	4
			Lion and the Mouse, The	4
Discovery World	Heinemann	Stage C	My Bean Diary	4
		Stage D	Fun Things to Make and Do	4
Discovery World Links	Heinemann	Stage C	Tractors	4
			What Can be Recycled?	4
Genre Range	Longman	Beginner Letters	Postcards	4
		Beginner Plays	I am Miss Cherry	4
			Poor Sam	4
		Beginner Trad Tales	Frog Prince, The	4
			Hare and the Tortoise, The	4
		Emergent Plays	Jumbo	4
Hotlinks	Kingscourt	10	Prickle, Crackle, Pop	4
		11	Shake and Shiver	4
Info Trail	Longman	Beginner Geography	Have You Seen My Bag?	4
			Pick Up That Crisp Packet!	4
			Up the Big Hill	4
		Beginner History	This House is Too Small!	4
			Were the Old Days the Best?	4
		Beginner Science	I Grew a Sunflower Big as My Dad	4
		Emergent Geography	Don't Throw it Away	4
			Pigeon Patrol, The	4
		Emergent History	How to Dress a Queen	4
		Emergent Science	From an Acorn to an Oak Tree	4
Lighthouse	Ginn	Blue: 1	Answer the Phone, Fiona!	4
		Blue: 2	Quiet Morning for Mum, A	4
		Blue: 3	Stop the Car!	4

SERIES	PUBLISHER	SET (OR AUTHOR)	TITLE	BAND
Lighthouse	Ginn	Blue: 4	Hullabaloo at the Zoo	4
		Blue: 5	It's a Gift	4
		Blue: 6	Lion's Lunch	4
		Blue: 7	No Running!	4
		Blue: 8	Sports Dictionary	4
Literacy Links Plus	Kingscourt	Contemporary Stories	Royal Dinner, The	4
			Sandwich That Max Made, The	4
			Sightseeing	4
			Who's in the Shed?	4
		Early A	Bang	4
			Can I Play Outside?	4
			Christmas Shopping	4
			Countdown	4
			Dad's Bike	4
			Goodnight Little Brother	4
			Just Like Grandpa	4
			Riddles	4
			Secret Soup	4
			Sleepy Bear	4
			Sneezes	4
			Words Are Everywhere	4
		Early B	Family Photos	4
			If You're Happy	4
			In the Garden	4
			Inside or Outside	4
			Mrs Bold	4
			Patterns	4
			Printing Machine, The	4
			Skin	4
			T J's Tree	4
			What's Around the Corner	4
			Wobbly Tooth, The	4
		Early C	BMX Billy	4
			Buffy's Tricks	4
			Ten Little Caterpillars	4
		Emergent B	Filbert the Fly	4
		Emergent C	Nests	4
		Emergent D	I Saw a Dinosaur	4
			Noises	4
			Noses	4
			Sitting	4
			When I Pretend	4
		Traditional Tales	Goldilocks and the Three Bears	4
			Lion and the Mouse, The	4
			Little Red Hen, The	4
Literacy Plus Topic	Kingscourt	Early A	What About Bennie?	4
		Early B	I Saw a Sign	4
			Jumper	4
			Out of Reach	4
			Wolf and the Seven Little Kids, The	4
		Early C	Footprints	4

SERIES	PUBLISHER	SET (OR AUTHOR)	TITLE	BAND
Literacy Plus Topic	Kingscourt	Early C	Postcards from Pop	4
		Emergent D	Good and Ready	4
National Geographic	Rigby	Blue Level	Cooking Dinner	4
			Hairy Harry	4
			Night Sky, The	4
			Park, The	4
New Way	Nelson Thornes	Green Core Book	Bad Cow & other stories	4
		Green Easy Start Set A	Film Star, The	4
			Hello	4
			Postcard, The	4
			Rob Goes to Hospital...	4
			Tim and Tom & Who Will Push Me?	4
		Green Easy Start Set B	New Tie, The	4
Oxford Literacy Web	OUP	First Non-fiction: Pack A	Why Do You Need to Read?	4
			Writing	4
		First Non-fiction: Pack B	Fruit	4
			Heating Food	4
			My Diary of an Oak Tree	4
		Stage 2 First Words NF	Building Site, The	4
			Emergency!	4
			How to Make a Party Hat	4
		Stage 4 (Duck Green)	Flying Footballs	4
			I'm Not Scared	4
			Twins, The	4
		Stage 4 (Variety)	Alex the Ant	4
			Gordon the Clever Goat	4
		Stage 5 (Duck Green)	Hiccups!	4
			Leela's Secret Plan	4
			Snow Surprise	4
			Where's Cheep?	4
		Stage 5 (Variety)	Sir Ben and the Dragon	4
			Stupid Ogre, The	4
Oxford Reading Tree	OUP	Stage 2 More Stories B	Floppy the Hero	4
			Kipper's Laces	4
			Wobbly Tooth, The	4
		Stage 2 Storybooks	Dream, The	4
		Stage 3 More Stories A	Kipper's Idea	4
		Stage 3 More Stories B	Barbecue, The	4
			Carnival, The	4
			Cold Day, The	4
		Stage 3 Sparrows	Pip at the Zoo	4
		Stage 3 Storybooks	Cat in the Tree, A	4
		Stage 4 More Sparrows	Lucky the Goat	4
			Yasmin and the Flood	4
		Stage 4 More Stories A	Nobody Got Wet	4
			Weather Vane, The	4
			Wedding, The	4
		Stage 4 More Stories B	Dragon Dance, The	4
			Scarf, The	4
		Stage 4 Playscripts	Balloon, The	4
		Stage 4 Sparrows	Joe and the Mouse	4

SERIES	PUBLISHER	SET (OR AUTHOR)	TITLE	BAND
Alphakids Plus	Horwitz Gardner	Transitional Level 13	Growing Strawberries	5
		Transitional Level 14	Fantastic Frog Facts	5
			Hungry Baby, The	5
			Our Classroom Pet	5
			Snip! Snap!	5
		Transitional Level 16	Stop That Dog!	5
AlphaWorld	Horwitz Gardner	Band 5: Green	Dangerous Plants	5
			In the Playground	5
			Kitchen Garden	5
			Rough and Smooth	5
			Wheels	5
			Wings	5
Beginner Books	Collins	Lopshire, Robert	Put Me in the Zoo	5
Book Project Fiction 2	Longman	Cluster B: Bean	Coldilocks and the Three Beans	5
			How Many Beans Make Five?	5
		Cluster F: Harry	Help Us Harry!	5
Book Project Fiction 3	Longman	Cluster A: Minnie	Minnie's Kite	5
		Cluster C: Monster Pack	Boasting Monsters, The	5
			Monster Birthday, The	5
		Cluster E: Once Upon A Time	Story Without End	5
			Two Silly Stories	5
Book Project Fiction 4	Longman	Cluster A: Poems	Come on, Wind	5
		Cluster B: Monster	Monster Who Loved Cameras, The	5
Bright and Early Books	Collins	Perkins, Al	Nose Book, The	5
		Seuss, Dr	Foot Book, The	5
Cambridge Reading	CUP	Bridging Book: A	Granny's Teeth	5
			Wrigglebottom	5
			You Can't Catch Me!	5
		Y1 A: Familiar Settings	Here Comes Everyone	5
			This is the Register	5
			What's the Time?	5
		Y1 A: Fantasy Worlds	Dan's Box	5
		Y1 A: Narrative Recount	Bad Boy Billy!	5
		Y1 A: Poetry	Two By Two	5
		Y1 A: Range of Cultures	Raven and the Fox, The	5
		Y1 B: Fantasy Worlds	Billy's Box	5
			Sophie's Box	5
			Yasmin's Box	5
		Y1 B: Range of Cultures	Clever Tortoise, The	5
			Little Red Hen, The	5
			Tortoise and the Hare	5
		Y1 C: Familiar Settings	Well Done, Sam!	5
		Y1 C: Poetry	Everyone is Reading	5
		Y1: Non-fiction	Seal	5
		Y1: Playscripts	Lion and the Mouse, The	5
Discovery World Links	Heinemann	Stage C	Animal Skeletons	5
			Victorian Seaside Holiday, A	5
		Stage D	Toys	5
Genre Range	Longman	Beginner Plays	What a Mess!	5
		Beginner Poetry	Nursery and Action Rhymes	5
			Songs and Riddles	5

SERIES	PUBLISHER	SET (OR AUTHOR)	TITLE	BAND
Genre Range	Longman	Emergent Comics	Bad Bert and the Bully	5
			Fatcat and the Mouse	5
			Frog Goes on Holiday	5
		Emergent Letters	Haircut Letters, The	5
			My Diary	5
		Emergent Plays	Duck Pond	5
			Sunita and the Wishing Well	5
		Emergent Trad Tales	Goldilocks and the Three Bears	5
Hotlinks	Kingscourt	13	Jeepers, Creepers	5
		14	In My Garden	5
Info Trail	Longman	Beginner Geography	Which Home?	5
		Beginner History	How to Write a Family Tree	5
		Beginner Science	Day I Felt Ill, The	5
			Don't Bite the Bottom off Your Ice-cream Cone!	5
			How to Make a Feely Box	5
			Scab on the Knee, A	5
		Emergent History	London's Burning!	5
		Emergent Science	Come and Visit the Moon!	5
Lighthouse	Ginn	Green: 1	Hats for the Carnival	5
		Green: 2	Whale's Year, The	5
		Green: 3	Jasmine's Duck	5
		Green: 4	Robby in the River	5
		Green: 5	Baked Beans	5
		Green: 6	Goal!	5
		Green: 7	Day the Sky Fell Down, The	5
		Green: 8	Laughing Hyena	5
Literacy Links Plus	Kingscourt	Contemporary Stories	Guinea Pig Grass	5
			Jessie's Flower	5
			Rat-a-tat-tat	5
		Early A	Moonlight	5
			Sally's Picture	5
		Early B	Grump, The	5
			If You Like Strawberries	5
			Lilly-Lolly-Littlelegs	5
			My Monster Friends	5
			Odd Socks	5
			Pete's New Shoes	5
			Wide Mouthed Frog, The	5
			Woolly, Woolly	5
		Early C	Bossy Bettina	5
			Crab at the Bottom of the Sea, The	5
			Dad Didn't Mind at All	5
			Dad's Bathtime	5
			Hungry Chickens, The	5
			In the Park	5
			No Extras	5
			What is Bat?	5
			Whatever Will These Become?	5
			When I'm Older	5
		Early D	Barnaby's New House, The	5
			Daniel	5

SERIES	PUBLISHER	SET (OR AUTHOR)	TITLE	BAND
Literacy Links Plus	Kingscourt	Early D	Friend, A	5
			My House	5
			Papa's Spaghetti	5
			Two Little Mice, The	5
		Emergent D	Tails	5
		Fluent D	In the City of Rome	5
		Traditional Tales	Enormous Watermelon, The	5
			Three Little Pigs, The	5
Literacy Plus Topic	Kingscourt	Early B	Secret Message, The	5
			Sending Signals	5
		Early C	Cat and the Dog, The	5
			Fishing Contest, The	5
			Never-Told Story, The	5
		Early D	Happy Birthday, Duckling	5
			How Lizard Lost His Colours	5
			Lizzie's Lunch	5
			Rainbow Parrot	5
			Tall Tales	5
			Time for a Family	5
National Geographic	Rigby	Green Level	How Does My Bike Work?	5
		Orange Level	Going Fishing	5
			Machines Make Fun Rides	5
		Turquoise Level	Jack's Boat	5
New Way	Nelson Thornes	Green Easy Start Set A	Bad Apple & The Carrot Field, The	5
		Green Easy Start Set B	Cup of Tea, A	5
			It's Not Fair	5
			Secret & The Birthday Surprise, The	5
			Three Kings & Kim's Star, The	5
		Green Platform Books	Big Box & other stories, The	5
			Camping Holiday & other stories, The	5
			Deb's Secret Wish & other stories	5
			Red Doll & other stories, The	5
			Three Billy Goats Gruff, The	5
Oxford Literacy Web	OUP	First Non-fiction: Pack A	How Do You Sleep?	5
			Ladybird, Ladybird	5
		Stage 4 (Variety)	Wizard's Hat, The	5
		Stage 5 (Duck Green)	Dragon Kite	5
			Wiz	5
		Stage 5 (Variety)	Forest Giants, The	5
			Genie in the Bottle, The	5
			Sir Ben and the Monster	5
			Sir Ben and the Robbers	5
Oxford Reading Tree	OUP	Stage 4 More Stories A	Balloon, The	5
			Camcorder, The	5
		Stage 5 More Stories A	Great Race, The	5
			Underground Adventure	5
			Vanishing Cream	5
			Whatsit, The	5
		Stage 5 More Stories B	Camping Adventure	5
			Mum to the Rescue	5
			New Baby, The	5

SERIES	PUBLISHER	SET (OR AUTHOR)	TITLE	BAND
Alphakids Plus	Horwitz Gardner	Transitional Level 16	Three Wishes, The	6
		Transitional Level 17	Amazing Ants	6
			Dancing Dudley	6
			Princess Jo	6
AlphaWorld	Horwitz Gardner	Band 6: Orange	After the Storm	6
			Present for Our Teacher, A	6
			Saving Up	6
			Storm is Coming, A	6
		Band 7: Turquoise	Seeds on the Move	6
Beginner Books	Collins	Berenstain, Stan & Jan	Bike Lesson, The	6
		Brown, Marc	Spooky Riddles	6
		Eastman, P D	Are You My Mother?	6
			Big Dog, Little Dog	6
		Heilbroner, Joan	Robert, the Rose Horse	6
		Sadler, Marilyn	It's Not Easy Being a Bunny	6
		Seuss, Dr	Great Day for Up!	6
			Green Eggs and Ham	6
			Hop on Pop	6
			I Can Read with My Eyes Shut	6
		Stone, Rosetta	Because a Little Bug Went Ka-choo!	6
Blue Bananas	Mammoth	Mooney, Bel	I Don't Want to Say YES!	6
		Wilson, Jacqueline	Monster Eyeballs	6
Book Project Fiction 1	Longman	Cluster B: Animals	Let's Go into the Jungle	6
		Cluster E: Ben Biggins	Ben Biggins' House	6
Book Project Fiction 2	Longman	Cluster C: Little Frog	Frog in the Throat, A	6
		Cluster F: Harry	Hurry Up, Harry!	6
Book Project Fiction 3	Longman	Cluster A: Minnie	Minnie and the Champion Snorer	6
		Cluster D: Doll's House	Keith's Croak	6
		Cluster E: Once Upon A Time	Pocketful of Gold	6
		Cluster F: Faraway Folk Tales	Handful of Corn	6
			King's Potatoes, The	6
Book Project Fiction 4	Longman	Cluster B: Monster	Monster Who Loved Toothbrushes, The	6
Bright and Early Books	Collins	Tether, Graham	Hair Book, The	6
Cambridge Reading	CUP	Bridging Book: A	When Dad Went Fishing	6
		Bridging Book: B	Flying Football, The	6
			Puppy Chase, The	6
			We're Going on a Picnic	6
		Y1 B: Familiar Settings	Follow My Leader	6
			Please, Miss!	6
		Y1 B: Poetry	Peas in a Pod	6
		Y1 C: Fantasy Worlds	Tom's Box	6
		Y1: Non-fiction	Osprey	6
		Y1: Playscripts	Little Red Hen, The	6
Discovery World Links	Heinemann	Stage D	Animal Rescue	6
Genre Range	Longman	Emergent Letters	Ben's Get Well Cards	6
		Emergent Trad Tales	Blue Jackal, The	6
Hotlinks	Kingscourt	12	Flip, Flap. Fly!	6
		15	By the Sea	6
Info Trail	Longman	Beginner Geography	How to Read the Sky	6
		Emergent Geography	Come to My Party!	6
			Is Lightning Most Frightening?	6

SERIES	PUBLISHER	SET (OR AUTHOR)	TITLE	BAND
Info Trail	Longman	Emergent Science	How to Look After a Rat	6
			Is Simba Happy in the Zoo?	6
Lighthouse	Ginn	Orange: 1	Try Again, Emma	6
		Orange: 2	Animal Tails	6
		Orange: 3	Greedy King, The	6
		Orange: 4	Jolly Hungry Jack	6
		Orange: 5	Jo the Model Maker	6
		Orange: 6	Dog from Outer Space, The	6
		Orange: 7	Dream Team, The	6
		Orange: 8	Two Baby Elephants	6
Literacy Links Plus	Kingscourt	Early A	Water Falling	6
		Early B	Grandma's Memories	6
		Early C	Boxes	6
			Brand-new Butterfly, A	6
			Gregor, The Grumblesome Giant	6
			Hippo's Hiccups	6
			Making Caterpillars and Butterflies	6
			Only an Octopus	6
			Philippa and the Dragon	6
			Pizza For Dinner	6
		Early D	Deer and the Crocodile, The	6
			Dinosaur's Cold, The	6
			Fastest Gazelle, The	6
			Frog Princess, The	6
			Half for You, Half for Me	6
			I Have a Question, Grandma	6
			Mice	6
			Queen's Parrot, The	6
			Rice Cakes	6
			Too Much Noise	6
			Why Elephants Have Long Noses	6
			Wind and Sun	6
		Fluent A	Knit, Knit, Knit, Knit	6
			Tommy's Treasure	6
		Traditional Tales	Gingerbread Man, The	6
			Jack and the Beanstalk	6
Literacy Plus Topic	Kingscourt	Early C	Fascinating Faces	6
			King's Pudding, The	6
			Sally's Surprise Garden	6
		Early D	Little Half Chick	6
			Rice	6
		Fluent A	Froggy Tale, A	6
		Fluent C	Big Catch, The	6
			Hat Came Back, The	6
National Geographic	Rigby	Green Level	Mighty Machines	6
			People Live in the Desert	6
		Orange Level	Wind Power	6
New Way	Nelson Thornes	Blue Core Book	Dressing Up & other stories	6
		Blue Parallel Books	Blue Rabbit & other stories, The	6
		Green Easy Start Set B	Big-head & The Greedy Dog	6
		Green Platform Books	Little Red Hen & other stories	6

SERIES	PUBLISHER	SET (OR AUTHOR)	TITLE	BAND
New Way	Nelson Thornes	Green Platform Books	Paper Boy & other stories, The	6
			Two Animal Stories	6
Oxford Literacy Web	OUP	Non-fiction - Toys	How to Make Toys from the Past	6
			My Toys, Gran's Toys	6
		Poetry Stages 1-5	Pit-a-Pat-a-Parrot	6
			This is the Mum	6
		Stage 6 (Duck Green)	Rescue, The	6
		Stage 7 (Duck Green)	Corker, The	6
			Magic Puppet, The	6
			Moon Cheese	6
			Year at Duck Green, A	6
Oxford Reading Tree	OUP	Stage 5 More Stories A	It's Not Fair	6
		Stage 6 & 7 More Owls B	Dad's Grand Plan	6
			Don't Be Silly	6
			Mirror Island	6
		Stage 6 More Owls	Christmas Adventure	6
			Fright in the Night, A	6
			Go-kart Race, The	6
			Laughing Princess, The	6
			Rotten Apples	6
			Shiny Key, The	6
		Stage 6 Owls	Kipper and the Giant	6
			Land of the Dinosaurs	6
			Robin Hood	6
		Stage 7 Playscripts	Broken Roof, The	6
			Joke Machine, The	6
			Lost in the Jungle	6
			Lost Key, The	6
			Red Planet	6
			Submarine Adventure	6
			Willow Pattern Plot, The	6
		Stage 8 Magpies	Kidnappers, The	6
		Stage 8 Playscripts	Kidnappers, The	6
			Viking Adventure	6
		Traditional Tales 5-7	Donkey That Sneezed, The	6
			Jack and the Beanstalk	6
Pathways	Collins	Year 1	Davina and the Dinosaurs	6
			Owl's Party	6
			Pirates	6
			Rainy Day	6
			Tadpoles	6
			Use Your Hanky, Hannah	6
			Watch Out	6
		Year 2	Grabber	6
			Miss Blossom	6
			My Secret Pet	6
			One Puzzled Parrot	6
			Red Riding Hood	6
		Year 3	Bee In My Bonnet, A	6
Pelican Big Bks	Longman	Dupasquier, Philippe	Dear Daddy…	6
		Palmer, Sue	Simple Rhyming Dictionary, A	6

SERIES	PUBLISHER	SET (OR AUTHOR)	TITLE	BAND
Oxford Literacy Web	OUP	Non-fiction - Animals	Elephant Diary	7
			Keep Your Hamster Happy	7
		Non-fiction - Toys	All Kinds of Dolls	7
			How My Bike Was Made	7
			Kites	7
		Poetry Stages 1-5	Beep Goes My Belly Button	7
			Teacher, Teacher	7
			Teeny Tiny Teddy, A	7
		Stage 6 (Duck Green)	Giants, The	7
			Leela and the Lost Shoe	7
			Lucky Ducks	7
			Songbird, The	7
Oxford Literacy Web	OUP	Stage 6 (Duck Green)	Sports Day	7
		Stage 7 (Duck Green)	Bird in the Bush, A	7
			Wolf Whistle, The	7
		Stage 7 (Variety)	Boy Who Talked to the Birds, The	7
			King's Ears, The	7
			Strange Dream, The	7
		Stage 8 (Duck Green)	Dinosaur Danger!	7
			Summer Fair, The	7
			Watch the Birdie!	7
		Stage 9 (Variety)	Daylight Robbery	7
			Dormouse Pot, The	7
			Miss Ross is Cross	7
Oxford Reading Tree	OUP	Stage 6 & 7 More Owls B	Joke Machine, The	7
			Submarine Adventure	7
			Willow Pattern Plot, The	7
		Stage 6 Owls	Outing, The	7
			Treasure Chest	7
		Stage 6 Robins	Dump, The	7
		Stage 7 More Owls	Bully, The	7
			Chinese Adventure	7
			Hunt for Gold, The	7
			Jigsaw Puzzle, The	7
			Motorway, The	7
			Roman Adventure	7
		Stage 7 Owls	Broken Roof, The	7
			Lost in the Jungle	7
			Lost Key, The	7
			Red Planet	7
		Stage 7 Woodpeckers	Kate and the Crocodile	7
		Stage 8 Magpies	Viking Adventure	7
		Stage 8 More Magpies	Flood!	7
		Stage 8 Playscripts	Day in London, A	7
			Flying Carpet, The	7
			Rainbow Machine, The	7
			Victorian Adventure	7
		Stage 8 True Stories	Travels with Magellan	7
		Stage 9 Magpies	Litter Queen, The	7
			Storm Castle	7
			Superdog	7

SERIES	PUBLISHER	SET (OR AUTHOR)	TITLE	BAND
Oxford Reading Tree	OUP	Stage 9 More Magpies	Dutch Adventure	7
			Flying Machine, The	7
			Key Trouble	7
Pathways	Collins	Year 1	Dips and Skips	7
			Hatseller and the Monkeys, The	7
			Hide and Seek	7
			Hop, Hop, Kangaroo	7
			In the Park	7
			Stretch, Curl and Twist	7
		Year 2	Hattie Hates Hats	7
			Make a Book Book, The	7
			Owl	7
			Rain Arrow, The	7
			Shoes	7
Pelican Big Bks	Longman	Body, Wendy	Absolutely Brilliant Crazy Party, The	7
		Cullimore, Stan	Turtle Who Danced with the Crane, The	7
		Purkis, Sallie	Looking at Teddy Bears	7
PM Storybooks	Nelson Thornes	Turquoise Set A	Cabin in the Hills, The	7
			Jonathan Buys a Present	7
			Monkey Tricks	7
			Nelson, the Baby Elephant	7
			Toby and the Accident	7
			When the Volcano Erupted	7
		Turquoise Set B	Bird's Eye View	7
			Hailstorm, The	7
			Little Dinosaur Escapes	7
			Number Plates	7
			Rescuing Nelson	7
			Seat Belt Song, The	7
		Turquoise Set C	Ant City	7
			Grandad's Mask	7
			Jordan's Lucky Day	7
			Nesting Place, The	7
			Race to Green End, The	7
			Riding to Craggy Rock	7
PM Traditional Tales	Nelson Thornes	Turquoise Level	Brave Little Tailor, The	7
			Elves and the Shoemaker, The	7
			Goldilocks and the Three Bears	7
			Little Red Riding Hood	7
			Stone Soup	7
			Ugly Duckling, The	7
Rigby Star	Rigby	Turquoise Level	Flyers	7
			Giant Jumperee, The	7
			Is the Wise Owl Wise?	7
			Korka the Mighty Elf	7
			Perfect Pizza, The	7
			That's Not My Hobby!	7
Spotlight on Fact	Collins	Y2 The Seaside	Along the Seashore	7
			Packing for a Holiday	7
Star Quest	Rigby	Purple Level	Peanuts	7
		Turquoise Level	Home for Bonnie, A	7

SERIES	PUBLISHER	SET (OR AUTHOR)	TITLE	BAND
Stopwatch	A&C Black		Broad Bean	7
			Chicken and Egg	7
			Tadpole and Frog	7
Story Chest	Kingscourt	Stage 4	Clever Mr Brown	7
			Just Like Me	7
			Where is My Spider?	7
		Stage 5	Captain Bumble	7
Story Steps	Kingscourt	Level 17 Benchmark Bk	Fairy-Tale Flowers	7
		Level 17 Collection	My Dog	7
		Level 17 Little Books	Dog Family, The	7
			Laughing Place, The	7
		Level 18 Benchmark Bk	Interesting Insects	7
		Level 18 Collection	Dandelion	7
		Level 18 Little Books	Diary of a Sunflower	7
			Giant Grass	7
			Little Red Riding Hood	7
		Level 20 Little Books	Top Cat	7
Story Street	Longman	Step 5	Wind and Fire, Part 1	7
			Wind and Fire, Part 2	7
		Step 6	Present for Jojo, A	7
			Snow Games	7
Storyteller	Kingscourt	Set 6	Please Don't Sneeze!	7
		Set 7	Amazing Tricks	7
			Bun, The	7
			Crocodile's Bag	7
			Fast Food for Butterflies	7
			Fowler's Family Tree	7
			Granny Garcia's Gifts	7
			Hat Chat	7
			It's About Time	7
			Lizzie's Lizard	7
			Parachutes	7
			Please Do Not Drop Your Jelly Beans	7
			Sarah's Pet	7
			Turtle Talk	7
Storyworld Plays	Heinemann	Stage 9	Big Barry Baker on the Stage	7
Storyworlds	Heinemann	Stage 8 Once Upon a Time	Little Red Riding Hood	7
			Three Wishes, The	7
			Tiger and the Jackal, The	7
		Stage 8 Our World	Highland Cattle, The	7
			Highland Games, The	7
			Lost in the Mist	7
			Rescue at Sea	7
		Stage 9 Animal World	Canal Boat Cat	7
Individual Titles	Little Mammoth	Ahlberg, Allan	Funnybones	7
	Puffin	Ahlberg, Allan	Miss Jump the Jockey	7
	Picture Puffin	Ahlberg, Janet & Allen	Starting School	7
	Walker	Alborough, Jez	Cuddly Dudley	7
	Picture Corgi	Allen, Jonathan	Chicken Licken (HB lift the flap)	7
	Picture Puffin	Allen, Pamela	Who Sank the Boat?	7
	Walker	Baron, Alan	Red Fox Dances	7

Band 9 GOLD

Reading Recovery Levels 21/22

NATIONAL CURRICULUM LEVEL 2B

WORKING WITHIN LEVEL 2: LEARNING OPPORTUNITIES

- Look through a variety of texts with growing independence to predict content, layout and story development

- Read silently or quietly at a more rapid pace, taking note of punctuation and using it to keep track of longer sentences

- Solve most unfamiliar words on the run

- Adapt to fiction, non-fiction and poetic language with growing flexibility

- Take more conscious account of literary effects used by writers

- Begin to make more conscious use of reading to extend speaking and writing vocabulary and syntax.

TEXT CHARACTERISTICS

- somewhat more challenging than in band 8

- sentence structures becoming longer and more complex

- story plot may be more involved and reflect the feelings of the writer

- wider variety of text genre but still illustrated

- some books with chapters for more sustained reading

- characters are more distinctive and rounded than at earlier levels

- widening vocabulary and range of terminology, but still a controlled proportion of unknown words used per paragraph/page

- non-fiction texts cover an increasing curriculum range, and involve a range of text type and formats

<table>
<tr><td>GUIDED READING</td></tr>
<tr><td>GOLD BAND</td></tr>
<tr><td>RECOUNT</td></tr>
</table>

WHALES ON THE WORLD WIDE WEB
Alphakids

Sarah Prince

Horwitz Gardner (2000)

ISBN 0 7253 1862 7

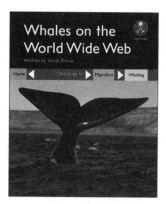

TEACHING OBJECTIVES

Provide opportunities for children to

- Skim-read title, illustrations and sub-headings to speculate what the book might be about
- Pose questions, and record these in writing, prior to reading non-fiction, to find answers
- Scan the text to find specific sections
- Locate parts of the text that give particular information
- Evaluate the usefulness of a text for its purpose
- Understand and use new words from reading.

TEXT SELECTION NOTES

A number of purposes are served in this small book illustrated with photos.

A class of children sets out to deepen their knowledge about whales by obtaining information from the web. They then construct their own web pages in order to share this information with other children. A boy recounts how he and his classmates carry out the project, and in doing so uses key word-processing vocabulary.

LINK TO WHOLE-CLASS CURRICULUM

There are links with a number of curriculum areas apart from English, including information technology, biology, ecology and geography. The book provides a simple, practical teaching model for project work in a modern school.

TEXT INTRODUCTION

Read the title and take a good look at the cover. What type of text do you think this is?

Let's write some questions we'd each like the answers to about whales or about the world wide web.

Now look through the book and see if you can spot the difference between the pages on the left hand side, and those on the right.

How could you describe the type of texts that you noticed? (Paragraphs, diagrams, maps, web-sites, email.)

STRATEGY CHECK

Read pages 2 to 5 and find out what the class decided to do. **Each child reads.** Describe their plans in your own words.

Now I want you to read in pairs pages 6/7, 8/9, 10/11, talk about what you read and prepare to tell the others about it.

Read slowly and think about the terms we've just used so that you can explain clearly, or prepare questions about those things you don't understand.

INDEPENDENT READING

This book contains quite a lot of new vocabulary for the children to work out. Teachers may find the following prompts helpful. For compound words such as **coastline, whalebone, Humpback**: split them into two parts and read each part separately, and then together.

For multi-syllabic words such as **designed, suggested, migrate, information**: find parts of the word you know, and try clapping the separate syllables. Now read right through the word. Re-read the sentence and check that it makes sense.

RETURN TO THE TEXT

Now you can report back to the group on the section you read. Can you show us where you found that information?

Let's return to our questions. Did we find the answers? Where could we go to find out more?

There were some words I'd like you to discuss: for example, **linked, scanned, migration, baleen, polluted**.

INDEPENDENT ACTIVITY

Check other sources including the web to satisfy unanswered questions, and record in diagrammatic form.

Use this model to create a group or class topic.

Band 10 WHITE

Reading Recovery Levels 23/24

NATIONAL CURRICULUM LEVEL 2A/
WORKING TOWARDS LEVEL 3

WORKING AT LEVEL 2A OR TOWARDS LEVEL 3: LEARNING OPPORTUNITIES

- Look through a variety of texts with growing independence to predict content, layout and story development

- Read silently most of the time

- Sustain interest in longer text, returning to it easily after a break

- Use text more fully as a reference and as a model

- Search for and find information in texts more flexibly

- Notice the spelling of unfamiliar words and relate to known words

- Show increased awareness of vocabulary and precise meaning

- Express reasoned opinions about what is read, and compare texts

- Offer and discuss interpretations of text.

TEXT CHARACTERISTICS

- widening range of genre and writing style

- story line or theme may be sustained over a longer period of time with chapters or sub-sections of text

- sentence structures may be longer with more subordinate phrases or clauses

- characters may be more fully developed

- more than one point of view expressed within the text

- information or action may be implied rather than spelled out

- texts may contain more metaphorical or technical language

- non-fiction texts placed in a broader context and include more detailed information

GUIDED READING
WHITE BAND
HUMOROUS FICTION

THE SINGING PRINCESS
Rigby Star

Judy Waite
Illustrated by Nick Schon

Rigby (2000)

ISBN 0433 04622 8

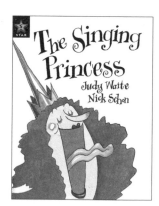

TEACHING OBJECTIVES

Provide opportunities for children to
- Read and respond imaginatively to a humorous story
- Identify and describe characters
- Discuss story settings and predict story endings
- Reinforce and apply word skills
- Discuss meaning of words and phrases that create humour.

TEXT SELECTION NOTES

No one dared to tell the Singing Princess how dreadful she sounded every time she opened her mouth. Life was very dull until Prince Dance-a-Lot turned up in his absurd armour. His attempts at dancing were no better than her singing. They exchanged colourful insults until the absurdity of the situation reduced them and the palace to helpless mirth.

Colourful language and amusing similes abound in this light-hearted tale, and children enjoy reading phrases such as 'cows burping' and 'trumpeting elephant with toothache'.

LINK TO WHOLE-CLASS CURRICULUM

Class discussions on alliteration, onomatopoeia, imagery and similes based on shared text, whether fiction or poetry, will supply children with the terminology they need to talk about the language in this book.

TEXT INTRODUCTION

Let's read the title and the blurb on the back cover.
Look through the book and talk about the atmosphere that the illustrator is trying to create. What makes you think that?
Does it remind you of another type of text? (comic strip)

STRATEGY CHECK

Read pages 2 to 5 to yourselves, and think about the two main characters in the story. Say the words that describe the princess's singing slowly to yourself and make pictures in your mind to match the words.

INDEPENDENT READING

Teacher asks individual children to read aloud quietly in turn, and acknowledges and prompts active problem-solving and fluent, well-phrased reading.

Some suggested prompts for unfamiliar vocabulary such as **earplugs**; **peered**; **toothache**; **spluttery**; **bumbly**:

Can you see parts of the word that you know? Start saying the word and think what would make sense.
Now start the sentence/line again, and see if it sounds right and makes sense.

Stop reading at page 5 and let's talk about the characters.
Now I'd like you to predict what's going to happen next. Let's jot down your ideas.
Now read up to page 11 and find out if there was really a monster.

What's going to happen when the princess sings and the prince dances?
Jot down your ideas and then read to the end. Were you right?

RETURN TO THE TEXT

What did you think about that story? Why? Do you think the ending worked well? Which parts do you think were amusing?
What do you think happened when Princess Melody started playing the trumpet and Prince Dance-a-Lot took up roller-skating?

INDEPENDENT ACTIVITY

Write a book review for other members of the class. Describe the characters, and make cartoon pictures of them insulting each other. Choose some similes from the story to write in the speech bubbles, or make up your own.

Make a chart of alliterative words from the story, e.g. **screech**; **spluttery**; **sparkly**; **swapped**; **snigger**.

TITLE	SERIES	PUBLISHER	SET (OR AUTHOR)	BAND
Barn Dance	Story Chest	Kingscourt	Ready-set-go Set BB	2
Barnaby's New House, The	Literacy Links Plus	Kingscourt	Early D	5
Barrel Of Gold, The	Story Chest	Kingscourt	Stage 4	5
Bath Time	Oxford Literacy Web	OUP	Starter Pack B (Variety)	1
Bath Water's Hot	Individual Titles	Walker	Hughes, Shirley	6
Bats	PM Non-fiction	Nelson Thornes	Gold Level	9
Be Quiet!	Rigby Star	Rigby	Yellow Level	3
Beaks	Literacy Plus Topic	Kingscourt	Emergent B	2
Beaks and Feet	Alphakids	Horwitz Gardner	Early Level 11	5
Beanbag	Literacy Plus Topic	Kingscourt	Fluent B	8
Beanpole Billy	Lighthouse	Ginn	Gold: 5	9
Bear and the Trolls, The	PM Traditional Tales	Nelson Thornes	Silver Level	10
Bear Hunt	Lighthouse	Ginn	Yellow: 6	3
Bear in the Park	All Aboard	Ginn	Stage 4 Set A: Sam & Rosie	5
Bear That Wouldn't Growl, The	Storyworlds	Heinemann	Stage 8 Animal World	6
Bears	Storyteller	Kingscourt	Set 2	2
Bears and the Honey, The	Storyworlds	Heinemann	Stage 2 Once Upon a Time	2
Bears' Christmas, The	Beginner Books	Collins	Berenstain, Stan & Jan	8
Bear's Diet	PM Storybooks	Nelson Thornes	Gold Set A	9
Bears In The Night	Bright and Early Books	Collins	Berenstain, Stan & Jan	2
Bear's Lunch, The	Individual Titles	Puffin	Allen, Pamela	6
Bears on Wheels	Bright and Early Books	Collins	Berenstain, Stan & Jan	3
Bears' Picnic, The	Beginner Books	Collins	Berenstain, Stan & Jan	8
Bears' Picnic, The	Story Chest	Kingscourt	Ready-set-go Set AA	1
Bears Who Stayed Indoors, The	Individual Titles	A & C Black	Gretz, Suzanna	10
Bears, Bears, Bears	Story Steps	Kingscourt	Level 7 Benchmark Bk	3
Beauty and the Beast	PM Traditional Tales	Nelson Thornes	Gold Level	9
Because a Little Bug Went Ka-choo!	Beginner Books	Collins	Stone, Rosetta	6
Beds	Book Project Non-fiction A	Longman	Homes	8
Bee In My Bonnet, A	Pathways	Collins	Year 3	6
Bee, The	Story Chest	Kingscourt	Ready-set-go Set B	2
Beep Goes My Belly Button	Oxford Literacy Web	OUP	Poetry Stages 1-5	7
Bees	Oxford RT Branch Library	OUP	Oxford Reds: Pack B	9
Bees and the Bear, The	Story Steps	Kingscourt	Level 11 Little Books	4
Before I Go to School	Storyteller	Kingscourt	Set 2	2
Ben and the Bear	Individual Titles	Walker	Riddell, Chris	6
Ben and the Bird	Story Street	Longman	Step 5	6
Ben and the Boxes	Story Street	Longman	Step 3	3
Ben and the Pop Star	Story Street	Longman	Step 4	5
Ben Biggins' Box	Book Project Fiction 1	Longman	Cluster E: Ben Biggins	3
Ben Biggins' House	Book Project Fiction 1	Longman	Cluster E: Ben Biggins	6
Ben Biggins' Playtime	Book Project Fiction 1	Longman	Cluster E: Ben Biggins	2
Ben Biggins' Socks	Book Project Fiction 1	Longman	Cluster E: Ben Biggins	2
Ben Biggins' Tummy	Book Project Fiction 1	Longman	Cluster E: Ben Biggins	2
Ben Biggins' Week	Book Project Fiction 1	Longman	Cluster E: Ben Biggins	3
Ben Gets a Hat	Story Street	Longman	Step 2	2
Ben Gets Cross	Story Street	Longman	Step 4	4
Ben the Bold	Literacy Links Plus	Kingscourt	Emergent C	3
Bendemolena	Spotlight on Plays	Collins	Age 7+	10
Ben's Amazing Birthday	Cambridge Reading	CUP	Y2 A: Narrative Recount	8
Ben's Dad	PM Storybooks	Nelson Thornes	Yellow Set A	3

TITLE	SERIES	PUBLISHER	SET (OR AUTHOR)	BAND
Ben's Get Well Cards	Genre Range	Longman	Emergent Letters	6
Ben's Red Car	PM Storybook Starters	Nelson Thornes	Set 2	1
Ben's Teddy Bear	PM Storybooks	Nelson Thornes	Red Set A	2
Ben's Tooth	PM Storybooks	Nelson Thornes	Green Set A	5
Ben's Treasure Hunt	PM Storybooks	Nelson Thornes	Red Set A	2
Berenstain Bears & Missing Dinosaur Bone, The	Beginner Books	Collins	Berenstain, Stan & Jan	8
Bertha's Secret Battle	Oxford RT Treetops	OUP	Stage 11 Pack A	10
Bertie and the Bear	Individual Titles	Picture Puffin	Allen, Pamela	6
Bertie Wiggins' Amazing Ears	Oxford RT Treetops	OUP	Stage 11 Pack A	10
Bertie Wiggins' Amazing Ears	Oxford RT Treetops	OUP	Stage 11 Playscripts	10
Best Cake, The	PM Storybooks	Nelson Thornes	Blue Set A	4
Best Children in the World, The	Story Chest	Kingscourt	Ready-set-go Set DD	3
Best Fish, The	Oxford Literacy Web	OUP	Stage 3 (Duck Green)	3
Best Nest, The	Beginner Books	Collins	Eastman, P D	7
Best Part, The	PM Storybooks	Nelson Thornes	Silver Set B	10
Best Pet, The	Lighthouse	Ginn	Purple: 3	8
Best Pizza in the World, The	Alphakids Plus	Horwitz Gardner	Emergent Level 5	3
Bet You Can't!	Individual Titles	Walker	Dale, Penny	3
Better Letter, A	Genre Range	Longman	Beginner Letters	2
Betty Boots	Alphakids	Horwitz Gardner	Extending Level 18	7
Bhalloo the Greedy Bear	Book Project Fiction 4	Longman	Cluster E: Favourite Stories	9
Bicycle, The	Story Chest	Kingscourt	Get-ready Set B	2
Bicycles Now and Fifty Years Ago	Book Project Non-fiction A	Longman	History of Transport	9
Biff's Aeroplane	Oxford Reading Tree	OUP	Stage 2 More Stories B	3
Big and Little	Storyteller	Kingscourt	Set 1	1
Big and Small	Alphakids Plus	Horwitz Gardner	Emergent Level 1	1
Big Bad Barney Bear	Individual Titles	Red Fox	Ross, Tony	8
Big Bad Bill	All Aboard	Ginn	Stage 6: Patt & Rhyme	6
Big Bad Raps	Crunchies	Orchard	Raps	8
Big Ball of String, A	Beginner Books	Collins	Holland, Marion	8
Big Balloon Festival, The	PM Storybooks	Nelson Thornes	Gold Set B	9
Big Barry Baker and the Bullies	Storyworlds	Heinemann	Stage 9 Our World	10
Big Barry Baker in Big Trouble	Storyworlds	Heinemann	Stage 9 Our World	9
Big Barry Baker on the Stage	Storyworld Plays	Heinemann	Stage 9	7
Big Barry Baker on the Stage	Storyworlds	Heinemann	Stage 9 Our World	9
Big Barry Baker's Parcel	Storyworlds	Heinemann	Stage 9 Our World	9
Big Bear's Bad Day	Oxford Literacy Web	OUP	Stage 2 (Variety)	2
Big Bear's Party	Oxford Literacy Web	OUP	Stage 2 (Variety)	2
Big Bear's Socks	Storyteller	Kingscourt	Set 3	4
Big Bo Peep	Lighthouse	Ginn	Gold: 4	9
Big Books and Little Books	Oxford Literacy Web	OUP	Stage 2 (Duck Green)	3
Big Boots	Storyworlds	Heinemann	Stage 6 Our World	6
Big Box & other stories, The	New Way	Nelson Thornes	Green Platform Books	5
Big Brother	AlphaWorld	Horwitz Gardner	Band 2: Red	2
Big Catch, The	Literacy Plus Topic	Kingscourt	Fluent C	6
Big Dog and Little Dog Visit the Moon	Blue Bananas	Mammoth	Young, Selina	8
Big Dog, Little Dog	Beginner Books	Collins	Eastman, P D	6
Big Dog, The	Alphakids	Horwitz Gardner	Transitional Level 14	6
Big Feet	Oxford Reading Tree	OUP	Stage 1+ First Sentences	2
Big Hill, The	Story Chest	Kingscourt	Get-ready Set B	2
Big Kick, The	PM Storybooks	Nelson Thornes	Red Set A	2

TITLE	SERIES	PUBLISHER	SET (OR AUTHOR)	BAND
Big Pig's Wig	Alphakids	Horwitz Gardner	Extending Level 23	10
Big Puddle, The	Oxford Literacy Web	OUP	Stage 3 (Duck Green)	2
Big Shapes and Little Shapes	PM Maths	Nelson Thornes	Stage A	1
Big Shrink, The	Cambridge Reading	CUP	Y2 A: Fantasy Worlds	9
Big Shrink, The	Cambridge Reading	CUP	Y2: Playscripts	9
Big Sister Rosie	All Aboard	Ginn	Stage 4 Set A: Sam & Rosie	5
Big Snowball, The	Storyworlds	Heinemann	Stage 5 Fantasy World	4
Big Surprise, The	Storyworlds	Heinemann	Stage 2 Animal World	8
Big Tease, The	Story Chest	Kingscourt	Stage 7	10
Big Things	PM Storybook Starters	Nelson Thornes	Set 1	1
Big Toe, The	Story Chest	Kingscourt	Small Read-together	4
Big Turnip, The	All Aboard	Ginn	Stage 3: Traditional Tales	4
Big Wide-Mouthed Frog, The	Individual Titles	Walker	Larranaga, Ana Martin	6
Big, Bad Cook, The	Literacy Plus Topic	Kingscourt	Fluent A	7
Biggest and Smallest	All Aboard Non Fiction	Ginn	Stage 5	6
Biggest Tree, The	PM Storybooks	Nelson Thornes	Orange Set A	6
Big-head & The Greedy Dog	New Way	Nelson Thornes	Green Easy Start Set B	6
Bike for Brad, A	PM Storybooks	Nelson Thornes	Purple Set B	8
Bike Lesson, The	Beginner Books	Collins	Berenstain, Stan & Jan	6
Bike Parade, The	Literacy Links Plus	Kingscourt	Emergent B	2
Billy Banana	Alphakids Plus	Horwitz Gardner	Early Level 11	4
Billy Beetle	Oxford Literacy Web	OUP	Stage 4 (Variety)	3
Billy Fishbone	Book Project Fiction 5	Longman		10
Billy's Baby	Story Street	Longman	Step 4	4
Billy's Box	Cambridge Reading	CUP	Y1 B: Fantasy Worlds	5
Bingo and the Bone	Storyworlds	Heinemann	Stage 2 Animal World	1
Bingo Wants to Play	Storyworlds	Heinemann	Stage 2 Animal World	2
Bird Feeder, The	Storyteller	Kingscourt	Set 2	2
Bird Hide, The	Alphakids	Horwitz Gardner	Extending Level 20	7
Bird in the Bush, A	Oxford Literacy Web	OUP	Stage 7 (Duck Green)	7
Bird Lady, The	Story Steps	Kingscourt	Level 20 Little Books	8
Bird Song	Storyteller	Kingscourt	Set 5	5
Bird Watchers	Storyteller	Kingscourt	Set 9	9
Birds	All Aboard Non Fiction	Ginn	Stage 2	3
Birds	Go Facts	A&C Black	Animals	8
Bird's Eye View	PM Storybooks	Nelson Thornes	Turquoise Set B	7
Birds of Prey	Storyteller	Kingscourt	Set 9	9
Birthday Balloons	PM Storybooks	Nelson Thornes	Blue Set B	4
Birthday Bug, The	Story Steps	Kingscourt	Level 2 Little Books	1
Birthday Cake for Ben, A	PM Storybooks	Nelson Thornes	Red Set B	2
Birthday Cake, The	Literacy Links Plus	Kingscourt	Emergent B	2
Birthday Cake, The	Story Chest	Kingscourt	Stage 2	5
Birthday Cakes	Alphakids	Horwitz Gardner	Emergent Level 4	2
Birthday for Bluebell, A	Crunchies	Orchard	Colour Crackers	9
Birthday Treasure Hunt, The	Info Trail	Longman	Emergent Geography	8
Black and White	Storyteller	Kingscourt	Set 2	2
Blackberries	PM Storybooks	Nelson Thornes	Yellow Set A	3
Blackberry Pudding	All Aboard	Ginn	Stage 4 Set B: Sam & Rosie	5
Blackbones Saves the School	Oxford RT Treetops	OUP	Stage 10 Pack C	10
Blow, Wind, Blow!	Story Steps	Kingscourt	Level 4 Collection	2
Blue Day	Literacy Links Plus	Kingscourt	Emergent A	2

TITLE	SERIES	PUBLISHER	SET (OR AUTHOR)	BAND
First Frog, The	Book Project Fiction 3	Longman	Cluster F: Faraway Folk Tales	7
First Morning, The	Literacy Plus Topic	Kingscourt	Fluent D	9
Fish	Star Quest	Rigby	White Level	10
Fish out of Water, A	Beginner Books	Collins	Palmer, Helen	7
Fisherman and His Wife, The	Literacy Links Plus	Kingscourt	Traditional Tales	8
Fishing	Alphakids Plus	Horwitz Gardner	Early Level 7	3
Fishing	PM Storybook Starters	Nelson Thornes	Set 2	1
Fishing	Story Chest	Kingscourt	Get-ready Set BB	1
Fishing Contest, The	Literacy Plus Topic	Kingscourt	Early C	5
Fishy Tale, A	Pathways	Collins	Year 1	4
Five and Five are Ten	PM Maths	Nelson Thornes	Stage B	3
Five Birds and Five Mice	PM Maths	Nelson Thornes	Stage A	2
Five Little Ducks	Individual Titles	Orchard	Beck, Ian	3
Five Little Men	Pathways	Collins	Year 1	4
Five Little Monkeys	Cambridge Reading	CUP	Y1 A: Poetry	4
Five Minutes' Peace	Individual Titles	Franklin Watts	Murphy, Jill	9
Fizz and Splutter	Story Chest	Kingscourt	Ready-set-go Set D	3
Fizzkid Liz	Rigby Star	Rigby	Orange Level	6
Flans Across the River	Oxford RT Treetops	OUP	Stage 11 Pack A	9
Flip, Flap. Fly!	Hotlinks	Kingscourt	12	6
Floating and Sinking	Alphakids	Horwitz Gardner	Early Level 11	4
Flock Watch	Story Steps	Kingscourt	Level 10 Little Books	4
Flood!	Oxford Reading Tree	OUP	Stage 8 More Magpies	7
Flood, The	PM Storybooks	Nelson Thornes	Green Set A	5
Floppy Floppy	Oxford Reading Tree	OUP	Stage 1 First Words	1
Floppy the Hero	Oxford Reading Tree	OUP	Stage 2 More Stories B	4
Floppy's Bath	Oxford Reading Tree	OUP	Stage 2 More Stories A	3
Flora to the Rescue	Storyworlds	Heinemann	Stage 6 Fantasy World	6
Floss	Individual Titles	Walker	Lewis, Kim	9
Flower Girl, The	PM Storybooks	Nelson Thornes	Red Set B	2
Flowers	AlphaWorld	Horwitz Gardner	Band 1A: Pink	1
Flutey Family Fruit Cake, The	Storyteller	Kingscourt	Set 9	9
Fly Away, Cheep	Oxford Literacy Web	OUP	Stage 4 (Duck Green)	3
Fly, The	Story Steps	Kingscourt	Level 5 Benchmark Bk	2
Flyers	Rigby Star	Rigby	Turquoise Level	7
Flying	Story Chest	Kingscourt	Ready-set-go Set B	2
Flying Carpet, The	Oxford Reading Tree	OUP	Stage 8 Magpies	8
Flying Carpet, The	Oxford Reading Tree	OUP	Stage 8 Playscripts	7
Flying Elephant, The	Oxford Reading Tree	OUP	Stage 4 More Stories B	3
Flying Fingers	Literacy Plus Topic	Kingscourt	Fluent B	8
Flying Fish, The	PM Storybooks	Nelson Thornes	Green Set B	5
Flying Football, The	Cambridge Reading	CUP	Bridging Book: B	6
Flying Footballs	Oxford Literacy Web	OUP	Stage 4 (Duck Green)	4
Flying Machine, The	Oxford Reading Tree	OUP	Stage 9 More Magpies	7
Flying Machines	Alphakids Plus	Horwitz Gardner	Early Level 11	6
Flying Tea Tray, The	Oxford Literacy Web	OUP	Stage 8 (Duck Green)	9
Flying Turtle, The	All Aboard	Ginn	Stage 5: Traditional Tales	5
Foggy Day, The	Oxford Reading Tree	OUP	Stage 2 More Stories B	3
Follow Me	Alphakids Plus	Horwitz Gardner	Emergent Level 4	2
Follow My Leader	Cambridge Reading	CUP	Y1 B: Familiar Settings	6
Food for All	First Explorers	Kingscourt	Level 1	8

TITLE	SERIES	PUBLISHER	SET (OR AUTHOR)	BAND
Food for Animals	AlphaWorld	Horwitz Gardner	Band 7: Turquoise	8
Food for Festivals	Pelican Big Bks	Longman	Witherington, Anne	8
Foot Book, The	Bright and Early Books	Collins	Seuss, Dr	5
Football at the Park	PM Storybooks	Nelson Thornes	Yellow Set B	3
Footprint Detective	All Aboard Non Fiction	Ginn	Stage 6	9
Footprints	Literacy Plus Topic	Kingscourt	Early C	4
For My Birthday	Lighthouse	Ginn	Pink A: 6	1
Forces of Nature	First Explorers	Kingscourt	Level 2	10
Forest Giants, The	Oxford Literacy Web	OUP	Stage 5 (Variety)	5
Forest, The	Cambridge Reading	CUP	Y1: Non-fiction	7
Forgotten Princess, The	Literacy Plus Topic	Kingscourt	Fluent D	8
Fortune for Yo-Yo, A	Crunchies	Orchard	Colour Crackers	9
Fossils	National Geographic	Rigby	Purple Level	9
Four Cars	PM Maths	Nelson Thornes	Stage A	2
Four Friends & other stories, The	New Way	Nelson Thornes	Yellow Platform Books	8
Four Ice Creams	PM Storybook Starters	Nelson Thornes	Set 2	1
Fowler's Family Tree	Storyteller	Kingscourt	Set 7	7
Fox and the Crow, The	Alphakids	Horwitz Gardner	Early Level 9	4
Fox and the Rabbit, The	Storyworlds	Heinemann	Stage 2 Once Upon a Time	2
Fox and the Snail, The	Alphakids Plus	Horwitz Gardner	Early Level 9	4
Fox and the Stork, The	Storyworlds	Heinemann	Stage 2 Once Upon a Time	2
Fox Who Foxed, The	PM Storybooks	Nelson Thornes	Green Set A	5
Foxes	PM Non-fiction	Nelson Thornes	Gold Level	9
Freddy's Teddy	Book Project Fiction 1	Longman	Cluster D: Teddy	3
Fried Piper of Hamstring, The	Crunchies	Orchard	Seriously Silly Stories	10
Friend for Kate, A	Cambridge Reading	CUP	Y1 C: Familiar Settings	7
Friend for Little White Rabbit, A	PM Storybooks	Nelson Thornes	Yellow Set A	3
Friend, A	Literacy Links Plus	Kingscourt	Early D	5
Friends and Families	Hotlinks	Kingscourt	17	7
Fright in the Night, A	Oxford Reading Tree	OUP	Stage 6 More Owls	6
Frisky and the Cat	Storyworlds	Heinemann	Stage 3 Animal World	2
Frisky and the Ducks	Storyworlds	Heinemann	Stage 3 Animal World	2
Frisky Plays a Trick	Storyworlds	Heinemann	Stage 3 Animal World	2
Frisky Wants to Sleep	Storyworlds	Heinemann	Stage 3 Animal World	2
Frog and Toad Are Friends	Individual Titles	Egmont	Lobel, Arnold	7
Frog and Toad Together	Individual Titles	Egmont	Lobel, Arnold	8
Frog Day	Storyteller	Kingscourt	Set 8	8
Frog Goes on Holiday	Genre Range	Longman	Emergent Comics	5
Frog in the Throat, A	Book Project Fiction 2	Longman	Cluster C: Little Frog	6
Frog Prince, The	Genre Range	Longman	Beginner Trad Tales	4
Frog Prince, The	Storyworlds	Heinemann	Stage 7 Once Upon a Time	6
Frog Princess, The	Literacy Links Plus	Kingscourt	Early D	6
Froggy Tale, A	Literacy Plus Topic	Kingscourt	Fluent A	6
Frogs	Storyteller	Kingscourt	Set 4	4
Frogs and Toads	All Aboard Non Fiction	Ginn	Stage 8	8
Frogs and Toads	Oxford RT Branch Library	OUP	Oxford Reds: Pack A	9
From a Bean to a Bar	Lighthouse	Ginn	Turquoise: 3	7
From an Acorn to an Oak Tree	Info Trail	Longman	Emergent Science	4
From One to Eight	PM Maths	Nelson Thornes	Stage B	3
Fruit	Oxford Literacy Web	OUP	First Non-fiction: Pack B	4
Fruit Salad	Alphakids	Horwitz Gardner	Emergent Level 1	1

TITLE	SERIES	PUBLISHER	SET (OR AUTHOR)	BAND
Fruits and Seeds	Oxford Reading Tree	OUP	Stage 10 Jackdaws	9
Fun and Games	Hotlinks	Kingscourt	19	7
Fun at the Beach	Oxford Reading Tree	OUP	Stage 1 First Words	1
Fun Run, The	All Aboard	Ginn	Stage 5 Set B: Sam & Rosie	6
Fun Things to Make and Do	Discovery World	Heinemann	Stage D	4
Fun With Fruit	Storyteller	Kingscourt	Set 1	1
Funny Ears	Star Quest	Rigby	Yellow Level	2
Funnybones	Individual Titles	Little Mammoth	Ahlberg, Allan	7
Fussy Freda	All Aboard	Ginn	Stage 7: Patt & Rhyme	9
G				
Gallo and Zorro	Literacy Links Plus	Kingscourt	Early D	8
Game with Shapes, A	PM Maths	Nelson Thornes	Stage A	2
Garden Friends	Book Project Fiction 1	Longman	Cluster B: Animals	3
Gardening for Beginners	All Aboard Non Fiction	Ginn	Stage 9	10
Gardening, The	Oxford Literacy Web	OUP	Starter Pack B (Variety)	1
Genie in the Bottle, The	Oxford Literacy Web	OUP	Stage 5 (Variety)	5
Get up, Webster!	Book Project Fiction 1	Longman	Cluster F: Webster	2
Getting Around	Alphakids Plus	Horwitz Gardner	Transitional Level 13	6
Getting Ready	Oxford Literacy Web	OUP	Stage 1 (Duck Green)	1
Getting Ready for the Ball	Literacy Links Plus	Kingscourt	Emergent A	2
Ghost and the Sausage, The	Story Chest	Kingscourt	Stage 6	9
Ghost in the Castle	All Aboard	Ginn	Stage 3: Sam & Rosie	4
Ghost Next Door, The	All Aboard	Ginn	Stage 7: Patt & Rhyme	9
Ghost Train, The	All Aboard	Ginn	Stage 2: Sam & Rosie	2
Ghost Tricks	Oxford Reading Tree	OUP	Stage 10 More Robins	10
Ghost, The	Story Chest	Kingscourt	Get-ready Set A	1
Ghostyshocks and the Three Scares	Crunchies	Orchard	Seriously Silly Stories	8
Giant and the Frippit, The	Rigby Star	Rigby	Orange Level	6
Giant Gingerbread Man, The	Alphakids	Horwitz Gardner	Early Level 9	4
Giant Grass	Story Steps	Kingscourt	Level 18 Little Books	7
Giant Jumperee, The	Rigby Star	Rigby	Turquoise Level	7
Giant Sandwich, The	All Aboard	Ginn	Stage 3 Set A: Patt & Rhyme	3
Giant Stromboli	Book Project Fiction 3	Longman	Cluster E: Once Upon A Time	9
Giant's Breakfast, The	Literacy Links Plus	Kingscourt	Emergent C	2
Giants, The	Oxford Literacy Web	OUP	Stage 6 (Duck Green)	7
Giddy Funfair	Book Project Fiction 4	Longman	Cluster D: Giddy House	7
Giddy Space	Book Project Fiction 4	Longman	Cluster D: Giddy House	10
Giddy Up and Away	Book Project Fiction 4	Longman	Cluster D: Giddy House	7
Gifts, The	Story Chest	Kingscourt	Get-ready Set DD	2
Giggle Box, The	Story Chest	Kingscourt	Ready-set-go Set DD	4
Ginger	Individual Titles	Safeway	Parker, Ant	3
Ginger, Where Are You?	Pathways	Collins	Year 2	8
Gingerbread Man, The	Cambridge Reading	CUP	Y1 A: Range of Cultures	4
Gingerbread Man, The	Literacy Links Plus	Kingscourt	Traditional Tales	6
Gingerbread Man, The	PM Traditional Tales	Nelson Thornes	Orange Level	6
Gingerbread Man, The	Storyworld Plays	Heinemann	Stage 6	4
Gingerbread Man, The	Storyworlds	Heinemann	Stage 6 Once Upon a Time	5
Give Me My Yam!	Individual Titles	Walker	Blake, Jan	9
Gizmos' Party, The	Rigby Star	Rigby	White Level	10
Gizmos' Trip, The	Rigby Star	Rigby	White Level	10
Glasses	Alphakids	Horwitz Gardner	Emergent Level 1	1

TITLE	SERIES	PUBLISHER	SET (OR AUTHOR)	BAND
Leaves	AlphaWorld	Horwitz Gardner	Band 2: Red	2
Leela and the Lost Shoe	Oxford Literacy Web	OUP	Stage 6 (Duck Green)	7
Leela's Secret Plan	Oxford Literacy Web	OUP	Stage 5 (Duck Green)	4
Legs	Literacy Links Plus	Kingscourt	Early A	2
Leonora and the Giddy House	Book Project Fiction 4	Longman	Cluster D: Giddy House	7
Leopard's Drum, The	Individual Titles	Frances Lincoln	Souhami, Jessica	9
Let Me in	Literacy Plus Topic	Kingscourt	Emergent D	2
Let Me in	Story Chest	Kingscourt	Stage 3	6
Let's Make Pancakes	Alphakids Plus	Horwitz Gardner	Transitional Level 12	5
Letang and Julie Save the Day	Book Project Fiction 6	Longman		9
Letang's New Friend	Book Project Fiction 6	Longman		9
Let's Build a Tower	Literacy Links Plus	Kingscourt	Emergent A	1
Let's Go Home, Little Bear	Individual Titles	Walker	Waddell, Martin	7
Let's Go into the Jungle	Book Project Fiction 1	Longman	Cluster B: Animals	6
Let's Have a Dog	Pathways	Collins	Year 1	5
Let's Play Board Games!	Spotlight on Fact	Collins	Y1 Toys and Games	4
Let's Play Monsters	All Aboard	Ginn	Stage 2: Sam & Rosie	2
Letters From Lucy	Pathways	Collins	Year 2	8
Lick of the Spoon, A	Cambridge Reading	CUP	Y2 B: Poetry	10
Lift, The	Story Chest	Kingscourt	Ready-set-go Set CC	4
Lights On	First Explorers	Kingscourt	Level 2	10
Lili's Breakfast	Storyteller	Kingscourt	Set 4	4
Lilly-Lolly-Littlelegs	Literacy Links Plus	Kingscourt	Early B	5
Lion and the Mouse, The	Cambridge Reading	CUP	Y1 A: Range of Cultures	4
Lion and the Mouse, The	Cambridge Reading	CUP	Y1: Playscripts	5
Lion and the Mouse, The	Literacy Links Plus	Kingscourt	Traditional Tales	4
Lion and the Mouse, The	PM Storybooks	Nelson Thornes	Blue Set A	5
Lion and the Rabbit, The	PM Storybooks	Nelson Thornes	Blue Set A	4
Lion Talk	Storyteller	Kingscourt	Set 6	6
Lions and Tigers	PM Non-fiction	Nelson Thornes	Turquoise Level	8
Lion's Dinner, The	Rigby Star	Rigby	Yellow Level	3
Lion's Lunch	Lighthouse	Ginn	Blue: 6	4
Lion's Roar, The	All Aboard	Ginn	Stage 6: Patt & Rhyme	7
Lisa's Letter	Book Project Fiction 2	Longman	Cluster E: Family	3
Litter Queen, The	Oxford Reading Tree	OUP	Stage 9 Magpies	7
Little Adventure, A	PM Storybooks	Nelson Thornes	Silver Set A	10
Little Angels	Oxford Literacy Web	OUP	Stage 3 (Duck Green)	3
Little Bear and the Wish Fish	Individual Titles	Frances Lincoln	Gliori, Debi	9
Little Blue, Big Blue	Rigby Star	Rigby	White Level	10
Little Bo Peep Has Knickers that Bleep	Crunchies	Orchard	Seriously Silly Rhymes	10
Little Brother	Story Chest	Kingscourt	Get-ready Set C	2
Little Brother's Haircut	Story Chest	Kingscourt	Stage 7	10
Little Bulldozer	PM Storybooks	Nelson Thornes	Yellow Set A	3
Little Bulldozer Helps Again	PM Storybooks	Nelson Thornes	Blue Set B	4
Little Dinosaur Escapes	PM Storybooks	Nelson Thornes	Turquoise Set B	7
Little Dragon, The	Oxford Reading Tree	OUP	Stage 3 More Wrens	2
Little Eight John	All Aboard	Ginn	Stage 7: Patt & Rhyme	9
Little Frog and the Dog	Book Project Fiction 2	Longman	Cluster C: Little Frog	3
Little Frog and the Frog Olympics	Book Project Fiction 2	Longman	Cluster C: Little Frog	4
Little Frog and the Tadpoles	Book Project Fiction 2	Longman	Cluster C: Little Frog	4
Little Girl and Her Beetle, The	Literacy Links Plus	Kingscourt	Fluent B	7

TITLE	SERIES	PUBLISHER	SET (OR AUTHOR)	BAND
Little Girl and the Bear, The	Storyworlds	Heinemann	Stage 9 Once Upon a Time	10
Little Half Chick	Literacy Plus Topic	Kingscourt	Early D	6
Little Hearts	Story Chest	Kingscourt	Ready-set-go Set AA	2
Little Inchkin	Individual Titles	Frances Lincoln	French, Fiona	9
Little Joe's Big Race	Individual Titles	Franklin Watts	Blackford, Andy	5
Little Meanie's Lunch	Story Chest	Kingscourt	Ready-set-go Set AA	3
Little Miss Muffet	Pathways	Collins	Year 1	5
Little Monkey	Alphakids	Horwitz Gardner	Early Level 11	4
Little Monster	All Aboard	Ginn	Stage 2 Set A: Patt & Rhyme	3
Little Monster Did it!	Individual Titles	Transworld	Cooper, Helen	8
Little Pig	Story Chest	Kingscourt	Ready-set-go Set B	2
Little Pig's Bouncy Ball	Individual Titles	Walker	Baron, Alan	5
Little Rabbit	Storyworld Plays	Heinemann	Stage 4	3
Little Rabbit	Storyworlds	Heinemann	Stage 4 Once Upon a Time	3
Little Red Bus, The	PM Storybooks	Nelson Thornes	Green Set A	5
Little Red Hen	All Aboard	Ginn	Stage 4: Traditional Tales	4
Little Red Hen & other stories	New Way	Nelson Thornes	Green Platform Books	6
Little Red Hen, The	Cambridge Reading	CUP	Y1 B: Range of Cultures	5
Little Red Hen, The	Cambridge Reading	CUP	Y1: Playscripts	6
Little Red Hen, The	Literacy Links Plus	Kingscourt	Traditional Tales	4
Little Red Hen, The	PM Traditional Tales	Nelson Thornes	Orange Level	6
Little Red Hen, The	Storyteller	Kingscourt	Set 5	5
Little Red Riding Hood	PM Traditional Tales	Nelson Thornes	Turquoise Level	7
Little Red Riding Hood	Story Steps	Kingscourt	Level 18 Little Books	7
Little Red Riding Hood	Storyworlds	Heinemann	Stage 8 Once Upon a Time	7
Little Red Riding Wolf	Crunchies	Orchard	Seriously Silly Stories	10
Little Snowman, The	PM Storybooks	Nelson Thornes	Red Set B	2
Little Things	PM Storybook Starters	Nelson Thornes	Set 1	1
Little Tiger's Big Surprise	Individual Titles	Little Tiger Press	Sykes, Julie	9
Living and Non-living Things	Alphakids	Horwitz Gardner	Emergent Level 2	1
Living Together	Alphakids	Horwitz Gardner	Extending Level 23	10
Lizard Loses His Tail	PM Storybooks	Nelson Thornes	Red Set A	2
Lizard's Tail	Alphakids Plus	Horwitz Gardner	Early Level 8	3
Lizzie and the Car Wash	All Aboard	Ginn	Stage 3: Sam & Rosie	3
Lizzie's Lizard	Storyteller	Kingscourt	Set 7	7
Lizzie's Lunch	Literacy Plus Topic	Kingscourt	Early D	5
Locked Out	PM Storybooks	Nelson Thornes	Blue Set A	5
London's Burning!	Info Trail	Longman	Emergent History	5
Lonely Giant, The	Literacy Links Plus	Kingscourt	Fluent B	8
Lonely Troll, The	Alphakids	Horwitz Gardner	Transitional Level 17	7
Long and Short	PM Maths	Nelson Thornes	Stage A	2
Long Journey, The	Oxford Reading Tree	OUP	Stage 7 More Robins	9
Long Live Roberto	Crunchies	Orchard	Colour Crackers	9
Look After Me	Oxford Reading Tree	OUP	Stage 1+ More First Sentences	2
Look at Me	Alphakids Plus	Horwitz Gardner	Emergent Level 1	1
Look at Me	Oxford Reading Tree	OUP	Stage 1+ First Sentences	1
Look at Me	PM Storybook Starters	Nelson Thornes	Set 1	1
Look at Me!	Lighthouse	Ginn	Pink A: 2	1
Look at the Ball	Storyteller	Kingscourt	Set 1	1
Look at the Tree	National Geographic	Rigby	Pink Level	1
Look Closer	Pathways	Collins	Year 1	8

TITLE	SERIES	PUBLISHER	SET (OR AUTHOR)	BAND
Look for Me	Story Chest	Kingscourt	Ready-set-go Set C	2
Look Inside	Storyteller	Kingscourt	Set 8	8
Look Out Fish!	Lighthouse	Ginn	Pink B: 2	1
Look Out For Bears	Literacy Plus Topic	Kingscourt	Emergent D	3
Look Out for Your Tail	Literacy Links Plus	Kingscourt	Fluent C	8
Look Out of the Window	Story Steps	Kingscourt	Level 4 Little Books	2
Look Out!	Literacy Links Plus	Kingscourt	Emergent B	1
Look Out! He's Behind You!	Individual Titles	Egmont	Bradman, Tony	5
Look Out, Dan!	Story Chest	Kingscourt	Get-ready Set CC	2
Look Out, Harry!	Book Project Fiction 2	Longman	Cluster F: Harry	4
Look Up	First Explorers	Kingscourt	Level 1	8
Look Up, Look Down	PM Non-fiction	Nelson Thornes	Red Level	3
Look What I Can Do	Individual Titles	Collins Pict Lions	Aruego, Jose	1
Look What I Found!	Lighthouse	Ginn	Pink A: 8	1
Look What You Can Make!	Story Steps	Kingscourt	Level 6 Little Books	3
Looking After Baby	Storyteller	Kingscourt	Set 2	2
Looking After Chickens	Alphakids	Horwitz Gardner	Transitional Level 15	6
Looking After Pip	Story Street	Longman	Step 5	5
Looking After the Egg	All Aboard Non Fiction	Ginn	Stage 7	10
Looking After Their Young	Alphakids	Horwitz Gardner	Extending Level 18	8
Looking at Teddy Bears	Pelican Big Bks	Longman	Purkis, Sallie	7
Looking Down	PM Storybook Starters	Nelson Thornes	Set 2	1
Looking for Fang	Alphakids	Horwitz Gardner	Emergent Level 5	3
Looking for Lucky	Genre Range	Longman	Beginner Comics	3
Looking Like Plants	Alphakids Plus	Horwitz Gardner	Transitional Level 12	6
Lord Mount Dragon, The	Cambridge Reading	CUP	Y2 B: Range of Cultures	10
Lord Scarecrow	All Aboard	Ginn	Stage 6: Sam & Rosie	6
Losing Lucky	Story Street	Longman	Step 6	6
Lost	Literacy Plus Topic	Kingscourt	Early A	3
Lost	Story Chest	Kingscourt	Ready-set-go Set B	2
Lost	Story Steps	Kingscourt	Level 13 Benchmark Bk	5
Lost	Story Street	Longman	Step 3	3
Lost and Found	Oxford Literacy Web	OUP	Stage 2 (Duck Green)	2
Lost at the Fun Park	PM Storybooks	Nelson Thornes	Blue Set B	4
Lost at the School Fair	All Aboard	Ginn	Stage 3: Booster Bks	4
Lost Coat, The	Storyworlds	Heinemann	Stage 3 Our World	2
Lost Costume, The	Storyworlds	Heinemann	Stage 6 Our World	6
Lost in the Forest	PM Storybooks	Nelson Thornes	Orange Set C	6
Lost in the Jungle	Oxford Reading Tree	OUP	Stage 7 Owls	7
Lost in the Jungle	Oxford Reading Tree	OUP	Stage 7 Playscripts	6
Lost in the Mist	Storyworlds	Heinemann	Stage 8 Our World	7
Lost in the Park	Alphakids	Horwitz Gardner	Transitional Level 13	6
Lost Key, The	Oxford Reading Tree	OUP	Stage 7 Owls	7
Lost Key, The	Oxford Reading Tree	OUP	Stage 7 Playscripts	6
Lost Mother, The	Alphakids	Horwitz Gardner	Early Level 6	3
Lost Puppy, The	Oxford Reading Tree	OUP	Stage 3 More Wrens	2
Loudest Sneeze, The	Alphakids	Horwitz Gardner	Transitional Level 16	6
Lucky Day for Little Dinosaur, A	PM Storybooks	Nelson Thornes	Yellow Set B	3
Lucky Ducks	Oxford Literacy Web	OUP	Stage 6 (Duck Green)	7
Lucky Goes to Dog School	PM Storybooks	Nelson Thornes	Yellow Set A	3
Lucky the Goat	Oxford Reading Tree	OUP	Stage 4 More Sparrows	4

TITLE	SERIES	PUBLISHER	SET (OR AUTHOR)	BAND
Pirate Gold	Oxford Literacy Web	OUP	Stage 9 (Variety)	10
Pirate Pete and the Monster	Storyworlds	Heinemann	Stage 4 Fantasy World	3
Pirate Pete and the Treasure Island	Storyworlds	Heinemann	Stage 4 Fantasy World	3
Pirate Pete Keeps Fit	Storyworlds	Heinemann	Stage 4 Fantasy World	3
Pirate Pete Loses His Hat	Storyworlds	Heinemann	Stage 4 Fantasy World	3
Pirates	Pathways	Collins	Year 1	6
Pirates Ahoy!	Story Street	Longman	Step 5	6
Pirates, The	Story Chest	Kingscourt	Stage 2	6
Pit-a-Pat-a-Parrot	Oxford Literacy Web	OUP	Poetry Stages 1-5	6
Pizza	Individual Titles	Wayland	Moses, Brian	10
Pizza For Dinner	Literacy Links Plus	Kingscourt	Early C	6
Pizza Princess	All Aboard	Ginn	Stage 4 Set A: Patt & Rhyme	5
Places to Visit	Spotlight on Fact	Collins	Y2 The Seaside	9
Places We Visit	All Aboard Non Fiction	Ginn	Stage 1	2
Planets, The	All Aboard Non Fiction	Ginn	Stage 8	9
Planning a Party	All Aboard Non Fiction	Ginn	Stage 6	10
Plants	Alphakids	Horwitz Gardner	Emergent Level 5	2
Plants	Go Facts	A&C Black	Plants	10
Plants All Round	First Explorers	Kingscourt	Level 1	8
Plants as Food	Go Facts	A&C Black	Plants	10
Platypus	Individual Titles	Viking	Riddell, Chris	8
Play with Me	All Aboard	Ginn	Stage 2 Set B: Patt & Rhyme	3
Play, The	All Aboard	Ginn	Stage 1: Sam & Rosie	2
Play, The	Oxford Reading Tree	OUP	Stage 4 Storybooks	4
Play, The	Rigby Star	Rigby	Pink Level	1
Playing	Alphakids	Horwitz Gardner	Emergent Level 1	1
Playing	PM Storybook Starters	Nelson Thornes	Set 1	1
Playing Outside	AlphaWorld	Horwitz Gardner	Band 1A: Pink	1
Playing with Pip	Story Street	Longman	Step 1	1
Playtime	Book Project Fiction 1	Longman	Cluster B: Animals	2
Please Do Not Drop Your Jelly Beans	Storyteller	Kingscourt	Set 7	7
Please Don't Sneeze!	Storyteller	Kingscourt	Set 6	7
Please, Miss!	Cambridge Reading	CUP	Y1 B: Familiar Settings	6
Please Mum!	Lighthouse	Ginn	Red: 9	2
Plop!	Story Chest	Kingscourt	Ready-set-go Set B	2
Plum Magic	All Aboard	Ginn	Stage 6: Sam & Rosie	6
Pocket Full of Pie, A	All Aboard	Ginn	Stage 9: Poetry	10
Pocket Money	Oxford Reading Tree	OUP	Stage 8 More Magpies	8
Pocketful of Gold	Book Project Fiction 3	Longman	Cluster E: Once Upon A Time	6
Pol and Pax	New Way	Nelson Thornes	Blue Parallel Books	7
Pol and Pax in the Salty Red Sea	New Way	Nelson Thornes	Orange Parallel Books	10
Pol and Pax on Earth	New Way	Nelson Thornes	Violet Parallel Books	9
Pol and Pax on the Third Moon	New Way	Nelson Thornes	Yellow Platform Books	8
Polar Bear, Polar Bear...	Individual Titles	Picture Puffin	Martin, Bill	7
Polar Bears	PM Non-fiction	Nelson Thornes	Silver Level	10
Polar Bears	Story Steps	Kingscourt	Level 8 Little Books	4
Poles Apart	Rigby Star	Rigby	Purple Level	8
Pollution	Alphakids	Horwitz Gardner	Extending Level 21	9
Polly the Most Poetic Person	Crunchies	Orchard	The One And Only	8
Pond Where Harriet Lives, The	Storyteller	Kingscourt	Set 4	4
Pond, The	Alphakids Plus	Horwitz Gardner	Emergent Level 5	2

TITLE	SERIES	PUBLISHER	SET (OR AUTHOR)	BAND
Ponds and Rivers	First Explorers	Kingscourt	Level 1	8
Pookie and Joe	Literacy Plus Topic	Kingscourt	Fluent D	7
Poor Bobby	All Aboard	Ginn	Stage 3: Booster Bks	4
Poor Old Mum!	Oxford Reading Tree	OUP	Stage 4 More Stories A	3
Poor Old Polly	Story Chest	Kingscourt	Small Read-together	4
Poor Sam	Genre Range	Longman	Beginner Plays	4
Pop! A Play	Rigby Star	Rigby	Yellow Level	3
Poppy's Pot	Oxford Literacy Web	OUP	Stage 1 (Duck Green)	2
Poppy's Puppets	Oxford Literacy Web	OUP	Stage 2 (Duck Green)	3
Postcard, The	New Way	Nelson Thornes	Green Easy Start Set A	4
Postcards	Genre Range	Longman	Beginner Letters	4
Postcards from Pop	Literacy Plus Topic	Kingscourt	Early C	4
Poupette	Book Project Fiction 7	Longman		10
Precious Potter	Crunchies	Orchard	Colour Crackers	8
Predators	Alphakids	Horwitz Gardner	Transitional Level 16	7
Present for Dad, A	Alphakids	Horwitz Gardner	Extending Level 22	9
Present for Jojo, A	Story Street	Longman	Step 6	7
Present for Our Teacher, A	AlphaWorld	Horwitz Gardner	Band 6: Orange	6
Presents	Storyteller	Kingscourt	Set 2	2
Presents	Storyworlds	Heinemann	Stage 5 Our World	4
Presents for Dad	Oxford Reading Tree	OUP	Stage 1+ More First Sentences	2
Prickle, Crackle, Pop	Hotlinks	Kingscourt	10	4
Princess and the Pea, The	Storyworlds	Heinemann	Stage 6 Once Upon a Time	5
Princess Jo	Alphakids Plus	Horwitz Gardner	Transitional Level 17	6
Princess Smartypants	Individual Titles	Puffin	Cole, Babette	9
Printing Machine, The	Literacy Links Plus	Kingscourt	Early B	4
Promise You Won't Be Cross	Blue Bananas	Mammoth		9
Proper Bike, A	Oxford Reading Tree	OUP	Stage 9 Robins	8
Psid and Bolter	Oxford Reading Tree	OUP	Tree Tops All Stars Pack 3	10
Pterosaur's Long Flight	PM Storybooks	Nelson Thornes	Orange Set B	6
Pudding	Book Project Fiction 2	Longman	Cluster D: Cat	4
Pumpkin House, The	Literacy Links Plus	Kingscourt	Fluent B	7
Pumpkin Man, The	Crunchies	Orchard	Little Horrors	9
Pumpkin Mountain & The Nightingale	New Way	Nelson Thornes	Yellow Platform Books	9
Pumpkin, The	Story Chest	Kingscourt	Ready-set-go Set C	3
Puppet Play, A	Storyteller	Kingscourt	Set 2	2
Puppet Show, The	Literacy Links Plus	Kingscourt	Emergent D	2
Puppy Chase, The	Cambridge Reading	CUP	Bridging Book: B	6
Purple Buttons	Oxford RT Treetops	OUP	Stage 10/11 Pack B	9
Push!	Oxford Reading Tree	OUP	Stage 2 Wrens	2
Puss-in-Boots	Literacy Links Plus	Kingscourt	Traditional Tales	8
Puss-in-Boots	PM Traditional Tales	Nelson Thornes	Purple Level	8
Pussy and the Birds	PM Storybooks	Nelson Thornes	Red Set A	2
Put Me in the Zoo	Beginner Books	Collins	Lopshire, Robert	5
Putting on a Magic Show	All Aboard Non Fiction	Ginn	Stage 7	9
Puzzle, The	Storyteller	Kingscourt	Set 1	1
Pyjama Party, The	Cambridge Reading	CUP	Y2 B: Familiar Settings	9
Pyjama Party, The	Cambridge Reading	CUP	Y2: Playscripts	8
Q				
Quack, Quack	Individual Titles	Walker	Casey, Patricia	2
Quarrel, The	Oxford Reading Tree	OUP	Citizenship Stories Stage 9/10	9

TITLE	SERIES	PUBLISHER	SET (OR AUTHOR)	BAND
Queen's Knickers, The	Individual Titles	Red Fox	Allen, N	10
Queen's Parrot, The	Literacy Links Plus	Kingscourt	Early D	6
Quest, The	Oxford Reading Tree	OUP	Stage 9 Magpies	9
Quiet Morning for Mum, A	Lighthouse	Ginn	Blue: 2	4
R				
Rabbit, The	Individual Titles	Red Fox	Burningham, John	5
Rabbits	Literacy Plus Topic	Kingscourt	Fluent C	10
Rabbits and Their Young	Book Project Non-fiction A	Longman	Animals	8
Rabbit's Surprise Birthday	Rigby Star	Rigby	Purple Level	8
Rabbit's Tail	Cambridge Reading	CUP	Y2 A: Range of Cultures	9
Rabbit's Trick	Oxford Literacy Web	OUP	Stage 4 (Variety)	3
Race to Green End, The	PM Storybooks	Nelson Thornes	Turquoise Set C	7
Race to the Pole	National Geographic	Rigby	White Level	10
Rachel Versus Bonecrusher the Mighty	Book Project Fiction 8	Longman		10
Rachel and the Difference Thief	Book Project Fiction 8	Longman		10
Racing Pigeons	All Aboard Non Fiction	Ginn	Stage 5	6
Racoons	PM Non-fiction	Nelson Thornes	Gold Level	9
Rain	Alphakids	Horwitz Gardner	Emergent Level 4	2
Rain Arrow, The	Pathways	Collins	Year 2	7
Rain Forest, The	National Geographic	Rigby	Purple Level	9
Rainbow Adventure, The	Oxford Reading Tree	OUP	Stage 8 Magpies	8
Rainbow Machine, The	Oxford Reading Tree	OUP	Stage 8 Playscripts	7
Rainbow Parrot	Literacy Plus Topic	Kingscourt	Early D	5
Rainforest Life	First Explorers	Kingscourt	Level 2	9
Rainforest Plants	Alphakids	Horwitz Gardner	Early Level 10	4
Rainy Day	Pathways	Collins	Year 1	6
Rainy Days	Hotlinks	Kingscourt	9	3
Rama and the Demon King	Individual Titles	Frances Lincoln	Souhami, Jessica	10
Rapunzel	Literacy Links Plus	Kingscourt	Fluent D	8
Rat-a-tat-tat	Literacy Links Plus	Kingscourt	Contemporary Stories	5
Rather Small Turnip, The	Crunchies	Orchard	Seriously Silly Stories	10
Rat's Funny Story	Story Chest	Kingscourt	Get-ready Set BB	1
Raven and the Fox, The	Cambridge Reading	CUP	Y1 A: Range of Cultures	5
Ready Steady Go	Individual Titles	Random House	Watanabe, Shigeo	4
Real Princess, The	Alphakids	Horwitz Gardner	Extending Level 19	8
Rebecca and the Concert	PM Storybooks	Nelson Thornes	Orange Set C	6
Recycle Michael	Storyteller	Kingscourt	Set 4	4
Red and Blue and Yellow	PM Non-fiction	Nelson Thornes	Red Level	3
Red Bird	Pathways	Collins	Year 1	4
Red Block, Blue Block	PM Maths	Nelson Thornes	Stage A	2
Red Doll & other stories, The	New Way	Nelson Thornes	Green Platform Books	5
Red Fox Dances	Individual Titles	Walker	Baron, Alan	7
Red Planet	Oxford Reading Tree	OUP	Stage 7 Owls	7
Red Planet	Oxford Reading Tree	OUP	Stage 7 Playscripts	6
Red Riding Hood	Pathways	Collins	Year 2	6
Red Riding Hood	Pelican Big Bks	Longman	Cullimore, Stan	5
Red Rose, The	Story Chest	Kingscourt	Large Read-tog Set 2	3
Red Ted at the Beach	Storyworlds	Heinemann	Stage 4 Our World	3
Red Ted Goes to School	Storyworlds	Heinemann	Stage 4 Our World	3
Reds and Blues	Oxford Reading Tree	OUP	Stage 1+ First Sentences	2
Reptiles	Alphakids Plus	Horwitz Gardner	Early Level 10	4